29 x 99

FASCIST AND LIBERAL
VISIONS OF WAR

FASCIST AND LIBERAL VISIONS OF WAR

Fuller, Liddell Hart, Douhet, and Other Modernists

Azar Gat

CLARENDON PRESS · OXFORD
1998

Oxford University Press, Great Clarendon Street, Oxford OX2 6DP

Oxford New York

Athens Auckland Bangkok Bogota Buenos Aires Calcutta
Cape Town Chennai Dar es Salaam Delhi Florence Hong Kong Istanbul
Karachi Kuala Lumpur Madrid Melbourne Mexico City Mumbai
Nairobi Paris Singapore Taipei Tokyo Toronto Warsaw

and associated companies in
Berlin Ibadan

Oxford is a registered trademark of Oxford University Press

Published in the United States
by Oxford University Press Inc., New York

British Library Cataloguing in Publication Data
Data available

Library of Congress Cataloging in Publication Data
Data applied for

ISBN 0-19-820715-8

1 3 5 7 9 10 8 6 4 2

Typeset by J&L Composition Ltd, Filey, North Yorkshire
Printed in Great Britain
on acid-free paper by
Bookcraft Ltd., Midsomer Norton
Nr. Bath, Somerset

To
Ruthie, Tamar,
and
Jonathan

PREFACE

This book is the third in a cultural history trilogy of modern strategic thought. Following on my earlier works, *The Origins of Military Thought from the Enlightenment to Clausewitz* (1989) and *The Development of Military Thought: The Nineteenth Century* (1992), it seeks to bring out some of the broader cultural assumptions and intellectual influences which have shaped strategic theory from the outset of the twentieth century. In view of the century's great complexity, however, the book can claim even less comprehensiveness than its predecessors. It focuses on two themes of seminal significance, to which separate studies are dedicated. Addressing fascism and liberalism, respectively, these studies revolve around the challenge of modernity. Underlying them is the question how did the ascent of modern, industrial, and technological mass society effect military theory.

The first study deals with the visions of machine warfare which appeared from the beginning of the century throughout the developed world. While these visions were of course primarily linked to the spread of industrialization, and especially to the advent of the internal-combustion engine, the study seeks to point out, and try to explain how it came about, that the earliest, most famous, and most far-reaching proponents of mechanized warfare were associated with proto-fascism and fascism. Both J. F. C. Fuller and Giulio Douhet, for example, the pioneering theorists of mechanized land and air warfare respectively, held proto-fascist ideas even before the First World War, and both joined fascist movements as soon as they were created. Indeed the same trend is discernible throughout the West. It will be suggested that the link here was not accidental. In the first decades of the twentieth century the modernist strands of proto-fascism and fascism celebrated technology and its achievements and futuristically envisioned the coming of a technocratic, efficient, and hierarchic Machine Age society. They thus attracted and inspired those who championed sweeping futuristic visions of mechanized war.

The second study combines a drastic re-evaluation of B. H. Liddell Hart's contribution to strategic theory with an analysis of the rise in the post-First World War liberal West of a new conception of war. The study suggests that the profound shock with which liberal Western societies reacted to the staggering human and material costs of the Great War spurred a radical reformulation of the classical strategic theory which had been crystallized in the climate of nineteenth-century nationalism. The new strategic conception revolved around the notions of containment and cold war, first formulated in the language of theory by Liddell Hart in his more mature and less-known writings of the second half of the 1930s. These notions were tried out by the Western powers against Germany, Italy, and Japan as a complement and alternative to appeasement, until the sudden collapse of their defences in Western Europe in May 1940 and in the Pacific in December 1941 virtually forced Britain and the United States into total war. Nuclear weapons immeasurably enhanced the logic of the new strategic concept, but, contrary to accepted assumptions, they neither created nor have been solely responsible for it. Indeed, arising as it did from the wider circumstances of the West's 'modern condition', this concept remains the preferred strategic option of Western powers even against non-nuclear adversaries. As the contours of the Cold War era are beginning to reveal themselves, it seems to have become the advanced world's strategic norm.

In writing this book I have had to deal with many historiographical questions which are related to its subjects and which have recently become the centre of controversy. These mainly concern the development of the doctrine of armoured warfare, Liddell Hart's role in that development, the influence of the British on the Germans, and the evolution of the Panzer arm. In all these I have found recent historiographical trends partly or wholly misleading. Since these questions significantly bear on, but do not directly belong to, my chosen subjects, I devoted to them special studies which I intended to append to the book. When this proved too cumbersome an arrangement, it was decided to keep them out of the book and have them published separately. Interested readers are thus referred to my 'Liddell Hart's Theory of Armoured Warfare: Revising the Revisionists', *Journal of Strategic Studies*, 19 (1996), 1–30, and 'British Influence and the Evolution of the Panzer Arm—Myth or Reality?', *War in History*, 4 (1997), 150–73, 316–38, for full-scale studies of the development of British and German interwar armoured doctrine.

ACKNOWLEDGEMENTS

In the course of my work on this book and its satellite studies, I have incurred many pleasant debts to people and institutions that have lent me their help and support. In Germany I was hosted by Militär-geschichtliches Forschungsamt, then in Freiburg i. Breisgau. I am particularly grateful to the institute's former Chief Historian, Professor Wilhelm Deist, who patiently and tactfully guided my steps into inter-war German military history. In addition, the warm friendship and hospitality which Professor and Frau Deist extended to my family and myself made our stays in Freiburg even more rewarding. During my periods of research at Yale I was hosted by the International Security Program under the directorship of Professor Paul Kennedy. In Britain my mentor, Professor Sir Michael Howard, as well as Professors Brian Bond and Robert O'Neill, shared with me their views and some personal recollections of Liddell Hart. Needless to say, the views expressed and the errors and faults that still remain in this book are my responsibility alone.

Of the many libraries and archives consulted in the course of my research, I am particularly thankful to the staffs of the Liddell Hart Centre for Military Archives at King's College, London, and of the Bundes Archiv-Militär Archiv, Freiburg, for their dedicated and patient service. The Trustees of the Liddell Hart Centre for Military Archives kindly gave me permission to cite from documents to which they hold copyright. I am also thankful to *War in History* and *War and Society* for allowing me to use material first published in these journals. Finally, my research in various countries over several years was made possible by the generous support of the Alexander von Humboldt Foundation, the United States–Israel Educational Foundation (Fulbright), and the British Council. I am most grateful to them all.

CONTENTS

PART I. FASCIST MODERNISM AND
VISIONARIES OF MACHINE WARFARE   1

1. Introduction: The 'Janus Face' of Fascism   3

2. J. F. C. Fuller: Positivism, Evolution, Fascism, and
   Future Warfare   13

3. Futurism, Proto-Fascist Italian Culture, and the
   Sources of Douhetism   43

4. German Right-Wing Radicalism, Strategic Adventurism,
   and Mechanized Warfare   80

5. Comparisons and Contrasts (I): American Populism,
   Progressivism, and Mid-West Technological Modernism   104

6. Comparisons and Contrasts (II): Marxism, Modernism,
   and the Doctrine of 'Deep Battle'   114

7. Conclusion   122

PART II. LIDDELL HART, MODERN, AND
'POST-MODERN' STRATEGY   125

1. Introduction   127

2. Background: The First World War in Western
   Consciousness   130

3. Theory: Limited War, Moderate Peace, and the
   Strategy of Indirect Approach   146

4. Policy: Defence of the West (I): Containment in
   the 1930s   178

5. Policy: Defence of the West (II): Hot War—Cold War   266

6. Conclusion: 'The Western Way in Warfare',
   Past and Future   306

Bibliography   311
Index   330

Part I

Fascist Modernism
and Visionaries
of Machine Warfare

I

Introduction:
'The Janus Face' of Fascism

This study suggests that a close affinity existed between the radical visions of machine warfare—inspiring and debated by soldiers and civilians during the first decades of the twentieth century—and the cultural and intellectual currents partaking of the proto-fascist and fascist outlook, or 'mood'. The mechanization of warfare was of course rooted in the general developments of the age, and was dependent upon tangible and material factors such as industrial capacity, technological advance, and geostrategic position. All the same, visions of machine warfare largely belonged to the domain of ideas and the imagination, flowering most vividly where their cultural and intellectual subsoil proved particularly fertile. Almost as a rule, they drew heavily from the modernist notions and visions, celebration of the machine, and ideals of action, vigour, and speed prominent within proto-fascism.

This proposition will probably not be foreign to historians of fascist ideas and imagery or to students of fascist-modernist artistic culture, as it might be to military historians. The role of the machine and the concept of a futurist machine-dominated society in the proto-fascist climate of ideas has become a well-recognized theme. Increasingly since the 1960s, indeed, fascism as a political and cultural phenomenon has been receiving far more serious scholarly attention than it had before. Two major revisions of earlier views have emerged. First, scholars have argued that although fascism became a potent political force in the wake of the political, social, and cultural dislocation brought about by the First World War—and in reaction against the spectre of Bolshevism—its growth dates from well before the interwar period, from as far back as the late nineteenth century. Second, rather than being a 'revolution of nihilism', led and carried out by gangs of thugs who were driven solely by a lust for power, fascism has been recognized as a comprehensive cultural 'mood', outlook, creed, or even ideology. It enjoyed strong appeal among intellectuals as a third way to modernity, an alternative to both liberalism and socialism.[1]

To be sure, as a generic term fascism is notoriously ambiguous. Italian Fascism and German National-Socialism differed from each other in some of their principal features; and these two central models were again different from the French, British, and other fascist variants which rose in industrialized Europe, to say nothing of the authoritarian-conservative regimes and right-wing radical movements in the predominantly agrarian countries of Eastern Europe, the Iberian peninsula, and Latin America, which from the 1930s adopted many features of fascist political culture. Concerned that ideological, chronological, and local diversity might render the concept itself dubious and unusable, some scholars have suggested a 'fascist minimum', of which the following is my own rough synthesis. Inevitably in view of our particular subject, it is tilted towards the intellectuals' outlook rather than towards the fascist rank and file or the practices of fascist regimes.

Fascism emerged on the heels of industrialization, urbanization, and the growth of mass society. Those who shared in the proto-fascist and fascist 'mood' rebelled against bourgeois culture, with its 'decadent' materialism, commercialism, atomistic and alienating individualism, and liberal-humanitarian values. They dreaded the further advance of plebeianism, mediocrity, and triviality expected with growing democratization. Espousing idealism and exalting youth, elementary dynamism, and vitalism, they called for comprehensive spiritual and cultural rejuvenation and the creation of a new man within a radically reconstructed society. They sought to overcome divisive parliamentarism, capitalism, and socialism through the application of communal solutions which would mobilize the energies and loyalty of the masses around unifying national traditions, myths, and ideals. At the same time, they held that government should firmly remain in the hands of a worthy élite, the creator and leader of the New Order.[2]

---

[1] References in these introductory remarks are necessarily sparing. See esp. G. Mosse, *The Crisis of German Ideology* (New York, 1964); *The Nationalization of the Masses* (New York, 1975); *Nazism* (Oxford, 1978); J. Weiss, *The Fascist Tradition* (New York, 1967); J. Gregor, *The Ideology of Fascism* (New York, 1969); A. Hamilton, *The Appeal of Fascism*, (London, 1971); Z. Sternhell, *Neither Right nor Left* (Berkeley, Calif., 1986); D. Carrol, *French Literary Fascism* (Princeton, NJ, 1995).

[2] In addition to the references in the previous note, two pioneering works are E. Nolte, *Three Faces of Fascism* (New York, 1969), and E. Weber, *Varieties of Fascism* (Princeton, NJ, 1964); most usefully, see: H. R. Trevor-Roper, 'The Phenomenon of Fascism', in S. J. Woolf (ed.), *European Fascism* (New York, 1969); A. Greil, 'The Modernization of

Fascist attitude towards the modern is a particularly ambivalent issue. The question of whether fascism was reactionary or radical and forward-looking is much debated. Here, most significantly, the considerable differences existing between the various movements and intellectual currents which partook of the fascist 'mood' are discernible. German National-Socialism remarkably demonstrated the 'Janus face' of fascism: hostile to Western rationalist tradition, deeply nostalgic, and steeped in *völkisch* and agrarian mythology, while also projecting a futuristic utopia, in which a vigorous German race would rule the vast territories of the new Reich and compete for global mastery, riding the most technologically advanced machines. On the other hand, the Italian Fascists, although also recalling the glories of ancient Rome, saw themselves as the modern movement *par excellence*—the true heirs of the 1789 revolutionary tradition, nineteenth-century Garibaldian republicanism, and the positivist vision of progress. From the turn of the century the poet Gabriele d'Annunzio, a precursor of the movement and its future artistic figurehead, celebrated the machine and modern technology, clothed in classical and mythological imagery, as a liberating and sublime aesthetic, moral, and spiritual vehicle of the new age. In a similar vein, one of the main sources of Italian Fascism was the Futurist movement in the arts, led by Filippo Tommaso Marinetti. The Futurists fiercely rejected any nostalgic yearnings for the past, aestheticized and worshipped the products of modern technology, and marvelled at the qualities of a modernist, machine-dominated society. For the Italian Fascists fascism was the order of the future, superseding obsolete parliamentary democracy in the new age of modern, industrial mass society. These notions were even more central to the Franco-Belgian fascist variety of Plannism, numbering among its theorists and adherents people like Henry de Man, Marcel Déat, Jacques Doriot, and the leading figure of Modernism in architecture, Le Corbusier. Equally, the followers of Sir Oswald Mosley in the British Union of Fascists claimed modernity as their own. For these movements fascism was predominantly the modern response to the needs of the modern era,

Consciousness and the Appeal of Fascism', *Comparative Political Studies*, 10 (1977), 213–38; A. J. Gregor, 'Fascism and the "Countermodernization of Consciousness"', ibid. 239–58; G. Mosse's Introduction to Mosse (ed.), *International Fascism*, (London, 1979), 1–41; S. T. Larsen, B. Hagtvet, and J. P. Myklebust (eds.), *Who Were the Fascists?* (Bergen, 1980); S. Payne, *Fascism: Comparison and Definition* (Madison, Wis., 1980); *A History of Fascism, 1914–1945* (Madison, Wis., 1995), esp. 3–19, 462–70, 487–95; R. Griffin, *The Nature of Fascism* (London, 1991).

transcending both capitalism and socialism. It would create a fully organized and efficient society, ruled by a meritocratic, managerial government of experts, both made necessary by the complexities of the new technological age.[3]

It is these modernist currents and aspects of proto-fascism and fascism that will concern us here. The futuristic aesthetization of the machine and of technological society (which has been amply highlighted by scholars) and the fascist-modernist view of the shape of the modern world (which has not) were both powerful cultural forces. Machine warfare visionaries may simply be thought to have identified with the fascist cult of violence, militarism, and quest for armament and for strong armed forces—and some of them certainly did. Yet these fascist attributes primarily hold true for the defeated and humiliated Germany of the 1920s and 1930s, and to a lesser degree for Fascist Italy. French fascism was mostly pacifist, and Mosley and his movement shared the general British reaction against the experience of the First World War. They genuinely regarded themselves as the 'party of peace', even before the prospect of war with Nazi Germany and Fascist Italy arose in the 1930s. Machine warfare visionaries were attracted to fascism for much broader reasons. Invariably, and almost by definition, they were people of strong intellectual bent. They were driven by, or were searching for, a comprehensive outlook, interpretation of history and the direction it was taking, and view of the current state of humanity, in which to anchor and from within which to develop their own specialized vision. More often than not, it was towards the modernist strands of proto-fascism and fascism that they gravitated.

Prelude: Positivism, Technology, and Future Society; Jules Verne and H. G. Wells

It is generally recognized that the late nineteenth century was characterized by a widespread so-called 'neo-Romantic revolt' against positi-

---

[3] Again, only briefly at this point: R. de Felice, *Fascism* (New Brunswick, NJ, 1977), 55, 103, 106; A. Cassels, 'Janus: The Two Faces of Fascism', and H. Turner Jr., 'Fascism and Modernization', in Turner (ed.), *Reappraisals of Fascism* (New York, 1975), 69–92 and 117–39 respectively; A. J. Gregor, 'Fascism and Modernization', *World Politics*, 26 (1974), 370–84; A. J. Joes, 'On the Modernity of Fascism', *Comparative Political Studies*, 10 (1977), 259–68; Sternhell, *Neither Right nor Left*, 141–212, on Plannism; J. Herf, *Reactionary Modernism* (Cambridge, 1984); Payne, *History of Fascism*, esp. 471–86; Griffin, *Fascism*, 47–8; A. Hewitt, *Fascist Modernism: Aesthetics, Politics, and the Avant-Garde* (Stanford, Calif., 1993). References to the much-debated National Socialist case reserved for the relevant chapter below.

vism. This is taken to signify growing doubts regarding the mid-nineteenth-century optimistic belief in a comprehensive, continuous, and accelerating progress, fuelled by the rapid advance of science, technology, and education, and leading to steady moral improvement and growing economic and social well-being. The revolt involved a rejection of the materialistic–mechanistic conception of reason, focusing instead on the elementary forces of life, the irrational springs of individual and communal psyche, and a cult of action and creativity. For all that, in some important respects the label 'revolt against positivism' is not altogether satisfactory and needs to be used with discrimination. Positivism may be loosely employed to denote the prevailing outlook of the progressive educated public in the West during the mid-nineteenth century, but more technically it consisted of the various and often widely varying doctrines of such thinkers as Saint-Simon, Fourier, Auguste Comte, Herbert Spencer, and their disciples. With them the element of the irrational, cyclical conceptions of history, and authoritarianism were as prevalent as secular materialism, linear optimism, and individualistic liberalism. The most diverse persuasions could draw from the positivist tradition, and did. The ideas of Jules Verne and H. G. Wells, the two most famous popular visionaries of the machine in the pre-fascist era, demonstrate this point.

The high tide of optimistic democratic-liberalism is exemplified by the inventor of the scientific novel and 'child of Second Empire positivism', Jules Verne (1828–1905). His internationally successful books shared and built upon the general enthusiasm for the remarkable feats of science, technology, and engineering, whose rapid advance was conspicuously changing daily life and firing the public's imagination during the second half of the nineteenth century. In an age of explorations the *Voyages extraordinaires* took his readers to the stretches of an unfolding globe and beyond, and dazzled them with the products and transforming effects of future technology, which Verne suggested lay not very far over the horizon. What he offered was not just spacecraft and aircraft, automobiles and submarines, gigantic cannons, huge projectiles, and gas shells, but also social visions. Verne was an 1848 liberal for his entire life, who would actively support the republic in 1870 and later run for the municipal council of Amiens on the republican-left ticket (while also being an anti-Dreyfusite). In his novels he stood for anti-authoritarian, humanitarian individualism, freedom for oppressed peoples, and international brotherhood, qualified only by strong, sometimes chauvinist, French patriotism. In his characteristically Saint-Simonian and

Fourierist utopian garden communities rational planning, enlightened social organization, electricity, and advanced sanitation brought about general welfare and happiness. For all that, even this progressive optimist succumbed to fits of anxiety and pessimism. We now know they had already marked one of his earliest, most prophetic but unpublished novels, *Paris au xx siècle* (completed in 1863), and they increased as he grew older and mid-century enthusiasm gave way to *fin-de-siècle* gloom. As the social, cultural, and environmental costs of industrialization and commercialism became more apparent, Verne's social and humanitarian utopias were repeatedly overshadowed by evil or alienating technology, whose sombre potential ran amok, threatening doom to both nature and humanity.[4]

Expressing the turn-of-the-century mood of both boundless belief in progress and deep anxiety was the most famous prophet of technology of his time and the practitioner of social futurology, H. G. Wells (1866–1946). Far more than Verne, whose British counterpart he was often regarded to be, Wells was a highly committed popular social philosopher as well as a novelist. A scientist by education, he was a student of the celebrated Thomas Huxley, Charles Darwin's champion in the great public debates that followed the publication of *The Origin of Species* (1859) and *The Descent of Man* (1871). An evolutionist like the rest of his generation, Wells none the less shared Huxley's objections to the social Darwinists' application of the categories of biology to the understanding of man's social life. Like Huxley, he held that the spectacular growth of human civilization once man's biological potential had evolved was primarily a cultural and historical process. This process was now entering a new stage. From his remarkable *Anticipation of the Reaction of Mechanical and Scientific Progress upon Human Life and Thought* (1902) onward, Wells sought to predict the shape of, and prepare humanity for, the industrial–commercial, urban, global, and scientific–technological civilization which was in the making. He believed that it would require radically new forms of human organization.

A friend of G. B. Shaw and the Webbs, and for a time a member of

---

[4] See esp. J. Chesneaux, *The Political and Social Ideas of Jules Verne* (London, 1972) (for his connections with the Saint-Simonians, see pp. 82–6); J. Noiray, *Le Romancier et la machine: l'image de la machine dans le roman français (1850–1900)*, ii (Paris, 1982) (a citation by Verne from Comte is printed on p. 220); J. Jules-Verne, *Jules Verne* (New York, 1976); A. Martin, *The Mask of the Prophet: The Extraordinary Fictions of Jules Verne* (Oxford, 1990), 130, 183.

the Fabian Society (which he failed to convert into a radical political order), Wells shared the Edwardian progressive–liberal–socialist quest for planned social reform. This was integrated, however, within his wider view of the course human history was taking, which he crystallized early on in his career and which became his lifelong panacea. He believed that the developments of the modern age, particularly the emergence of a global economy and the revolution in communications (he predicted the proliferation of the automobile and the coming of air flight), were leading towards a world state. In this new global community a culture of science and technology, education, freedom, and enlightened humanitarianism would prevail. Yet, like the French positivists of the previous century—Saint-Simon, Fourier, and Comte, who had advanced a remarkably similar views of the direction and ultimate destination of human development—and unlike Spencer, whom he criticized on that account, Wells thought modern society and the new world state would be neither democratic nor characterized by individualistic, unregulated *laissez-faire*. He shared the educated class's growing suspicions of the rationality of the masses, expressed for example by Wells's close friend, the famous social psychologist Graham Wallace, and by Gustave le Bon, whose highly influential works Wells often cited. Wells's élitism, while of a heroic and individualistic character, was of a different sort from that of a Carlyle, a Nietzsche, or a Shaw. For him, democracy was only a historical phase, mainly because the evolving highly advanced scientific, technological, and industrial society would require sophisticated coordination and planning, which could only be carried out by a government of experts, a Platonic meritocratic élite of managers and scientists.[5]

Wells held that a world state was becoming an overriding necessity because the enormous potential destructiveness of modern technology threatened to bring about the end of civilization if the existing antagonistic state system continued. Most of Wells's technological novels dealt with war. His early success, *The War of the Worlds* (1898), with its extraterrestrial instruments of war, was still innocent 'scare' science

---

[5] A good study of Wells's political and social outlook is W. Wagar, *H. G. Wells and the World State* (New York, 1961); see also H. G. Wells, *Experiment in Autobiography* (New York, 1934). Two excellent studies of some relevant aspects of the intellectual background of the time are G. R. Searle, *The Quest for National Efficiency* (Oxford, 1971), and P. Crook, *Darwinism, War, and History* (Cambridge, 1994). For Wells's military ideas, see T. H. E. Travers, 'Future Warfare: H. G. Wells and British Military Theory, 1895–1916', in B. Bond and I. Roy (eds.), *War and Society* (London, n.d.), 67–87.

fiction. But Wells was dead serious in his later works. In *Anticipations* he cited Ivan Bloch's analysis of the shape of future war, predicting that the rapid rise of firepower would create a tactical and strategic stalemate which in turn would bring about the collapse of the closely knit world economy, famine, and breakdown of the warring societies. To Bloch's analysis Wells added a great struggle for the conquest of the air by aircraft, whose appearance at around 1950 or 2000 he had been anticipating since the mid-1890s (the mistaken prediction of the date was shared at that time even by Wilbur Wright). The air fleets would then proceed to attack land targets. After great upheavals, the general calamity would lead to the creation of a world state.

Indeed, Wells's analysis of modern war went further than Bloch's. In *Anticipations* he considered that a progressively mechanized war would bring forth a new type of highly trained professional army, the product of the new technological and scientific age. The old mass armies of amateurs and recruits were doomed. The modern trend was to link the new type of soldier 'with the engineer and doctor and all the continually developing mass of scientifically educated men that the advance of science and mechanism is producing'. In the public debate in Britain in the years preceding the First World War, Wells would reject the idea of a conscript army in favour of an élite force.[6] In 'The Land Ironclads', published in *The Strand Magazine* in 1903, he prophesied mechanized land warfare, with land ships manned by soldier-engineers.[7] It was, however, aircraft that figured most prominently in his work. They became the subject of his novel *The War in the Air* (1908), a stark warning issued against the background of mounting international tensions. In this novel the airships and aircraft of the great powers crossed oceans and continents in a truly global world war. They sank fleets of dreadnoughts (whose days, Wells believed, were coming to a close because of the torpedo boat, submarine, and aircraft)[8] and attacked the enemy's heartland, his centres of population and industry. This was again followed by a collapse of modern advanced civilization, and opened decades of anarchy and endemic strife. Wells's novel *The World Set Free* (1914), published before the war, starts with a positivist history of man's ascent from his ancient origins up to his present-day wealth-

---

[6] Travers, 'Wells', 68–9.

[7] Ibid. 69, 72–3; also H. G. Wells, *Italy, France and Britain at War* (New York, 1917), 153.

[8] Travers, 'Wells', 79; A. J. A. Morris, *The Scaremongers: The Advocacy of War and Rearmament, 1896–1914* (London, 1984), 346–7.

creating and emancipating, science- and technology-based civilization.[9]
It then describes the invention of an atomic bomb (*sic*) in 1933 and of
atomic power stations (*sic*) for civilian use in 1953. (This is not as
startling as it may sound: Wells took his inspiration from the recent
advances in nuclear physics made by Ramsay, Rutherford, and Soddy.)[10]
A short time later in the mid-century, an atomic war between the great
powers, which were governed by mediocracies, racked civilization. This
disaster led to the emergence of a new world republic in which atomic
weapons and other armament were banned.

By the end of the First World War Wells was campaigning for the
creation of a League of Nations, and during the interwar period he
dedicated all his energy to popularizing the ideas of a world state and
élite government. By the 1930s he ceased to concern himself with
anything else. His *The Shape of Things to Come* (1933), filmed by
Alexander Korda in 1936, merely repeated his by now constant theme:
the rise of modern civilization; its collapse in destructive wars leading to
mass epidemics and medieval anarchy; its tortuous regeneration; and
the establishment of a world state. The new civilization would possess a
regulated economy, would be led by a class of managers, experts, and
aviators, would exercise far-reaching control of the environment,
including bio-molecular engineering of plants, and would organize
society and education with the view of promoting general happiness.
The Second World War, which seemed to confirm Wells's worst fears,
broke his heart.

In some important respects, in which he echoed the French positivists of the first half of the nineteenth century, Wells's cast of mind
made him a typical potential recruit for fascism. He thought democracy
mediocre and unsuitable for the modern world. He rejected economic
liberalism in favour of communalism and social planning, while also
rejecting Marxism. He called for the creation of a new type of élite
government, which in *Modern Utopia* (1905), for example, he even
suggested should engage in breeding on eugenic principles. He believed
the modern world would bring about new forms of social ethics and
secular religions. In his more pessimistic moods he thought that civilization was in a structural crisis and that present culture was sick. Even
his doctrine of free love (which again echoed Saint Simon and Fourier)
was reminiscent of a characteristic streak within the proto-fascist mood.

---

[9] This would be fully developed in Wells's brilliant positivist work *The Outline of
History* (London, 1920).   [10] H. G. Wells, *The World Set Free* (London, 1927), 25.

On the other hand, Wells's differences with the fascist cast of mind were also of a fundamental nature, and explain why he never came within the fascist orbit. He was anti-authoritarian, humanistic, pacifist, and cosmopolitan. On the whole he rejected social Darwinism, racism, and flights into the mystical—all typical, though individually not necessarily indispensable, components of the fascist mix. Other intellectuals, from both left and right, who shared many of Wells's views but were a generation younger, hovered much closer to fascism.

2

J. F. C. Fuller:
Positivism, Evolution, Fascism, and
Future Warfare

John Frederick Charles Fuller's (1878–1966) intellectual intensity,
wide-ranging interests, and literary scope have been fully documented
in his own vast output and autobiography, and by his biographers.[1]
None the less, for students of military affairs they still appear as an
interesting, piquant, but largely unconnected addendum to his military
work. In particular his involvement in Oswald Mosley's British Union
of Fascists during the 1930s has been viewed as an unfortunate accident
in his career, to be mainly attributed to his famously eccentric personality or to the fascist emphasis on order and all things military.[2] By
contrast, this study aims to advance the following propositions, some of
which have long been known: Fuller developed as an intellectual well
before he became a military thinker; the nature of this development
made him a characteristic participant in the proto-fascist mood; his
interest in and major contributions to his own military profession
evolved distinctively out of his general intellectual development; his
vision of future mechanized armies in particular drew its inspiration,
breadth, and vigour from his general outlook and interests; thus his
formal fascist phase was only the logical conclusion of a lifelong intellectual bent.

The Forming of a Proto-Fascist Intellectual

The undistinguished child of an Anglican clergyman, Fuller was sent
into an army career by his family. Upon entering Sandhurst in 1897, he

---

[1] J. F. C. Fuller, *Memoirs of an Unconventional Soldier* (London, 1936); and two
excellent intellectual biographies: A. J. Trythall, *'Boney' Fuller: The Intellectual General*
(London, 1977); B. H. Reid, *J. F. C. Fuller: Military Thinker* (London, 1987).

[2] Even Reid, *Fuller*, 176–7, seems to espouse this view, even though it goes against the
drift of his book; but see Trythall, *Fuller*, 181–3; also J. Luvaas, 'Major General J. F. C.
Fuller', in *The Education of an Army* (London, 1965), 364–5.

was little interested either in his profession or in the customary social pursuits of regimental life in the light infantry. But, a loner and introvert, he found the army's dull routine convenient for the satisfaction of a newly developed hunger for books, mostly of a philosophical nature. He became, and would ever remain, an intense autodidact. His reading first made him agnostic and anti-religious: 'this pronounced mental change coincided with the last lap of the great theologico-Darwinian controversy, and in consequence I soon became immersed in Huxley, Lecky, Samuel Laing and other rationalist writers.'[3] Brian Holden Reid has admirably analysed Fuller's extensive reading lists during 1898–1901, the years of the Boer War in which he participated:

During these years something approaching 200 volumes found their way into his hands. . . . An interest in Carlyle was already evident before Fuller left for South Africa, as he read *Sartor Resartus* in 1898, followed a year later by *Heroes and Hero Worship* and the *History of Frederick the Great* in 1902. He also devoured Laing's *Problems of the Future* and *Human Origins*, Darwin's *Descent of Man* and Freeman's *History of the Norman Conquest*. . . . From 1899 onward religious books held his attention. These included Laing's *A Modern Zoroastrianism*, Allen's *Evolution of the Idea of God*, Arnold's *Death and Afterwards* and *Science and the Christian Tradition*, Wiedemann's *The Ancient Egyptian Doctrine of the Soul*, and 'Saladin', *Why am I an Agnostic?* . . . Fuller continued to read widely in philosophy. He read Paul Carus's *A Primer of Philosophy* and Kant's *Dreams of a Spirit Seer*. An interest in science is noteworthy and titles like Laing's *Modern Science and Modern Thought* are found in his notebooks. . . . Fuller reflected seriously on what he had read. After reading Carlyle's *History of the French Revolution* . . . he speculated that man is but a 'veneered brute' and once the veneer wore off, man's latent savagery 'springs forth' in all its ghastly ferocity. This view of man's inherent animalism was fortified some months later when Fuller thought he had discovered the full implications of Darwin's Theory of Evolution. 'I am a great believer in Darwin and Evolution[,] the whole theory is so grand, so beautiful and true.' He then turned to Wall's *Darwinism and Race Progress* and made some jottings on the universal application of the theory. Further grist to his Darwinist mill was provided by his study of two books by the Social Darwinian, Benjamin Kidd, *The Control of the Tropics* and *Social Evolution*.[4]

---

[3] Fuller, *Memoirs*, 458–9.

[4] Reid, *Fuller*, 11–12; the reading lists are in Fuller's material deposited at the Liddell Hart Centre of Military Archives, King's College, London (hereafter King's), IV/4/1. They range widely over history, art history, and literature.

Among the earliest books Fuller read during that period was *The First Greek Philosophers*, containing the surviving fragments of Heraclitus. Heraclitus' dialectics and celebration of war, 'the father of all things', made him popular among social-Darwinists of all countries during that time.[5] As Fuller's biographer has aptly concluded: 'Thus at [from] the beginning of his career Fuller identified himself with a major intellectual current, and one that owed little to the democratic, empirical English tradition.'[6]

Apart from evolutionism, several other intellectual traits which the young Fuller exhibited and which he maintained for life connected unmistakably with ideas and sentiments which, although enjoying a much wider currency, were all feeding the evolving proto-fascist mood. One of these traits was anti-socialism and élitism. Fuller wrote to his brother in 1906:

That the masses are socialistic is not very grave danger; for socialism is but the scum on the democratic cauldron. Socialism is anti-progressive, tending to level the higher to the lower, true democracy is diametrically the reserve it raises: the former is but a passing phase bubbling to the surface, a cleansing, a semi-education, the latter a step in the evolutionary ladder.[7]

As Reid again points out, Fuller 'absorbed the ideas of Benjamin Kidd and Karl Pearson as to the need for order, efficiency and discipline in the administration of all departments of state. This Edwardian vision of a technocratic élite of functional men was widely popularized in the years immediately before the First World War.'[8]

A second and even more fundamental trait was anti-materialism, about which Fuller wrote to his mother while still a young subaltern: 'the generality of people are cold, unfeeling, unloveable. And why? simply because Mammon bosses the show.'[9] Again, this widespread sentiment in turn-of-the-century Europe was expressed, for example, by the social-Darwinist and popular writer Benjamin Kidd, whom Fuller avidly read. Even more than Huxley, Kidd 'wanted a massive shift of human consciousness away from the dominating values of Mammon, ego, agnostic science, appealing to the 'emotion of the ideal', to man's capacity for self-transcendence and higher spirituality'.[10]

[5] Reid, *Fuller*, 9–10; Fuller, *Memoirs*, 7.   [6] Reid, *Fuller*, 10.

[7] King's, IV/3/139b, quoted by Trythall, *Fuller*, 20–1.

[8] Reid, *Fuller*, 19; see also G. R. Searle, *The Quest for National Efficiency*.

[9] King's, IV/3/4, quoted in Reid, *Fuller*, 9.

[10] P. Crook, *Darwinism, War, and History* (Cambridge, 1994) 70.

Indeed, third and closely linked to anti-materialism came the search for a new spirituality, which in turn led Fuller to mysticism. During the years 1903–6 he was stationed in India. Breaking away from religious conventions and accepted social mores, he was at that time preoccupied with sexual morality, reading extensively and embracing the doctrine of free love.[11] During that period he also immersed himself in the study of Indian culture. 'I studied the *Vedas* and the *Upanishads*—in translations, of course—and took a deep interest in the Yoga philosophy.' He then read George Berkeley's idealist philosophy and Spencer's *First Principles*, about which he wrote:

this noted book brought me into contact with his idea of the Unknowable. I then began to realize that, though conventional religion might be nauseating, crudely it stood for something which was neither rational nor irrational, but wonderful; a something which was beyond all things. . . . the only true course of reform lay in replacing an old worn-out spirituality by a new.

Spencer himself was an atheist and the most rationalist of the positivist major figures, but in his concept of the Unknowable he demarcated the limits of scientific knowledge, beyond which religion and metaphysics reigned. He also echoed his French predecessors, who had held that religion was not merely superstition but *inter alia* an archaic mode for expressing ideas about the world and the nature of being. In describing his own intellectual transformation from critical agnosticism to new spirituality, Fuller used the positivist terminology from Saint-Simon onward regarding the constant rotation of cultural epochs from the 'iconoclastic' to the 'synthetic', or from the 'destructive' to the 'constructive'.[12] Believing that their era called for a new 'synthetic' religious revival, Saint-Simon, Comte, and their disciples had turned with great zeal to creating a new positivist Religion of Humanity or of the 'Great Being', and to establishing its church and elaborate cult.

In 1905 Fuller's first two published articles appeared in the *Agnostic Journal*, but by then he was moving beyond his anti-religious phase. It was to the search for the hidden meaning and unity behind the appearance of phenomena, and for illuminating secret wisdom, that he had now turned.[13] In 1905 he made contact with Aleister Crowley, who

[11] Reid, *Fuller*, 13. Fuller read Lecky, *History of European Morals*, Ellis, *Studies in the Psychology of Sex*, Huston, *A Plea for Polygamy*, Rosenbaum, *The Plague of Lust*, *The Blight of Respectability*, and Westermark, *The History of Human Marriage*.
[12] All citations are from Fuller, *Memoirs*, 17, 459–60.
[13] Ibid.; Trythall, *Fuller*, 20.

would become known as 'the most notorious magician of the century
. . . the best-equipped magician to emerge since the seventeenth
century'.[14] The long tradition of occultism enjoyed a great revival
throughout the West at the turn of the century as part of the neo-
Romantic wave. It drew on an extensive series of magical and mysterious texts, actually or supposedly derived from a variety of ancient
sources: Egyptian Hermetism and cults, Greek myths and Pythagorean
and Platonic teaching, Jewish Cabbala, Christian Rosicrucianism, Far
Eastern wisdom, and so on. It sought to decipher and to unite with the
cosmic forces operating behind reality by interpreting the secret mean-
ings within mysterious symbols, words, and numbers, through the use
of ecstasy, and through liturgy. Crowley began his involvement with the
occult as a member of the magical order of the Golden Dawn, where he
soon quarrelled with the founder of the order and with other members,
such as the poet W. B. Yeats, another would-be fascist sympathizer. He
then started his own independent career. Whereas the Golden Dawn
mainly emphasized texts and liturgy, the tempestuous, domineering,
and brilliant Crowley would increasingly use drugs and sexual ecstasies.
He claimed to have had a series of encounters with ancient demons, and
wrote a number of books in which he proclaimed himself the founder of
a new religion which would replace Christianity and transcend its
boundaries of good and evil.[15]

Towards the end of his stay in India, Fuller responded to an adver-
tisement by Crowley promising a £100 prize for the winning writer of a
book on Crowley's teaching. Fuller entered as the sole competitor and
won the prize (which Crowley never paid). The book he wrote, his first,
The Star in the West (1907), was full of the enthusiasm of the convert,
announcing to the world the new gospel in an archaic, mystical, and
elevated style. According to Fuller, Crowley's new religion synthesized
the wisdoms of East and West and reconciled all conflicting philosophical positions.[16] Returning to Britain in 1906, Fuller became
Crowley's closest disciple, wholly absorbed in the activities of his group,
and co-editor and contributor to his journal, *The Equinox*. He had

---

[14] R. Cavendish, *A History of Magic* (London, 1977), 147–8; on Fuller, see p. 148.

[15] See E. Howe, *The Magicians of the Golden Dawn: A Documentary History of a
Magical Order, 1887–1923* (London, 1972); J. Symonds, *The Great Beast: The Life and
Magic of Aleister Crowley* (London, 1971); R. Cavendish, *The Magical Arts* (London,
1984).

[16] In Fuller's view, Crowley synthesized Plato, Aristotle, Bacon, Descartes, Spinoza,
Malebranche, Berkeley, Hume, Kant, Fichte, Schelling, Hegel, Comte, Spencer, and
Huxley, as well as Cabbala, Buddhism, Yoga, and agnosticism.

several mystical experiences but, faithfully married from 1907, he left his doctrine of free love behind him.[17]

All this is not an irrelevant curiosity. As Reid has rightly pointed out in respect to the mystics of that period: 'Before 1939 these groups were largely right wing in political complexion.'[18] Recent research has revealed the spread of occult sects in the West at the turn of the century, with which Crowley and his followers maintained close contact. It highlighted the mystical influences on the young Adolf Hitler, on other Nazi leaders such as Heinrich Himmler, Alfred Rosenberg, and Rudolf Hess, and on Nazi ideology, which cannot be fully understood without these influences. In Germany and the German-speaking parts of the Habsburg empire these sects mixed occultism with Wagnerian *völkisch* nationalism and racism. They depicted a mythological past in which a bright Aryan order of priests ruled inferior dark races. That archaic order was disrupted by the destructive and chaotic Jews, spreading Christianity as one of their poisonous weapons, and carrying out an eternal Manichaean struggle against the Aryans. Here is an element that is discernible not only in the Nazis' racism and murderous demonization of the Jews but in their apocalyptic fantasies, utopian millenarianism, and vision of the SS as a semi-religious warrior order.[19] All over the West, leading modernist poets and novelists who were attracted to proto-fascism and fascism (and were virulent anti-semites), like Ezra Pound, T. S. Eliot, W. B. Yeats, Wyndham Lewis, and, more ambivalently, D. H. Lawrence, were also deeply involved with the occult.[20]

---

[17] Capt. J. F. C. Fuller, *The Star in the West: A Critical Essay upon the Works of Aleister Crowley* (London, 1907); Symonds, *The Great Beast*, esp. 96–7, 121; Trythall, *Fuller*, 20–1, 24–6; Reid, *Fuller*, 14–16. Most of Fuller's occult library is at Rutgers University. Galley proofs of mystical books published in 1908, which Fuller apparently helped to proof read, are in Box XI.   [18] Reid, *Fuller*, 14.

[19] The most comprehensive and impressive study is J. Webb, *The Occult Establishment* (La Salle, Ill., 1976); for the fascist connection in Britain, see pp. 125–36, and for Germany and the Nazis, pp. 275–344, esp. pp. 299–330; also N. Goodrick-Clarke, *The Occult Roots of Nazism* (New York, 1985); and E. Howe, *Astrology and the Third Reich* (Wellingborough, Northants, 1984). The whole theme was pioneered and developed by G. Mosse, *The Crisis of German Ideology* (New York, 1964), 313–14; *The Nationalization of the Masses* (New York, 1975), 197–9; *Nazism* (Oxford, 1978), 59–61; 'Introduction' to G. Mosse (ed.), *International Fascism* (London, 1970), 7–10; and, most fully, 'The Mystical Origins of National Socialism', in his *Masses and Man: Nationalist and Fascist Perception of Reality* (Detroit, 1987), 197–213.

[20] Of the considerable literature on this subject, see most recently: L. Surette, *The Birth of Modernism: Ezra Pound, T. S. Eliot, W. B. Yeats, and the Occult* (London, 1993); G. M. Harper (ed.), *Yeats and the Occult* (Canada, 1975); G. Hough, *The Mystery Religion of W. B. Yeats* (Brighton, Sussex, 1984); W. Chace, *The Political Identities of Ezra Pound and T. J. S. Eliot* (Stanford, Calif., 1973).

While Fuller was never a 'hard' biological racist, his anti-Semitic article 'The Cancer of Europe', published in the first issue of *The Fascist Quarterly* (1935), blamed the Jews, portrayed as a meta-historical force, for a thousand years' Manichaean struggle to destroy Christian civilization. Quoting from the Cabbalist book *The Zohar* and from the prophets, Fuller claimed that the Jews were materialists and anti-spiritualists, successively using magic, money, and psychoanalysis to further their cause.[21] Although he quarrelled with Crowley in 1911, and the two parted ways, Fuller retained for life his mystical bent. Among his many books were one on Yoga and one on Cabbala.[22] He carried forward from his preoccupation with the occult to his other interests, including the military, a holistic and dialectical outlook, a search for the fundamental that underlay the appearance of reality, and an emphasis on the moral and on the exercise of conflicting wills.[23]

In 1907–12 Fuller served as the adjutant of a Volunteer, and later Territorial, battalion, where he proved to be a successful leader and trainer. In 1912 he returned to his regular regiment as a company commander. He also acted as rail transport officer to the Aldershot command and as brigade machine-gun officer—all valuable experiences in view of the nature of the approaching war. In 1911, after his break with Crowley, he suddenly decided to enter the Staff College. Failing the examination in 1912, he got in the next year. For the first time his mind focused on his own military profession, bringing to it the same intellectual absorption which had characterized his earlier activities and the intellectual equipment he had acquired in them: 'during the years in which I attacked conventional religion, subconsciously I was forging a piece of mental machinery wherewith I could thresh the grist from the chaff of the conventional theories of war . . . '[24] Fuller possessed the strong, independent mind of the autodidact, sharpened by more than a decade of critical contemplation, some experience in writing, and, above all, the knowledge and conceptual frameworks he had absorbed from his

---

[21] 'The Cancer of Europe', *Fascist Quarterly*, 1 (1935), 66–81; the occult nature of his anti-Semitism has been noted by Webb, *The Occult Establishment*, 127, 220.

[22] Fuller, 'The Black Arts', *Occult Review* (Apr. 1923); *Yoga: A Study of the Mystical Philosophy of the Brahmins and Buddhists* (London, 1925; 2nd edn 1933); *The Secret Wisdom of the Qabalah: A Study of Jewish Mystical Thought* (London, 1936). Two manuscripts, 'The Hidden Wisdom of the Illuminati' (1926) and 'Four Dimensional Man' (1930), can be found at King's, IV/14 and IV/16. Fuller's story of his involvement and break with Crowley is at Rutgers, V/5. [23] See Reid, *Fuller*, 19–20.

[24] *Memoirs*, 459–60.

extensive, if haphazard, reading. Inevitably, his work would always swing between brilliant originality and dilettantism, and in his early literary efforts the latter was often more conspicuous.

Fuller's literary remains held at Rutgers University include what appears to be his first substantial military work, a typescript of a book, 'The Foundation of an Imperial Army', composed in 1910–11. Written in a vague, semi-mystical, and somewhat tiresome style, it was never published and has remained unknown. It is a good catalogue of Fuller's intellectual makeup and roots. It advocated imperial unity, national efficiency, and a mass conscript army and reserve on the European pattern in addition to the professional colonial army. It called for a unity of 'body, mind and spirit', and for the cultivation of 'a vigorous and virile race' in a revived Empire. It put forward elaborate schemes for national regeneration and for the regimentation of society, the economy, and professional training. Fuller suggested, for example, that from the age of 4 all boys and girls should start to receive semi-military and patriotic education. All these themes were common enough among right-wingers in Edwardian Britain, and so were even the more radical ideas expressed by Fuller. He wrote that 'capitalists and paupers are the offsprings of a degenerate race', while rejecting socialism as a levelling doctrine. Specifically citing Wells's *Anticipations*, he wished to 'destroy ultimately and for ever the cancer of party-politics'. Wells's influence was clearly also responsible for a glaring inconsistency in Fuller's work and anticipated his later ideas: while advocating the creation of a British conscript army, Fuller claimed that the German mass army reflected early nineteenth-century democracy, whereas now the world was moving into the scientific–commercial epoch.[25]

Positivism and the Science of War

Fuller's published career as a military writer started with several humbler but more useful technical articles and booklets on training and organization, which stemmed from his experience with the volunteers,

---

[25] Fuller, 'The Foundation of an Imperial Army', (Rutgers), quotations from pp. 32, 41, 51–2. Tim Travers in his 'Future Warfare: H. G. Wells and British Military Theory, 1895–1916, in B. Bond and I. Roy (eds.), *War and Society* (London, n.d.), 81–2 and n. 90, has commented on the striking similarity of ideas between Wells and Fuller, expressing surprise that there was no evidence of recognition between the two. Fuller's typescript now leaves no doubt that he borrowed heavily from Wells.

Territorials, and Regulars.[26] This also led him to study Sir John Moore's innovative, flexible, and humane system of training during the wars of the French Revolution.[27] Soon, however, these interests developed deeper, into battlefield psychology and tactics. Here Fuller found two major themes from his intellectual background readily applicable: one of these was the positivist tenet that 'the physical and social sciences were governed by identical forces and could be treated in the same way';[28] the other was the then fashionable interest in crowd psychology. Fuller's *Training Soldiers for War* (1914), composed before but published after the outbreak of the war, opened with the statement that the training of soldiers was a science as much as an art, based on the psychology of individuals and of crowds. The booklet was wholly derived from two interrelated sources. As the author frankly admitted: 'I consider it preferable to base this work on the clear reasonings of such men as de Maud'huy, de Grandmaison and Langlois, and the many other French writers, who are too little known or studied in this country.'[29] And influencing the French school itself was the highly popular psychology of the crowd, especially that of Gustave le Bon, whom Fuller again cited extensively.[30]

Le Bon's *La Psychologie des foules* (1895), translated into English as *The Crowd* (1896), went through forty-five editions in France alone, and was translated into sixteen languages. A positivist in his approach to science, fiercely anti-socialist, and dreading the entrance of the masses into politics, Le Bon described the collective behaviour of the crowd as impulsive, driven by primal instincts, irrational, and open to manipulation. As such it was dangerous but also left an opportunity for skilful control by a small leading élite, which, according to Le Bon, had always been the sole agent of progress in any society. Highly popular, a biological racist, vulgar, and suspect in academic circles, Le Bon was read with great interest by Mussolini, and by Hitler, who borrowed

---

[26] Capt. Fuller, 'The Mobilization of a Territorial Infantry Battalion', *Army Review*, 5 (1913), 1–32; *Hints on Training Territorial Infantry* (London, 1913); 'The Three Flag System of Instructing Infantry Fire Tactics', *Army Review*, 6 (1914), 119–22; 'Notes on the Entrainment of Troops to and from Manoeuvres', *Army Review*, 7 (1914), 184–213.

[27] Taken up before the war, this study was worked into an article, 'The Training of the New Armies, 1803–1805', *Journal of the Royal United Services Institution*, 61 (1916), 779–90, and then expanded into 2 volumes, *Sir John Moore's System of Training* (London, 1924), and *British Light Infantry in the Eighteenth Century* (London, 1925).

[28] Reid, *Fuller*, 19.

[29] *Training Soldiers for War* (London, 1914), p. vii and *passim*.

[30] Le Bon is cited e.g. ibid. 10, 21, 23. As chief instructor at the Staff College in 1923–5, Fuller would place Le Bon's *The Crowd* on the required reading list: Trythall, *Fuller*, 103.

much from him in *Mein Kampf.* Le Bon was also in close touch with some of the leading professors at the École de Guerre, like Henri Bonnal and Louis de Maud'huy, whom he influenced by his educational and psychological theories. By the mid-1900s courses in military psychology were established in the French military schools. Within a sweeping cultural wave of vitalism and Bergsonianism in France in the decade before the war, Le Bon's teaching provided much of the psychological basis for the doctrines of the younger French offensive school grouped around Grandmaison.[31]

For Fuller, Le Bon's teaching probably coincided with the instinct theories of the founders of functional psychology, the American William James, whom Fuller is known to have read, and the British William MacDougal, author of *Introduction to Social Psychology* (1908). They were also in tune with the writings of Karl Pearson, the positivist, social-Darwinist Galton Professor of Eugenics at the University of London, and another of Fuller's favourites. In 'The Foundation of an Imperial Army' Fuller had already written about the necessity of turning the 'mob' into a 'dynamic crowd', and it was on these psychological foundations that he now based his work on training and tactics. Though highly complex, he argued, human nature was based on the same principles which underlay every living organism. Sensations, memories, and emotions form the mind, and are processed by imagination and reason. Constant repetition creates instinctive behaviour, stamped into the species through natural selection during evolution. Like Grandmaison, whose *Dressage de l'infanterie en vue de combat offensif* (1906) he followed closely, Fuller maintained that it was the function of drill to turn an unformed crowd into disciplined soldiers. Repeated training would create battlefield-conditioned reflexes, counter the natural instincts of fear and self-preservation, and habituate the soldiers to closing with the enemy. Like Langlois, Fuller suggested that the increase in firepower brought about by the quick-firing gun and the machine-gun might favour the offensive by overwhelming the defender in the chosen sector of attack. Thus, to the disdain of his commanders

---

[31] G. Le Bon, *The Crowd: A Study of the Popular Mind* (London, 1896); also *The Psychology of Peoples* (London, 1899). R. A. Nye, *The Origins of Crowd Psychology: Gustave Le Bon and the Crisis of Mass Democracy in the Third Republic* (London, 1975), provides ample evidence for Le Bon's influence on the French military (pp. 123–53; Fuller is mentioned on p. 144); I was unfamiliar with this source when writing my *The Development of Military Thought: The Nineteenth Century* (Oxford, 1992), 114–72. See also Mosse, *Nazism*, 58; R. de Felice, *Fascism* (New Brunswick, NJ, 1977), 74; M. Billig, *Fascists* (New York, 1978), 20–3.

at the Staff College, he advocated penetration rather than envelopment as the preferable method of attack. In his memoirs Fuller presented this as an example of foresight about the nature of the First World War, barely mentioning the unrealistic reasoning behind his views and passing in silence over their sources in the by then discredited French offensive school.[32]

During these years Fuller's military thinking was also developing in another, related direction. Preparing himself for the Staff College, he read in the beginning of the *Field Service Regulation*: 'The fundamental principles of war are neither very numerous nor in themselves very abstruse, but the application of them is difficult, and cannot be made subject to rules.'[33] Naturally, the conception of principles of war awoke his deepest interest. Descending from the military thinkers of the Enlightenment, it was engraved in military textbooks during the nineteenth century, especially in those countries most influenced by positivism, the Enlightenment's direct heir and Fuller's own creed. The positivist view that the methods which had been crowned with success in the sciences should now be applied to achieve comparable results in the human sciences was clearly expressed by Fuller in a letter to his father in 1916. He thought it

an extraordinary thing [that] whilst every science is run on a few definite principles, war today should be run on the dice-box of luck. . . . We can predict certain events in war as surely as Darwin could in life directly he grasped the fundamental principles of evolution. However we have no military Darwin as yet, let us hope the Germans will not discover one.[34]

This was practically a verbatim restatement of the views of the military thinkers of the Enlightenment, only with Darwin substituted for Newton. However, as Fuller complained, he had found no principles stated after the promising start of the *Field Service Regulations*, and his instructors at the Staff College had proved no help in this respect either. Surprisingly, he mentioned neither Jomini's celebrated set of principles, which had been studied throughout Europe and in the United States during the nineteenth century, nor Edward Hamley's

---

[32] Fuller, *Training Soldiers*; also, both from before the war and specifically citing Grandmaison, 'The Procedure of the Infantry Attack: A Synthesis from a Psychological Standpoint', *JRUSI*, 58 (1914), 63–8; 'The Tactical Penetration', ibid. 59 (1914), 378–89; in addition, *Memoirs*, 23–6; Trythall, *Fuller*, 26–31; Reid, *Fuller*, 22–7, 31, 138–9; Crook, *Darwinism, War, and History*, 132–6.   [33] Fuller, *Memoirs*, 28.
[34] King's, IV/3/190; quoted by Trythall, *Fuller*, 38.

widely circulated *Operations of War*, which neatly and elegantly presented Jomini's principles to generations of British Staff College students. By the coming of the twentieth century both had suffered a decline in popularity, caused both by the spread of the anti-positivist Prussian-German military theory and by the transformation of war itself. The principles that Jomini had abstracted from the Napoleonic system of operations but considered universally applicable had largely been rendered irrelevant by rapidly changing conditions.[35] In any event, Fuller started afresh, returning to Napoleon for inspiration but moving on to a higher level of abstraction. He had read Napoleon's *Maxims* back in 1901, and had been led to study the history of Napoleon's campaigns and his voluminous *Correspondence* by the Edwardian scholar-soldier, Lt. Col. F. M. Maude, to whom he had been introduced by Crowley in 1909. A child of the Enlightenment, Napoleon had repeatedly expressed in his writings the belief in military science based on a few immutable principles. And Maude, himself interested in military science, an evolutionist, and apparently a mystic, was an important source of influence on Fuller.[36]

By the outbreak of the First World War Fuller had crystallized the following list of six principles:

The principle of the Objective—the true objective being that point at which the enemy may be most decisively defeated; generally this point is to be found along the line of least resistance. The principle of Mass—that is, concentration of strength and effort at the decisive point. The principle of the Offensive; the principles of Security, Surprise and Movement (i.e. rapidity).[37]

As Reid has shown, in developing the principles of war Fuller consciously borrowed from Spencer's *First Principles*, as for example the latter's assertion that 'motion follows the line of least resistance or the line of greatest traction or the result of the two'.[38] At the Staff College, during the war, and for a decade later, Fuller worked on his principles, repeatedly rearranging them to make them truly primary and comprehensive. In the early 1920s his list of principles was incorporated into the British *Field Service Regulations*, became standard, and was copied

[35] See my *The Origins of Military Thought from the Enlightenment to Clausewitz* (Oxford, 1989); *Military Thought: The Nineteenth Century*, esp. ch. 1.

[36] King's, IV/12/35; Trythall, *Fuller*, 25; Reid, *Fuller*, 20–2; 89–90; Gat, *From the Enlightenment to Clausewitz*, 133–5.   [37] *Memoirs*, 28; *Training Soldiers*, 42.

[38] Reid, *Fuller*, 35, 93.

with slight variations by the Americans and by many other armies.[39] The heuristic and pedagogic value of these principles of war remains a matter of debate. In comparison to those of Jomini, for example, they claim greater universality—which was achieved, however, at the price of greater abstraction from any concrete reality.

The principles of war represented 'the tip of an iceberg in his [Fuller's] thinking, an iceberg labelled Science of War'.[40] In his writings during and after the First World War, culminating in *The Foundations of the Science of War* (1926), Fuller continuously worked towards the crystallization of such a science. He rediscovered the military thinkers of the Enlightenment, such as Maurice de Saxe, Henry Evans Lloyd, J. A. H. Guibert, and Robert Jackson, whose pleas for the formation of a universal theory of war he repeatedly cited and used (as they themselves had done in respect to each other) to prepare the ground for the coming of his own theory of war:[41]

In a small way I am trying to do for war what Copernicus did for astronomy, Newton for physics, and Darwin for natural history. My book, I believe, is the first in which a writer has attempted to apply the method of science to the study of war; for Lloyd, Jackson, Clausewitz, Jomini, and Foch did not do this.[42]

Informing his readers that he had read extensively in philosophy and science in his youth, Fuller cited Spencer, Huxley, Pearson, and a variety of popular scientific writers for their definitions of science and of the scientific method. He blamed the lack of a scientific approach to the study of war for the dismal failure of prewar military thinking (with the exception of Ivan Bloch) to predict the nature of the First World War. As Bacon, Descartes, and Locke had taught the modern world, he wrote, authority must give way to scientific study, based on an observation of historical experience, description, classification, critical thought, and generalization. War must pass from the alchemical to the

---

[39] Fuller, 'The Principles of War, with Reference to the Campaigns of 1914–15', *JRUSI*, 61 (1916), 1–40; 'Gold Medal (Military) Prize Essay for 1919: "The Application of Recent Developments in Mechanics and Other Scientific Knowledge to Preparation and Training for Future War on Land"', ibid. 65 (1920), 244; *Memoirs*, 28, 54, 388–9; *The Foundations of the Science of War* (London, 1926), 13–15; Trythall, *Fuller*, 108–9; Reid, *Fuller*, 94–5.   [40] Trythall, *Fuller*, 35.

[41] See e.g. Fuller, *The Reformation of War* (London, 1923), 24, 76; *The Foundations of the Science of War*, 18–25; Jomini, Clausewitz, and Foch are also cited; 'The Discipline of Robert Jackson', *Army Quarterly*, 10 (1925), 98–109; 'Major General Henry Lloyd: Adventurer and Military Philosopher', ibid. 12 (1926), 300–14; and repeatedly after in Fuller's later work; Gat, *From the Enlightenment to Clausewitz*, 25–135.

[42] *The Foundations of the Science of War*, 18.

scientific stage, from which it could then be applied to concrete problems through art.[43]

As had been the case with the military thinkers of the Enlightenment, the actual fruits of Fuller's programmatic rhetoric regarding the science of war were, at best, mixed. Apart from his principles, there were several other components to his proposed military science. These included interesting evolutionary theories—mainly derived from James, Kidd, and Pearson, and written in a social-Darwinist vein—regarding the biological and anthropological origins of war and its fundamental cultural–historical role in relations between and within societies.[44] There was a scholastic and cumbersome exposition of the 'elements' of war: men, movement, weapons and protection, each having negative and positive spheres of action, and all effected by 'conditions', such as time, space, ground, weather, numbers, morale, communications, supply, armament, and the like. In *The Foundations of the Science of War* Fuller even attempted a comprehensive speculative system, according to which war, like reality in general, was governed by what he called 'the Threefold Order', in which everything was divided into threes that came together in higher entities.[45] The system was embarrassingly artificial, the worst example of amateur metaphysics, and it was rightly received with perplexity and ridicule by readers of the book. It had its source in the dialectical and holistic ideas that Fuller had shared with Crowley and other turn-of-the-century mystics, which in turn had been vaguely inspired by German idealism. As Reid rightly points out, it was reminiscent, for example, of the system and ideas of the mystical social thinkers G. I. Gurdjieff and his disciple P. D. Ouspensky, who enjoyed great vogue in Western salons during the 1920s and 1930s and whom we shall repeatedly encounter on the following pages.[46] Finally, Fuller's book incorporated elaborate, sometimes useful but mostly clumsy and immature schemes for reorganizing and making efficient all the departments of the defence establishment. As mentioned before, the advancement of schemes for a sweeping overhaul of state apparatus had been characteristic of the movement for national efficiency before the First World War, and it would later

---

[43] Fuller 17, 20–47; cf. Fuller, *Tanks in the Great War, 1914–1918* (London, 1920), 297–9.

[44] See esp. Fuller, *The Reformation of War*, 6–23, 56–74.

[45] Fuller, 'Prize Essay', 240–4; 'The Foundations of the Science of War', *Army Quarterly*, 1 (1920), 90–111; *The Reformation of War*, 24–55; *The Foundations of the Science of War*, 48–62 and *passim*.   [46] Reid, *Fuller*, 12, 15, 17.

become a prominent feature of fascist programmes.[47] Soon Fuller was to advocate the systematic use of scientific management and scientific production techniques—Taylorism and Fordism—whose gospel was powerfully spreading from America during the 1920s.[48] The pervasive and intricate relation of Taylorist and Fordist ideology to fascist ideas will be discussed more fully later on.

But, of course, it was mainly for the way Fuller applied his positivist view of history and his *Kulturkritik* to form a comprehensive vision of the potential of a new mechanical invention—the tank—that he acquired his intellectual pre-eminence and worldwide reputation as Britain's leading military theorist. Within his sweeping interpretation of modern developments both machine armies and fascism were perceived as the trends of the future, the products of the machine age and of machine-dominated societies.

Machine Age Armies

Fuller was nominated GSO2 and then GSO1 to the newly created Heavy Branch of the Machine Gun Corps, later the Tank Corps, at the end of 1916. He had played no role in the invention and early evolution of the tank, in which Ernest Swinton, Winston Churchill, and Maurice Hankey had figured most prominently on the British side. He soon established himself indisputably as the brain of the new corps, developing its tactical doctrine and devising its operational schemes during the years 1917–18, as the corps grew from infancy to become a crucial weapon for the *Entente*. In general, however, his ideas were not altogether unique.

The first question that preoccupied people's minds both inside and outside the tank corps was how this completely new, untried, and fragile instrument was to be integrated most effectively in the battle against the German fortified line on the Western Front. Tactical methods, the details of cooperation with infantry, artillery, and aircraft, and the elaborate procedures of supply and communication had all to be worked out from scratch and continuously developed with experience. Fuller played a leading role in performing this task, but unknown to him, many of the ideas he developed in a series of staff papers and helped implement in practice had already been advanced by Swinton in his

---

[47] 'Prize Essay', 257–61; *The Reformation of War*, 229–55; *The Foundations of the Science of War*, 78–92; Searle, *The Quest for National Efficiency*.

[48] Fuller, *The Generalship of Ulysses S. Grant* (London, 1929), 15.

prophetic memoranda during 1915 and 1916. Both men recommended that the tank be employed offensively, in large numbers, with the aid of surprise, on suitable dry land, on a wide enough front of attack, and in cooperation with the other arms. Both believed its mobility, armour, and firepower could carry it through as far as the German second and third lines of defence, several miles deep. It would protect the infantry advance, create and threaten exposed enemy flanks, and prevent the attack from losing momentum as it moved out of the range of its artillery support. Hopefully, the tactical impasse of the war would thus be broken.[49]

From the summer of 1917 Fuller's staff papers on the employment of tanks reveal a clear progression towards a more ambitious conception. As the original heavy tanks were supplemented by medium models, he increasingly considered that the breaking of the enemy's trench lines should be followed by a pursuit and deeper exploitation of success by medium tanks, armoured cars, cavalry, and tractor-drawn artillery. In the summer of 1917 he proposed only raids and limited battles until greater superiority over the Germans could be built, and a decisive offensive in 1918, later postponed to 1919. His raid concept fore-shadowed the Battle of Cambrai in November 1917, the tank's first major success. For the later, decisive offensive Fuller gradually developed an operational scheme, of which the famous so-called 'Plan 1919' of May 1918 was only the ultimate version. The scheme was based on a 1000-strong tank army, divided into three. In the final version, 'Plan 1919', one force was intended for a conventional all-arms attack on the enemy defensive lines, while another was to be deployed in a direct breakthrough against the enemy's command system deep in his rear to create paralysis, panic, and complete breakdown of control. In Fuller's characteristic imagery, this was described as a shot at the enemy's brain and nervous system. Large-scale strategic pursuit by a third mechanized force would then turn the enemy's defeat into total collapse.

As Fuller himself admitted, many of these ideas were, again, not exclusively his own. Medium tanks, including the advanced Medium D,

---

[49] Ernest Swinton's papers, 'The Necessity for Machine-Gun Destroyers' (1 June 1915) and 'Notes on the Employment of Tanks' (Feb. 1916), are both cited in his *Eyewitness* (London, 1932), 129–34, 198–214. For Fuller, see 'Training Note No. 16' (Feb. 1917) and 'Projected Bases for the Tactical Employment of Tanks in 1918' (11 June 1917), in the bound volume of Tank Corps documents entitled 'Tank Strategy and Tactics 1916–1918', King's, TS TCO I/6 and I/16; this and the other volumes contain some of the most important source material on the development of Tank Corps tactics; also Fuller, *Memoirs*, 96–8, 122–30.

on which 'Plan 1919' was based, had been developed specifically for follow-up operations. The *Entente* powers were producing tanks by the thousand and at an accelerating rate during the last phase of the war. Ideas for a massive tank offensive in 1919 were entertained by the spring of 1918 by Field Marshals Henry Wilson and Ferdinand Foch, and by several of those concerned with tanks at the staffs of the *Entente* powers. These ideas developed simultaneously, though Fuller certainly played a significant role in advancing the concept.[50]

Finally, 'Plan 1919' already contained the germs of an even more advanced vision of war, that of a fully mechanized and highly mobile army. Originally, this vision had not been conceived by Fuller either, but by his subordinate, the GSO3 Captain Giffard Le Q. Martel. As early as November 1916 Martel wrote a paper entitled 'A Tank Army', in which he suggested that in the future great powers' armies would take the form of armoured forces whose characteristics would much resemble those of navies. Unhindered by geographical obstacles, they would be capable of operating freely across the land (and across water obstacles), supplied and defended in fortified bases, behind trenches and minefields. For the various functions Martel envisioned a variety of armoured vehicles which he labelled 'torpedo-tank', 'destroyer-tank', and 'battle-tank', as well as specialist and supply tanks. When he showed this paper to Fuller in March 1917, the latter at first objected on the grounds that the tank was merely an auxiliary to the infantry.[51] Gradually, however, Fuller took up the idea in its entirety and anchored it within a wider philosophy of history.

Indeed, that precisely was the point which made Fuller the leading prophet of the new epoch of warfare. More than single-mindedness, an obsessive streak of character, unorthodox personality, and presence at the right time and place were needed for the part. Swinton moved on to other tasks at the Committee of Imperial Defence after launching the

---

[50] Fuller, 'Projected Bases for the Tactical Employment of Tanks in 1918', 'Tank Operations Decisive and Preparatory, 1918–1919' (Jan. 1918), King's, TS TCO I/40, envisioning the employment of more than 10,000-tanks, and 'The Tactics of the Attack as Affected by the Speed and Circuit of the Medium 'D' Tank' (May–June 1918), King's, TS TCO I/50; 'Tank Raids' (6 Aug. 1917), in the bound volume of documents 'The Battle of Cambrai 1917', King's, I/BC I/2/2; *Memoirs*, 126–7, 172–5, 234–7, 318–41. See also most recently J. P. Harris, *Men, Ideas and Tanks: British Military Thought and Armoured Forces, 1903–1939* (Manchester, 1995), 47–172.

[51] G. Le Q. Martel, 'A Tank Army' (Nov. 1916), King's, TS TCO I/9; *In the Wake of the Tank* (London, 1931), 15–16; *An Outspoken Soldier* (London, 1949), 14; Fuller, *Memoirs*, 111–12, 318.

tank, and would later become Chichele Professor of Military History at Oxford. Martel was an engineer, and his main interest after the war would be tank design. But Fuller was a positivist student of war, and, like Wells, it was through this perspective that he would interpret the wider significance of the tank as one aspect of a comprehensive historical development.

Less than three months after Martel had shown him his tank army paper, Fuller wrote in his tactical memorandum:

The one thing to realise is, that mechanical warfare is going to supersede muscular warfare. That is to say, more and more is war going to depend on the engine than on man's legs. In the administrative services this war has already largely replaced horse traction by motor traction. Except for the armoured car, the tank is the first application of this means of movement to the fighting units. The tank to-day carries forward the riflemen of the future. These riflemen, or machine gunners, must be supported by tank artillery and tank bayonet-men, so as to occupy and make good what the tank riflemen render possible. If this is sound reasoning, then we should forthwith prepare to raise the mechanical army we shall require.[52]

Six months later Fuller suggested that the new epoch opening in land warfare was bringing forward developments which had already taken place not only at sea but in the whole sphere of economic production: 'the application of petrol to land warfare will prove as great a step in tactics as that of steam in naval warfare. . . . the application of machinery to land warfare is as great a saver of man-power as its application to manufacture.'[53] Man-carried and horse-drawn rifle and cannon armies were rapidly declining into obsolescence, to be wholly superseded in the end by mechanical armies and mechanical warfare.[54] As 'Plan 1919' stated, the old and the new could not be harmonized, as the tactics of the First World War had attempted to do, because mechanical armies represented an entirely new level of capabilities. Old arms, such as infantry and artillery, would become mechanical, and the former in particular would be reduced in size and importance. Cavalry would disappear. Aircraft would closely cooperate with the mechanical land armies.[55]

These were the ideas that Fuller continued to develop in a series of

---

[52] 'Projected Bases for the Tactical Employment of Tanks in 1918' *Memoirs*, 129–30.
[53] 29 Dec. 1917, quoted in *Memoirs*, 228.
[54] 'Tank Operations Decisive and Preparatory, 1918–1919' *Memoirs*, 235–6.
[55] 'The Tactics of the Attack as Affected by the Speed and Circuit of the Medium "D" Tank'; *Memoirs*, esp. 322–4, 330–3.

lectures and articles in the aftermath of the war. From August 1918 he headed a new branch in the War Office responsible for the organization and establishments of the Tank Corps, and he soon won himself a reputation as an intellectual maverick and propagandist of futurist mechanized warfare. In August 1919 he submitted to his superiors a memorandum entitled 'A New Model Army'. This became the core of an essay, 'The Application of Recent Developments in Mechanics and Other Scientific Knowledge to Preparation and Training for Future War on Land', which won the gold medal at a special competition announced by the Royal United Services Institute for Defence Studies. The development of war, Fuller stated, followed the general development of civilization as a whole. This had been profoundly affected by recent advances in the sciences, especially in the fields of electricity, chemistry, and mechanics. Their application to war produced the two leading land inventions of the First World War: poison gas and the petrol-engined tank. A new epoch in military history had opened in which manpower would be replaced by machine-power. The slow and vulnerable manual mass armies would give way to mechanical armies relying on scientific and industrial infrastructure at home. Fuller outlined a programme for an evolutionary transformation of the old-style army, according to which its transport and fighting echelons were to be gradually mechanized, and the traditional arms reduced in size. In the last stage the army would become fully mechanized. He borrowed the analogy Martel had drawn with naval warfare, where mechanization had already taken place, to project fleets of armoured vehicles possessing naval designations.[56] In his later works he would further pursue this analogy, suggesting that the armoured fleets would freely travel the face of the earth, barely hindered by either geography or logistics. Fuller even invaded the naval sphere itself, entering and outrageously winning the Naval Prize Essay competition for 1920. Then and throughout the interwar period he predicted the decline of the Dreadnought before the aircraft, the aircraft carrier, and the submarine.[57]

Fuller continued with his historical interpretation of the rise of the tank. To get the proper perspective on the confounding development of warfare during the First World War, he wrote in 1920, one should ask

---

[56] 'Prize Essay', esp. 240, 246–8, 255, 261–74; *Memoirs*, 392–9, 408–10; also *Tanks in the Great War*, 302–5, 313–15.

[57] *Naval Review*, 10 (1922), 73–104; *Memoirs*, 393–4; *The Reformation of War*, 136–48, 176–9; *On Future Warfare* (London, 1928), 215–18; *Towards Armageddon* (London, 1937), 133–5, 196–208.

what had been happening in civil life? a mechanical evolution, so rapid that no revolution in the whole world's history can compare to it. Every day brought to birth some new invention, every hour civilisation gathered greater speed; epochs crumbled away, epochs sprang up in the night, science was sweeping brute force off the face of the earth, and was replacing muscle by mechanical energy.[58]

Communications were one aspect of this rapid transformation. As Fuller would later suggest, the First Industrial Revolution, motivated by steam power, was followed by a second, powered by oil and electricity.[59] In the first wave, 'the locomotive, the railway, and the steamship, the great mechanical movers of civil life', made possible the assembly, transportation, and supply of armies of millions. Then, the invention of the internal-combustion engine and the lorry made it possible to 'mechanically link up the strategic base of operation, which consists of a network of railways, with the battlefield itself'. At the end of this highly advanced system there remained, however, the old foot armies—supported by riding and pack animals—of the pre-mechanized epoch. Is it any wonder that, despite all their efforts and sacrifices during the First World War, these armies proved so pathetically immobile and ineffective? The remedy lay with the proliferation of the internal-combustion engine. 'The next link to forge is a mechanical tactical striking force.'[60]

This wide historical perspective within which the mechanization of war was to be understood is now fairly well recognized. But so is any interpretive perspective once it has been formulated and absorbed into people's way of thinking. At the time, Fuller's ideas were eye-opening. It should be remembered that people were in real difficulty as to what to make of the tank. It did not fit into any previously known category. It was variously regarded during and after the war as a historical freak, a specialized mechanical instrument designed to overcome trenches and barbed wire, or, at best, a useful auxiliary arm to infantry or a substitute for cavalry in reconnaissance and pursuit. Fuller's interpretation proved so powerful because it offered a broad context within which the emergence and future development of the tank were understood as an integral, and in a way inevitable, aspect of the evolution of modern industrial society as a whole.[61] Heinz Guderian's later summary of the

---

[58] 'The Introduction of Mechanical Warfare on Land', *Royal Engineers Journal* (Jan. 1921), repr. in Fuller, *On Future Warfare*, 114–15.   [59] *Grant*, pp. viii, 26.
[60] 'The Introduction of Mechanical Warfare on Land', 115–22.
[61] Cf. Fuller, *Memoirs*, 452–3.

influence Fuller and his friends had on him testifies to precisely that sort of effect: 'They envisaged it [the tank] in relationship to the growing motorization of our age, and thus they became the pioneers of a new type of warfare.'[62]

Machine Age Armies and Machine Age Societies

Indeed, Fuller's main interest shifted increasingly from his attempt to develop a positivist science of war to an effort to put forward a positivist interpretation of military history. His mind and work were dominated throughout the interwar period by two closely related themes. First, he strove to lay out the main features of the new mechanical epoch. Next, he struggled to develop more deeply, both by means of *Kulturkritik* and in historical–positivist terms, how the new epoch fitted into the general evolution of modern society and, further, into the course of universal history. This he called 'the natural history of war'. Nominally, he wrote more than forty books during his lifetime, some of them—after he had left the army—for commercial reasons. But programmatically, he was now to write only two works, corresponding to the themes mentioned above and repeatedly reworked in sequences of conceptually similar books. First was *The Reformation of War* (1923), whose vision of machine warfare was reproduced with little variation in *On Future Warfare* (1928), and again in *Lectures on FSR III* (1932). Second was the cultural critique of *The Dragon Teeth: A Study of War and Peace* (1932), repeated in *The First of the League Wars* (1936) and again echoed in *Towards Armageddon* (1937). This category was also developed in a more historical form in *War and Western Civilization, 1832–1932: A Study of War as a Political Instrument and the Expression of Mass Democracy* (1932), later to be refurbished (and politically somewhat redressed) as *The Conduct of War, 1789–1961: A Study of the Impact of the French, Industrial and Russian Revolutions on War and Its Conduct* (1961). Fuller's other books amplified the same themes. By the 1930s his ideas and historical senses considerably widened and gained in depth, as he strove to develop the notions he had gradually evolved since his youth.

Dominated by science and by a revolution in communications, the new epoch, according to Fuller, would be moral, intelligent, mobile, and

---

[62] H. Guderian, *Panzer Leader* (London, 1952), 20. More fully on this contentious subject, see my 'British Influence and the Evolution of the Panzer Arm: Myth or Reality?', *War in History*, 4(2) (1997), 150–73; 4(3), (1997) 316–38.

élitist—in many ways the opposite of its predecessor—in war as in peace. As Condorcet had already foreseen in the 1790s, nineteenth-century mass armies were the product of the evolving mass society, or mass democracy—an era reflected in the writings of Clausewitz and Marx. Manual at first, like the agricultural epoch to which they belonged, these armies were later supported by the mass-production capabilities of the emerging industrial era. Thrown against one another, they relied on numbers and brute force. Their characteristic mode of operation was physical destruction of the enemy's armed forces. How-ever, with the further expansion of scientific and industrial society, and as the laboratory was increasingly taking over the workshop at the forefront of civilization, both armies and the nature of war itself were being transformed. The armies of the new age would rely on highly advanced machines, especially cross-country armoured vehicles incor-porating the old arms, supported by gas and by aircraft. Further into the future, as early as 1928 Fuller prophesied, lay automated, electric [electronic], 'robotic' warfare. Quality would be more important than numbers, and as sophisticated equipment was expensive, the old con-script armies would give way to smaller, professional, élite forces. Extremely mobile, these would seek to dislocate, paralyse, and cause the disintegration of their enemy by rapidity of movement and man-oeuvre, rather than destroy him in a direct clash of forces and costly attrition.[63]

According to Fuller, this transformation of field warfare corre-sponded to a deeper change in the nature of war and of the interna-tional system in the industrial–commercial era. One of the earliest critics of the First World War, Fuller was quick to embrace Keynes's influential ideas in *The Economic Consequences of the Peace* (1920). As Keynes stressed, in the highly advanced, interdependent global econ-omy that had emerged since the late nineteenth century, the enemy's

[63] See esp. Fuller, 'The Last Lap of the Physical Epoch' and 'The First Lap of the Moral Epoch', in *The Reformation of War*, 75–119, 229–55, and *passim*; *On Future Warfare*, pp. v–vii, 83–197 and *passim*; *Armoured Warfare* (London, 1943; originally *Lectures on FSR III*, 1932), 7–12, 32–42, and *passim*; *War and Western Civilization* (London, 1932), *The Dragon's Teeth: A Study of War and Peace* (London, 1932), 212–23, 229, 296–9 (robotics in the last two page references; also the TS 'Electrical Battles' (1928): Rutgers, II/12); *The First of the League Wars* (London, 1936), 99–106, 111–15, 125–8, 169–76 and *passim*; *Towards Armageddon*, 92, 132 (robotics); all repeated in later books during and after the Second World War. A similar conceptual framework has been recently advanced in A. and H. Toffler's *Third Wave* (New York, 1980) and *War and Anti-War* (New York, 1993); and, directly influenced by Fuller's work, R. Simpkin, *Race to the Swift: Thoughts on Twenty-First Century Warfare* (London, 1985).

ruin was no longer his problem alone, as it had been in agricultural, generally autarkic societies, but was seriously damaging to one's own economic prosperity and social well-being. War had to be cut short and made less destructive if it were not to become wholly counter-productive and lose its political rationale: the creation of a better peace.[64]

Of course, the logic of the economic argument had long led liberals to the conclusion that war was no longer an advantageous instrument of international relations and must therefore be abolished. Fuller was ambivalent about this prospect. As an anti-liberal and social-Darwinist he regarded war as biologically, socially, and metaphysically necessary and even beneficial, an antidote to degeneration and decadence—at least until humanity developed much further. He was particularly hostile toward the League of Nations. He criticized the League for attempting forcibly to freeze the global status quo to the advantage of the strong by pressing down on and papering over the dynamic currents and deep sources of discontent that lay at the roots of conflict. The treatment of the symptoms rather than the causes of the disease would never work. If the elimination of war was to be seriously attempted, its deeper sources had to be exposed and treated. In Fuller's opinion they sprang from the ills of modern society, and thus could only be approached in a wider context. In his view, the First World War was the product of the uncontrolled materialistic order of industrial civilization which set all against all. Fierce competition over global spaces for economic growth fuelled national anxieties in the international arena. Widening social gaps, poverty, and a loss of spiritual values bred social discontent, a fear of civilization, and a quest for moral transcendence. To remove these causes of strife and war, one had to abolish the old sick civilization for a new harmonious order. All forms of protectionism and tariff barriers had to be removed, to allow free trade and universal access to international resources and markets. European integration, federation, and unity, as well as the establishment of a just world state, based on genuine harmony rather than force, had to be pursued. Internally, chaotic and degenerating materialism must be replaced by a new spiritual revival and well-regulated order. For Fuller,

---

[64] Fuller, *The Reformation of War*, 75, 144, 187–8; Keynes is cited e.g. on p. 270, and repeatedly in Fuller's later works; *The Foundations of the Science of War*, 63, 76–7; *On Future Warfare*, 166–8, 212; *Armoured Warfare*, 41.

the instrument and expression of this comprehensive cultural transformation was fascism.[65]

Fuller's critique of mass democracy was scathing. In his official memorandum 'Tank Operations Decisive and Preparatory, 1918–1919', forwarded to the Chief of the General Staff, Field Marshal Henry Wilson, at the beginning of 1918, he wrote: 'Our destiny, as a great nation, lies in the hands of an ignorant and discontented proletariat, which is swayed by words.'[66] To be sure, similar views were not uncommon among the military (including C. G. S. Wilson himself) during the war, but intellectually and ideologically their significance in Fuller's case was much deeper. For him democracy was not the distasteful but inevitable trend of the future but, on the contrary, a doomed order belonging to a passing phase of civilization and collapsing on account of its ills and patent inadequacy for modern times. Democracy was predicated on quantity, whereas modern scientific society was based on quality. Truth and understanding were beyond the masses' reach. While still formally in the army, and even before the British Union of Fascists was created, Fuller wrote in a Nietzschean vein that Christianity, democracy, and socialism were the enemies of the forces of life and of true morality. Alien to knowledge and excellence, they represented the rule of ignorance and weakness. Sickly humanism and pacifism were among their more recent products. The growing standardization of life oppressed the individual, the ingenious, and the spiritual. Rampant materialism and false, barren rationalism bred nihilism, hedonism, and a return to bestial instincts. The new mass entertainment was passive and corrupting. The rise in the number of the poor degenerated the race. Demagoguery and emotionalism masqueraded as the will of the people. What the world needed was authority. The masses had to be controlled by the intelligent minority and by some mystical ideal.[67] It was no accident that Fuller joined the Fascists when the party was established.

---

[65] Fuller, *The Reformation of War*, 6–23, 211, 256–83; 'The Progress of War', *The Nineteenth Century and After*, 100 (1926), 483–94; *Grant*, pp. vii, 392–412; *The Dragon's Teeth*, 1–179; *War and Western Civilization, 1832–1932* (London, 1932), 7–9, 245–66; *Empire Unity and Defence* (London, 1934) 'The World at a Dead End', *Fighting Forces*, 10 (1934), 551–6; 'The Foundation of European Order', ibid. 11 (1934), 23–9; 'Fascism and War', *Fascist Quarterly*, 1 (1935), 140–55; *Memoirs*, 464–77; *The First of the League Wars*, pp. v–vii, 106–11, 123–4, 154–61.   [66] Quoted in Fuller, *Memoirs*, 237.

[67] Fuller, *War and Western Civilization*, 7–9, 224; *The Dragon's Teeth*, 7–13, 22–39, 58–9; *India in Revolt* (London, 1931), 134, 240, 244.

After joining the British Union of Fascists Fuller wrote that, whereas democracy had its origin in the agricultural and early industrial age, fascism was the expression of the new scientific epoch. While democracy was based on uncontrolled individual freedom which in practice led to exploitation, anarchy, and maldistribution of wealth by finance, fascism would rationally organize society for the common good and for a true, higher form of reasoned freedom. Admittedly, Continental fascist regimes of his time were still crude and experimental, but that was only their beginning. Against American capitalism and Soviet Bolshevism, both materialistic and Jewish-inspired, Europe was taking up fascism which promoted something beyond material needs—a unifying national and religious ideal. Virile, youthful, and full of energy and creativity, fascism would counter the forces of decadence, passivity, and corruption that had engulfed Western civilization. While peaceful and non-militaristic, it would infuse the military virtues of courage, honour, self-sacrifice, comradeship, and solidarity into civil life.[68]

These views, which Fuller had crystallized long before the creation of the British Union of Fascists, remarkably resembled the ideas of the man who founded the party, gave it its doctrines and public stature, was in effect the party—Sir Oswald Mosley (1896–1980). One of the most brilliant men in British politics, minister at the age of 33 and widely regarded as destined for greatness before he left the Labour Party in 1931, Mosley was a positivist and an evolutionist for whom fascism was the modern order, the new synthesis for the industrial–scientific age. Mosley espoused Keynesian economics and admired American efficiency and industrial methods. He wanted a well-regulated society and economy, ruled by a technocratic élite of managers, professionals, and technicians which would replace capitalist–democratic anarchy. Influenced by Goethe, Hegel, Nietzsche, Spengler, and Shaw, he called for Faustian vitality to counter decadence and decline. He was not particularly racist, and his anti-Semitism developed only in the 1930s, partly in response to Jewish hostility to his party. From the 1920s Mosley saw the balance of power system and commercial rivalry as the root cause of the First World War, and he wanted them, and war, eliminated. While initially supporting collective security and the League of Nations, he later blamed the League for perpetuating the Great War's

[68] Fuller, *The First of the League Wars*, 7–8, 88, 120–39, 148–54, 251–301; *Empire Unity and Defence*, 62, 82–3, 287, 294; *Towards Armageddon*, 236–7; 'Dictatorship and Generalship', *Army Quarterly*, 35 (1937), 57–8.

rivalry. Instead, he called for European political cooperation and economic union.[69]

Scholars agree that Mosley's, and Fuller's, advocacy of peace, of genuine European cooperation and conciliation, pre-dated not only their own formal fascist phase but also the rise of the National-Socialists to power in Germany. It became one of the BUF's main principles during the 1930s as 'the party of peace', not because of subservience to foreign interests. The BUF's leaders were unquestionably patriotic, and, while looking at the fascist regimes in Italy and Germany as welcome partners, maintained a British reserve towards all things foreign and certainly felt no inferiority towards them. Both Mosley and Fuller, who became a member of the BUF's Policy Committee in 1934 and Mosley's chief adviser on defence, advocated imperial unity and rearmament for strong defence. But once Germany and Italy were given their due in Europe, the BUF looked to close and peaceful cooperation with those countries in the interests of European civilization. Both believed that Hitler did not want war, and that German autarky was merely an expediency forced upon him by conflict.[70]

As international tensions mounted, Fuller, like Mosley, wanted Britain to stay out of Continental conflicts and leave Germany hegemonious in Europe and a bulwark against Russian communism. Otherwise, Fuller feared the coming of a new comprehensive world war of a quasi-religious nature, a new Armageddon, whose winner would impose its rule on Western civilization. For Fuller, the winner would either be fascism, the expression of the new scientific age, or communism, the culmination of the era of industrial democracy, 'the early coal and steam age'—both in violent forms, due to an unnecessary and ruinous war—but not parliamentary liberal-democracy, whose time had passed.[71] If war came, it would assume the character of 'totalitarian warfare', which was not Ludendorff's total war of endurance but a lightning one,

---

[69] C. Cross, *The Fascists in Britain* (London, 1961); R. Benewick, *The Fascist Movement in Britain* (London, 1972); R. Skidelsky, *Oswald Mosley* (London, 1981); K. Lunn and R. Thurlow (eds.), *British Fascism* (London, 1980); O. Mosley, *My Life* (London, 1968). Leslie Susser's regrettably unpublished Oxford dissertation, 'Fascist and Anti-Fascist Attitudes in Britain between the Wars' (1988), importantly expands on the cultural background of British fascism.

[70] Cf. Mosley, *My Life*, 382–8; Fuller, *Empire Unity and Defence*; *The First of the League Wars*, 145–7, 183–5; *Towards Armageddon*, 43–4.

[71] Fuller, *The First of the League Wars*, 159–65; *Towards Armageddon*, 236–8; 'The Soviet-Spanish War to September 1938', *Army Quarterly*, 37 (1939), 312–21.

launched by surprise, using high-quality mobile machine armies to paralyse and disarm the enemy.[72]

Positivist, evolutionary, and dialectical interpretations of history found expression not only in linear views of progress but also in cyclical and spiral conceptions. For Fuller, old forms and values, like spirituality or social cohesion, seemingly lost during the evolution of civilization, reappeared in new guises and higher syntheses to fulfil crucial functions. In the military field Fuller suggested that European history had seen two grand cycles of warfare: the Classical and the Christian. These divided respectively into three tactical cycles: cavalry, infantry, and artillery, which he later redesignated 'shock', 'shock and missiles', and 'missiles'. Roughly, both grand cycles reflected the transformation from rural to urbanized and industrialized civilization. Equally, they were motivated by an 'evolutionary pendulum of weapon power, slowly or rapidly swinging from the offensive to the protective and back again in harmony with the speed of civil progress'. Every measure enjoys a period of success following its introduction, but thereby provokes countermeasures to redress the balance. Fuller called this 'the constant tactical factor' which lay at the root of the 'law of military evolution'.[73] As his biographer points out, Fuller again drew extensively on the ideas and vocabulary of Spencer, Darwin, James, and Pearson in formulating his evolutionary scheme of military development and in explaining the psychological tension between aggressiveness and fear, impulse and inhibition, that fuelled it. Later on he found support for his views before in the works of Oswald Spengler and Arnold Toynbee.[74] Fuller suggested that the artillery, or projectile, cycle of the Christian era, which had started with the Industrial Revolution and which stretched from the middle of the nineteenth century to the First World War, was subsiding. The tank heralded a new (cavalry or shock) tactical cycle, thus implicitly opening a new grand cycle of civilization to supersede the Christian. In

---

[72] *The First of the League Wars*, 51–89, 165–225; *Towards Armageddon*, 48–54.

[73] Fuller, 'The Influence of Tanks on Cavalry Tactics', *Cavalry Journal*, 10 (1920); 'Science and War', *The Nineteenth Century and After*, 103 (1928), 88–96; *The Dragon's Teeth*, 212–49, quotation from p. 213.

[74] Although at times Fuller expressed scepticism about the rich and complex conceptions incorporated in Spengler's *Decline of the West* (London, 1926), he shared the latter's pessimistic *Kulturkritik* of Western civilization and the notion of its decline, prevalent among right-wing intellectuals before and after the First World War. For his scepticism, see Fuller, *India in Revolt*, 33; both Spengler and Toynbee are extensively cited e.g. in *Thunderbolts* (London, 1946); James is quoted in e.g. *Empire Unity and Defence*, 107; see the perceptive discussion in Reid, *Fuller*, 134–40.

one variant on the theme of élite modern society, Fuller speculated that armour might bring about a new, quasi-feudal regime run by a new mechanized aristocracy.[75] All the same, aware of the dialectical development of weapon power, by the late 1920s he wrote that the tank would soon have to contend with anti-tank devices such as the gun and the mine, which (in a new 'shock and projectile' cycle) would limit its rule and constantly vie with it for supremacy.[76]

Conclusion

This summary—perhaps any summary—of Fuller's ideas can never substitute for the original, levelling as it does the dazzling heights and embarrassing lows of his content and style. It cannot do justice to the wealth of tantalizing ideas, brilliant insights, original flashes of inspiration, and extremely suggestive historical interpretations which flow incessantly from Fuller's untamed, self-taught, and amateurish but ingeniously creative mind. At second hand they all lose much and pale somewhat, though gaining perhaps in coherence and readability. Stylistically, Fuller's works were always breathtaking, provocative, and engaging, but often obscure, mystifying, or mystical, at times deliberately so, as he thought wisdom was not intended for the masses. It was his friend, junior partner, and rival, Liddell Hart, who communicated many of his ideas to a wider public in a simplified and marketable form—and free from fascist overtones—taking much of the credit in the process.

Confining ourselves to the strictly military aspect, Fuller's ideas have attracted considerable criticism. In his remarkable critique *The 'Mechanization' of War* (1927) Victor Germains foreshadowed the opinion formed at the British War Office during the 1930 and anticipated virtually every point raised by later historians. Serialized and abstracted at the time by the Germans and Russians, his book has been undeservedly forgotten today. While expressing support for the tank and for mechanization, Germains claimed that Fuller and his disciples had been guilty of exaggeration, distortion, and oversimplification. He argued that mechanization did not economize on the overall number of people engaged—as the history of industrialization had

---

[75] *Thunderbolts*, 132.

[76] Fuller, 'One Hundred Problems of Mechanization', *Army Quarterly*, 19 (1929), 256–7; *The Dragon's Teeth*, 289–90; *Armoured Warfare* 20, 27, 85–94; 'The Problem of Tank and Anti-Tank Weapons', *Fighting Forces*, 14 (1937), 42–5; *Towards Armageddon*, 140–1.

shown—but merely redirected their contribution. In addition, he dismissed the claim that mechanized armies would be cheaper than their predecessors, or that civil industry and civil vehicles could be easily converted to military use. Thus he held that in the foreseeable future large-scale and necessarily unmechanized armies would be essential for supporting the mobile forces, in both offence and defence, in what was bound to be a protracted war. Mobile war did not necessarily promise quick decision. Modern industrial nations possessed vast resources and great endurance, and they would not succumb to rapid manœuvre alone. Further, Germains preceded and perhaps influenced Fuller in claiming that the development of the anti-tank gun and mine would considerably limit the tank's mobility. He also held that the naval analogy was false and misleading. Mobile forces would never be capable of travelling freely in any direction. Because of cost/effectiveness the railway would retain its primacy as a means of communication on land, followed by the lorry, and only lastly by the tractor. Roads were essential for land mobility, and much preferable even for cross-country vehicles. Unavoidably, they would face heavy pressure. Logistics, practically ignored by the mechanization enthusiasts, would remain a major restriction on manœuvre. Finally, in many non-European theatres and for policing the empire, unmechanized forces would be best.[77]

In any case, it is not our purpose here to evaluate Fuller's ideas but to bring out the intellectual thread running though his work. His anti-materialism and hostility towards bourgeois/mass society placed him within the ranks of the revived turn-of-the-century European right. His evolutionism and positivism indicated that he belonged to its radical and future-oriented, rather than conservative and nostalgic wing. He was a typical recruit to the modernist brand of proto-fascism and fascism, particularly powerful within the springs of Italian fascism, but noticeable everywhere in Europe, and later characteristic of Oswald Mosley's movement. He believed that the train of history was rapidly advancing towards a new qualitative scientific–technological–industrial age which would require a new, efficient, and highly organized form of social and economic regime, ruled by a professional–technocratic–meritocratic élite. Correspondingly, moral revival, new dynamism, and vitalism would replace democratic decadence. This wider trend of civilization development also provided the framework within which

[77] V. W. Germains, *The 'Mechanization' of War* (London, 1927), 43–4, 74–89, 94–5, 129–41, 166, 168–217, 225, 229, 244, and *passim*.

the future shape of armed forces was to be understood. They would be designed, organized, and run by scientific methods. They would become fully mechanized, making use of the latest products of industry and the laboratory, while reducing in numbers to become élite forces. Rapidity of movement, sophisticated control, and a highly discriminate mode of operations would make the moral dislocation and physical paralysis of the enemy their aim. Fuller was not the only one to hold these views. Throughout the West proto-fascists and fascists thought along similar lines.

3

Futurism, Proto-Fascist Italian Culture, and the Sources of Douhetism

The positivist vision of a modern, highly organized, and efficient society that we have seen most strikingly expressed in Fuller's (and Mosley's) brand of fascist modernism was matched by yet another strand, derived mainly from artistic sources, which aestheticized and celebrated the machine and the attributes of futurist society as a mighty force for moral liberation and human elevation. It is this strand of fascist modernism that we shall now examine more closely. Nowhere did it flourish more powerfully than in proto-fascist Italian culture; and in its arsenal of dynamic machines nothing equalled the symbolic potency of the aeroplane.

D'Annunzio, Marinetti, and the Air

It is widely recognized that one of the main sources of post-First World War Italian Fascism was pre-war Italian avant-garde culture. A forerunner of both was Italy's most famous poet, novelist, and playwright, the flamboyant and charismatic Gabriele d'Annunzio (1864–1938), whose international artistic celebrity was matched by the publicity raised by his extravagant love life and tempestuous politics. A parliamentary deputy for the conservatives from 1897, he swung to the left in 1900 to become a socialist deputy. In fact, no more a socialist than an ordinary conservative, he (as a considerable number of intellectuals would do in the following decade) was searching for a new form of politics and a new spiritual synthesis, to be discovered somewhere between extreme right and extreme left. Anti-democratic, influenced by Wagner and Nietzsche, and a Darwinist, d'Annunzio closely identified himself by the mid-1880s with the fashionable apprehensive literature then coming out regarding the psychology of the masses. He called for the defence of aristocratic values and high culture against the 'barbarians'.[1] Yet with the coming of the twentieth century d'Annunzio's contempt for the masses blended with a new attitude. At the same time as political theorists like Vifredo Pareto, Gaetano Mosca, and Robert Michels were developing their élite theories, d'Annunzio came to the conclusion that the masses could be mobilized, controlled, and harnessed by the élite for the achievement of great spiritual, nationalist, and imperialistic aims. This was the notion that he would perfect with the techniques of charismatic leadership and perpetual public liturgy characterizing his ominous nationalist-revolutionary rule in Fiume in 1919–21, techniques which were to be closely learnt and imitated by Mussolini.[2]

This political shift was also evident in d'Annunzio's art. During the 1880s and 1890s he had won international renown in the style of *fin-de-siècle* 'Decadence' and 'aestheticism'. His attitude towards the modern had been at best ambivalent. By the closing years of the century, however, he embraced modernity with enthusiasm. His elevated language and rich classical imagery were now blended with an exaltation of the power generated by industrial society and by the machine. In 1900 he wrote characteristically in an envious article on Germany:

All of . . . its cities have become glowing refineries, centres of magnificent industries; the men of . . . its countryside have been attracted to the precise and shining machines; the smokestacks of the factories are myriad in . . . its skies . . . Upon the old Prussian military tradition the novelty of the industrial age has been miraculously grafted.

In the same vein d'Annunzio now celebrated the train, the street-car, the warship, and the torpedo boat:

> Ship of steel, flashing ahead straight and swift
> and beautiful as an unsheathed weapon,
> living and pulsing
> as though the metal enclosed a terrible heart.

By the first decade of the twentieth century, however, it was the dynamism and heroic individualism promised by the fast car and then by the aeroplane that most captivated d'Annunzio. For enthusiasts

---

[1] J. M. Becker, *Nationalism and Culture: Gabriele D'Annunzio and Italy after the Risorgimento* (New York, 1994) is particularly instructive here.

[2] G. Mosse, 'The Poet and the Exercise of Political Power: Gabriele d'Annunzio', in his *Masses and Man: Nationalist and Fascist Perception of Reality* (Detroit, 1987), 87–103; M. Ledeen, *The First Duce: D'Annunzio at Fiume* (Baltimore, 1977).

at the beginning of the century these were not merely machines but the engines of a new age of boundless revolutionary potential, moral and civilization-transforming forces. Much like Wells, d'Annunzio now believed that a new élite of technocrats and virile technological knights would replace the old élite at the head of modern society.[3] These were the attitudes that d'Annunzio shared with the young avant-garde artists who launched a crusade against the bastions of established culture in Italy in the decade before the First World War, and whose relation to him mixed the conflicting sentiments of imitation, rejection, and envy. In Florence the group around the writers Giovanni Papini (1881–1956) and Giuseppe Prezzolini (1882–1983), the painter and critic Ardengo Soffici (1879–1964), and their journals *Leonardo* and *La Voce*, rebelled against the preoccupation of Italian culture with its past heritage, denounced decadence, and called for a virile spiritual, artistic, and moral regeneration. They proclaimed that the age of democracy had come to an end and that a new aristocratic age was beginning. The young socialist Benito Mussolini (1883–1945), already deeply influenced by Nietzsche, Sorel, and Pareto, corresponded with the leaders of the group, reading and contributing to its journals. However, the Florentine group was largely overshadowed by, and from 1913 began to cooperate with, another avant-garde group—which had been gaining international fame—Marinetti's Milanese Futurism.[4]

The poet Filippo Tommaso Marinetti (1876–1944) launched Futurism in a great public relations gesture that would become characteristic of his movement's mode of operation. His 'Manifesto of Futurism' was published on 20 February 1909 on the front page of one the most respected newspapers of Europe's cultural capital, *Le Figaro* of Paris. In the coming months it was echoed by other newspapers throughout Europe. It read as follows:

1. We intend to sing the love of danger, the habit of energy and fearlessness.
2. Courage, audacity, and revolt will be essential elements of our poetry.
. . .
4. We say that the world's magnificence has been enriched by a new beauty: the beauty of speed. A racing car whose hood is adorned with great pipes, like

---

[3] Becker, *D'Annunzio*, 183–202, is again especially good here; quotations from 184, 185, the latter from 'Naval Odes' (1892).

[4] W. Adamson, *Avant-Garde Florence: From Modernism to Fascism* (Cambridge, Mass., 1993); 'The Language of Opposition in Early Twentieth-Century Italy: Rhetorical Continuities between Prewar Florentine Avant-Gardism and Mussolini's Fascism', *Journal of Modern History*, 64 (1992), 22–51.

serpents of explosive breath—a roaring car that seems to run on grapeshot—is more beautiful than the *Victory of Samothrace.*

5. We want to hymn the man of the wheel, who hurls the lance of his spirit across the Earth, along the circle of its orbit.

. . .

8. We stand on the last promontory of the centuries! . . . Why should we look back? . . . We already live in the absolute, because we have created eternal, omnipresent speed.

9. We will glorify war—the world's only hygiene—militarism, patriotism, the destructive gesture of freedom-bringers, beautiful ideas worth dying for, and scorn for woman.

10. We will destroy the museums, libraries, academies of every kind, will fight moralism, feminism, every opportunistic or utilitarian cowardice.

11. We will sing the great crowds excited by work, by pleasure, and by riot; we will sing of the multicolored, polyphonic tides of revolution in the modern capitals; we will sing of the vibrant nightly fervour of arsenals and shipyards blazing with violent electric moons; greedy railway stations that devour smoke-plumed serpents; factories hung on clouds by the crooked lines of their smoke; bridges that stride the rivers like giant gymnasts, flashing in the sun with a glitter of knives; adventurous steamers that sniff the horizon; deep chested locomotives whose wheels paw the tracks like the hooves of enormous steel horses bridled by tubing; and the sleek flight of planes whose propellers chatter in the wind like banners and seem to cheer like an enthusiastic crowd.[5]

Unlike many of the widely diverging artistic styles coming under the title 'Modernism', the nature and programme of Futurism claimed to reflect the lexical meaning of the concept. Rather than apprehend and shrink from the products of modernity, from industrialization, urbanity, and their attendant social forms (an attitude that was widespread among Western cultural élites), Futurism embraced them with enthusiasm. Perhaps, as was suggested to Marinetti by the painter, writer, and would-be fascist Wyndham Lewis (1884–1957) who together with his friends founded Vorticism in Britain under Futurist influence, Futurism's modernistic enthusiasm was due to Italy's industrial backwardness when compared to Britain, France, or Germany.[6] This backwardness shamed her élite and made it eager to catch up. Futurist poets, painters, sculptors, and architects celebrated the rhythm and glitter of the 'electrified' metropolis, the functional beauty and radiating

[5] F. T. Marinetti, *Selected Writings* (New York, 1972), 39–44.

[6] Cited by D. Edgerton, *England and the Aeroplane: An Essay on a Militant and Technological Nation* (London, 1991), 13; more generally, F. Jameson, *Fables of Aggression: Wyndham Lewis, the Modernist as Fascist* (Berkeley, Calif., 1979), 5 and *passim.*

power of the industrial plant, the exhilarating, Dionysian speed of the car, and the boundless new horizons opened by the aeroplane. Rejecting democracy, parliamentarism, and mediocrity, Marinetti believed that the future belonged to a new vigorous élite, composed of artists, inventors, and technicians, that would engage in creative struggle—and war. In the often-cited words of the art critic and left-wing social theorist Walter Benjamin, Marinetti's work most strikingly reveals the nature of fascism as the aesthetization of politics and war.[7] In *War: The World's Only Hygiene* (1911–15) Marinetti depicted almost biological hybrids of man and machine and, as one essay was titled, a futurist 'Electrical War'. Having described a world dominated by science and technology, the essay went on:

Intelligence finally reigns everywhere. Muscular work ceases to be servile, now having only three goals: hygiene, pleasure, and struggle . . . Twenty five great powers govern the world, fighting over the markets of a superabundant industrial production. And this is why we finally arrive at the first electric war. No more of those old explosives! Then we will know what to do with the rebellion of imprisoned gases that throb angrily beneath the atmosphere's heavy knees. Steel elephants, bristling with shining trunks pointed to the enemy, advance from two directions on the border between the two peoples—enormous pneumatic machines rolling down their tracks. . . . These slip away soon afterwards, to right and left along their tracks, making way for locomotives armed with electric batteries. . . . Twenty electric explosions in the sky, now a measureless glass chamber pneumatically emptied, have echoed the brave torments of two rival peoples with the fullness and splendor of their frightful interplanetary electric volleys.[8]

Marinetti and the Futurists reserved their most emotive imagery for the aeroplane. Recent studies have comprehensively described the decisive role the aeroplane and flight played in Western consciousness during the first decades of the twentieth century, which is similar to the later fascination with the exploration of space. The aeroplane promised the conquering of time and space, the vast extension of man's rule over nature and of the white man's domination over the world. It would usher in a new age of immense potential. The work of the Wright brothers after their first historic flight in 1903 initially attracted little attention. But in late summer 1908 Wilbur Wright came to France for a series of public flights that demonstrated the unrivalled performance of

---

[7] W. Benjamin, 'The Work of Art in the Age of Mechanical Reproduction', in his *Illuminations* (New York, 1968), 243–4.　　　　[8] Marinetti, *Writings*, 106–7.

the Wright machine and awoke the vivid interest and enthusiasm of the Europeans. Royalty, aristocracy, artists, and literati came to Le Mans, Issy-les-Moulineaux, near Paris, and other sites to watch the fabulous machine in flight, have their photo taken with Wilbur Wright, and sometimes, for those who dared, join him in the air. In July 1909 Louis Blériot's flight across the Channel aroused excited public response. International air meetings now followed one another, attracting similar attention. In September 1909 one of the first such meetings was opened in Brescia, near Milan. Celebrities of all sorts attended, including d'Annunzio. He managed to persuade Glenn Curtiss and Mario Calderara to take him for a flight. He had been writing his first novel in ten years, *Forse che sì forse che no* (Perhaps Yes, Perhaps No), published in February 1910. Its heroes were flight pioneers whose supreme experience and daring were celebrated in d'Annunzio's elevated, heavily ornamented style. Like Wells, the German air novelist Rudolf Martin, and the French Émile Driant, d'Annunzio proclaimed that flying would change civilization, create a new ruling aristocracy of aviators, and revolutionize war.[9]

Marinetti was flying in the same direction. As d'Annunzio had done in *Alcyone* (1904), where he had portrayed himself as Icarus, Marinetti had been using images of flying in his poetry even before publishing his 'Manifesto of Futurism' in Paris in the wake of Wilbur Wright's flights. As he explained, the intention of the 'Manifesto' was 'to replace in people's imagination the silhouette of Don Juan with that of Napoleon, Andrée [a Swedish balloonist], and Wilbur Wright'. His 1909 play *Poupées électriques* (Electric Puppets) was dedicated to Wright. From the start the aeroplane was for Marinetti at once a leverage for human liberation and elevation from earthly confines and an engine of war. In 'Let's Murder the Moonlight' (1909) the aeroplane performs as the hero's mythological vehicle of war, where flesh and metal amalgamate. Taken for a flight for the first time in September 1910, over Milan, Marinetti sang the praises of the new epoch; he was an 'aeropoet', bestowing 'aeropoetical praise'. The flight over Milan opened his 'Technical Manifesto of Futurist Literature' (1912), calling for the transformation of language to suit the new mechanical age. His disciples, poets such as Mario Bètuda and Paolo Buzzi, followed in

---

[9] F. P. Ingold, *Literatur und Aviatik: Europäische Flugdichtung, 1909–1927* (Basle, 1978), 26–49; R. Wohl, *A Passion for Wings: Aviation and Western Imagination, 1908–1918* (New Haven, Conn., 1994), 115–22.

his footsteps in writing 'winged verses'.[10] The aeroplane figured prominently in Futurist painting, and even in Futurist cookery. Yet neither Marinetti nor d'Annunzio was content with words and images alone. They celebrated war, and they meant it.

In 1911–12 Italy waged war on Turkey for the conquest of Libya. The war was highly controversial, and Marinetti defended it from its critics on the left and in the Catholic establishment. In his political poem *Le Monoplan du pape* (The Pope's Monoplane) he flew over Italy singing the glory of war as the way to greatness through creative destruction. In real life he went to Libya and then to Turkey to watch the fighting and the first use of the aeroplane in war. Covering the war for European newspapers, he was filled with lyrical adulation of the Italian aviators who participated in the war and whose names were becoming nationally famous. His modernist poem *Zang tumb tumb* (1914) sought to convey the sounds and sights of war viewed from an aeroplane flying above the battlefield around Adrianople in 1912.[11] In his 'Electrical War' he again celebrated the monoplane and 'man having become airborne'.[12] The book which contained that essay, *War: The World's Only Hygiene*, comprising his works from the years 1911 to 1915, was intended as a propaganda weapon in the noisy campaign of agitation that radical nationalists were waging for Italy's entry into the First World War. As the title of the book implied, they believed that the war was a crucial cleansing process for decadent Italian society, politics, and culture—a heroic enterprise in which Italy could discover its mission and forge a renewed greatness. D'Annunzio and Mussolini agitated for the same cause, the latter departing from the Socialist Party on that account. When Italy finally entered the war, they all enthusiastically rushed to enlist.

While Marinetti—39 in 1915—and his Milanese group served together in the trenches on the Alpine front, as did Mussolini, d'Annunzio carved for himself a role of an entirely different order of glamour. Determined to live up to his reputation as a daredevil, the poet—52 in 1915—became Italy's most decorated war hero. He switched between the élite and technically most advanced units of the Italian armed forces, participating in the most extraordinary missions. At the outbreak of the war he was commissioned as a lieutenant in the

[10] Marinetti, *Writings*, 53, 84, 253; Inglold, *Literatur and Aviatik*, 59–80, 278–99, 342–5; Wohl, *A Passion for Wings*, 2, 138–44, 264–7.

[11] Ingold, *Literatur und Aviatik*, 238–47; Wohl, *A Passion for Wings*, 140–2, 264.

[12] *Writings*, 106.

cavalry, but being the national institution that he was he went where he pleased. As early as July–August 1915 he twice flew over Trieste, dropping leaflets and carrying out reconnaissance. He also joined a submarine on an active combat mission. The Adriatic coast and the air would remain his main theatre of operations, but on occasions he would leave to join land offensives, always striving to be at the forefront of danger. In the autumn of 1915 he fought on the ground at San Michele. He raided Trento from the air in September and Aisonizza in October, flew in support of the land war at the turn of the year, and again raided Trieste in January 1916. The next month he was seriously wounded in a forced landing, losing one eye and becoming incapacitated for six months. He bombed Parenzo in September 1916 and fought on the ground at Veliki in October. Between January and May 1917 he fought on the ground on the rivers Isonzo and Timavo. In August 1917 he led the three squadrons that bombed Pola, and in October led the aerial raid on Cattaro. In February 1918 he participated in a night raid by three high-speed torpedo boats on Austrian warships lying in a defended anchorage in the Adriatic. That year he was appointed commander of the 'First Naval Squadron of Torpedo-Carrying Airplanes'. In July 1918 he bombed Pola, and in August, after earlier failed attempts, he led an audacious air raid on Vienna, dropping leaflets. A major from 1917, he was raised to lieutenant-colonel in 1919.[13]

The air raids on Austrian cities, especially the long-range ones, required more than mere audacity and bravado. One had to have the machines. Together with Russia, Italy was the most industrially backward of all the great powers involved in the war. Yet tellingly, together with Russia, where futurist enthusiasm for the air matched Italy's, Italy pioneered the development of the heavy bomber. In the years preceding the war, the Russian Igor Sikorsky and Turin manufacturer Giovanni Battista Caproni had been separately working on the development of the world's only heavy-load, long-range, multi-engine aeroplanes. Sikorsky's giant four-engine plane entered active service with the Russian army in late 1914, and by the summer of 1915 the Caproni trimotor went into action with the Italian air service. If Russia was slightly ahead in terms of time and size, it was no match for Italy in numbers. Some

---

[13] D'Annunzio's wartime reports and letters are printed in G. Po (ed.), *Gabriele d'Annunzio: combattente al servizio della regia marina* (Rome, 1931); *Gabriele d'Annunzio: scritti, messaggi, discorsi e rapporti militari* (Rome, 1939). Mostly from the literary perspective is A. Bonadeo, *D'Annunzio and the Great War* (Madison, Wis., 1995).

800 Capronis, roughly equally divided between twin-motors and trimotors, were built by 1918, as compared with only 73 Sikorskys. The other great powers developed their heavy bombers considerably later. The famous German Gotha, ordered in 1915, entered service in 1916, and went into action over Britain in the spring and summer of 1917, after the failed Zeppelin offensive. But it was a twin-motor. The giant multi-engine R planes (*Riesenflugzeuge*), also participating in the raids on Britain, had the same career dates, but only 55–65 were built. The British equivalents to the Gotha, the twin-motor Handley-Page 100 and DH9, were also developed over the same years. Multi-engine British giants only went into service in 1918.

From their total backwardness of only a few years earlier, the Italian aeronautical and engine industries made great strides, and kept abreast of technological developments during the war, winning lucrative contracts from their *Entente* allies up to the end of the war. The 1913 version of Caproni's trimotor was still powered by Gnome 80 hp rotaries. But by 1914 it switched to Fiat 100 hp engines, and by 1915 to Isotta-Fraschini 150 hp units, upgraded to 200 hp in 1916. In 1916–18 250 and 300 hp engines were developed and mass produced by Fiat, simultaneously with the German, British, and French designs. Units of 500 hp were developed by all Italian engine manufacturers by the end of the war.[14]

It was on the heavy Caproni trimotors that d'Annunzio based a scheme for the future of air operations. In May 1917 he drew up a memorandum to General Luigi Cadorna, chief of the Italian army's general staff. The air force, he suggested, would support the other arms through reconnaissance and bombing; but primarily it had the potential for an even more promising line of action. The giant planes were capable of striking at the centres of the enemy's industrial production. They would destroy and disorganize the armament and munitions plants and irreparably disrupt the work process. D'Annunzio calculated the carrying loads and distances for great air raids from France on Essen, which would deliver more than 100 tons of bombs. Closer to

---

[14] J. Morrow, *The Great War in the Air* (Washington, 1993) is particularly rich here; see also G. H. Haddow and P. Grosz, *The German Giants: The Story of the R Planes, 1914–1919* (London, 1969); P. Vergano, *Origins of Aviation in Italy, 1783–1918* (Genoa, 1964); A. D. Harvey, *Collision of Empires: Britain in Three World Wars, 1793–1945* (London, 1992), 394. For Russian Futurist enthusiasm for the aeroplane and air pioneering, see Ingold, *Literatur und Aviatik*, 133–89 and p. 114 below.

home he specified the Adriatic main port of Pola, and Vienna, as prize targets.[15]

To be sure, 'strategic' bombing on targets deep in the enemy's rear had been taking place since the beginning of the war. The French, under the influence of Commandant Barès, pioneered the idea as early as 1914, but doubts about the efficacy of the bombing and production difficulties rapidly lowered French interest in such efforts. The Zeppelin raids on Britain were conceived in 1914 and carried out in earnest from the spring of 1915. The Gotha and R plane raids on London began in the spring and summer of 1917, at the time d'Annunzio submitted his memorandum to Cadorna. Following these raids, the British moved to create an independent strategic bombing force within their newly constituted independent air force. This bomber force began its raids on Germany in the autumn of 1917 and intensified them from the summer of 1918.[16] Still, d'Annunzio's memorandum derived from the plans and and memoranda of Colonel Giulio Douhet, a friend of Caproni and d'Annunzio, who had encouraged the industrialist to take up the production of his heavy bombers in the first place, well before the Great War.[17] For, again, in order to have the heavy bomber, one had first to conceive the idea of it.

Douhet: Science, Poetry, Fascism, and Mechanized War

It was against the background of the intense modernist fascination with the latest advances of science and technology—with the automobile, with electricity, with gas, and finally with the aeroplane—prevalent in prewar Italian proto-fascist avant-garde culture that Giulio Douhet (1869–1930) evolved his visions of future mechanized and air warfare. Although widely known as the most extreme and most famous of the air theorists, and as closely associated with the idea of air warfare as Fuller is with that of mechanized land warfare, Douhet has received little

---

[15] The memorandum, dated 11 May 1917, is reprinted in Po, *D'Annunzio: scritti militari*, 75–88.

[16] See esp. Morrow, *The Great War in the Air*; L. Kennett, *The First Air War, 1914–1918* (New York, 1991); M. Cooper, *The Birth of Independent Air Power* (London, 1986). Still useful are H. A. Jones, *The War in the Air*, v and vii (Oxford, 1935 and 1937), 1–159 and 101–74 respectively; J. Cueno, *The Air Weapon, 1914–1916* (Harrisburg, Penn., 1947), 351–77.

[17] Some correspondence between d'Annunzio and Douhet is printed in A. Monti (ed.), *Giulio Douhet: scritti inediti* (Gennaio, 1951), 230–4. Also see for their cooperation n. 40 below and related text.

serious study.[18] Famous for his works during the 1920s, he had in fact developed the kernel of his later ideas and emerged as a military theorist of the first order well before the First World War. Himself an amateur novelist, poet, painter, and playwright—as well as a professional soldier—he was closely attuned to the dominant themes of his intellectual milieu, which he expressed in his own field in the more precise and practical language of technical, organizational, and operational schemes. His ardent Fascism, which he espoused from the movement's very inception in 1919, was the natural extension of the opinions and sentiments he had expressed long before the war.

Douhet came from a Piedmontese family of strong military and patriotic tradition. In 1888 he graduated from the artillery academy of the Italian army first in his class, and later entered Turin polytechnic, from which he again graduated with distinction. From the start he acquired a reputation of brilliance, and in 1900 was posted to the army's general staff. As with d'Annunzio and Marinetti, his first enthusiasm prior to the advent of the aeroplane was for electricity, chemistry, and the automobile, the exciting new products of the unfolding 'Second Industrial Revolution'. While Italian avant-garde artists marvelled at the power and glitter of electricity, Douhet studied it scientifically. His final paper at the polytechnic, 'The Calculation of Rotating Field Engines', was published, as was his 'Summary of the Current State of Electric Technology'.[19] In a scientific conference at the Sorbonne in Paris he read a paper, 'Separation of Oxygen and Hydrogen from Air by Means of a Fractional Distillation of Liquid Air' (1905).[20]

However, by the first years of the new century Douhet was preoccupied with the automobile and its military applications. By European, not only Italian, standards, he had been a leading advocate

---

[18] Most summaries of Douhet's life have appeared in Italian as introductions to the various collections of his writings. In English the sole accessible summary is E. Warner, 'Douhet, Mitchell, Seversky: Theories of Air Warfare', in E. M. Earle (ed.), *Makers of Modern Strategy from Machiavelli to the Second World War* (Princeton, NJ, 1943), 487–97, and the only comprehensive one is F. Cappelluti, 'The Life and Thought of Giulio Douhet' (doctoral dissertation, Rutgers University, 1967), which regrettably has not been published. See also Claudio Segrè, 'Douhet in Italy: Prophet without Honor?', *Aerospace Historian*, June 1979, 69–80; 'Giulio Douhet: Strategist, Theorist, Prophet?', *Journal of Strategic Studies*, 15 (1992), 351–66.

[19] For the first study, see Cappelluti, 'Douhet', 4, and for the second, G. Douhet, *Cenno sommario sullo stato attuale dell'elettrotecnica* (Turin, 1905; date of composition 1903); one chapter is devoted to the electric automobile.

[20] C. Ranieri, 'General Giulio Douhet', introduction to Douhet, *The Command of the Air* (Rome, 1958), p. ix.

of the mechanization of armies well before turning his attention to the air. In a series of lectures and pamphlets delivered and published from 1901 onward, when the automobile was barely beginning to develop from infancy into a commercial product, the then Captain Douhet envisaged the mechanization of whole armies. In *Mechanization, from the Military Point of View: A Scheme of Mechanization for Military Use* (1902) he wrote that every new invention had implications for the conduct of war. The essence of mechanization was the substitution of mechanical energy and mechanical work for animal-powered transportation. Mechanical energy could be extracted from a variety of sources: chemical (coal and petrol), electric, or dynamic (compressed gas), each potentially capable of powering automobiles. Comprehensively comparing their respective qualities on the basis of mathematical and physical computation, Douhet unequivocally supported the electric engine, his old favourite. This was not as misguided as it may appear in view of the ensuing development of the car, for at the turn of the century petroleum and electric engines still ran neck and neck as the preferred power for automobiles. Leading car pioneers such as Ferdinand Porsche, whose electric car was the sensation of the Paris Salon de l'Automobile of 1900, initially regarded the electric engine as more promising. In any case, Douhet's thoughts were on the largest scale from the outset. His pamphlet consisted of detailed schemes for the mechanization of complete army corps, elaborately working out payloads and speeds. The armies of the future would undoubtedly be mechanized, though Douhet thought in terms of mechanical mobility into the battlefield rather than for the fighting itself. He did not envisage the tank.[21] In the following years he became one of the foremost advocates of mechanization in the Italian general staff,[22] and was appointed first commander of a newly constituted élite mechanized Bersaglieri battalion. All this, it will be remembered, had begun more than a decade before the First World War. At least in *ideas* Italians were ahead of anyone else. Then, during the great years of breakthrough for aviation, 1908–9, Douhet

---

[21] G. Douhet, *L'Automobilismo, sotto il punto di vista militare: schema di un sistema automobilistico per uso militare* (Turin, 1902); *A proposito dell'articolo: gli automobili e la loro applicazione nell'arte della guerra* (Rome, 1902); *Automobilismo militare e pesante* (Genoa, 1904). For the electric car at the turn of the nineteenth century, see S. Bayley, 'Dead as a Flat Battery', *Times Literary Supplement*, 18 Aug. 1995, 25.

[22] See L. Ceva and A. Curami, *La Meccanizzazione dell'esercito italiano dalle origini al 1943* (Rome, 1989), 21–3.

too, like d'Annunzio and Marinetti, was taken by the prospects opened up in the air.

Douhet's 'The Problems of Air Navigation' was written in 1909 and published in the service journal *La Preparazione*, as well as in pamphlet form, in 1910. It was more or less contemporaneous with the works of the air novelists all over Europe and no different in its general messages. His work, however, was not a novel but a military tract, albeit of a visionary nature. The title of the work might be misleading: far from dealing with navigation in the strictly technical sense, it was an outline of future war in and from the air. As in any other new field, Douhet stated, at first the idea of flight required fantasy to realize its potential. And as with the mechanization of armies, he thought big from the outset. After surveying the history of flying, emphasizing the achievements of the Wright brothers and Blériot, Douhet predicted that air fleets would become a dominant feature of future war. He rejected the dirigible as too vulnerable to be used for military purposes, and for years would fight in the Italian army against any investment in it as sheer waste of money. But he viewed the aeroplane as having a tremendous potential for bombing over land and sea, as well as possessing great reconnaissance capability for all branches of the armed forces. He also claimed that the aeroplane was relatively cheap: 3,000 could be bought for the price of one battleship. Great air fleets would be deployed in the future, operating much as in sea warfare. Industrial preparation at home during peacetime would be required to produce the necessary equipment for the air force and keep it supplied.[23] In general this was a fair forecast of things to come. Unlike Douhet's later ideas, it did not assume the complete dominance of air power to the practical exclusion of armies and navies, nor did it prescribe 'strategic' bombing of the enemy's production centres and population as the only appropriate mission for air power. All the same, Douhet was later justified in proudly citing his early work as evidence that his main ideas went back to 1909–10, well before the First World War.

The work of 1909–10 was only the beginning, for Douhet now converted to the air. He was posted to the aviation battalion of the Italian army, created in Turin in 1912, and in the same year became its second commander. On the request of the war ministry he submitted a

---

[23] Maj. G. Douhet, *I Problemi dell'aereonavigazione* (Rome, 1910); a reprint can be found in the most significant collection of his works, the posthumous *Le Profezie di Cassandra* (Genoa, 1931), 61–87.

report detailing an organizational scheme for the air units. In this official report his tone was again relatively modest. He did not yet advocate an independent air force. He also held that it was too early to determine exactly how the aeroplane would be used in war, whether for reconnaissance, bombing, or air battle. For this reason he suggested the development for the time being of an 'all-purpose' aircraft, an idea to which he would return in the 1920s. He again emphasized close industrial cooperation as the most essential prerequisite for the development of a strong air force.[24] Douhet was a man who backed words with deeds. During his tenure of command in Turin he befriended Caproni, who became a close associate for life. It was under his urging and promise of support that Caproni took up the development of his heavy bomber. At the end of 1914 Douhet was removed from his post and made chief of staff to an infantry division for ordering Caproni's aircraft without authorization from his superiors or from the war ministry.[25]

But it was not engineering alone that gave wings to Douhet's imagination, nor was the dry prose of official reports his only language. In a lecture at the Turin polytechnic in 1913, following the war in Libya, he sang the glory of future air warfare, and 'sang' is the appropriate word here. Echoing d'Annunzio and Marinetti, Douhet waxed poetic in words worth quoting at some length:

All of a sudden Italy was stricken by a new shudder meandering all over her, all the brows bent for so long were risen, its hearts pulsed more excitedly; a new unknown strength infused everyone: War!
. . .
Any doubt was silenced, any wavering disappeared in this emergency; spreading their wings the adventurous airway researchers flew toward the unknown.

> . . . The bent wings
> of men are passing, Daedalus's
> large devices, the field machines
> made of stretched hemp-close and light
> wood, which will carry man and his
> dreadful thunderbolt on fragile supports.

The delicate machines were reset on the new homeland of Italy, leaving the light trail of their talons on the wet sand of our seas; like new human eagles they rose against the enemy, the very first ones in the world, amazing all.

---

[24] Cappelluti, 'Douhet', 46–54.
[25] For the Douhet–Caproni relationship, based on archival material, see ibid. 56–61.

Uncertain machines struggling in the wind, guided by steady hands, as if made of bronze, and hearts steadier than bronze. Man and his machine with one strong pulsation in one single heart; a single tangle of nerves and steel shrouds in the large clever birds . . .

All the new Italian land, so much hoped for, was discovered before it became Italian, by their eyes which were burnt by both wind and sun, over the propeller's whirling star; and they discovered ambushes and traps, unexpected help for their brothers fighting on earth and sea, and they brought their message of peace and their message of death.

> Moizo, Gavotti from your light glacis,
> bowed in the danger of the winds
> over the enemy who ignores the new assault!
> . . .

A new weapon arose: an air weapon; a new battlefield opened: the sky; so very present everywhere that a new event took place in the history of war: the principles of war in the air.[26]

Douhet quoted air poetry again in a chapter dedicated to air warfare in his book *The Art of War* (1915), comprising a series of lectures he had given earlier at the Popular University of Turin.[27]

Indeed, although Douhet, like most self-styled prophets, failed to cite anybody who may have stimulated his inspiration, he none the less left a clear enough trail. For example, in September 1914, shortly after the outbreak of the First World War, he published an article entitled 'Futurism', in which he applied the message of the celebrated artistic movement to his own field, the art of war. He rejected both bourgeois values and the reliance on the past. Again, lengthy quotations are called for:

We love the Futurists. This advanced movement of unconventional youngsters who intend breaking every tradition and rejecting every old rubbish is likable, and it is likable even when it goes to extreme in order to 'épater le bourgeois', that poor bourgeois, secluded in dog's bed, with a tail stump between his trembling legs, begging for mercy, forgetful of all his past strength, and who has become the laughing stock of today's strong spirits.

Yes, we love those impetuous forerunners of tomorrow, because, in them, one finds something true. We often forget that we are living in the present, that the door of the past is closed while that of the future is wide open in front of us, and

---

[26] 'Prolusione al corso preparatorio di aviazione' (29 Jan. 1913), in *Profezie di Cassandra*, 88–101, quotations from 90–2. I am most grateful to Signor Renato Orsini, who made these artistic translations for me.

[27] Lt.-Col. Douhet, *L'Arte della guerra* (Turin, 1915), 127.

we are inexorably pushed towards it by a continuous power pressing behind our shoulders. . . .

History for example, which was called the teacher of life, it is a chain instead, to which life is tied and carried backwards. . . .

Never again will we find ourselves in the conditions of the battle of Salamis, Canne, Austerlitz and Sedan; let us leave once and for all those poor dead in peace . . . Hannibal is dead, Napoleon is dead, Moltke is dead; tomorrow we shall be dead too; let us respect the past, but let us create the future. . . .

The present war cannot be compared to the wars of the past . . . Judging it with old-fashioned methods is a mistake, the same as it would be mistaken to try and measure an electric potential with a double decimeter; it was absurd to prepare it with a backward look, the same as it would be absurd to try and build an induction coil with a string. . . .

All true geniuses of war . . . broke all past traditions, revolutionizing the present, anticipating the future. . . .

There is room for everybody. Archaeology to scholars, the present and the limits of the future, to men of action.[28]

The unanswered question of 'Futurism' regarding the direction of the future was answered two weeks later with the publication in the same journal of Douhet's 'Man and the Machine'. Modern war, he wrote, was machine war, everywhere replacing muscular labour with the latest products of science and technology—the rapid-firing gun, the machine-gun, the enhanced chemical energy of modern explosives, the railway, the armoured car, and the aeroplane—all exponentially increasing human power. The whole nation becomes a great factory of war. While Douhet's article was coached in a realistic military language as opposed to the sham-mythological science fiction of Marinetti's 'Electrical War' written about the same time, the parallels between the two visions are striking. It ought to be borne in mind that both pre-dated the growing mechanization of warfare that would take place during the later course of the First World War.[29]

Direct evidence linking Douhet to Marinetti also exists. Marinetti's literary remains, in the possession of the Beinecke Library at Yale, include two books by Douhet. One is *How Did the Great War End?* (1919), itself an insignificant history written in November 1918, immediately after the Central Powers' collapse, but personally dedicated to

---

[28] 'Futurismo', *Gazzetta del Popolo*, 24 Sept. 1914, repr. in *Profezie di Cassandra*, 189–92. Cf. e.g. Marinetti's 'Futurist Manifesto' above.

[29] Douhet, 'L'Uomo e le macchine', *Gazzetta del Popolo*, 7 Oct. 1914, repr. in *Profezie di Cassandra*, 207–11.

Marinetti by the author. The other book is fictional, *The Honourable Who Could No Longer Lie: A Story from Pre-War Times* (1921).[30] It may be that the *personal* connection between Douhet and the aeropoets began or crystallized during the agitation to bring Italy into the war in 1914–15. In his journalistic articles Douhet, although a regular soldier, barely masked his desire to see Italy join the war, evoking the famous '*sacro egoismo*'.[31] Even before 1914, and after, he repeatedly urged the need for total national and industrial mobilization of all spiritual and physical resources for the purpose of war. Modern war, he emphasized time and again, was national and total.[32] Like other nationalist critics of parliamentary Italy, he castigated the widespread corruption of his country and complained that 'Italy is ruled by mediocrity'.[33] His highly critical stance towards the incompetence of the authorities only intensified after Italy entered the war.

Carefully following the strategic development of the war, analysing its features, and continuously drawing up schemes for action in a stream of private notes and memoranda to his superiors, Douhet sought a way around the stalemate of the trenches. As Fuller would do, he claimed that the belligerents were anachronistically trying to repeat 1870–1. Very early in the war he became convinced that the murderous offensives on the enemy's fortified lines were futile and had to be stopped. The army ought to assume the defensive until the necessary *matériel* was made available. On 3 July 1915, barely a month after Italy had declared war, he suggested that the air represented the most promising strategy for victory. Modern technology, he wrote, had made possible heavy multi-engine aircraft with a carrying capacity of up to 1,000–1,500 kg. These were able to strike hundreds of kilometres behind the front lines and against the enemy's vital industrial centres, upon which the strength of nations in modern war depended. The secret of success lay in the massive concentration of all available resources at the decisive point for a grand air offensive against the Central Powers. A great armada of 500 aircraft, each carrying some 500 kg. of explosives to a range of between 300 to 500 km., should be assembled. It would be sent

---

[30] Col. G. Douhet, *Come finì la Grande Guerra* (Rome, 1919); id. *L'Onorevole che non potè più mentire. Racconto dei tempi ante-guerra* (Rome, 1921).

[31] See e.g. 'Il sacro egoismo', *Gazzetta del popolo*, 20 Oct. 1914, repr. in *Le Profezie di Cassandra*, 212–16.

[32] *L'Arte della guerra*, 1–4; 'La Preparazione industriale', 12 Nov. 1914, also 28 Aug. 1914, repr. in *Profezie di Cassandra*, 149–54, 227–30.

[33] See e.g. 9 Nov. 1914, repr. in Monti, *Douhet: Scritti inediti*, 7.

to attack arsenals, ports, magazines, industrial plants, military centres, banks, and government ministries, inflicting immense, irreparable, and decisive damage on the enemy. In Douhet's calculation the whole proposition was relatively inexpensive, costing no more that 50 million Italian lire. (Optimistic claims that mechanization actually *saved* money were common among its pioneers.) The required type of machine was available in the shape of the Caproni 300. All that was needed was a strategic decision and the allocation of resources for its mass production.[34]

Douhet's scheme for an all-out air offensive was only the first in a series of plans. In January 1916 he submitted a memorandum to Generals Brusati and Cadorna. As before, he showed a firm grasp of the industrial and technological character of modern war. The memorandum began with the same broad historical reasoning that Fuller espoused later on: 'war follows the evolution of industry in the application of the machine. In the same way that the machine multiplies production, its introduction into the modern army multiplies destruction.' 'The modern army derives its strength from the machines it possesses. . . . Neither the genius of the commanders nor the valour of the soldiers can substitute for mechanical means.' Military power now rested on industrial and commercial might.[35] Again surveying the deadlock on land, Douhet returned to his proposal for a grand air offensive against the Central Powers:

> Modern armies represent the armoured shield behind which the nations at war work to prepare the means appropriate to feed the war; the powerful aeroplane is able to pass over such armour and strike at the nation itself in its centres of production and along the lines of supply running from the country to the army. Thus it is the best weapon to strike a fatal blow . . . the new weapon attacks not only the fist but the heart, and cuts the nerves and veins of the arm.[36]

An air fleet of 1,000 aircraft was capable of dropping 500 tons of explosives in one flight. It could destroy the Austrian navy in Pola, and completely cut off Austrian communications through the Tirol. More systematically, the priorities of the air offensive should be as follows: (*a*) to destroy the means of production of the enemy's nation, its wealth, resources, and morale; (*b*) to cut off the communications of

---

[34] 3 July 1915, in *Diario critico di guerra* (2 vols., Rome, 1921–2), i. 65–9; in an exception to his general rule, Douhet cites Wells's ideas.

[35] Jan. 1916, ibid. ii. 14, 17.

[36] Ibid. 16, 19–21; quoted in Harvey's excellent *Collision of Empires*, 393–4.

the enemy's army, isolating it from supplies and reinforcements; (c) to devastate its rear areas; and (d) to attack its front line. Industry should be organized to mass-produce aeroplanes in the same way as Fiat mass-produced trucks.[37]

During these years Douhet was kept away from any position related to the air. In his repeated criticism of the army's unpreparedness and strategy, his requests for resources for the air, and his demands for total mobilization of the nation's industry and morale, he made himself a nuisance in the eyes of his superiors. Far from restricting his criticism to army channels, he secretly briefed parliamentary deputies. On one such occasion he left behind in a railway carriage a confidential document criticizing the army. After it had been found and turned over to the authorities he was arrested, and sentenced by court martial in October 1916 to one year's imprisonment, which he duly served.[38]

All the same, in June 1917, while still in prison and a month after d'Annunzio had submitted his own memorandum to Cadorna, Douhet again put forward a revised scheme for a grand Allied aerial offensive against the Central Powers. His recommended order of priorities was now, first, to win air superiority by bombing the enemy's aircraft, aeronautical installations, and plants for aeroplane production. Then, the enemy's rear and front could be attacked and his morale broken. A huge aerial armada, including 1,000 Italian aircraft, 3,000 French, 4,000 British, and 12,000 American, was capable of hurling 1,000 ton of bombs on Hamburg, Essen, Berlin, and Vienna, in one drop. In the not too distant future air power would dominate war.[39] A few days later, on 3 July 1917, in a memorandum co-signed by Douhet, d'Annunzio, and Caproni and submitted to the Chief of the Army's General Staff, General Carlo Porro, the three called for the creation of an independent air force.[40] In January 1918 Douhet was appointed Director of Technical Services in the Aeronautical Bureau, but in June he resigned from the post on the grounds that it lacked any power. Shortly afterwards he left the army. He was promoted to general in 1921.

Douhet incorporated the ideas he had developed during the war in

---

[37] Ibid. 21–2; see also Douhet, 'Proposte al generale Cadorna sull'impiego dell'aviazione', 19 Feb. 1916, in Monti, *Douhet: scritti inediti*, 14 ff.

[38] In addition to the Diary, see relevant material in *Le Profezie di Cassandra*, 299–350.

[39] Douhet, 'La Grande Offensiva aerea', 23 June 1917, in Monti *Douhet scritti inediti*, 114–31.

[40] This unpublished document, contained in Douhet's file in the ministry of war, is cited by Cappelluti, 'Douhet', 151.

his programmatic book *The Command of the Air* (1921). Since the book is known well enough and adds little to what we have already described, it can be briefly summarized. Air power is the offensive weapon *par excellence*. Whereas civilian population had traditionally been protected by the army, air power now made it vulnerable to attack. The modern nation's centres of industry, transportation, and government could be obliterated swiftly and with relative ease, perhaps within days or even hours, by bomber fleets of medium speed and heavy-load carrying capacity. There is practically no effective defence against such an attack, because the attacker is always free to choose the time and place of the raid. Pre-emptive strike to gain air superiority by destroying the enemy's air force on the ground is the only defence. Although Douhet still left a subsidiary role for auxiliary aviation to support the army and navy, he held that the role of these services was quickly diminishing, and that they should be progressively reduced and the air force expanded. The latter should be constituted as an independent service, with its own ministry responsible for the development of the country's aeronautical infrastructure and civil aviation.[41]

But writing on strategic and air matters was only one aspect of Douhet's activity in the immediate aftermath of the war. He painted, wrote literature, and established a nationalist weekly, *Il Dovere* (Duty), which he edited between 1919 and 1921. He also participated in the activity of the *Arditi*, the élite Italian storm troops of the war that became the nucleus of the extra-parliamentary opposition to the post-war liberal government and soon joined hands with Mussolini. In 1922 Douhet took part in the 'March on Rome', and after the Fascists seized power he was sent to d'Annunzio by Mussolini, together with two other army generals, carrying a letter of invitation that called upon the national poet to join the new regime.[42] Douhet's fortunes and that of his ideas seemed to have changed radically. As he wrote in the introduction to the second edition of *Command of the Air* (1926), conditions had become much more favourable to his ideas. Indeed, in the new political and intellectual climate he radicalized his rhetoric even further.[43] For, like the avant-garde artists with whom he associated and by whom he was influenced, Mussolini had been an enthusiast for the aeroplane from its beginning. He exalted its wider futurist and

---

[41] *Il Dominio dell'aria* (Rome, 1921), trans. as *The Command of the Air* (London, 1943), 1–79.   [42] Cappelluti, 'Douhet', 153, 159.
[43] *The Command of the Air*, introduction to 2nd edn. (1926), 5, 80.

spiritual significance, and was eager to identify it with the Fascist movement. The aeroplane and flight were among the Fascists' most potent symbols.

Mussolini, Balbo, and the Fascist Cult of Flying

In the mid-1930s Guido Mattioli lauded Mussolini's relationship to the aeroplane and flying in his book *Mussolini aviatore*, which the Italian authorities took care to translate into German and English. While obviously propagandistic, the work is doubly significant, as it remarkably testifies to the sort of image the Fascists sought to project as well as documenting the very real nature of Mussolini's interest in the aeroplane. The introduction to the book stated that, unlike the great leaders of the *Risorgimento*, the Duce did not merely send people to action but personally led them himself. He was a man of action and irresistible will, qualities for which flying provided a singular showcase. The book strove to demonstrate that Mussolini had not only, as it stated, realized General Douhet's theories by building one of the world's strongest air forces but was himself an aviator, personally leading the daring conquest of the skies. Numerous photographs of the Duce in full flying gear cleverly drove this point home. Mussolini was taken up in the air for the first time in 1918 and learnt to fly the year after. He established an 'aeronautical parliamentary group' in the Italian Chamber of Deputies when first elected, and made extensive use of the aeroplane for travelling during his campaign for power and after becoming the dictator of Italy. Moreover, he had been writing about the aeroplane since 1909. The record in Mattioli's book, to be sure partly coloured for effect but none the less resting on documentary evidence, has been summarized as follows by Robert Wohl:

in July 1909, Mussolini wrote an article for a regional Italian newspaper in which he expounded on the meaning of the Channel flights. Exploits like that, the young Mussolini insisted, could not be understood simply in terms of sport. They were an expression of the deepest tendencies of the new century. Our age was heroic, perhaps even more so than the Ancient World. The word that summed up the new century was movement. 'Movement towards the icy solitude of the poles and toward the virgin peaks of the mountains, movement toward the stars and toward the depths of the seas . . . Movement everywhere and acceleration in the rhythm of our lives.' And when Blériot succeeded in flying the Channel, Mussolini saluted him as one of the first champions of a new race of Nietzschean *dominatori*, one of those restless figures who give meaning to life through the pursuit of an ideal. The war, which Mussolini experienced from the immobility of the trenches, only increased his reverence for aviators. . . . Even before the war ended, Mussolini had begun to seek out the company of military pilots and aces. Several would be at his side when he came to power in October, 1922. . . . The ace Mario Stoppiani, who took Mussolini up for one of his first flights, remembered him as being in a state of 'enthusiastic delirium'. . . . Driving away from the airfield with a group of aviators, it occurred to Mussolini that these men represented 'the new Italian race of producers, builders, and creators'. They were the Italians of the future who would conquer the land, the sea, and the sky.[44]

'Aviation must remain the privilege of the spiritual aristocracy,' Mussolini wrote in 1909. 'Not every Italian can or should fly,' he said in a speech at the Aero Club of Italy in November 1923. 'But all Italians should envy those who do and should follow with profound feelings the development of Italian wings.'[45]

That this was the language of d'Annunzio and Marinetti which Mussolini borrowed and integrated in his political rhetoric is well recognized. The three men, all prima donnas with megalomaniac political ambitions—and increasingly playing on similar political grounds— had always paid the closest attention to one another. Their relationships were characterized by competition, envy, and tentative cooperation. Both Marinetti and Mussolini came to visit d'Annunzio in his hour of glory, after he had established his revolutionary regime in Fiume, where they were able to see, apart from everything else, his use of aeroplanes as a central element of his perpetual political carnival. They loathed the fact that he had caught the nation's attention, whereas he wanted no partners to share the glory with. In turn, d'Annunzio, who was himself entertaining plans for a march on Rome, was pre-empted by Mussolini.[46] For all that, Mussolini made him the cultural hero of Fascist Italy, a position he held for the duration of his life, and that of the regime.

Things were even more complex between Marinetti and Mussolini. Mussolini was quick to pick up the messages and learn from the public-relations techniques of Futurism. In addition, as he later wrote,

[44] Wohl, *A Passion for Wings*, 287–8; the evidence is derived from G. Mattioli, *Mussolini Aviator, and His Work for Aviation* (Rome, 1939), esp. pp. vii, 5, 8–10, 16–18, 41–4, 71–85. See also Mussolini's speech in the Italian senate on 30 Mar. 1938, in which he gave tribute to 'Douhet's vision' as the precursor of the Italian doctrine of air warfare: cited by Cappelluti, 'Douhet', 238, from Mussolini, *Opera omnia* (Florence, 1963), xxix. 81.

[45] Cited by Mosse, 'Fascism and the Avant Garde', in his *Masses and Man*, 230–1; Wohl, *A Passion for Wings*, 288.   [46] Ledeen, *The First Duce*.

Marinetti 'gave me the feeling of the ocean and the machine'. The agitation for war brought them together, and the two cooperated most closely in 1915–19. In 1918 Marinetti founded a political party, *Italia Futurista*, but Mussolini's Fascist Party founded a year later proved more successful. Marinetti was presented as the second candidate, after Mussolini, on the Fascist list for parliament in the elections of 1919. From then on their relations cooled. Marinetti strongly objected to Mussolini's compromises with the monarchy, the church, and the magnates of industry in order to win power, and the two broke with one another. Only in 1924 did Marinetti return to the ranks of the victorious Fascists. Although Mussolini discarded the radical edge of Futurism, and of his own youth, and increasingly preferred d'Annunzio and neo-classicism to artistic avant-garde, Marinetti joined his *Accademia d'Italia*, became secretary of the Union of Fascist Writers, rushed to volunteer for the war in Ethiopia at the age of 60, and remained loyal to the regime to the very end.[47]

Douhet too believed his time had come when the Fascists came to power, and he also would be at least partly disappointed. The new regime, which he had helped build and in which he held a place of honour, stood for vigour, efficiency, modernization, mobilization of the national effort, and the air—all of which he had preached for years. Mussolini made him commissioner of aviation and considered making him secretary of state for the newly constituted air ministry in 1923— the second to be created anywhere. But he decided against it in the end, and Douhet resigned from office after a few months.[48] Maintaining close relations with the regime, he returned to writing on defence matters and propagating the air gospel. As with other right-wingers all over Europe, the First World War only strengthened his conviction that modern war was a total national and industrial affair, requiring concerted effort in peacetime for thoroughly preparing the nation's material infrastructure and cultivating moral cohesion. He now urged

---

[47] For Marinetti's politics and fascism, see J. Joll, 'F. T. Marinetti: Futurism and Fascism', in his *Three Intellectuals in Politics* (New York, 1965), 133–78; C. Tisdall and A. Bozzolla, *Futurism*, 200–9; J. Davis, 'The Futures Market: Marinetti and the Fascists of Milan', in E. Timms and P. Collier (eds.), *Visions and Blueprints: Avant-Garde Culture and Radical Politics in Early Twentieth-Century Europe* (Manchester, 1988), 82–97; W. Adamson, 'Modernism and Fascism: The Politics of Culture in Italy, 1903–1922', *American Historical Review*, 95 (1990), 359–90; 'Fascism and Culture: Avant-Garde and Secular Religion in the Italian Case', *Journal of Contemporary History*, 24 (1989), 411–35.

[48] Douhet, *La Guerra integrale* (Rome, 1936), p. xv; some correspondence with Mussolini is printed in Monti, *Douhet: scritti inediti*, 238–45; also Cappelluti, 'Douhet', 160.

the creation of a combined ministry of defence to coordinate this effort. Furthermore, he held that modern war was technological and scientific. Very much as Fuller had done, Douhet developed his historical interpretation of the growth of mechanical warfare to be understood in terms of the overall industrialization of Western society. Production had been mechanized and rationalized, and could turn out commodities in mass volume. The railway had transformed military communications. The machine-gun and other mechanical machines of death had been rapidly propagating during the First World War, increasingly taking the place of the traditional arms, cavalry and infantry. The latest advances of science—electricity, gas, and the aeroplane—would soon achieve dominance. War had become the industry and science of destruction, and air power was the weapon of 'integral destruction'. In order to prepare for the future, armed forces had to reduce their personnel while increasing the lethality of weapons, cut down the army and navy, and invest in air and chemical warfare.[49]

It was the publication of the second edition of *The Command of the Air* in 1926 (to which a second part was added, basically repeating the same ideas) that really brought Douhet's vision of air warfare to the forefront of the strategic debate in Italy and won him increasing international celebrity. His *War of the Future* (1928), *The War of 19—* (1930), and many articles in which he answered his critics depicted a future war that was conducted and quickly decided almost entirely from the air by means of strategic bombing.[50] As with Fuller in respect to mechanized land warfare, it was Douhet's radicalism and sweeping vision that captured universal attention and stamped his name on the idea of air warfare, making 'Douhetism' a generic concept. At the same time, this inherent radicalism also often appeared, and later proved to be, fanciful and unrealistic.

It should be noted, for example, that, although Douhet was becoming a national monument and from 1926 was again officially employed by the air ministry to advance the cause of the air in public, his vision of air warfare was far from being fully accepted even by the independent Italian air force. During the late 1920s his writings were often criticized in the service journal *Rivista Aeronautica*, and Douhet, for his part, took

---

[49] G. Douhet, *La Difesa nazionale* (Rome, 1925).

[50] *Probabili aspetti della guerra futura* (Palermo, 1928); his articles during the last years of his life are reprinted in *Le Profezie di Cassandra* and *La Guerra integrale*; also in the British edn. of *The Command of the Air*.

on his critics with relish.[51] The Regia Aeronautica naturally upheld its independence and favoured the role of strategic bombing, but it did not share Douhet's rejection of fighter aircraft and his dismissal of the role of tactical air support for the army and navy. Under-Secretary and later Secretary of State for the Air, Italo Balbo—who had been maintaining close, warm, and respectful relations with Douhet, whom he treated as the grand old master of air warfare—fought vigorously to increase the allocation for the air force at the expense of the army and navy. He thought, for example, that investment in battleships and aircraft carriers was a waste of money because their roles could be better filled by land-based aircraft. At the same time, however, he held that both the strategic and tactical aspects of air power must have their share in the building of the air force: 'Neither of these theories can be altogether discarded. . . . I think there is virtue in both.' In an article to the *Enciclopedia italiana*, 'Air Warfare', published in 1938 after he had left office, Balbo maintained that, though Douhet was the 'precursor' of a 'new' and 'purely Italian' concept of 'total aerial warfare', whose ideas were discussed worldwide, 'not all of the Italian general's deductions are to be taken literally'. Douhet's theory applied mainly to wars between two industrial powers but not to other sorts of conflicts, such as the Ethiopian War, the Spanish Civil War, or the Sino-Japanese War.[52]

Italo Balbo himself (1896–1940) was an outstanding example of the fascist as airman syndrome. Coming to Milan from his native Ferrara to attend high school, he edited a literary journal just before the war. Like the other young rebels in literary circles, he considered d'Annunzio, who would later become his friend, to be decadent; was fascinated by the aeroplane and by the remarkable feats of the flight pioneers; and took to the streets to agitate for Italy's entry into the First World War. During the later part of the war he served as a storm platoon commander on the Alpine front, becoming involved after the war in nationalist activities both as a journalist and on the streets. He joined the Fascists in 1921, excelled as a blackshirt leader, and after the Fascist seizure of power, he was made governor of Ferrara. In 1926 he was appointed under-secretary for the air, becoming secretary in 1929, a position he held until 1933. Learning to fly in 1927, he personally led the daring

---

[51] Monti, *Douhet: scritti inediti*, 255 ff.; Douhet, *La Guerra integrale*, 3–70; Cappelluti, 'Douhet', 200–29; Sergè, 'Douhet in Italy'; L. Kennett, *A History of Strategic Bombing* (New York, 1982), 40, 56, 82.

[52] I. Balbo, 'Guerra aerea', in *Enciclopedia italiana*, xviii (Rome, 1938), 92–3; C. Sergè, *Italo Balbo: A Fascist Life* (Berkeley, Calif., 1987), 154–5, 189.

mass flights that earned Italian aviation worldwide renown and made Balbo himself—dashing, charming, and lovable—an international celebrity. His bearded face in flying headgear became a regular feature on the front pages of journals and magazines. In 1928 his group of sixty-one aeroplanes cruised the western Mediterranean. The next year he led thirty-five aeroplanes to the eastern Mediterranean, all the way to Odessa. In 1931 he went much further, crossing the Atlantic to Rio de Janeiro at the head of twelve aircraft. Two years later he led twenty-five aircraft in a double crossing of the Atlantic, to Chicago and back. (Like many Fascists, he was fascinated by American dynamic modernism.)

These flights had a double purpose. They were propaganda feats, intended to foster Fascism's image as an advanced, dynamic, and virile movement; and they were also designed to test the doctrine of strategic bombing. In August 1931 Balbo supervised a week-long, large-scale air manœuvre in which two aerial armies, totalling 860 aeroplanes, were pitted against each other. Mass day and night raids on La Spezia, Ancona, Genoa, Florence, Bologna, and Terni were carried out. The manœuvre was declared a complete success by the air ministry, but the supreme general staff under Marshal Pietro Badoglio was far less enthusiastic, and in the following year's manœuvres the Regia Aeronautica cooperated with the army.[53]

By the early 1930 Balbo wanted to take over Badoglio's position, and it is the platform on which he ran that is of interest to us. He wanted to see the Italian armed forces thoroughly mechanized. In the words of his biographer, 'Balbo was the leading candidate of the "modernists" within the Italian high command, who thought Badoglio, who was not a Fascist, to be 'both militarily and politically too conservative to remain at the head of a revitalized "fascist" military machine'. In a meeting with Mussolini in the summer of 1933, Balbo

favored reorganizing the armed forces into a series of highly flexible and mobile forces. The army was to be reduced in size to twenty divisions, of which five would be Alpine, five armored, and ten motorized. Balbo viewed the new army as an ensemble of 'expeditionary forces' ready to embark at a moment's notice, primarily by rail or by sea, for Italy's four shores. These units would be well equipped, armed with the latest weapons, and trained in amphibious warfare. The Aeronautica's budget would be quadrupled. . . .[54]

[53] We now have a biography of Balbo in English: Sergè, *Balbo*, esp. 16, 148–9, 182. A contemporary biography which is in itself a document of the fascist mood is R. Italiaander, *Italo Balbo* (Munich, 1942).   [54] Sergè, *Balbo*, 279–80.

Nothing came of Balbo's plans for a military machine based on aircraft and armoured and mechanized formations, if only because it was Balbo, rather than Badoglio, that was replaced by Mussolini. Concerned that Balbo's great popularity might overshadow his own and position Balbo as the Duce's successor (an ambition that was not foreign to Balbo), Mussolini kicked him upward to the post of governor of Libya. Douhet's widow was among those who protested to Mussolini, but to no avail.[55] Later during the 1930s Balbo would wholly oppose Italy's alliance with Germany, adoption of racial policies, and involvement in the Second World War. In 1940 he was mistakenly shot down and killed by Italian gunners when landing in his aircraft in Tobruk.

Balbo's removal from the Regia Aeronautica illustrates the limitations of the Fascist modernist and Futurist rhetoric and the weakening of the movement's revolutionary stance which began once it assumed power. On the symbolic and propagandist level the Fascist affinity with the air was intensely cultivated. The regime financed and boasted of a series of major Italian triumphs in international air races that heightened the country's prestige during the second half of the 1920s. Flying aces like Francesco de Pinedo, Arturo Ferrarin, and Mario de Bernardi set international records for speed and distance flying and won numerous trophies, the Schneider Cup of 1926 being the most prestigious. Between 1927 and 1939 Italians set 110 flight records, and even at the latter date Italians kept thirty-six of the eighty-four records established by the International Aeronautical Federation. The Regia Aeronautica held a special place among the armed forces as the 'Fascist service', and during the first years of his regime Mussolini not only made the air force independent but also increased its budget sevenfold from its insignificant postwar amount. All the same, in budgetary terms the air force remained a poor third, far behind the army and navy. In this respect it was in no better and perhaps even in a slightly worse position than the French and British air forces, claiming only some 15 per cent of the total defence budget. Apart from everything else, Mussolini did not want to alienate the army and navy whose support for his regime was crucial. Only in the late 1930s, as in the other European powers, did appropriations for the Regia Aeronautica grow sharply, overtaking those of the navy in budget share. None the less, Italy's economic and industrial base had all along been much smaller than that of the other great powers. The achievements of pioneering

[55] Ibid. 283.

theorists and innovative designers that had given her a place of honour in the world of aviation could not be sustained for long once the other great powers began to rearm in earnest.[56]

Influence, Echoes, and Parallels

It is not the aim of this study to chart Douhet's 'influence' abroad, which was as ambivalent as it was at home. The fact remains, however, that from the late 1920s in France, Germany, and the Soviet Union—and in the United States even before then—his name and work increasingly came to symbolize the idea of a war-winning 'strategic' air force—whether this idea was accepted, rejected, or somewhere in between, as was most often the case. Translation dates of his books are misleading in this respect. For example, although Douhet's *The Command of the Air* was only translated into German in 1935, by the late 1920s future air warfare had become the hottest stuff on the pages of *Militär-Wochenblatt*, the German army's semi-official journal. It was regularly and intensely discussed, and Douhet's name and ideas were often cited. Prohibited from possessing aeroplanes, the Reichswehr eagerly watched developments abroad. In the mid-1930s the new and independent Luftwaffe was attracted to strategic bombing (albeit as one among several roles) and was paying considerable attention to Douhet's ideas. It was chiefly supply shortages, problems with the production of powerful engines, and the political drive for speedy production of a large number of aircraft that gradually swayed the Luftwaffe away from the heavy bomber.[57]

Things were even more intriguing in respect to the United States. In the spring and summer of 1917, as it entered the war in Europe, the world's most advanced industrial power, in which flight had been pioneered, was seriously looking for the machines and theory of air warfare not only to the *Entente*'s hitherto strongest industrial powers, Britain and France, but also to its least developed partner, Italy. To be sure, from the outset the United States embarked on a huge industrial mobilization that was ultimately planned to supply not only its own air force but also that of her allies. Yet, as the historian of American ideas of air warfare makes clear, 'on 6 April 1917, the American Army did not

---

[56] Sergè, *Balbo*, esp. 149, 157–66, 182–5.

[57] See E. Homze, *Arming the Luftwaffe* (Lincoln, Nebr., 1976), 34, 51–4, 121–5, 264; R. Overy, 'From Uralbomber to Amerikabomber: The Luftwaffe and Strategic Bombing', *Journal of Strategic Studies*, 1 (1978), 154–78; W. Murray, *Luftwaffe* (Baltimore, 1985), 4–15.

possess a single modern combat aircraft'. Furthermore, before producing aircraft one had to decide what aircraft ought to be produced and for what purposes.

To determine such questions a special Aeronautical Commission, headed by Maj. Raynal C. Bolling, was sent to Europe in June 1917. There its members worked in close cooperation with Lt.-Col. William ('Billy') Mitchell, who had arrived in France in May as an observer to the Allies' air forces and who had assumed the post of chief of the air service, American Expeditionary Forces, in June. Both the Bolling Commission in its report of 15 August and Mitchell's 'General Principles Underlying the Use of the Air Service', issued in the autumn of 1917, saw the air force as playing a double role, both in the tactical zone of operation in direct support of the ground forces and deeper, in 'strategic' bombing. On the whole this conception was modelled on British thoughts and practice at that stage of the war; the Bolling Commission was in touch with the British Air Board, and Mitchell spent a few days visiting the headquarters of Maj.-Gen. Hugh Trenchard, the Royal Air Force Commander in France. Yet the radical edge of the American concept came from contact with the Italians:

As a result of a visit to Italy, the Bolling Commission was evidently favorably impressed with Italian bombing raids against Austria, and the commission recommended that the United States should purchase Caproni biplanes and the license to manufacture Caproni triplanes. . . . Major Edgar S. Gorrell . . . was detailed in charge of the Air Service Technical Section in Paris . . . his studies led him to believe that the United States should purchase or build a sufficiently large number of night bombers to carry out a 'systematic bombardment' of Germany. What the influence of Count Caproni had been on the original Bolling mission report may only be speculative, but in October 1917 both Bolling and Gorrell were in active correspondence with the Italian aircraft manufacturer. Sometime during October, Caproni collaborated with his friend Captain Giulio Douhet in the preparation of a 'Memorandum on the "Air War" for the U.S. Air Service' which urged that mass attacks made at night by long-range Allied bombers against industrial targets deep within Germany and Austria could definitely overwhelm the enemy by substantially reducing his war production at the same time that Allied production was increasing. That same month, Caproni gave Gorrell a little book signed by Nino Salveneschi and entitled *Let Us Kill the War; Let Us Aim At the Heart of the Enemy*. Evidently written by a journalist to represent Caproni's views, this small English-text book was a further exposition of the concept of strategic bombardment. In November 1917, Bolling personally advised Howard Coffin, the Chairman of the Aircraft Production Board in Washington, that the United States ought to give a higher priority to the production and procurement of bomber aircraft than to observation and fighter aircraft . . . the United States initially undertook to manufacture Caproni bombers, but it was also decided to produce British-designed Handley-Page bombers.

By the end of the war, however, very little had come of this strategic plan.[58]

A World War hero, chief of the training and operations group at the headquarters of the postwar United States Army Air Service, and assistant chief of the Service, Billy Mitchell, leading a group of radicals within the Service, became the United States's foremost theorist of air warfare. He won national acclaim for his outspoken public crusade for the air force after the war and eventual trial for violation of military discipline, which resulted in his dismissal from the army. However, while his career so remarkably parallelled that of Douhet, historians and his biographer agree that he developed late as an air theorist, and that the evolution of his thought was crucially influenced (and thoroughly radicalized) by the ideas of Douhet and the Italians.[59]

While the Bolling Commission envisaged an independent status and an independent role for the air force as early as the summer of 1917, Mitchell arrived at that position only from 1919 on, partly under the pressure of the postwar cuts in the armed forces which practically eliminated the air service. During the war neither he nor his fellow American airmen in France ever thought that the air force should become anything other than an auxiliary arm of the army. By the end of the war, Mitchell's only original idea had been for a large-scale paratroop assault beyond the German lines, to be carried out in conjunction with a large tank offensive to end the war.[60] Even as he developed further, Mitchell's views in the immediate postwar period regarding the roles and capabilities of the aircraft initially remained admirably discriminating. He saw that air flight was going to transform

[58] R. F. Futrell, *Ideas, Concepts, Doctrine: A History of Basic Thinking in the United States Air Force, 1907–1964* (Maxwell Air Force, Ala., 1971), 10–14. This is based on the archival research of J. L. Atkinson, 'Italian Influence on the Origins of the American Concept of Strategic Bombardment', *Airpower Historian*, 4 (1957), 141–9. (I have been unable to obtain: Key, 'Some Papers of Count Caproni di Taliedo: Controversy in the Making?', Supplement to *Pegasus* (1955), 7–11.)

[59] A. Hurley, *Billy Mitchell: Crusader for Air Power* (New York, 1964); R. Flugel, 'United States Air Power Doctrine: A Study of the Influence of William Mitchell and Giulio Douhet at the Air Corps Tactical School, 1921–1935' (doctoral dissertation, University of Oklahoma, 1965).

[60] W. Mitchell, *Memoirs of World War I* (New York, 1960), 268–9.

both civil communications and war. He believed that a huge civil and military aeronautical infrastructure would have to be built and co-ordinated. He thought the air force must become an independent service and either have its own independent ministry to advance and protect its interests or work under a unified defence department incorporating all three armed services. He maintained that command of the air would be essential for the operation of the other services and be the first task of the air force. He believed air warfare was going to transform land and sea warfare. Yet he did not view the air force as being able to replace the army and navy. On the ground in particular, army targets were too numerous, diffuse, and capable of concealment for the air force to decide anything by itself. On the sea, large armoured warships had become too vulnerable to aircraft operating from aircraft carriers or from land bases, and their days were over. Much like Richmond and Fuller in Britain, and like eminent American admirals such as William Fullam, William E. Sims, and Bradely Fiske, Mitchell believed that the navy of the future would be composed of aircraft carriers and submarines. The air force itself would consist mostly of pursuit aircraft to protect the American continent and the land and sea theatres of war abroad. The remainder of the force would be divided between observation aircraft belonging directly to the army and navy, attack aircraft, and bombers. This mixture of types and missions was pretty much along the lines common during the later stage of the First World War in Europe. The bombers would constitute only a small part of the air force, although Mitchell believed that mostly night raids on the civil rear would cause massive destruction of cities and would become an integral aspect of future war, a threat to which the United States would not be immune. These were the ideas he developed and propagated, in collaboration with his friends, in a stream of memoranda, testimonies before Congress, and newspaper articles between 1919 and 1921, and incorporated in his book *Our Air Force* (1921).[61] Inevitably, he too had his share of errors and exaggerations, but on the whole his was an impressive forecast of the shape of things to come. Apparently, by this time he had not come into contact with Douhet or the Italians in any significant way, although this was soon to change.

In the winter of 1921/2 Mitchell was sent to Europe at the head of an

---

[61] *Our Air Force* (New York, 1921); see I. D. Levine *Mitchell: Pioneer of Air Power* (New York 1943), 83, and esp. Hurley, *Mitchell*, 1, 17, 39–55, 58, for his late development; Futrell's excellent *Ideas, Concepts, Doctrine*, 13–21, is particularly good on the opinions in the Air Service around Mitchell.

inspection group on air matters. In his report he described France as the strongest air force and Italy as the weakest. Nevertheless, he singled out the latter as possessing special excellence:

> Mitchell knew Caproni and probably saw him again during this visit, but ten years passed before Mitchell ever mentioned having had 'frequent conversations' with Douhet. Mitchell was probably referring to Caproni and Douhet when he reported meeting 'more exceptional ability in Italy than we did in any other country'. . . . If he had heard nothing about *The Command of the Air* while he was in Italy, he nevertheless became aware of its main points a few months later. Lieutenant Colonel A. Guidoni, the Italian Air Attaché in Washington, sent an Italian aviation journal's summary of the book to Air Service Headquarters and to Lester Gardner, the editor of *Aviation* magazine. Gardner discussed the piece with Mitchell, called attention to it in his journal, and planned to publish a translation of the entire book. In a letter to Douhet, Guidoni quoted Gardner as saying that Mitchell was greatly impressed by the ideas of Douhet.[62]

Mitchell's contacts with Douhet and his work must have had a significant share in the transformation and radicalization of his views during the 1920s, which in the end became barely distinguishable from Douhet's. Thus, while Mitchell's *Winged Defence* (1925) mainly repeated the ideas of his *Our Air Force*, it incorporated some new thoughts and contained much more radical overtones. In the preface to the book Mitchell predicted, as Douhet had done, that the battle of attrition on land and at sea would diminish in importance because the air force would mount a direct strategic attack on the enemy's sources of power. He now claimed that air power would prevent and replace the transportation of troops by sea. Like the Italians, he no longer even believed in the aircraft carrier, claiming that it stood little chance against land-based aircraft.[63] In the introduction to his war memoirs, which he prepared for publication in 1926, Mitchell advanced similar views, misleadingly creating the impression that he had held them during the war. Here too he claimed that the struggle of attrition and

---

[62] Hurley, *Mitchell*, 75, also 76, 81–2; Guidoni's letter to Douhet is printed in Monti, *Douhet: scritti inediti*, 236–7. The translation promised by Gardner never appeared. However, a 5-page extract of *The Command of the Air* was prepared by the War Department Military Intelligence Division on 23 Mar. 1922 and found its way into the files of the Air Service Plans Division. A typescript translation of the first 100 pages of the book was received by the Air Service Field Officers' School on 3 May 1923; see Futrell, *Ideas, Concepts, Doctrine*, 21–2; the case for Douhet's influence on the air force from the late 1920s is made by Flugel, 'United States Air Power Doctrine'.

[63] *Winged Defence* (New York, 1925), esp. pp. xvi, 5–6, 99–138.

total destruction which had characterized the World War would be replaced by a direct, swift, inexpensive, and decisive air strike against the enemy's industrial centres, making extensive use of gas. By the mid-1920s Mitchell, too, had adopted an exclusive vision of air warfare.[64] In 1927, after his dismissal from the army, Mitchell again went on a tour of inspection of European aeronautics. He found all doors open to him, and in Italy his host was Italo Balbo. As in his earlier tour, he reported that the French had the strongest air power in Europe, but 'Italian aviation was in his view even more progressive'.[65] Mitchell repeated his forecast of future war in his *Skyways* (1930).[66] In his journalistic articles during the 1930s he consistently argued that a strategic air offensive from Midway and Alaska was the only effective course open to the United States in a war with Japan. He thought the navy's only contribution would be submarines, and regarded the aircraft carrier as a waste of money.[67]

Britain did not need Douhet or the Italians to adopt the idea of an independent, 'strategic', and even war-winning air force. In the wake of the German raids on London and following the recommendations of a board headed by Jan Christian Smuts, a separate air ministry was created in December 1917, and the world's first independent air force, the RAF, was established in April 1918. From the summer of 1917 the British air force in France under Trenchard was bombing strategic targets in the German rear. Air Minister William Weir and the RAF's Chief of Staff, Frederick Sykes, wanted this to become its principal mission, and Trenchard, Chief of the Air Staff in 1919–29, soon converted to this view and during the interwar period advocated strategic bombing as Britain's most promising strategy. In his *Reformation of War* (1923) Fuller made the aerial bombing of cities, especially with gas, one of the principal features of future warfare, and Liddell Hart copied his ideas for his *Paris* (1925). Later Liddell Hart rightly claimed that he had never heard Douhet's name until he saw his book in French translation in the mid-1930s, and that British thoughts on the use of air power had developed

---

[64] *Memoirs of World War I*, 4–5. His unjustified claim for hindsight wisdom has not escaped his biographer: Hurley, *Mitchell*, 117. Although based on Hurley, D. MacIsaac's brief reference to Mitchell in 'Voices from the Central Blue: The Air Power Theorists', in P. Paret (ed.), *Makers of Modern Strategy from Machiavelli to the Nuclear Age* (Princeton, NJ, 1986), 631, underestimates Mitchell's transformation during the 1920s.

[65] Hurley, *Mitchell*, 114, citing Mitchell's manuscripts.

[66] (Philadelphia, 1930), 253–70.   [67] Hurley, *Mitchell*, 122–3.

independently.[68] All the same, as some historians have noted, active public enthusiasm for the air in interwar Britain was disproportionately associated with the radical right. Thus the seemingly mysterious 'second career' of T. E. Lawrence, 'Lawrence of Arabia', who in the 1920s first joined the Tank Corps and then the RAF under the pseudonyms 'Aircraftman Ross' and 'Private Shaw', is incomprehensible when separated from the intellectual outlook which brought it about. Lawrence stood on the fringes of and had a special status in radical British right-wing culture. Like the Italian Futurists, not only did he see the aeroplane, the fast motorcycle (on which he eventually died in a road accident), and the fast motor-boat (which he tested for the RAF) as exhilarating instruments of speed and a source of emotional elation; for him they, and especially the aeroplane, opened new frontiers and new horizons. The few who were engaged with the aeroplane were the heroic pioneers of a new age. As he told a friend, the air was 'the only first-class thing that our generation has to do. So everyone should either take to the air themselves or help it forward.' He joined where he believed the great drama of the future was unfolding.[69] As David Edgerton has written in his interesting study *England and the Aeroplane*: 'It is important to note the aristocratic basis of these ideas . . . "reactionary modernist" feeling was very widespread in the interwar years.'[70]

Edgerton's survey of some of the radical right-wing enthusiasts for the air runs as follows:

Rear-Admiral Murray Sueter, a leading wartime naval aviator, was elected to Parliament as a candidate of Lord Rothermere's Anti-Waste League and Horatio Bottomley's Independent Parliamentary Group in 1921. He remained in the House as a Conservative until 1945, being knighted in 1934. His name crops up in all the main pro-air and pro-German organizations of the late 1930s. . . . Colonel the Master of Sempill was a senior member of the Air League, the Anglo-German Fellowship and the Link. He entered the House of Lords in the 1930s as Baron Sempill, and in 1939 was one of the hard core of German enthusiasts who urged publicly for peace with Germany from the Lords. But

---

[68] Fuller, *The Reformation of War*, 136–51; B. H. Liddell Hart, *Paris* (London, 1925), 41–62; for the interwar period, see mainly R. Higham, *The Military Intellectuals in Britain: 1918–1939* (New Brunswick, NJ, 1966), 119–259; H. Montgomery Hyde, *British Air Policy between the Wars* (London, 1976); M. Smith, *British Air Strategy between the Wars* (Oxford, 1984), esp. 64–6.

[69] Edgerton, *England and the Aeroplane*, 46; Wohl, *A Passion for Wings*, 1; and for Lawrence and the radical right, Susser, 'Fascist and Anti-Fascist Attitudes in Britain', 145–57.   [70] Edgerton, *England and the Aeroplane*, 46.

the most politically important pro-German peer after 1935 was Lord Londonderry, Secretary of State for Air, 1931–1935. He was a member of the Anglo-
German Fellowship, but while still friendly to Germany was not a member of
the Link. . . . Lord Rothermere was a particularly enthusiastic promoter of
aviation in the interwar years . . . he had been Britain's first Secretary of State
for Air, though he did not stay in the job long. . . . He called for an 'Air
Dictator' to take control of aircraft production. . . . In 1935 Rothermere created
a National League of Airmen, which was active in the General Elections of that
year, though it was supposedly non-political. It was headed by Norman
Macmillan, Fairey's test pilot, and had among its supporters the Duke of
Westminster, Major-General Fuller and Admirals Sir Murray Sueter and
Mark Kerr. . . . Rothermere's air campaign was part of a larger imperialist
programme which was deeply hostile to the League of Nations. In the early
1930s he briefly supported Oswald Mosley and his British Union of Fascists,
and his abandoning of Mosley did not make him any less a figure of the hard
Right. It was not just ultra-right politics which they had in common. Mosley
had flown for the RFC in the war, and saw in aircraft that combination of
modern science and the Faustian, heroic spirit which was so central to his idea
of the 'Modern Movement'. Mosley formed Fascist flying clubs in 1934.
Several historians have noted that aviators formed a disproportionate element
in the membership of the British Union of Fascists. . . . The connection
between fascist politics and aviation in the interwar years may be considered
at the level of lesser personalities too. A. V. Roe was a prominent financial and
moral supporter of Mosley. Lady Houston, the wealthy widow of a Liverpool
shipowner and Tory MP, was very well known as a pro-Italian fascist through
her *Saturday Review*. . . . She did not at first like the Nazis but changed her
mind in 1936. . . . Lady Houston is still remembered as the generous benefac-
tress of the famous 1931 Schneider Trophy Race. This was not her only
benefaction: she offered to give almost £200,000 to the British Union of
Fascists and attempted to give equally large sums to the nation for the air
defence of London.[71]

Richard Griffiths, also emphasizing the Fascists' special connection
with aviation, adds other names to the list: 'the Secretary-General
and the Secretary of the Air League, Air Commodore J. A. Chamier
and Colonel Norman Thwaites, were members of the [fascist] January
Club, the latter (who was editor of the journal *Air*) becoming its chairman in late 1934.' From the pages of *Aeroplane* which he edited from
1911 to 1939, C. G. Grey eulogized Nazi Germany, hailed her rearmament and the creation of the Luftwaffe, believed she defended
Europe against communism, and called Britain to ally with her and

[71] Ibid. 47–9.

abandon France, 'essentially a feminine nation'.[72] On the whole, according to Edgerton, Winston Churchill's position, enthusiastically supporting air armament but opposing the 'active pro-German, pro-aviation Right' was 'a lonely one'. By the late 1930s even someone like Bertrand Russell, who had not hovered into or close to the fascist orbit, echoed Wells, d'Annunzio, Marinetti, Fuller, and Lawrence:

> We seem now, through the aeroplane, to be returning to the need for forces composed of comparatively few highly trained men. It is to be expected, therefore, that the form of government, in every country exposed to serious war, will be such as airmen will like, which is not likely to be democracy.[73]

It is this conclusion that we he have encountered again and again all over Europe. Those who expected a new fascist age were also the most enthusiastic for the aeroplane and for flying. Antoine de Saint-Exupéry, France's most famous airman-novelist during the interwar period, escaped this syndrome, even though he shared much of the spiritual yearning that led many of his friends to fascism. It has been charged that his 'code of hardship, duty, discipline, and sacrifice made him susceptible to the ideal of Airman-as-Fascist'. However, his conception of the flying machine was essentially developed in a 'Christian, pacifist, human' direction. By contrast, his good friend and fellow pilot, Jean Mermoz, became vice-president of the fascist *Croix de Feu*.[74] In the late 1920s and early 1930s, like many others, the most prominent pioneer of modernist architecture in Europe, Le Corbusier (1887–1965), was moving from syndicalism towards semi-fascism and fascism in the *Redressement Français* and *planisme*, editing the journals of this vein *Plans* and *Prélude*. Like those movements, he was inspired by the French Utopian Socialists and impressed by Taylorism. He held that the modern technological republic of producers, interconnected in complex economic and urban systems, could only be hierarchic and rationally run by a paternalistic, authoritarian, technocratic élite, for which Le Corbusier planned grandiose skyscrapers, centred in his designed modernist metropolises. He believed a harmonious Second Machine Age was coming, replacing the First, which had been divisive and fuelled by greed and which had collapsed with the Great Depression. Increasingly anti-democratic, Le Corbusier dedicated his book *La Ville radieuse* (1935) 'To Authority'. During the Second World War he

---

[72] R. Griffiths, *Fellow Travellers of the Right* (London, 1980), 137–40.
[73] Edgerton, *England and the Aeroplane*, 46, 49.
[74] L. Goldstein, *The Flying Machine and Modern Literature* (London, 1986), 139–44.

looked in vain to Vichy to realize his modernist urban plans. In his introduction to his photo album *Aircraft* (1935) he described the aeroplane as 'the advance guard of the conquering armies of the New Age', the age of the 'machine' or 'mechanical civilization', of which the automobile was another symbol. He, too, traced his first encounter with the aeroplane to Paris in 1909.[75] As we shall see, the war hero, famous writer, and modernist right-wing radical Ernst Jünger wrote in the same vein in Germany. Finally, although Nazi Germany was a latecomer to aviation and far more ambiguous in its attitude to modernity than Italian Fascism, the Nazi mystique of the air and the role of the Luftwaffe in the regime's political liturgy were as prominent as they were in Fascist Italy, and with far more powerful industrial muscle to back them.

[75] See esp. R. Fishman, *Urban Utopias in the Twentieth Century: Ebenezer Howard, Frank Lloyd Wright, and Le Corbusier* (New York, 1977), 213–52; Le Corbusier, *Aircraft* (New York, 1988, original 1935), 5–13.

4

German Right-Wing Radicalism,
Strategic Adventurism, and
Mechanized Warfare

Any discussion of German fascism is inevitably dominated by Nazism, whose long shadow falls across modern German, Western, and world history. Yet the National Socialist Party and its fanatical leader, Adolf Hitler, only became a significant political force in Germany at the outset of the 1930s, when complex and somewhat conjunctural circumstances brought them into power and gave them the means to play out on such a grand scale their gruesome part in history. To be sure the party expressed and throve on deep and powerful currents within German national and political culture; but that precisely also meant that it had begun as only one element within a much wider phenomenon. Drawing on even earlier national traditions, German right-wing radicalism had been taking shape from the late nineteenth century, with the advent of mass society in the wake of Germany's industrialization.

The growth of the popular radical right in Germany before the First World War as a cultural and political force mixing nostalgic, *völkisch*, and pessimistic sentiments with modernist and vitalist notions, is fairly recognized and needs no elaboration here. Within the armed services, officers like Colamr von der Goltz, Friedrich von Bernhardi, August Keim, Erich Ludendorff, and Alfred Tirpitz spoke and acted for those among their civilian and military peers who sought ways of overcoming and exploiting the modern condition, which the traditional ruling and official classes had long viewed with alarm and despair. Skilfully using such modern devices as the media and mass popular movements, they wished to bridge class divisions and mobilize the masses behind the state in a new popular and nationalist unity. While the First World War brought about, under Ludendorff's orchestration, an unprecedented degree of social and industrial mobilization, it was widely believed in right-wing circles that Germany had ultimately lost the war because that degree had not been high enough. As with the Prussian reformers a century earlier, who had faced similar conditions of defeat and national humiliation, the need to create a modern *Volksgemeinschaft* (which might be imperfectly translated as 'popular national community') was widely regarded in these circles by officers and civilians alike as essential for Germany's military and political regeneration. It was also viewed as necessary for the survival and rejuvenation of her traditional élite's ethos, self-identity, and hold over the state under modern conditions.

Within the Reichswehr the generation that had been born during the last two decades of the nineteenth century, served as junior and middle-rank officers in the First World War, and was now rising into higher positions was generally inclined towards this view.[1] The more radical element of this generation aspired to a new, modern, totalitarian regime that would maximize the nation's cohesion, boost its morale and harness its resources for power politics and war. It was mostly these people that were particularly susceptible to, and active in implementing, radical visions of mechanized warfare. Not for the first time in her history, modernization was urged on Germany by the need to meet the demands of war. The Reichswehr as a whole, like all parts of the Reich's traditional élite, lent its more or less qualified support to Hitler's rise to power in the hope that he would bring the support of the masses, rejuvenate the nation, and undo Versailles. But within the Reichswehr the radicals were his most enthusiastic supporters.

Jünger: Machine Warfare and Machine Societies

Before turning to serving regular officers of the Reichswehr and Wehrmacht, one might start with one of their peers who had left the army after the First World War as a war hero to become a best-selling author and one of Germany's most distinguished writers of the twentieth century. From his youth Ernst Jünger (b. 1895) rebelled against his bourgeois background, searching for adventure, action, and purpose. At 17 he ran away from home to join the French Foreign Legion, only to be returned from North Africa on his parents' request. Fortunately for him, the war came soon after. He enlisted, underwent basic training, and served at the front for one month before being sent for officer training. Returning to the front in 1916, he was wounded seventeen times, four times critically, and was awarded the *Pour le Mérite*,

---

[1] See most notably M. Geyer, *Aufrüstung oder Sicherheit: Die Reichswehr in der Krise der Machtpolitik, 1924–1936* (Wiesbaden, 1980).

Germany's highest decoration. During the last year of the war he trained and commanded a platoon and a company of élite storm troops, participating in some of the fiercest battles of that year. He was among the few selected to remain in the small Reichswehr after the war, and contributed to the infantry sections of the German post-war field-service manual, *Führung und Gefecht der verbundenen Waffen.* His *In Stahlgewittern, Storm of Steel* (1920), based on his war diaries and describing his front-line experience, immediately made him famous, running through several editions during the 1920s. In 1923 Jünger left the army to start a career as a radical right-wing writer.[2]

Like Erich Maria Remarque, Robert Graves, Siegfried Sassoon, and other late-1920s authors in the war literature genre, Jünger described the trench warfare experience in a factual, quasi-realistic style. But the similarity ends here. Theirs would fundamentally be a liberal–pacifist attitude, evoking fear, exhaustion, horror, misery, brutalization, degradation, mutilation, disgust, and purposelessness. But for Jünger war was an exhilarating experience approached with relish, an opportunity to master fear and transcend bodily limits, the ultimate virile sport, a supreme fulfilment of one's self.[3] His unquestioned personal heroism aside, Jünger's attitude, like theirs, only acquires its meaning when seen in terms of his wider world-view, which he set out to develop in his later books.

In his extended essay *The Battle as Inner Experience* (1922), Jünger analysed the psychological qualities and emotions involved in battle. He also presented war as 'the father of all things', a force of crucial moral, historical, and social significance.[4] Three years later came his third war book, *Copse 125*. This he also based on his war memoirs, this time from a small section of the Western Front facing the British from the end of June to mid-July 1918. The memoirs, however, were intertwined with his reflections on the war, on war in general, and on what it stood for. Mostly, these reflections were of the all too familiar stuff of the German idealist and nationalist tradition, mixed with the influence of Nietzsche and Spengler, and they can be briefly summarized. War was the ultimate

---

[2] On Jünger, see esp. J. P. Stern, *Ernst Jünger* (New Haven, Conn., 1953); H.-P. Schwarz, *Der konservative Anarchist: Politik und Zeitkritik Ernst Jüngers* (Freiburg, 1962); G. Loose, *Ernst Jünger* (New York, 1974); J. Herf, *Reactionary Modernism* (Cambridge, 1984), 70–108.

[3] *In Stahlgewittern* (1920), reprinted in his *Sämtliche Werke,* i (1978); trans. as *Storm of Steel: From the Diary of a German Storm-Troop Officer on the Western Front* (New York, 1929).

[4] *Der Kampf als inneres Erlebnis,* reprinted in *Sämtliche Werke,* vii (1980).

moral and spiritual test for the greatness of a nation and for the ideas it represented. It was nature's way of selection, and the cleanser of internal weakness, corruption, and decadence for which economic or cultural competition could never substitute:

We have never stopped it and never shall, because war is not the law of one age or civilization, but of eternal nature itself, out of which every civilization proceeds, and into which it must sink again if it is not hard enough to withstand the iron ordeal. For this reason those who seek to abolish war . . . a belated rearguard of an enlightenment . . . are the real pest of civilization though they have it always on their lips. . . . May they ever be a laughing-stock to the youth of our land . . . let us be hard and merciless on ourselves and on others.

According to Jünger, the First World War should have been fought until the end, rejecting any compromise. The defeat was only a breathing-space before the next struggle.[5]

But what form would the next war take and, hence how to prepare for it? Here Jünger had novel things to say. In the first place it would be machine war. *In Stahlgewittern* had already conveyed the notion that man was now operating under a 'storm of steel', within an overpowering *Materialschlacht*, in a new machine war epoch. In this world natural and artificial were mixed.[6] This notion was radically developed in 'The Technique of Future Battle', an article which Jünger published in October 1921 in *Militär-Wochenblatt*, the army's semi-official journal, and incorporated—further developed and expanded—in *Copse 125*.[7] He wrote that the spring of 1918 saw the fully fledged appearance of mechanized warfare. From then on,

the theory of mobile war was gaining the upper hand and soon to be seen in action. With this arises the question of the further development of war. . . . What this war emphasizes again and again as the new and decisive factor is the entry of the machine into battle and the corresponding retirement of purely manual work. Of our three main arms, to which aviation was added as a fourth, two, infantry and cavalry. . . were wholly occupied in what I call manual work in distinction from machine work. Of these two, the cavalry will soon disappear altogether from the field of battle . . . The infantry will, perhaps, hold out

[5] *Copse 125: A Chronicle from the Trench Warfare of 1918* (London, 1930), 56–7, and similarly pp. viii–xii, 128, 181–4; the German original, *Das Wäldchen 125* (1925), is reprinted in *Werke*, i.

[6] See interestingly B. Hüppauf, 'The Birth of Fascist Man from the Spirit of the Front', in J. Milford (ed.), *The Attraction of Fascism: Social Psychology and Aesthetics of the 'Triumph of the Right'* (New York, 1990), 45–76.

[7] 'Die Technik der Zukunftsschlacht', *Militär-Wochenblatt* [*M–W*], 1 Oct. 1921, 287–90.

longer; but it, too, is threatened by a process of disintegration that has begun already. . . . As mobility increases, the exaggerated importance of artillery will fall away.[8]

As Jünger stated: 'The machine is more powerful than muscle':[9]

we shall have to break away from the idea of a massed attack in its old form . . . It is a question no longer of launching men in mass but machines . . . The solid earth, in default of roads, and with its changing contours, presents greater difficulties to the passage of machines than do the air and the sea, where the machine has finally established itself in the picture of war. But the peace-time invention of the motor-plough and the war-time one of the tank have made the first steps in overcoming these difficulties.[10]

Sea warfare 'where the mechanical problem came long ago and decisively to the front', serves as the best guide to the future of land war, though the latter will probably favour smaller machines.[11]

the tank is the most important invention of a war rich in contrivances, though it will not perhaps in this war reach by a long way its final stage. . . . Mobility, fire and cover are combined in it . . . For this reason and other too, in its further development it is bound to be the decisive engine of the battle of to-morrow with all other arms as its mere accompaniment.

Jünger went on to speculate that the development of the tank might be followed in the future by the development of flying tanks.[12] Scientific and technological innovation was moving fast, and now counted the most:

It is scarcely to be expected that European nations whose civilization proceeds from one mighty source will encounter one another with radically different methods of war, as in the case for example of the Spaniards and the Aztecs. But there will, all the same, be ideas in the air, such as the automatic steering of aeroplanes or wireless telephony, that one side will develop more quickly than the other. And it can never be foreseen what surprises of deadly nature may be expected. . . . It is precisely in a short war that such surprises are the more dangerous.[13]

Partly for that reason, the technological age will make armies not only mechanical but smaller, placing the emphasis on the most modern advancements of science and the most sophisticated and agile forms of organization:

---

[8] Copse 125, 4, 128–9, 133.   [9] Ibid. 131.   [10] Ibid. 130.
[11] Ibid. 130–1.   [12] Ibid. 132–3.   [13] Ibid. 136–7.

sheer mass, whether of men or material, will have little influence on the out-come of a war such as we are considering. . . . We see every day in all branches of industry how a new miracle of mind, fused into steel, abolishes at a stroke all that has gone before. . . . Why should it be otherwise in war? No, an army, too, in its entirety, is more than ever before a machine in which cog grips cog and every ounce of energy is transmitted to the driving belt of the attack. . . . For this an instrument is required so highly polished and fraught with spirit that the notion of mass is utterly foreign to it.[14]

These ideas, concepts, and general outlook, indeed the phrases themselves, ring all too familiar. In this author's opinion, their near one-to-one similarity to Fuller's is no coincidence. By 1921, when Jünger wrote the original article on the technique of future battle, he may have read Fuller's *Tanks in the Great War* (1920), either in English or in a German translation made at an unknown date during the 1920s and circulated in the Reichswehr in typescript for internal use. He also may have read Fuller's Gold Medal essay, published in the RUSI journal the year before. From 1924, as Jünger further developed the theme of mechanized warfare for *Copse 125*, Fuller's ideas, mainly through his disciple Liddell Hart, were prominently reviewed in *Militär-Wochenblatt*. Thus, like Liddell Hart, Jünger may have owed his conversion from an infantry specialist to a proponent of mechanized war to Fuller's influence.[15] In any event, already a right-wing radical himself, Jünger now worked out independently the wider social implications of machine warfare and, like Fuller, was soon to expand from the military field to consider the character of the machine epoch as a whole. In *Copse 125* he wrote:

---

[14] Ibid. 134.

[15] For translated copies of Fuller's *Tanks in the Great War*, see Bundesarchiv-Militärarchiv, Freiburg im Breisgau [BA-MA Freiburg], 8/v. 1745 and 1939. Liddell Hart's article 'The Next Great War' was abstracted as the opening piece of *M–W*, 25 July 1924, 713–15, after having been briefly reviewed on 5 May, ibid. 578. His 'The Development of a "New Model" Army' was briefly reviewed in *M–W*, 11 Nov. 1924, 501, and recommended for translation. On 18 Dec. 1924 another opening piece in *M–W*, 649–51, described the new thoughts in Britain of replacing the muscle armies by machine ones, leading to an all-armoured army and a reduction of 60% in manpower. Fuller was cited in the journal here and there, e.g. 15 Apr. 1924, 531. Jünger contributed an article on infantry tactics on 10 Aug. 1923, 51. Kurt Hesse wrote about him on 15 Mar. 1924, 451. Jünger's books were prominently advertised in the journal. His only divergence from Fuller's views in respect to future mechanized warfare was his belief that gas would lose its importance: *Copse 125*, 133–4. See also my 'British Influence and the Evolution of the Panzer Arm: Myth or Reality?', *War in History*, 4(2) (1997), 150–73, and 4(3) (1997), 316–38.

I hate democracy as I do the plague—besides, the democratic ideal of an army would be one consisting entirely, not of Fahnenjunker, but of officers with lax discipline and great personal liberty. For my taste on the contrary, and for that of young Germans in general to-day, an army could not be too iron, too dictatorial, and too absolute—but if it is to be so, then there must be a system of promotion that is not sheltered behind any sort of privilege but opened up to the keenest competition.

In addition, old barriers must come down so that officers could get in touch with their men in order to feel their pulse, inspire them, and enhance solidarity.[16] The intention was clear: old-fashioned conservative Prussianism would not do either, for it, too, had become obsolete and out of step with the needs of the modern age:

We young Germans would be the last to reject Prussianism so far as its moral side goes. We know well that the inspired and practical founders of it had an unsurpassed wisdom in setting men to a job. They built up a machine that worked economically, exactly, and reliably, and one that could inspire enthusiasm in spite of bleak outlines, because its aim was not self but the greatness of the country . . . generation after generation was reinforced by this will of steel. . . . But it is no longer in tune with our time nor with an army composed as ours is, not with the resources that decide a battle of to-day.[17]

What was needed in the machine age was the fusion of men and machines into an integrated whole—modern, machine-like animated military and social bodies. Like Marinetti and the Futurists, Jünger did not hold that this fusion devaluated man. On the contrary, he glorified it as a new and enhanced opportunity for man to thrive, spiritually, morally, and aesthetically. It was towards this point of view that he strove to stir the German nationalist right, within which conservatism and a general fear of modernity had always been prominent elements:

where does the common man come in in all this? Is not all this a soulless and crushing business? A cold exalting of mechanical forces, an array of formulae in physics, chemistry, and the higher mathematics? Is this to be the test of life? Is it not giving the intellect and big business the mastery of the earth? . . . This is the question put now and then by the cultured German who prizes Weimar above Essen, and by the soldier too when he sees the instincts of the hero subdued to the technique of war. . . . But what do we, the coming generation, care for all this? . . . Every civilization has been great in creations that can be set

---

[16] *Copse 125*, 83.
[17] Ibid. 158–60; also 'Die Technik der Zukunftsschlacht' (1921), 289–90.

beside our own, but the machine is what we ourselves have created and we have a right to be proud of it . . . is it not we ourselves who stand behind it? Is it not our life and our blood that provide its impulse? . . . Good equipment is prized only by people whose virile nerve is still vigorous.[18]

Experience proves that the best warriors are produced by the most advanced industrial nations—the French, the British, and, above all, the Germans:

it is the man of Central Europe by whom the best machines are made, that also stand up for them best when they are in operation. The hardiest sons of the war, the men who led the storm-troops, and manipulate the tank, the aeroplane and the submarine are pre-eminent in technical accomplishment . . . accustomed to serve the machine and yet its superior at the same time.[19]

Modern power stemmed from society as a whole. If the army was to become 'a machine in which cog grips cog and every ounce of energy is transmitted to the driving belt', if it was 'to weld the pick of human and mechanical energy into one whole of such tempered force',[20] then so must society as a whole. A new machine-age society was in the making. How would it look like? *Copse 125* offered only glimpses. Like the army, it would be authoritarian, disciplined, meritocratic, and highly co-ordinated and cohesive. Like the army, it would be psychologically manipulated:

It is an important task of modern psychology to study these spheres of activity that invisibly and yet powerfully permeate the mass and magnetize it into changing formations like a heap of iron filings. There are laws here whose workings must be explored. . . . [It is] a very simple resource that must be put at the disposal of the leader as part of his equipment. For we must learn to practice a kind of demagogy from above . . .[21]

These again were the ideas of mass psychology that so fascinated anti-liberal radicals throughout the West, including Jünger's friend, the military writer. Kurt Hesse. In any event, like Fuller, Jünger now turned to analyse the historical growth and central features of the coming machine age—in war and, increasingly, in society as a whole.

In his article 'Fire and Movement' (1930) Jünger traced the development of warfare in the fast-changing mechanical era since the nineteenth century. The growth of fire-power had been progressively paralysing armies, a process already apparent in the wars in South

[18] Ibid. 138–9.   [19] Ibid. 48.   [20] Ibid. 134.   [21] Ibid. 173–4.

Africa and Manchuria and reaching its zenith on the Western Front during the First World War. Aircraft and, more importantly for land battle, the tank then revived movement on the battlefield, heralding a new machine age.[22] In another article written in the same year, 'Total Mobilization', Jünger traced the development of national war mobilization from the French Revolution to its logical conclusion in modern society. The production programmes of the latter part of the First World War, most impressively the massive American cooperation between army and industry, and, further still, the Soviet Five-Year Plan, showed the way towards a new centralized and planned economy. In disciplined societies and electrified cities of millions, transport systems, plants, engines, and aeroplanes were now intertwined with men into one complex which was working towards one goal. Following the wars of the knights, kings, and citizens successively, the twentieth century ushered in the war of the workers (*Arbeiter*), a special concept denoting functionaries and technocrats at all levels of a hierarchic organism, the human cogs of the new machine society.[23]

Jünger outlined the features of the new society in his next book, *The Worker* (*Der Arbeiter*, 1932). He claimed that humanity was about to enter a new age. The era of the bourgeois Third Estate would soon be superseded by that of the worker, as liberal democracy developed and evolved into the working state (*Arbeitsstaat*). The former had only the appearance of mastery and control which in reality hid internal divisions, lack of purpose, petty individualism, and moral weakness. By contrast, the latter would embody integral and cohesive power, replacing both the amorphous masses and the individualistic bourgeoisie. In the worker a new human type and a new social ethics would come into being—sturdy, 'post-critical', unreflectively dedicated to its mission—expressing the new *Arbeitsstaat*, in which everything was mobilized in peace and in war within a comprehensive working programme. Military mobilization, born in the age of the bourgeoisie, would now grow into total labour mobilization. Again, the Soviet Five-Year Plan showed the way to the future, though Jünger was not a Marxist internationalist.[24]

---

[22] 'Feuer und Bewegung' (1930), repr. in Jünger, *Werke*, vii. 107–17.

[23] Jünger, 'Die Totale Mobilmachung' (1930), repr. ibid. 121–42; see esp. 127–9. It was in reference to Jünger's work that Walter Benjamin first developed his interpretation of fascism as the aestheticization of politics, war, and technology—each becoming its own end—which he later applied to Marinetti: 'Theorien des deutschen Faschismus', in *Walter Benjamin: Gesammelte Schriften*, iii (Frankfurt, 1977), 238–50; trans. in *New German Critique*, 6 (1979), 120–8.

[24] *Der Arbeiter* (1932) is reprinted as vol. viii of his *Werke* (1981).

Jünger's literary career was matched by his intense public involvement in radical right-wing organizations. He participated in *Freikorps* activities during the early 1920. After his release from the army he exalted the nationalist saboteurs operating against the French occupation of the Ruhr: 'the men who are in love with dynamite'.[25] He became involved with the *Stahlhelm*, the largest ex-servicemen right-wing, anti-republic, anti-democratic, and anti-communist organization, to whose paper, *Die Standarte*, he regularly contributed agitating pieces. When the paper was closed down by the government, he helped to establish another right-wing paper, *Arminius*. At first, Jünger praised Hitler's nascent movement and sent him dedicated copies of his war books. Hitler reciprocated with a copy of *Mein Kampf* and in 1927 offered Jünger a National Socialist seat in the Reichstag, which he declined. Like the Italian Futurists in respect to Fascism, Jünger deplored any compromise with the existing order, disapproved of Hitler's decision to adopt legal methods, and feared that he was following in Mussolini's footsteps. In the way it had developed, Jünger now regarded Italian Fascism as no more than 'a late form of liberalism . . . Fascism is little suited to Germany as Bolshevism'. By the early 1930s Jünger became associated with a small group known as the 'National Bolsheviks'. This group sought to synthesize nationalism and planned centralized economy and society in a sort of 'Prussian socialism', and supported the cooperation with the Soviet Union against the West which was then reaching its zenith.[26] When the Nazis came to power, he remained aloof from politics—as the Futurists in Italy had initially done—regarding National Socialist rule as vulgar and plebeian, a caricature of his vision of a vigorous and cohesive modern machine society. Unlike the Italian Futurists, he retained his aloofness up to the end of the National Socialist regime. However, other right-wing radicals took a different attitude.

Indeed, this is one reason why Jünger merits our attention at such length. Although a writer of national reputation, he had little practical influence either inside or outside the army. Nevertheless, in his work the historian of ideas can find, developed in literary form, *all* the dominant themes also espoused by others, who wrote less but who were more strategically positioned and more closely involved with the practical affairs of army and state. General Werner von Blomberg

---

[25] Quoted in Stern, *Jünger*, 10.
[26] Schwarz, *Jünger*, 97–130; A. Hamilton, *The Appeal of Fascism* (London, 1971), 122–4.

(1878–1946) and Colonel Walter von Reichenau (1884–1942)—both future field marshals—accepted by Hitler in 1933 as war minister and chief of the ministerial office respectively, are the most prominent examples.

The Army Modernists and the Nazis

In discussing the army's attitude towards the National Socialist rise to power and regime, historians have emphasized the difference between Blomberg and Reichenau, on the one hand, and the rest of the army's high command, in particular Generals Fritsch and Beck, the army's commander-in-chief and chief of the General Staff, on the other.[27] What was this difference? After all, as mentioned earlier, the wide consensus in the Reichswehr welcomed the new regime. On the whole the Reichswehr's leadership was anti-democratic and anti-republican, and it stood for the reinstatement of Germany as a great power. Its members hoped Hitler would be able to begin rearmament and foster the desired *Volksgemeinschaft*. Still, historians agree, the army's high command was mostly composed of conservative-nationalists, heirs to the old Prussian tradition, however modified, whereas Blomberg and Reichenau represented something new and radical. Though also belonging to the right side of the political spectrum, theirs was the sort of right that conservatives found suspect. This difference pre-dated the National Socialist rise to power. It consistently found expression in attitudes towards the army's role in the new National Socialist state, operational planning for war, and mechanized warfare.

Chief of the Reichswehr's disguised general staff (*Truppenamt*) in 1927–9, Blomberg had always been somewhat suspect to the majority of his peers. As the later Field Marshal Gerd von Rundstedt, a quin-tessential representative of the old army, would testify in Nurenberg: 'Blomberg was always somewhat strange to us; he hovered in other spheres. He adhered to Steiner's way, somewhat theosophic and so on. No one really liked him.'[28] But Blomberg, a cultured man of many interests with a lively mind, was suspect not only for his attraction to

---

[27] The standard books on the subject are J. Wheeler-Bennett, *The Nemesis of Power: The German Army in Politics, 1918–1945* (New York, 1967); R. O'Neill, *The German Army and the Nazi Party, 1933–1939* (London, 1966); K.-J. Müller, *Das Heer und Hitler: Armee und nationalsozialistisches Regime, 1933–1940* (Stuttgart, 1969); M. Messerschmidt, *Die Wehrmacht im NS-Staat: Zeit der Indoktrination* (Hamburg, 1969).

[28] Quoted in Müller, *Das Heer und Hitler*, 51.

the spiritual. Ever since the 1920s he had been searching for unorthodox ways of breaking out of the post-war mould which perpetuated Germany's military and political submission. As a leading historian of the Reichswehr in the 1920s has shown, in 1924–5, following the French occupation of the Ruhr, the then Head of the Operations Branch (T1) of the general staff, Colonel Joachim von Stülpnagel, advanced schemes for a war of national liberation, based on a sweeping popular uprising against the invaders. It would intensify the campaign of sabotage and civil resistance already taking place into a wide-scale, semi-regular, and guerrilla war of total patriotic commitment, which would engulf the whole nation. This concept was wholly at odds with that of the army's commander-in-chief (*Chef der Heeresleitung*), the conservative Hans von Seeckt. Like the schemes of the radical, modernizing Prussian reformers after Jena for popular insurrection against French rule, Stülpnagel's plan went beyond the regular army and regular warfare and presupposed total social mobilization. As in Napoleon's time, it promised to be ruinous for the country and possessed dubious prospects of success. In any event, Stülpnagel's ideas were shared by Blomberg, then head of the training branch (T4), later head of the operations branch, and, finally, chief of the General Staff. In the late 1920s, in case of war against a French–Polish coalition, Blomberg devised a two-tiered idea, based on total popular resistance and swift mobile operations. War games and manoeuvres held in 1928–9 to test the plan demonstrated that it had little chance of success. War Minister Wilhelm Gröner, working for a *rapprochement* with the republic, declared it hopeless. But Blomberg continued to advocate radical operational schemes. In 1935, with the German army only at the very beginning of its expansion, he initiated a study in the war ministry on the possibility of a swift war of movement to overwhelm Czechoslovakia before France or the Soviet Union could come to her support. The initiative was blocked by Chief of the General Staff Beck, who protested strongly against the encroachment on his professional domain, arguing at the same time that the idea was strategically impractical. None the less, the ministry returned to raise similar ideas in 1937.[29]

Blomberg's radical operational schemes went hand in hand with

---

[29] M. Geyer, *Aufrüstung oder Sicherheit*. For the Czechoslovakian issue in 1935 and 1937, see also K.-J. Müller, *General Ludwig Beck: Studien und Dokumente* (Boppard a.m., 1980), 226–31, 240–5, 440–4.

radicalism in two attendant fields: the socio-political and the techno-logical. Starting with the former, if popular national war was to be waged, absolute cohesion and patriotic dedication on the part of the people, a true *Volksgemeinschaft*, had to be achieved. To be sure, many in the army wanted that, but not everybody was prepared to go to the same length or to pay the price for it. Most members of the army's high command also wanted to preserve as much as possible of the Prussian conservative tradition, the status of the old élites, and their own self-identity. By contrast, Blomberg—and Reichenau—rejected a great deal of this as anachronistic, and were willing to look for wholly new and modern forms of social order to achieve the goal of national cohesion, efficiency, and power.[30] During the 1920s the techniques of either Bolshevism or fascism seemed capable of achieving these ends, with the mighty energies of *Amerikanismus* also casting a strong, albeit ambivalent, spell. In 1928, at the height of Soviet–German military cooperation, Blomberg, in his capacity as chief of the General Staff, travelled to the Soviet Union for an extensive tour. He wrote a long report on what he had seen, analysing both the Red Army's consider-able advances and its lingering backwardness. However, above all he was deeply impressed by the degree of social mobilization, discipline, and energy he had found in the Soviet Union. This was a model of how a modern nation could be totally harnessed to produce immense power for peace or for war. As he would later confess only half-jokingly, Blomberg returned from the Soviet Union almost a Bolshevik. He wanted a military alliance with the Soviet Union. More significantly, he asked himself who in Germany could bring about a similar reorientation of society?[31] By the early 1930s he believed that Hitler and his movement had the potential to bring this about. In 1932 Reichenau, his chief of staff in the East Prussia military district (Wehrkreis I), of which Blomberg was given command after his tenure as chief of the General Staff, communicated with Hitler in order to learn about his intentions.[32]

In 1930 Blomberg led a German military delegation on a two-month

[30] K.-J. Müller, *The Army, Politics and Society in Germany, 1933–45* (Manchester, 1987), esp. 31–4, makes this point very well.

[31] J. Erickson, *The Soviet High Command* (London, 1962), 263–8, 307; Wheeler-Bennett, *Nemesis of Power*, 295–7; F. Carsten, *The Reichswehr in Politics 1918 to 1933* (Oxford, 1966), 281–2, 289–90; Geyer, *Aufrüstung*, 320–1. I have not been given access to Blomberg's MS autobiography in BA-MA N 52.

[32] T. Vogelsang, 'Hitlers Brief an Reichenau vom 4. Dezember 1932', *Vierteljahrshefte für Zeitgeschichte*, 7 (1959), 429–37.

tour to the United States, as official guests of the US Army. The delegation was taken across the country and shown all parts of American military establishment. Both Blomberg and Colonel Külental, head of the intelligence branch (T3) of the General Staff, who also participated in the tour, wrote a detailed report on what they saw. In his report Blomberg emphasized the war potential of the American system of Reserve, National Guard, and industry. 'The mission of the army today', he wrote, 'is to train commanders and weapon experts in large numbers, as well as to prepare for industrial mobilization'. 'The army, National Guard, organized reserves, and the preparation of war industry are cut out for the creation of an army of millions.'[33] The might of American industry had been particularly impressive for the Germans both on account of their First World War experience and in view of the United States' dominating economic power during the 1920s, on which the Locarno *détente* was based. On the one hand, American Mammonism, mass popular culture, and racial diversity had always been viewed with repugnance and alarm by the European élites, in Germany more than anywhere else. During the 1920s, as American popular culture in the shape of Hollywood and (black) jazz music was making strong headway, these impressions grew even stronger. On the other hand, German awe and admiration for the modernity, efficiency, and dynamism of American industry, symbolized by Detroit, was boundless. American scientific production and scientific management techniques were avidly studied by German industrialists: 'Taylorismus + Fordismus = Amerikanismus'.[34] In 1930 Captain Walter Warlimont was the first foreign officer to participate in the course of the US Army Industrial College.[35] Yet by that year the United States had been thrown deep into the Great Depression, and the mystique of her power was greatly diminished. As he had in the Soviet Union, Blomberg saw in the United States what he was looking for:

The National Guard and the organized reserves are the bearers of a country's healthy, future-assured militarism . . . in the face of powerful, pulsating economic forces, there lives in the youth the feeling of commitment to military

[33] Reports in BA-MA RH 2/1825.
[34] See extensively in C. Maier, 'Between Taylorism and Technocracy: European Ideologies and the Vision of Industrial Productivity in the 1920s', *Journal of Contemporary History*, 5(2) (1970), 27–61; T. Hughes, *American Genesis: A Century of Invention and Technological Enthusiasm, 1870–1970* (New York, 1989), 284–94.
[35] Geyer, *Aufrüstung*, 162.

preparedness, to the defence of the country and, unexpressed but instinctive, an imperialistic will for the growth of American world position.[36]

All the same, the masses of the unemployed that Blomberg had seen and commented upon in his official report help explain why it was after all the totalitarian and cohesive Soviet Union, with its gigantic Five-Year Plan, that had left the greater impression on him.

For Reichenau, Blomberg's new chief of staff, a visit to the United States in 1913 with the German Olympic committee was a formative experience. Different in character from his chief, Reichenau nevertheless held a similar political outlook. While Blomberg's intellectual ability was not matched by a strong will and political astuteness, Reichenau was cold-minded, calculating, and possessed a clearer sense of where he was going. He too, was disliked and distrusted by many of his peers in the army. He, too, had been unorthodox in his attitudes towards tradition and modernity. From his visit to the United States Reichenau returned particulary impressed by the vitalism, sense of the future, realism, industrial might, informal manner, and sporting pursuits which permeated American culture. Some of these he conspicuously imported to Germany. In contrast to the Prussian tradition, he introduced a more open, face-to-face contact with the rank and file under his command. To the dismay of his fellow officers, he initiated and personally participated in field runs and games with his troops.[37] (The traditional school may have had a point: Reichenau would die in the field at the age of 58 of heart failure.) These almost trivial examples serve to demonstrate a point: Reichenau thought Prussian traditions old-fashioned, and modernization essential. But, like his chief, while he was egalitarian, it was not liberal–democratic values that he brought over from the United States.

It was probably their sympathetic attitude to the prospect of National Socialist rule that facilitated the nomination of Blomberg and Reichenau to the war ministry by agreement between Hindenburg and Hitler when the National Socialists came to power in 1933. In the ministry they were instrumental in bringing the army more closely under the new regime. Whereas the army's high command sought to preserve its traditional autonomy within the state, Blomberg and Reichenau worked to integrate it with the state. In a series of directives that effectively

---

[36] Ibid.
[37] W. Görlitz, 'Reichenau', in C. Barnett (ed.), *Hitler's Generals* (London, 1989), 209–10; Wheeler-Bennett, *Nemesis of Power*, 298.

extended the Reich's *Gleichschaltung* to the armed forces, they introduced Nazi insignia, Nazi political indoctrination, Nazi racial legislation, and the personal oath of allegiance to Adolf Hitler.[38] Neither of them had been or would ever become a confirmed Nazi. 'Fellow travellers' of National Socialism, they regarded it as an answer to the needs of a modern nation competing for power in the international arena. To be sure, in time both would find Hitler's strategic planning too risky even for their own tastes, and in consequence they lost favour in his eyes. At the famous conference in November 1937, recorded by Hossbach, where Hitler outlined his far-reaching plans for European expansion to high-ranking officers and officials, Blomberg was among those who expressed reservations about the risks of provoking a general European war. Shortly afterwards he was forced to resign after it became known that his new second wife possessed a dubious sexual past. During the winter of 1939/40 Reichenau, commanding the 6th Army, joined the universal resistance in the army's high command—which became conspiratorial—to Hitler's demand for a general offensive in the West, whose prospects of success the generals judged to be slim. In consequence, Hitler, who on earlier occasions had been keen to have Reichenau nominated as chief of the army's general staff, would now rule him out as a successor to Halder.

In any event, the same quest for a revival of Germany's status as a great power that had led Blomberg and Reichenau to seek unorthodox solutions in radical military schemes and radical modernist totalitarian politics also made them from very early on interested in, and enthusiastic for, the potential of modern mechanized forces. In May 1926 in a memorandum he wrote as head of the operations branch in the General Staff, Blomberg was among the first high-ranking German officers to emphasize the significance of the revolutionary advances in mechanization and armoured doctrine made in Britain at that time.[39] In 1928, during his tenure as chief of the General Staff, while Blomberg outlined his plans for a war of popular resistance and swift movement, the army took the decision to convert its motorized transportation units into combat units.[40]

[38] See esp. Messerschmidt, *Die Wehrmacht im NS-Staat*, 1–209.

[39] 29 May 1926, in RH 2/2195; the memorandum was abstracted in *M-W*, 4 Aug. 1926, 146.

[40] M. Geyer, 'German Strategy in the Age of Machine Warfare, 1914–1945', in P. Paret (ed.), *Makers of Modern Strategy from Machiavelli to the Nuclear Age* (Princeton, NJ, 1986), 559; W. Nehring, *Die Geschichte der deutschen Panzerwaffe, 1916 bis 1945* (Berlin, 1969), 54–6.

A year later, Blomberg drafted plans and asked for the resources needed for the creation of an independent tank regiment and motorized infantry unit, a step which was eventually intended to lead—when political conditions became favourable—to the creation of 'independent tank formations'.[41]

Thus it is not surprising that while leading the German delegation to the 1932 Geneva Disarmament Conference, Blomberg asked to meet Liddell Hart, who covered the conference for the *Daily Telegraph*, and told him of his admiration for his work.[42] Later that year Reichenau wrote to Liddell Hart to inform him that he was translating *Foch*, a book that was 'not following obsolete theories, but setting new rules'.[43] Fuller was a frequent official guest in Germany during the 1930s, invited both as a fellow fascist and as the leading expert on modern mechanized warfare, and extensively meeting with the country's political and military leadership. Col. Sir Andrew Thorne, the British military attaché in Berlin from 1932 to 1935, recalled after the war:

during that time there I could not fail to be impressed by the extent to which both Liddell Hart's and 'Boney' Fuller's books were being studied by officers of all ranks and arms in the German Army. I knew both Blomberg (Minister of War) and Reichenau (Chief of the Defence Staff) very well, and they were both engaged in translating books by these two authors for use for non-English speaking German officers.[44]

As Guderian, who played a leading role in the creation of the Panzer force during the 1930s, was to testify, the promotion of Blomberg and Reichenau following Hitler's rise to power had 'an immediate effect on my work. Both these generals favoured modern ideas, and so I now found considerable sympathy for the ideas of the armoured force, at least at the highest levels of the Wehrmacht.' In 1938 Reichenau assumed command over Group Command 4, the army incorporating all the then existing armoured and mechanized corps of the German army.[45] Blomberg not only was very favourable towards the armoured forces but also lent his unqualified support to the nascent Luftwaffe, to

---

[41] T4 (signed Blomberg), 1 Sept. 1929, in BA-MA Freiburg RH 39/115; see also Geyer, 'German Strategy', 559.
[42] B. H. Liddell Hart, *Memoirs* (2 vols., London, 1969), i. 171–2; his records at the time: 7 and 8 Mar. 1932, in the Liddell Hart Centre of Military Archives, King's College, London [King's], 11/1932/1 and 11/1932/9.
[43] Reichenau to LH, 28 Nov. 1932, 9/24/87/R.
[44] Thorne to Hankey, 22 Mar. 1946, King's, 13/45.
[45] H. Guderian, *Panzer Leader* (London, 1952), 29, 37, 48.

which he made sure that élite army officers would be transferred.[46] In his testimony after the war before Allied interrogators in Nuremberg, Blomberg himself tied together the various aspects of his differences with the army conservatives during the National Socialist era (understandably failing to mention his radical war plans):

The unification of the Higher Command of the Wehrmacht, the characteristic features of the 'Volksarmee' as compared with an isolated professional army (Reichswehr), the question of the mechanization of the army, the unaccustomed competition of the new 'Luftwaffe', these were, according to my impression, the facts that many Generals could not easily assimilate.[47]

The respective roles of British influence, Guderian, and the German general staff in the creation of the Panzer arm have all become contentious subjects in recent years, to which I have dedicated a separate special study. Here I shall only touch upon the themes relevant to our subject, referring interested readers to that study.[48] Chief of the army's General Staff Beck, accused in Guderian's memoirs of being a constant obstacle to his radical plans,[49] has been shown by recent scholarship to have played a crucial role in the creation of the Panzer force, including that of the first three armoured divisions in 1935. However, the fact remains that Beck came to the subject late, much under the stimulus of others, and moving cautiously, dispersed a large part of the tank force for cavalry-type and infantry support missions. The army's commander in chief, Fritsch, was favourably mentioned in Guderian's memoirs as a supporter of armour; and, indeed, as early as 1927, as chief of the operations branch in the general staff in succession to Blomberg, Fritsch had emphasized the independent use of armour as an operationally decisive weapon.[50] All the same, being the 'old Prussian gentleman' that he was, he could not help but accept 'reluctantly what he is said to have called "all those damnable innovations, cars, tanks, etc." '. As the historian who has done the most to make Beck's case in respect to armour concludes; the difference between Blomberg and Reichenau at the war ministry, on the one hand, and Fritsch and Beck at the army's high command, on the other, reflected a 'different attitude to the

[46] L. W. Murray, *Luftwaffe* (Baltmore, 1985), 7.
[47] 'Niederschrift Blomberg über seine Einstellung zu Adolf Hitler und dem Nationalsozialismus': Nov. 1945, BA-MA N 52/7, p. 2.
[48] Gat, 'British Influence and the Evolution of the Panzer Arm'.
[49] Guderian, *Panzer Leader*, 32–3.
[50] Ibid. 31–2; Geyer, 'German Strategy', 559.

modern world. General von Fritsch represented more a stance rooted in pre-industrial feudalism. . . . The armed forces command, on the other hand, was of the opinion that the world had changed.'[51] Blomberg and Reichenau were modernists and in general favourably disposed towards the machine. They were also looking for any revolutionary means that might make it possible for Germany to break the ring around her and tilt the European balance of power in her favour. It is again significant that Guderian named the radical General Joachim von Stülpnagel, who had originated the idea of a popular war of national liberation and who retired from the army in 1931, as particularly favourable to the nascent mechanized force.[52]

Michael Geyer has suggested a distinction between the 'idealist' school and the 'technicians' in the German high command both before and during the Second World War. In this distinction the former was represented by Beck and his colleagues and continued the tradition of the old general staff. Allegedly, this school was accustomed to considering strategy within an overall perspective of the European and international balance of power, and duly assessed by the late 1930s that Hitler was leading Germany into a general European and world war which it had no chance of winning. By contrast, according to this view, the 'technicians'—mostly, like Guderian, of a younger generation— were totally preoccupied with technologies and techniques of warfare, losing sight of the overall strategic picture. Less constrained in this manner, they were more eager for war, and in general abdicated its overall strategic direction to Hitler.[53]

While partly helpful, this distinction seems to me to be somewhat off the mark and potentially misleading as to the more substantial nature of the difference between the two groups, which essentially lay in the degree of their political radicalism. The same mistake was for a long time made in regard to Schlieffen of the old school. He also was dubbed a 'military technician' in comparison to the elder Moltke, notwithstanding the (misconceived) German political agenda at the turn of the nineteenth century for European hegemony and a status of world power that underlay his (misguided) military plan for total victory in a two-front war.[54]

---

[51] K.-J. Müller, *Army, Politics and Society*, 34.   [52] Guderian, *Panzer Leader*, 25.

[53] Geyer, *Aufrüstung*, 79, but also 93; id., 'German Strategy', in Paret (ed.), *Makers of Modern Strategy*, 572, 584–6—much, in my opinion, against the general drift of his argument.

[54] A. Gat, *The Development of Military Thought: The Nineteenth Century* (Oxford, 1992), 96–9.

The younger generation in the Reichswehr and Wehrmacht was on the whole simply more radical than the older, convinced as it was that the goal of Germany's revival would necessitate more forceful means, more extreme measures, and more risky initiatives. 'Beck', as Guderian revealingly wrote even in his post-war memoirs, 'was above all a pro-crastinator in military *as in political matters*.'[55] It was because of their political radicalism, not only for the career opportunities he opened to them, that most members of the younger generation in the army supported Hitler and enthusiastically followed his plans of expansion and war. Only the onset of defeat made them more critical of his direction of the war, if mostly not of his overall aims. From the 1890s onward foreign policy and, correspondingly, also domestic attitudes in Germany underwent further radicalization with every successive generation.

It was within this broader perspective that the fiercely nationalistic Guderian, working to advance his radical conception of armoured warfare, immediately recognized Hitler as an ally. The setting of their first meetings, stressed by Guderian, are noteworthy:

I saw and heard Hitler for the first time at the opening of the Berlin Automobile Exhibition, at the beginning of February [1933]. It was unusual for the Chan-cellor himself to open the exhibition. And what he had to say was in striking contrast to the customary speeches of Ministers and Chancellors on such occasions. He announced the abolition of the tax on cars and spoke of the new national roads that were to be built and of the *Volkswagen*, the cheap 'People's Car', that was to be mass produced.[56]

According to Guderian, in addition to Blomberg and Reichenau, 'it soon became apparent that Hitler himself was interested in the problem of motorisation and armour'. At the army's demonstration ground for weapon development at Kummersdorf—which, as Guderian stressed, Hitler was the first chancellor to attend in fifty years—Guderian gave Hitler a half-hour demonstration of his troops. He elicited from him the famous enthusiastic and repeated response: 'That's what I need! That's what I want to have!' As Guderian wrote in his memoirs: 'As a result of this demonstration I was convinced that the head of the government would approve my proposals for the organization of an up-to-date *Wehrmacht*, if only I could manage to lay my views before him.' Guderian went on to complain that the rigidity of

---

[55] Guderian, *Panzer Leader*, 32; my emphasis.   [56] Ibid. 29.

military procedure, especially as things stood in the 1930s, made it difficult for him to appeal directly to Blomberg and Hitler.[57] None the less, it is widely agreed that Hitler's known interest in the mechanized forces and in radical operational doctrines proved a major spur to their development in Germany, as well as providing a personal safety net for Guderian's career.

The Nazi Nostalgic Mechanized Utopia

In general, the attitude of the Nazis and Hitler towards the modern was ambivalent.[58] Of all the fascist movements Nazism was probably the least modernist, even though it operated in Europe's most advanced industrial, technological, and scientific nation. Its strong *völkisch*, nostalgic, and mystical bent cast its futurist utopia in a mythological agrarian and pastoral past.[59] Like Mussolini, Hitler turned to suppress the most radical and avant-garde elements in his movement after coming to power. At a rally of the National Socialist Motor Corps in the summer of 1933, Guderian heard Hitler talking of the need for every revolution to become evolution at a certain point.[60] While a *Gleichschaltung* of the Reich was carried out, the SA was decimated and the social

---

[57] Guderian, 29–30.

[58] The debate here does not seem to be ebbing; see esp. R. Dahrendorf, *Society and Democracy in Germany* (London, 1968); D. Schenbaum, *Hitler's Social Revolution* (New York, 1966); K. D. Bracher, 'Tradition und Revolution im Nationalsozialismus', in *Zeitgeschichtliche Kontroversen* (Munich, 1976), 62–78; H. Mommsen, 'Nationalsozialismus als vorgetäuschte Modernisierung', in *Der Nationalsozialismus und die deutsche Gesellschaft* (Hamburg, 1991), 405–27; M. Rauch, 'Anti-Modernismus im Nationalsozialistischen Staat', *Historisches Jahrbuch*, 107 (1987), 94–121; N. Frei, 'Wie modern war der Nationalsozialismus?', *Geschichte und Gesellschaft*, 19 (1993), 367–87; A. Schildt, 'NS-Regime, Modernisierung und Moderne', *Tel Aviver Jahrbuch für deutsche Geschichte*, 23 (1994), 3–22; M. Prinz and R. Zitelmann (eds.), *Nationalsozialismus und Modernisierung* (Darmstadt, 1995); M. Roseman, 'National Socialism and Modernisation', in R. Bessel (ed.), *Fascist Italy and Nazi Germany: Comparisons and Contrasts* (Cambridge, 1996), 197–229.

[59] For the following, the best overall discussion is provided by G. Mosse, 'Fascism and the Avant Garde', in *Masses and Man: Nationalist and Fascist Perception of Reality* (Detroit, 1987), 230–4; also his 'Introduction' to Mosse (ed.), *International Fascism* (London, 1979), 7, 24–5; M. Eksteins, *Rites of Spring: The Great War and the Birth of the Modern Age* (New York, 1990), 322–8. For more specialized studies, see M. Renneberg and M. Walker (eds.), *Science, Technology and National Socialism* (Cambridge, 1994); A. D. Beyerchen, *Scientists under Hitler* (New Haven Conn., 1977); S. Wollgast, ' "Technikphilosophie" während der Herrschaft des deutschen Faschismus', in Wollgast and G. Kovács (eds.), *Technikphilosophie in Vergangenheit und Gegenwart* (Berlin, 1984), 115–35; J. Shand, 'The Reichsautobahn: Symbol for the Third Reich', *Journal of Contemporary History*, 19 (1984), 189–200; A. Rabinbach, 'The Aesthetics of Production in the Third Reich', in Mosse (ed.), *International Fascism*, 189–222.   [60] Guderian, *Panzer Leader*, 30.

radicals Ernst Röhm and Otto Strasser were eliminated. Whereas
Futurism remained the semi-official artistic style of Fascist Italy—
grudgingly sharing that status with Roman neo-classicism—Hitler's
parochial and petty-bourgeois sensibilities were directed against artistic
modernism. A brief flirtation with Expressionism, which the poet
Gottfried Benn (1886–1956)—who, unlike most of his friends, supported National Socialism—hoped to make the official style of the new
regime, was interrupted in 1934.[61] Realistic neo-classicism would
henceforth occupy that rank. Despite efforts of the Bauhaus's director
Mies van der Rohe and the support of Nazi intellectuals around Joseph
Goebbels in Berlin, much the same happened regarding modernist
architecture. Still, 'But for Hitler's interest in architecture, Albert
Speer believed, modernism—as promulgated by the Weidemann–NS
Students Association faction—would have developed as the 'official'
style of National Socialism.'[62]

On the other hand, Hitler and National Socialism exalted the most
spectacular and dynamic products of modern technology. Like Mussolini and the Italian Fascists, they associated themselves with and made
extensive use of the aircraft and the fast car. The *Autobahn*, top-of-the-
range Mercedes, and the popular Volkswagen symbolized their modernist programme. Radio and film played a similar role, as well as being
one of the regime's most effective means of propaganda and political
mobilization. While Nazi ideology had always contained an element of
hostility towards industry and science, the regime inevitably acknowledged their necessity for the building of German national power. They
were promoted, while harnessed to further the regime's ends and made
to conform to its ideological principles, some of which, like racism and
anti-Semitism, entailed considerable scientific penalties. Above all,
science and industry were to produce the modern equipment for the
revived armed forces, with an emphasis on revolutionary means which
would intimidate Germany's neighbours and, in case of war, make it
possible for her to escape the prospect of stalemate and attrition. As
early as 28 February 1934, addressing army and SA leaders at the
Reichswehr ministry, Hitler predicted that in order to gain living space
in the east for the German people in the teeth of international opposition, 'short, decisive blows to the West and then to the East could be

---

[61] Hamilton, *The Appeal of Fascism*, 135, 149–52, 158–9.
[62] E. Hochman, *Architects of Fortune: Mies van der Rohe and the Third Reich* (New York, 1989), 311.

necessary'.[63] Only recently have scholars begun to realize that the famous 'Blitzkrieg' was not developed before the war in any formal or orderly manner, indeed, was not even a German term but one created by foreign media.[64] None the less, the notion that revolutionary means would assist Germany to prevail against a superior coalition was imprinted in the minds of Hitler, Blomberg, and many of the younger generation in the army. In *Mein Kampf* (1925) Hitler had written about 'the universal motorization of the world, which in the next war will be overwhelmingly decisive in the struggle'.[65] From very early on the mechanized forces in the army were among the beneficiaries of this notion, although by far the principal benefactor was, of course, the Luftwaffe.

Modernist enthusiasm and mystique went hand in hand with strategic considerations in the cultivation of the Luftwaffe. As everywhere else, the aeroplane was regarded in Germany, particularly by fascists, as the most potent symbol of the new age. Like the Italian Futurists, like Wells, and like Lawrence, Ernst Jünger celebrated the flyer as 'the new man, the man of the twentieth century.' Flyers, he wrote, would constitute the new aristocracy of the future. Flying was a vitalistic and dynamic force which countered decadence. It also had the potential to impose world power and order on barbarism. Here too Germany must break the Versailles restrictions and conquer the air.[66] Much as Mussolini had done during and after his struggle for power, Hitler flew 30,000 miles during the election campaign of 1932. Going from town to town under the slogan 'Hitler over Germany', he attended 200 meetings. He was the first German politician to use the aeroplane in this manner, and the propaganda value of this campaigning technique was as important as its efficiency. After coming to power, 'Hitler wanted the largest air force in the World and the best pilots. War in the air would be viewed as a Germanic form of battle.' Like Italo Balbo in Italy, Herman Goering, the First World War ace, second in the Nazi hierarchy and commander-in-chief of the Luftwaffe, held a special status in the

---

[63] R. O'Neill, *The German Army and the Nazi Party, 1933–1939*, (London, 1966) 127.

[64] Gat, 'British Influence and the Evolution of the Panzer Arm'.

[65] Cited by E. Bennett, *German Rearmament and the West, 1932–1933* (Princeton, NJ, 1979), 319.

[66] 'Der Flieger', *Der Tag*, 15 (1928); 'Nation und Luftfahrt', *Vormarsch*, 1 (1927–8), 314–17; cited in Herf, *Reactionary Modernism*, 85. Similarly in Jünger's introduction to the book he edited in the late 1920s, *Luftfahrt ist Not!* A fascinating study is P. Fritzsche, *A Nation of Fliers: German Aviation and the Popular Imagination* (Cambridge, Mass., 1992); Jünger is cited throughout and the Nazis are extensively covered.

regime, and the service he headed possessed a special aura.[67] Similar to the Regia Aeronautica in Mussolini's regime, the Luftwaffe was the Nazi service *par excellence*, unlike the Prussian army and Wilhelmine navy, with which Hitler jibed that he had to deal.

To conclude, irrespective of Nazism, the German armed forces sought to break the Versailles restrictions, expand, and modernize. Yet Nazi political support and the orientation of right-wing radicals within the armed forces were a significant factor in directing German rearmament—particularly the emphasis on the Luftwaffe but also the development of the Panzer arm—towards modern means of war, revolutionary doctrines, and radical operational schemes.

[67] Eksteins, *Rites of Spring*, 322, citing Rauschning, *Hitler Speaks*, 18–19; Mosse *International Fascism*, 24.

Comparisons and Contrasts (I):
American Populism, Progressivism, and
Mid-West Technological Modernism

Every picture gains in clarity when set against comparisons and contrasts. Having covered much of the proto-fascist and fascist spectrum, we might, finally, try to gain further insight into the connection between fascist modernism and visions of machine warfare by turning to examine two other pronouncedly modernist ideologies: American Progressivism and Marxism.

The Nazi's enthusiastic embrace of Charles A. Lindbergh (1902–74) was one expression of the fascists' effort to identify themselves with the images of youth, vigour, potency, advanced technology, and the conquest of the air, for which Lindbergh had become the greatest living symbol. With his upright character and sharp mind he slipped almost naturally into the role of the international superhero into which he had been launched by his trans-Atlantic flight in 1927. Everywhere he went he was showered with honours and acclaim, and much to his peril he found himself ever the focus of attention for the world's media. Everybody who was anybody, from royalty down, was eager to meet and talk with him. Governments, air forces, and industrialists sought his cooperation, advice, or simply the aura of his association. Civilian and military establishments alike in all countries were open to him, as they were for nobody else. So his value for Nazi propaganda is clear. His own part in the relationship is less clear, however. This chapter seeks to suggest a more general explanation for the Lindbergh affair, broadening our perspective to the United States and to some features of American Populism, Pragmatism, Progressivism, and Mid-West modernism.

It is widely held that fully fledged fascism never took root in America in any significant way, remaining confined to marginal immigrant associations such as the German–American Bund.[1] Yet scholars have

---

[1] See M. Schonback, *Native American Fascism During the 1930s and 1940s* (New York, 1985); also C. Sokol, *The German–American Bund as a Model of American Fascism: 1924–1940* (Ann Arbor, Mich., 1979).

discerned some family resemblance between fascism and aspects of American Populism and 'nativism', movements which grew in force and assumed political forms from the late nineteenth century in response to the pressures of modernity. Particularly strong among the agricultural communities of the Mid-West which found the new environment of international markets economically inhospitable, intellectually incompressible, and culturally alien, Populism and American nativism responded to the encroaching forces of the outside world with resentment, distrust, and anxiety. They exhibited the rising xenophobia and offended religious sensibilities that are all too characteristic of the reactions of small, parochial communities to the challenge of modernity. The arch-enemy in their eyes was international finance, whose greedy tentacles stretched around the world—sucking its wealth—from its centres in the City of London and Wall Street. Somewhere behind the conspiracy stood the demonic figure of the international Jew. More generally, there was animosity towards West Coast politicians, intellectuals, and urban megalopolises, swamped by alien immigrants.

However, side by side with these sentiments and their political manifestations, and not far removed demographically and geographically, there also arose from the turn of the century the Progressive movement, whose campaign against political corruption and rampant big-business capitalism and whose cult of modernism and efficiency had a profound effect on American public life. Here too the Mid-West was one of the main strongholds of the movement. And if engineers, lawyers, and other professionals were more prominent among the ranks of Progressivism than among those of Populism, then it is a telling fact that these professionals had mainly grown up in the farms of rural America, and affectionately carried with them both its memory and much of its ethics and ideals. Finally—and this fact perhaps has not been sufficiently recognized—it was in the rural communities of these very same provinces of the Mid-West that the mythological heroes of American technological modernism grew up, all cherishing for life this formative experience. Thomas Alva Edison was born in a Ohio village and grew up in a small Michigan community; Henry Ford was born and raised on a Michigan farm; the Wright brothers came from Dayton, Ohio; Frank Lloyd Wright was born and raised on his grandfather's farm in Wisconsin; Billy Mitchell was the son of a Wisconsin senator, and grandson of a railroad and banking magnate; and Charles A. Lindbergh was the son of a Progressive Congressman from Minnesota.

These American technological pioneers not only had similar roots, but some of them shared political ideals and even collaborated with one another in their political work. Henry Ford is surely the most famous of the lot for his public and political activities. Having built his fabulous manufacturing empire in the decade before the Great War—transforming the automobile industry, becoming the guru of modern industry with his techniques of mass production and management, and turning into a symbol of modernity world-wide—he increasingly styled himself the authentic voice of popular America' and the representative of true American values. Poorly educated and intellectually simple but also reflective, idealistic, and thoroughly convinced of his mission, he was able to use his fame and vast fortune for amplifying the mood, ideals, and prejudices of his native region and times. He first ventured into the public arena during the drive to keep the United States out of the First World War, a campaign in which Mid-West pacifists and isolationists (like the elder Lindbergh) were particulary active. He financed and led the 'Peace Ship' whose planned cruise of anti-war activists ended in failure.[2] It was, however, mainly after the war that Ford offered himself through the media to large audiences as a popular philosopher with the answers to the great challenges of modernity, and even considered running for the presidency. He preached a Jeffersonian popular democracy, in which a new, decentralized industrial society would be synthesized with—without fundamentally altering—the traditional values and life-style of rural America. The engine of his programme was of course the automobile which, as his life ambition had been, should come to every household in America, making it possible to spread industry to the small communities throughout the nation rather than concentrate it, and the people, in monstrous cities of millions. Ford attacked high finance, and became an extreme anti-Semite.

During the 1920s Ford published and distributed *The Protocols of the Elders of Zion*, a fake composed by the Czarist secret police and alleging a Jewish conspiracy to win control over the world. His newspaper, the *Dearborn Independence*, read mainly in the Mid-West, was thoroughly anti-Semite. In addition, by 1920 his reputation for benevolence toward his workers was tainted by his hard-line anti-unionist stance. Finally,

---

[2] See B. Kraft, *The Peace Ship: Henry Ford's Pacifist Adventure in the First World War* (New York, 1978); and, for Lindbergh the elder, B. Larsen, *Lindbergh of Minnesota* (New York, 1973).

during the 1920s and 1930s he strengthened his relations with quasi-fascists and fascists both at home and abroad. Heinz Spanknoeble, organizer of the Teutonia Society, Fritz Kuhn, would-be leader of the German–American Bund, and others of similar views worked for the Ford Company in Detroit, apparently not by coincidence. Ford himself was sympathetic to Fascist Italy and had particularly good relations with Nazi Germany, where he had long been admired and by which he was decorated. After the outbreak of the Second World War in Europe he again became one of the leading members of America First, the isolationist association that campaigned to keep America out of the war. All the same, during the war his factories poured automobiles, aircraft, ships, and other armaments for the war effort in the mass volume that had made Ford synonymous with American industrial–military might.[3]

So what does all this show? Ford himself was never a fascist and neither were any of the other figures that will be discussed here. Yet in the distinctively Mid-West American blend of agrarian nostalgia, nativist Populism, Progressivism, and celebration of technology there were many elements that resonated with fascist sentiments and ideas. These made Ford and people of similar outlook at least attentive and responsive, if not sympathetic, to the fascist regimes abroad. What would be the character of the emerging advanced industrialized society? How could its pains be alleviated by social planning, and how could it be reconciled with traditional communal values? These questions were at the root of the fascist mood, and it was much the same questions that preoccupied Ford and other Mid-West pundits of modernism and technology with whom he cooperated.

One of the people Ford admired deeply, befriended, and cooperated with was Thomas Edison. The two had much in common. Both were self-made men who came from small Michigan communities, received little formal education, but were endowed with technological genius that brought them to world fame. Both also shared the same basic outlook. Like Ford, Edison detested Wall Street, the banks, and high finance. He was anti-Semitic, and was ascetic in character and conduct.[4] Another man with whom Ford cooperated was the leading American

---

[3] See esp. Schonbach, *Native American Fascism*, 47, 68, 123; Kraft, *The Peace Ship*, 278–83; R. Wik, *Henry Ford and Grass Roots America* (Ann Arbor, Mich., 1972); D. Nye, *Henry Ford: 'Ignorant Idealist'* (New York, 1979); and R. Lacey, *Ford: The Men and the Machine* (Boston, 1986), 132–236.

[4] M. Josephson, *Edison* (London, 1961), 435–7, 463, 465–6.

figure of architectural Modernism, Frank Lloyd Wright. As Wright made his great comeback in the 1930s, after almost two decades of professional and public retreat, he came armed with a social philosophy which he preached and practised. Always evoking his childhood in his grandfather's farm in Wisconsin—'born in the prairie', as he liked to describe himself—he made this the cornerstone of his ideal for modern America. Like Ford, he wanted a decentralized Jeffersonian democracy and a revival of the disappearing qualities of rural life. His third wife, the power behind his return to architecture and public life, was a follower of the fashionable mystical thinkers and occultists Gurdjieff and his disciple Ouspensky, who preached a return to the harmonies of nature. While rejecting their mysticism, Wright was influenced by their social philosophy. He and his wife established a quasi-monastic institution, the Taliesin Fellows, in the wilderness of Wisconsin. Teaching holistic and organic architecture, the institution became a magnet for young and aspiring architects who came to live and work there as apprentices, and for many other guests, like the novelist and popular philosopher of Nietzschean individuality, Ayn Rand. Under the impact of the Great Depression Wright prophesied the demise of the metropolis and of the North-East model of anonymous, alienated, mass urban and industrial society. The cities were to remain as economic centres and work places, but they were not fit for human habitation. Like Ford, Wright developed his grand vision of life in America, a new 'integration', the so-called Broadacre scheme. People would move to the suburbs and to small towns spread out in the countryside, where the qualities of agrarian America and closeness with nature would be revived. A network of highways would link all parts of the nation together. The car, aeroplane, and radio had made it possible to combine dispersion with modern civilization. Retreat from excessive industrialism would also involve the forsaking of colonialism and trade conflicts. The United States ought to resume a pacifist and isolationist stance. In collaboration with Ford, Wright campaigned against American involvement in the Second World War.[5]

Wright was a democrat, who stood for individual freedom and rejected both forms of 'central European' totalitarianism—as he regarded them—fascism and Bolshevism. But he was also an anti-

---

[5] See esp. R. Fishman, *Urban Utopias in the Twentieth Century: Ebenezer Howard, Frank Lloyd Wright, and Le Corbusier* (New York, 1977), 97–150; Donald Leslie Johnson, *Frank Lloyd Wright versus America: The 1930s* (Cambridge, Mass., 1990).

capitalist communitarian. The first two tenets in his 'American' pro-gramme read: 'No private ownership of public needs. No landlord or tenant.' Another of his lists began: '1. No very rich nor very poor to build for—no gold. 2. No idle land except for common landscape—no real estate exploiters. . . . In short no speculation in money, land, or ideas.'[6] Most technological modernists in the United States who took a critical stand towards capitalism—especially during the 1930s—remained within the democratic camp, yet aspects of their teachings were congruent with fascist ideas and appealed to fascists, as was true in the opposite direction. The self-taught popular social thinker and anti-fascist Lewis Mumford, for example, inclined toward communitarism, environmentalism, and social planning. His brilliant *Technics and Civilization* (1934) greatly impressed Fuller, coinciding as it did with his own approach to the tracing of the 'natural history of war', taken up in his books from 1932 on.[7] Scepticism regarding the rationality of capit-alism and suspicions of its wastefulness had been harboured in America long before the Depression and the New Deal. Before the First World War such sentiments were expressed by the exponents of American Pragmatism and rational social science. These included philosophers, sociologists, popular writers, politicians, and industrialists like Lester Frank Ward, Thorstein Weblen, Charles Sanders Pierce, John Dewey, George Herbert Mead, William James, Theodore Roosevelt, Frederick Taylor, Herbert Hoover, Graham Wallace, and Walter Lippman.[8] While they mostly remained within the democratic and sometimes even liberal sphere, it has long been recognized that their ideas of scientific manage-ment, social engineering, efficiency, planning, control, and social order contained Comtean-Positivist, non-liberal, and non-democratic elements. It has been hyperbolically remarked that the most radical schemes for the building of modern cities were initiated by Stalin, Mussolini, Hitler, and General Motors.[9]

We have already seen how Billy Mitchell was impressed and influ-enced by Italian ideas and by Douhetism after his visits to Europe and Italy in 1921–2 and again in 1927. On his second visit his host was Italo Balbo and he was granted an audience by Mussolini. According to

[6] Ibid. 115, 295.
[7] L. Mumford, *Technics and Civilization* (London, 1934); *The Culture of Cities* (London, 1934); T. Hughes and A. Hughes (eds.), *Lewis Mumford* (Oxford, 1990); J. F. C. Fuller, *The First of the League Wars* (London, 1936), p. viii.
[8] J. M. Jordan, *Machine-Age Ideology: Social Engineering and American Liberalism, 1911–1939* (Chapel Hill, NC, 1994).   [9] Fishman, *Urban Utopias*, p. xiii.

Mitchell's biographer, relying on his manuscripts of the time: 'The Fascist movement also caught Mitchell's attention. He came away from an interview with Benito Mussolini believing that the dictator "stands as one of the greatest constructive powers for good government that exists in the world today".'[10] Favourable opinion of Fascist Italy was much too widespread in the West during the 1920s to indicate any deep affinity with fascism, and the evidence in the matter is too slim anyhow. Yet Mitchell's emphasis on 'good government' is symptomatic of the concerns of American Progressivists and of 'efficiency movements' throughout the West. After his dismissal from the army, Mitchell, like Fuller, continuously advanced schemes for the reorganization not only of the defence establishment but of the whole machinery of federal government.[11]

The man who succeeded Mitchell as America's most popular aviator was Charles A. Lindbergh. And if sympathy for Fascist Italy in the 1920 was too widespread to be indicative of much, admiration for Nazi Germany in the 1930s was a different matter. Unlike Henry Ford, with whom he worked closely in America First, Lindbergh was a refined person who felt at ease in the best of companies. He too, however, looked back with affection on his 'boyhood on the upper Mississippi', as one of his biographies is called, and he bore the mark of the ideas with which he had grown up in his father's house. Progressive Congressman Lindbergh had been a champion of the American farmer, an enemy of the Money Trust, and an active member of the opposition to the United States' entry into the First World War.

After the sensational murder of his elder son in 1931, Charles Lindbergh and his family moved to Europe to escape the press, living in France and Britain. In 1936 Lindbergh was asked by the American military attaché in Berlin to go to Germany to assess the strength and capability of the Luftwaffe. By 1939 he had visited Germany five times, was accepted with state honours and great clamour, and was decorated by Goering. His reports and journals, as well as the writings of his wife, the novelist Anne Morrow Lindbergh, who shared his views, are a remarkable testimony to the sort of ambivalent fascination people like the Lindberghs felt towards fascism.

The Lindberghs were decent and well-meaning people—humanitarian, idealistic, sensitive, caring, pacifistic, and on the whole

---

[10] A. Hurley, *Billy Mitchell: Crusader for Air Power* (New York, 1964) 115.
[11] Ibid. 122.

driven by the best of motives. Like their peers of the enlightened post-First World War generation in the West, they felt that another world war was too horrific to contemplate, would bring about the end of Western civilization, and was wholly unacceptable. Yet Charles Lindbergh's belief in the need of the white race to keep its unity in order to defend itself against the Asian and Mongol hordes and against 'the infiltration of inferior blood', though also common enough among his generation, revealed another streak in his mind. While living in Britain, for which the Lindberghs felt deep affection and respect, Charles Lindbergh found the British depressingly inefficient, slow, indulgent, and increasingly slipping behind the modern world. Moulded during the age of the ship, their national character was in his opinion inadequate for the speed and precision of the new air age. In France, of which the Lindberghs were as fond as they were of Britain, Charles Lindbergh was equally troubled by the country's profound political divisions, general sense of aimlessness, and loss of spirit. Of the Soviet Union, where he was again lavishly entertained, Lindbergh had the worst opinion. He believed it was backward and inherently mediocre, and prophesied the imminent collapse of the communist system. By contrast, the Lindberghs were impressed by German efficiency, drive, unity, collective spirit, purposefulness, and modernist enthusiasm for science and technology. Charles Lindbergh reasonably assessed in 1937–8 that the Luftwaffe was the strongest air force in the world; and the air was in the 1930s the 'high-tech' field by which the level of advancement of any modern nation was measured. According to Lindbergh, Nazi Germany was a 'virile' nation that escaped the general 'softness' and decadence of the democracies.

The Lindberghs were well aware of the brutality of the Nazi regime. They were sincerely dismayed by it, and never 'liked' Nazi Germany. All the same, contemplating Nazi Germany, the Lindbeghs asked if their scruples were not merely the indulging of a passing age, the one that had proved itself bankrupt with the Great Depression. And, further, were not Nazi brutalities merely the labour pains of a new age, surface expression of the inevitable currents of history, of the forces that were fundamental to, and would inherit, the modern world? As Lindbergh wrote:

Modern Germany does not permit a superficial judgment. She challenges our most fundamental concepts. . . . What measures the rights of men and of a nation? . . . Are we deluding ourselves when we attempt to run our governments by counting the number of heads, without a thought of what lies within them? Are our standards true? . . . Is it possible to perpetuate a government, or a League of Governments, unless representation is clearly proportional to the strength which is available to support it?[12]

Anne Morrow Lindbergh recorded similar thoughts in her diaries.[13] She developed them further in her book *The Wave of the Future* (1940), a title that speaks for itself:

In recent years, my generation has seen the beliefs, the formulas, and the creeds, that we were brought up to trust implicitly, one by one thrown in danger, if not actually discarded: the sacredness of property, the infallibility of the democratic way of life, the efficiency of the capitalist system . . . innocent people are being punished, and peaceful nations overrun by force of aggression, which we were taught to believe were outmoded forms of action in our stage of civilization.[14]

How were these upheavals to be interpreted? According to Anne Morrow Lindbergh, in international relations they were largely the sour grapes of the unjust treatment on the part of the 'have' powers: the United States, Britain, and France, towards the 'have-not' powers: Germany, Japan, and Italy. And the same line of thought extended further, to the Western democracies' domestic order:

A world in which there were widespread depressions, millions of unemployed, and drifting populations was not going to continue indefinitely. A world in which young people, willing to work, could not afford a home and family, in which the race declined in hardiness, in which one found on every side dissatisfaction, maladjustment and moral decay—that world was ripe for change.

Something, one feels, is pushing up through the crust of custom. One does not know what—some new conception of humanity and its place on the earth. I believe that it is, in its essence, good; but because we are blind we cannot see it, and because we are slow to change, it must force its way through the heavy crust violently—in eruptions. Some of these eruptions take terrible forms, unrecog-

---

[12] *The War Time Journals of Charles A. Lindbergh* (New York, 1970), 11, 22–3, 172, 450, and *passim*; anecdotal perhaps, but typical of the generation's search for direction, is the account that Lindbergh too read Ouspensky's *A New Model of the Universe*: ibid. 490; E. Lindbergh, *Autobiography of Value* (New York, 1978), 145–62, and *passim*; W. Cole, *Charles A. Lindbergh and the Battle against American Intervention in World War II* (New York, 1974), 26–31, 35 (citation), 38, 80–1, and *passim*; L. Goldstein, *The Flying Machine and Modern Literature* (London, 1986), 107–9.

[13] *The Flower and the Nettle: Diaries and Letters, 1936–1939* (New York, 1976), esp. 100–1; *War Within and Without: Diaries and Letters, 1939–1944* (New York, 1980), esp. 80–1.

[14] *The Wave of the Future: A Confession of Faith* (New York, 1940), 7–8.

nizable and evil forms. 'Great ideas enter into reality with evil associates and with disgusting alliances. But the greatness remains, nerving the race in its slow ascent.'[15]

The struggle of the past against the future, she wrote, called to mind the old European élites' shocked reaction and opposition to the French Revolution and Terror. New social and economic forces were at work. 'There is no fighting the wave of the future . . . All you could do was to dive into it or leap with it. Otherwise, it would surely overwhelm you and pound you to the sand.' Rather than fight abroad, Anne Morrow Lindbergh urged the United States to revolutionize itself domestically. It must come up with a distinctive American solution to the challenges of the future, which would address the same fundamental problems that had given rise to fascism and communism abroad, while avoiding their brutality and excesses.[16]

To sum up our discussion, American social history has been widely regarded as unique and distinct in many ways from that of European societies—more so than the national uniqueness, and distinctiveness that have distinguished these societies from one another. There was very little native fascism in the United States, as well as very little organized socialism. However, if fascism, as developed in Europe, never really took root in the United States, many of the ideas, concerns, and sentiments it expressed had American equivalents. Interestingly, some of them came together in Mid-West Populism, Progressivism, and technological modernism. None of the great American heroes of technology examined here, who figured as potent symbols of modernity world-wide, was fascist. Yet it so happened that Mid-West enterprise, pragmatism, and industrial opportunity dominated American technological inventiveness; at the same time and often expressing themselves through the same people, Mid-West Populism and American nativism responded to the onset of modernity with an ambivalence and anxiety that sought ways of integrating the great advances of technological society with traditional communal and rural values. The Great Depression awoke in many Mid-West pundits of technological modernism long-held doubts regarding the efficiency, morality, and unity of capitalist and liberal-democratic society and its general adequacy to cope with the world of tomorrow. It is not surprising that some of them looked at the fascist regimes abroad with interest and even sympathy, and that the fascists, for their part, embraced them with enthusiasm.

[15] Ibid. 12–15, 17, 22.   [16] Ibid. 18–19, 34–5, and *passim*.

6

Comparisons and Contrasts (II): Marxism, Modernism, and the Doctrine of 'Deep Battle'

Whereas fascism was ambivalent and 'Janus-faced' in respect to modernity—some of its strands more than others—Marxism was the modernist ideology *par excellence*, wholly directed towards the future and regarding itself as the ultimate conclusion of the era of the machine and industrial society. Indeed, many if not most of Europe's fascist leaders (Mussolini and Mosley being the best-known examples) had arrived at their new creed from the ranks of the left, particularly from French and Italian revolutionary syndicalism, and had often developed out of Marxist assumptions and a Marxist interpretation of history. As we have seen, many in fact remained on the fence between the two movements, hesitant or seeing no need to choose, some even claimed by both. Georges Sorel, a post-Marxist revolutionary syndicalist and author of *Reflection on Violence* (1908), inspired and was honoured by both Lenin and Mussolini. Marinetti hailed the Bolshevik Revolution in Russia, although he ultimately rejected its class-based character. He, too, was favourably regarded by Lenin and by the founder and theorist of the Italian Communist Party, Antonio Gramsci. His dynamic, anti-bourgeois, machine-dominated Futurism was viewed by the Soviets, before its alliance with Fascism became complete, as a potential artistic ally.[1] The Russian Futurists, like the poet Vladimir Mayakovsky, the poet and aviator Vasily Kamensky, and the painter Kazimir Malevich, celebrated the aeroplane every bit as much as Marinetti and his Italian circle. Lenin himself had taken great interest in the aeroplane ever since his stay in Paris, from December 1908, where he lived through the first

---

[1] C. Tisdall and A. Bozzolla, *Futurism* (London, 1977), 200–1, 205–6; J. Davies, 'The Futures Market: Marinetti and the Fascists of Milan', in E. Timms and P. Collier (eds.), *Visions and Blueprints: Avant-Garde Culture and Radical Politics in Early Twentieth-Century Europe* (Manchester, 1988), 82.

memorable years of enthusiasm for aviation.[2] On his road to fascism from his syndicalist position in France of the late 1920s, Le Corbusier looked favourably on Bolshevism as the creator of a new, centralized, authoritarian, meritocratic regime, suitable for the modern age. He was courted by the Soviets, honoured by the Soviet modernist architects— Konstantin Melnikov, the Vesnin brothers (Alexander, Victor, and Leonid), Moses Ginsburg, and N. A. Miliutin—and commissioned to build large projects in the Soviet Union.[3] It was not without reason that his American rival Frank Lloyd Wright denounced Le Corbusier's centralized, gigantic, and crushing urban utopias as being appropriate to fascist, Nazi, or communist authoritarianism, long before this charge was adopted by post-modernist architects. Wright too, however, was courted by the Soviets and by the Soviet modernist architects.[4] Ironically, like Hitler and, less severely, Mussolini—and as if to validate the 'totalitarian model'—by the mid-1930s Stalin had suppressed architectural and artistic modernism in favour of monumental classicism and 'socialist realism'. In Germany, Jünger was reproached by his friend Oswald Spengler for not being able to free himself from Marxist analysis in his portrayal in *Der Arbeiter* (1932) of a future machine-dominated society.[5] Like Blomberg, Jünger saw the Soviet Union as a model for his modernist right-wing designs. During the 1920s Lenin's and Soviet enthusiasm for American Taylorism and Fordism dwarfed even that of the Germans. In Lenin's slogan: 'Electrification + Soviet Rule = Socialism'.[6] In 1946, admittedly after horrendous trials, Stalin, like Fuller, proclaimed that Clausewitz had belonged to the 'hand-tool period of warfare', whereas it was now the machine age.[7] Fascist and Soviet modernism had much in common.

If Marxism as an ideology was so thoroughly modernist, even less

[2] F. P. Ingold, *Literatur und Aviatik: Europäische Flugdichtung, 1909–1927* (Basel, 1978), 52–9, 133–89; R. Wohl, *A Passion for Wings: Aviation and Western Imagination, 1908–1918* (New Haven, Conn., 1994), 145–53, 157–78. A detailed general study is V. Markov, *Russian Futurism: A History* (Berkeley, Calif., 1968).

[3] B. B. Taylor, *Le Corbusier: The City of Refuge, Paris 1929/33* (Chicago, 1987), 9.

[4] D. L. Johnson, *Frank Lloyd Wright versus America: The 1930s* (Cambridge, Mass., 1990), 176, 179–230, 244.

[5] A. Hamilton, *The Appeal of Fascism* (London, 1971), 124.

[6] C. Maier, 'Between Taylorism and Technocracy: European Ideologies and the Vision of Industrial Productivity in the 1920s', *Journal of Contemporary History*, 5(2) (1970), and extensively in T. Hughes, *American Genesis: A Century of Invention and Technological Enthusiasm, 1870–1970* (New York, 1989), 249–84.

[7] A. Gat, *The Development of Military Thought: The Nineteenth Century* (Oxford, 1992), 244.

ambivalently than fascism, then why were the pioneering visionaries of machine warfare before, during, and immediately after the First World War mostly associated with proto-fascism and fascism rather than with Marxism? It might be claimed that fascism was simply overtly militaristic whereas socialism was ideologically humanitarian and pacifist; but Marxist and socialist thinkers had been considering the issue of war since the nineteenth century, if only for the transition period when socialist revolutions would have to be carried out and defended. A more significant reason for the difference in question would be that, from Engels to Jaures (for all the former's brilliant analysis of the evolution of technology, society, and war)[8] the thinkers of the Second International and socialist movements had been heavily committed to militias and mass popular armies on the model of the French Revolution, and opposed regular élite forces. An unceasing debate along these lines between the left and the right had been going on in France since 1871 (if not 1815). It provided the political background for the way the idea of a small, élite, professional, armoured force was received when proposed (unoriginally) in 1934 by Charles de Gaulle, himself a dubious republican. In Russia, learning by experience during the Civil War, War Commissar Trotsky created a centralized regular Red Army much against party mood, and defended it against advocates of local militias and partisan warfare. However, once the war was over, it was Trotsky himself who requested that the army be converted into a locally based militia, winning the debates against the 'red commanders', Frunze, Gusev, and Tukhachevsky, in successive party congresses during the early 1920, though ultimately losing the political power struggle itself.[9]

From 1923 to 1924 a group of officers largely influenced by Mikhail Tukhachevsky began to synthesize the lessons of modern war—the First World War, the Civil War, and the Russian–Polish War—into a systematic strategic and operational doctrine. But it was only from around 1928–9 that radical modern ideas of mechanized warfare were gradually absorbed, progressively turning the old concept of war on broad fronts into the advanced and innovative conception of 'deep battle' and 'deep operations'. Several studies of these developments are currently under way in the newly opened Soviet archives, which should much extend our knowledge of them. But to anyone familiar

---

[8] Ibid. 233–4.
[9] J. Erickson, *The Soviet High Command* (London, 1962), 113–43.

with the evolution of mechanized doctrine from a comparative perspective throughout the developed world during the 1920s, it is not difficult to discern where at least the initial stimulus for the Soviets' newly awakened interest in radical conceptions of mechanized warfare came from at that particular moment. It originated with the path-breaking manœuvres of the British Experimental Mechanized Force in 1927–8, which made use of the world's first operational fast and long-range tank, the Vickers Medium, and were perceived in conjunction with the revolutionary theories and propagandist writings of Fuller and his disciples, chief among them Liddell Hart. All armies of the industrial world closely studied these manœuvres, translated the British writers, and established experimental armoured formations of their own. In 1928, on the instruction of Secretary of State for War D. Davis, who had witnessed the British 1927 manœuvres, the US army formed and tried out for the first time its own experimental armoured brigade. The French were quickening the mechanization of their cavalry. The Italians, too, were closely studying and much influenced by the British manœuvres.[10] The first Soviet mechanized regiments intended for independent use were created in 1929–30. The Red Army's Field Service Regulations of 1929 stipulated that, in addition to their traditional role of direct infantry support, tanks would be incorporated into independent groups (DD) to be used for penetration into tactical depths against the enemy's artillery. This was the first step in the development of the concept of mechanized 'deep battle'.[11]

Fuller's *Tanks in the Great War* had already been translated into Russian in 1923. His seminal *The Reformation of War* was translated in 1931, edited and prefaced by Tukhachevsky, who quoted liberally from the range of Fuller's writings. Apparently Fuller's *Lectures on FSR III* or *On Future Warfare*, or both, were also translated during the 1930s. *The Remaking of Modern Armies* (1927) by Liddell Hart, regarded at first as Fuller's disciple, was translated in 1930. Martel saw many translated copies of his own book *In the Wake of the Tank* (1931) during his visit to the Soviet Union in 1936. As was the case in

    [10] R. Ogorkiewicz, *Armoured Forces* (London, 1970), 17–18, 87; J. Hendrix, 'The Interwar Army and Mechanization: The American Approach', *Journal of Strategic Studies*, 16 (1993), 77–81; L. Ceva and A. Curami, *La Meccanizzazione dell'esercito italiano dalle origini al 1943* (Rome, 1989), 113–32; and for the Germans again, see extensively my 'British Influence and the Evolution of the Panzer Arm: Myth or Reality?', *War in History*, 4(2) (1997), 150–73 4(3) (1997), 316–38.
    [11] Erickson, *The Soviet High Command*, 316.

Germany, regular periodical translations were as, if not more, important. 'Each issue of *Voina i revolyutsiya* contained a highly technical commentary on the tactics and technology of "foreign armies", e.g. French military organizations, Polish military regulations, *British writings on tank warfare*.' In 1932 Karl Radek, the editor of *Izvestiya* and an expert on military affairs in his own right, told Fuller and Liddell Hart in Geneva that they were the best-known foreign military experts in the Soviet Union, and that Fuller's book (unclear which) sold there more than 100,000 copies. According to Liddell Hart, Radek told him that the Red Army was then creating its first armoured corps, and invited him to come to the Soviet Union as an official adviser.[12]

From 1928 Tukhachevsky began to develop the concept of large-scale mechanized battle. His fellow theorist Viktor K. Triandafillov's admirable book *The Nature of the Operations of Modern Armies* (1929), which summarized the Soviet theorists' early work on successive large-scale operations ('operational art') and provided a seminal formulation of the concept of deep battle, only began to acknowledge the operational potential of the new fast, long-range tank and to evolve towards a more radical conception of mechanized warfare. But at that time Triandafillov was already making great progress, and by the time of his death in an air crash in 1931 he was rewriting his book in that direction.[13] All the same, if British theory and practice provided an initial and crucial stimulus for Soviet development, their reception was by no means slavish, but dialectic and innovative. Both Tukhachevky and Triandafillov advanced similar and striking critiques of Fuller's conception of the nature of modern mechanized warfare. Both were extremely capable, and Tukhachevsky in particular was a man of broad intellectual interests. Familiar as they were with Victor Germains's book, both echoed his principal points.

---

[12] All existing studies more or less recognize the British precedent and influence: Erickson, *The Soviet High Command*, 270, 308; id. 'The Soviet Union', in E. May (ed.), *Knowing One's Enemies: Intelligence Assessment before the Two World Wars* (Princeton, NJ, 1984), 395 (quotation; my emphasis); R. Simpkin, *Deep Battle: The Brainchild of Marshal Tukhachevsky* (London, 1987), 46; and Tukhachevsky on Liddell Hart and Martel, ibid. 126, 130, 132; D. Glantz, *Soviet Military Operational Art: In Pursuit of Deep Battle* (London, 1991), 19. See also B. H. Liddell Hart, *Memoirs* (2 vols., London, 1965), i. 196–8, reproducing his notes at the time, Liddel Hart Centre for Military Archives, King's College, London, 19 Feb. 1932, in 11/1932/6; 26 Feb. 1932, in 11/1932/1; A. J. Trythall, *'Boney' Fuller: The Intellectual General* (London, 1977), 175, 210.
[13] V. K. Triandafillov, *The Nature of the Operations of Modern Armies*, with foreword by J. Kipp and Introduction by J. Schneider (Ilford, Essex, 1994), esp. 20–2, 91, 110; Simpkin, *Deep Battle*, 38. See also *The Evolution of Soviet Operational Art*, i: *1927–1964* (London, 1995), trans. H. S. Orenstein, foreword and introd. by D. Glantz.

To be sure, a hostile, xenophobic, and polemic style was the mandatory norm of Soviet commentary on foreign, non-socialist works. Without such commentary a book simply could not appear in the Soviet Union, the very fact that it did indicating that it was regarded as useful.[14] No capitalist-bourgeois writer could expect better, and Fuller was not merely that but a fascist, a fact that Tukhachevsky saw clearly in 1931 three years before Fuller joined the BUF when it was founded in 1934, from a book published eight years earlier than that.[15] All the same, none of this should be taken as diminishing the sincerity of Triandafillov and Tukhachevsky in criticizing Fuller's ideas. Both their strategic and Marxist viewpoints converged in their critique.

Small, élite, fully mechanized, high-technology armies, wrote Triandafillov and Tukhachevsky, might perhaps be suitable for Britain's needs, both on account of her insular position and because of the shortcomings of capitalist societies in mobilizing the masses (also evident in Seeckt's ideas in Germany). But such armies would not do for large-scale continental wars, nor express the strength of a socialist state. This was the mistake of A. I. Verkhovskii, who advocated them, in Fuller's footsteps, in the Soviet Union. From the wider historical–economic perspective Tukhachevsky, like Germains, questioned Fuller's analysis of modern developments, claiming that wherever mechanization had taken place it had not reduced manpower but only redirected its employment while vastly increasing productivity. The same would hold true for armies. Machine armies would be big, not small, with a larger part of the manpower absorbed in a much-expanded and essential services and maintenance sector. Strategically, Triandafillov and Tukhachevsky argued that Fuller's great merit had been that he had raised the idea of deep penetration by armour, giving Britain the lead in respect to future warfare. Such penetration, however, could not alone decide the outcome of battle, or of war as a whole. Small armoured forces risked isolation and destruction. The massive human and industrial resources possessed by modern states promised protracted struggle and staggering attrition rates. For these reasons the largest armoured forces possible (together with aircraft and air-mobile forces, which Tukhachevsky, like Liddell Hart, criticized Fuller for neglecting) would have to work side by side and in inter-arms cooperation with masses of foot infantry and

---

[14] Simpkin in *Deep Battle*, 82, perceives this clearly.
[15] Tukhachevsky's preface to Fuller's *The Reformation of War*, printed in Simpkin, *Deep Battle*, 125-6.

conventional artillery within armies of millions.[16] It was the scheme for such cooperation that the authors of 'deep battle' and 'deep operations' masterfully developed during the 1930s until Stalin's purges of 1937–8 broke them.

The doctrine of 'deep battle' had its weaknesses. In particular, its missions definition for armour was highly differentiated. Three specialized armour group types were envisaged, destined respectively for close and long-range infantry support and long-distance penetration. More crucially, there were to be specialized tank types for each mission. Thus, as in the French and British armies, the Soviet fast, long-range tanks were unable to cooperate effectively with the slow, infantry-support models. After learning this to their cost in the opening campaigns of the Second World War, the Soviets (faster than the British) abandoned the old categories for good, adopting the main battle tank (medium and heavy) for all mission types. Indeed, this was exactly the point that the creators of the Panzer arm during the 1930s had criticized in Soviet armour, which they otherwise held in esteem. Walter Nehring concluded that the Soviet permanent functional splitting of armour was schematic and inflexible. Guderian wrote that while 'there is something to be said' for it, it 'demands a whole inventory of specialized tanks, with all the attendant disadvantages'.[17] On the other hand, whereas Guderian and the creators of the Panzer arm concentrated primarily on their armoured divisions, while Beck strove for a more comprehensive approach but was not as radical and advanced as the Soviets, 'deep battle' was from the beginning both comprehensive and advanced. It was the only fully developed doctrine of mobile warfare consciously and systematically devised from above before the Second World War for the use of a modern mass army which was only partly mechanized. The Germans only confronted the problems entailed by a partly mechanized army when they actually encountered

[16] Triandafillov, *Modern Armies*, 26–9; Tukhachevsky's preface to Fuller, *The Reformation of War*, in Simpkin, *Deep Battle*, 127–33; Tukhachersky, 'New Questions of War' (1931–2), in Simpkin, *Deep Battle*, 135–58, echoing Fuller in many ways; see also ibid. 159–60.

[17] W. Nehring, *Kampfwagen an die Front!* (Leipzig, 1934), 26; H. Guderian, *Achtung Panzer* (London, 1992; German original 1937), 153; 'Schnelle Truppen einst und jetzt', *Militärwissenschaftliche Rundschau*, 4 (1939), 237–8. The German criticism in the 1930s of the Soviet armour doctrine has been well noted by H. Senff, *Die Entwicklung der Panzerwaffe im deutschen Heer zwischen den beiden Weltkriegen* (Frankfurt a.M., 1969), 22. See also my 'British Influence and the Evolution of the Panzer Arm', 322–3.

these problems in 1940–1, during their campaigns in the West and against the Soviet Union.

To be sure, during the 1930s the Germans, too, wanted as big an army as possible and total mobilization. But for Hitler, Blomberg, or Guderian the desire to escape a full-scale war of attrition, which German resources could not sustain, by gambling on swift, short, and unconventional coups was overwhelming. Soviet Russia, on the other hand, was not similarly constrained. Russia's traditional reliance on mass and space remained good, in a modern form, for the Soviet Union. In addition, Soviet strategic ideas were largely shaped by socialist precepts. Taken together, these factors constituted the foundations upon which the doctrine of 'deep battle' and 'deep operations' was built. Ever attacked for their fascination with mechanization by the army conservatives around Defence Commissar Klementi Voroshilov, the authors of 'deep battle' advocated, not futuristic élite machine armies on the model of Fuller or Douhet, but modern machines *cum* the masses.

7

Conclusion

Fascism is primarily associated with Mussolini's regime in Italy and with that of Hitler in Germany, the two major Western countries where it reached power, with explosive effect. Yet this study deals only marginally with the actual practices of these regimes, or with the debated question of their 'modernizing' nature and impact, or with their part in perpetrating the Second World War. Its main concern is with fascism as an idea and a cultural mood which attracted intellectuals well before the First World War and before fascism was transformed into mass political movements. Among early twentieth-century intellectuals proto-fascism and fascism enjoyed widespread appeal. To be sure, fascism inclined towards nationalism. In countries like Italy and Germany, which felt themselves deprived in the international arena, it also possessed a strong revisionist foreign policy element and a militaristic tendency, which constituted an important part of its appeal and helped it into power. On the whole, however, fascism was perhaps even more about domestic affairs. First and foremost, it was a cultural and political response to the rise of mass society, urbanization, and secularization which took place during the closing decades of the nineteenth century. While not all those born in the last quarter of the nineteenth century were fascists, practically all fascists were born during that period (d'Annunzio, born in 1863, was an exception and in this respect, too, is rightly regarded as a forerunner). The fascists were looking for a 'Third Way' to modernity that would preserve 'civilization' and élite culture from the threat of democratic and socialist plebeianism, that would encompass the masses without being dominated by them, and that would counter the 'disenchantment of life' associated with modern rationalism. As such, fascist varieties mixed varying degrees of pre-industrial nostalgia and agrarian mythology with the most strident modernist and futurist visions. It is this latter streak of fascist modernism, in its intimate relation to visions of modern machine warfare, that has concerned us here.

The fact that most if not all of the radical visionaries of machine warfare were associated with fascism does not indicate that it was more modernist than liberalism (the Marxist–socialist comparison has already been discussed); it was simply more enthusiastically so. By nature fascist modernism was avant-gardist, utopian, futuristic, and inclined to deploy sweeping rhetoric and flamboyant imagery. This is exactly the stuff of which visions are made and with which headlines are captured. By the same token, however, these qualities do not necessarily translate all that well into reality. For vision—and the word has been deliberately chosen—is different, has in it both more and less than doctrine. It is a prophetic and inspiring picture, strikingly sketched with compelling rhetorical devices, but with little systematic elaboration of detail. As such, visions are often partly or wholly far-fetched, poorly grounded in experience, and divorced from existing conditions, and they ignore the complexity of circumstances, sometimes deliberately. They may prove a sound bridge to the future, or they may not.

To be sure, whatever precedent fascists could claim in developing radical conceptions of machine warfare, such ideas were also adopted, for good or for ill, by others. What is more, when we move from the domain of abstract ideas to reality, the deployment of mechanized armies in a large-scale great-power war depended on industrial weight, and here Britain and the Soviet Union were each roughly equal to Germany, while the United States was far superior to all, and Italy did not count. Furthermore, in the ultimate test of war production the fascist regimes did not prove to be the model of efficiency that fascist modernists had envisaged they would be and that others, too, at the time believed they were. War production was far more systematically and efficiently organized by their enemies.

As it happened, contrary to Fuller's prediction and that of other radical modernists, it was neither fascism nor communism that emerged victorious from the Armageddon of the twentieth century but—as of today—the outdated and expected loser, liberal democracy. This was so perhaps because liberal democracy was after all more in tune with the nature of modernity than its rivals; or alternatively, maybe because the liberal democratic United States was simply so much more powerful than the other great powers that it decided in favour of the coalitions it joined all three great power conflicts of the twentieth century. Either way, as the twentieth century progressed, the world's greatest concentration of power, and the world's technologically most advanced societies, were increasingly to be found in the liberal democratic camp—in the West and among those who emulated its model. It remained for Fuller's disciple, Liddell Hart—who, unlike his mentor, had become a staunch liberal—to develop a strategic blueprint designed to fit the aims, capabilities, and limitations of a liberal West moving at the forefront of modernity.

Part II

Liddell Hart, Modern, and 'Post-Modern' Strategy

I

Introduction

Basil Henry Liddell Hart (1895–1970) is perhaps the most famous strategic theorist of the twentieth century. Yet since his death (which coincided with the opening of the British archives of the interwar period), his ideas have come under searching scholarly criticism, and his reputation has suffered heavy blows. The influential doctrines he advocated in the 1930s—such as the 'British Way in Warfare', Limited Liability, and the superiority of defence—have been criticized as historically dubious, politically unrealistic, and strategically harmful.[1] His (and Fuller's) reformist rhetoric, which blamed mostly conservatism and vested organizational interests for the British army's failure to adopt the British-pioneered doctrine of armoured warfare, has been qualified and revised.[2] The predominant role that he claimed in the development of that doctrine has been judged to be overstated.[3] Furthermore, strong evidence has been produced that Liddell Hart considerably exaggerated his influence on the creators of the German Panzer arm.[4] Indeed, most damaging of all, in these and other cases he has been found guilty of a recurring tendency to manipulate evidence, and people, in order to protect and enhance his reputation. The

---

[1] See esp. C. Barnett, *Britain and Her Army, 1509–1970* (London 1970); *The Collapse of British Power* (London, 1972), 497–503, 581; M. Howard, 'Liddell Hart' (1970) ['LH'] and 'The British Way in Warfare: A Reappraisal' (1974), reprinted in *The Causes of War* (London, 1984), 237–47, 189–207; P. Kennedy, *The Rise and Fall of British Naval Mastery* (London, 1976); B. Bond, *Liddell Hart: A Study of His Military Thought* (London, 1977) [*LH*], 65–118; *British Military Policy between the Two World Wars* (Oxford, 1980); J. Mearsheimer, *Liddell Hart and the Weight of History* [*LH*] (London, 1988); D. French, *The British Way in Warfare, 1688–2000* (London, 1990); H. Strachan, 'The British Way in Warfare', in D. Chandler (ed.), *The Oxford Illustrated History of the British Army* (Oxford, 1994), 417–34.

[2] M. Howard, *The Continental Commitment* (London, 1972); H. Winton, *To Change an Army: General Sir John Burnett-Stuart and British Armoured Doctrine, 1927–1938* (Lawrence, KS, 1988); Bond, *Military Policy*.

[3] Winton, *To Change an Army*; K. Macksey, *The Tank Pioneers* (London, 1981); Mearsheimer, *LH*, 42–4; J. P. Harris, *Men, Ideas and Tanks: British Military Thought and Armoured Forces, 1903–1939* (Manchester, 1995).

[4] K. Macksey, *Guderian: Panzer General* (London, 1975), 40–1; *The Tank Pioneers*, 118, 216; picked up and developed by Mearsheimer, *LH*, 160–7, 184–201.

unattractive side of Liddell Hart's character, his long-observed vanity and obsession with fame, was harshly exposed in the most recent full-scale study of his work, John Mearsheimer's *Liddell Hart and the Weight of History* (1988), overshadowing his more praiseworthy qualities and casting a sinister light on his entire career.

There has now developed heightened awareness of Liddell Hart's knack for self-advertisement and genius for cultivating contacts and personal relationships, all the more surprising in such a self-conscious, highly strung, and socially awkward man. This genius is testified to by the nearly 1,000 individuals whose files of correspondence with Liddell Hart, preserved in his huge archive, read like an international *Who's Who* of military, political, and academic personae. In his large country house Liddell Hart entertained a constant march of guests from all over the world, including most of the rising generation of young military historians. Although highly egocentric, he took genuine interest in their work, encouraged them, and invested enormous effort in helping them. In the process, however, they were chained to him by the 'hoops of steel' of friendship, respect, and gratitude, disarming them as potential critics, at least during his lifetime.[5] Since Liddell Hart, as Churchill jested about himself, decisively shaped scholarly and popular perceptions by writing so much of the history of his times and of his own deeds himself, the process of critical reassessment has been natural and more than necessary.

In my research I have discovered a great deal of new and unflattering information about Liddell Hart. Yet I have also found that the most serious charges levelled against him are factually erroneous and based on almost incredible historiographical slips on the part of his chief critic, John Mearsheimer. Most of this relates to Liddell Hart's theory of armoured warfare and his influence on the creators of the German Panzer arm, to which I have dedicated separate studies.[6] Therefore, in view of the distortions introduced both by Liddell Hart himself and by his critics, which cast doubt on all that supposedly was known about him, no less than a full-scale reconstruction of his work and influence has become necessary. Nothing could be taken for granted as accepted fact. However, while putting the record straight was an indispensable

---

[5] In addition to Mearsheimer, see the superb commentary in Howard, 'LH' (the quotation is from p. 238); and Bond, *LH*, 1–10.

[6] A. Gat, 'Liddell Hart's Theory of Armoured Warfare: Revising the Revisionists', *Journal of Strategic Studies*, 19 (1996), 1–30; 'British Influence and the Evolution of the Panzer Arm: Myth or Reality?', *War in History*, 4(2) (1997) 150–73, and 4(3) (1997), 316–38.

preliminary condition for the present study, it is not in itself its purpose. The critical wave against Liddell Hart has been so sweeping that the idea that he holds a pivotal place in the development of twentieth-century strategic theory might appear strange and wholly outdated to many in the scholarly community. Yet this is precisely what this study sets out to establish. It will be argued here that Liddell Hart's life-work, whose full development remains largely unrecognized, was far weightier than it is commonly considered today. Moreover, it will be claimed that it reflected and foreshadowed, in the field of strategic theory, the conditions and outlook of a society and an age: the evolving Western liberal democracy, whose expanding orbit would increasingly dominate the twentieth century, and seems likely to extend further into the future. The strategic paradigm of an epoch is offered here through the intellectual biography of a man.

Our starting-point is the Great War, which during the past decades has been snatched from the hands of military historians by cultural historians, who have turned it into a growth industry. While not the beginning of modernity, the war is now widely regarded as a towering landmark in the growth of modern consciousness.[7] As John Mueller has argued in his *Retreat from Doomsday: The Obsolescence of Major Wars* (1989), the war signalled a profound change of attitude to the phenomenon of war and its conduct. However, in contrast to Mueller, it will be claimed here that it was predominantly liberal opinion that was strongly affected by this change for reasons that are inherent in the development of modern liberal societies.[8] Our location is thus the first, and historically the most deeply rooted, mass liberal–democratic great powers of the West, and in particular Britain. It was then and there that the problem of war for modern liberal societies first imposed itself in all its starkness, and that a distinctive strategic response began to evolve.

---

[7] See below, but also, for an important qualification stressing the continuity of traditional values and images, J. Winter, *Sites of Memory, Sites of Mourning: The Great War in European Cultural History* (Cambridge, 1995).

[8] J. Mueller, *Retreat from Doomsday: The Obsolescence of Major War* (New York, 1989). For criticisms somewhat like my own, see C. Kaysen, 'Is War Obsolete? A Review Essay', *International Security*, 14 (1990), 42–63; R. Schweller, 'Domestic Structure and Preventive War: Are Democracies More Pacific?', *World Politics*, 44 (1992), 235–69.

2

Background: The First World War in Western Consciousness

Historical

The First World War was a landmark in Western consciousness, yet its significance for the various nations involved differed greatly. A formal and vague consensus in favour of international reconciliation and co-operation and against the use of force in international relations, which appeared to have crystallized from the mid-1920s, proved fragile and short-lived. With the collapse of the international economic system, it was shaken off by those countries to whom the postwar order gave the least reason to be satisfied with the Locarno territorial status quo, and whose deep-seated national traditions made them less receptive to the so-called Locarno spirit. It proved more durable, however, in the countries which emerged on the winning side of the war, whose interests were less directly or obviously under threat, and in which internationalist and liberal notions were a far more important part of the national make-up. Indeed, rather than generating anything fundamentally new, the war effectively accentuated and polarized long-standing differences in national attitudes. Crudely put, one was moving along an attitude spectrum as one was travelling west, mentally as well as geographically. And it is with the westernmost parts of the West that this study is concerned. As early as the First World War, President Wilson's internationalist and liberal crusade had forced evasive tactics and clever rhetoric on the other, more cynical participants in the war and in the peace-making, thus producing a tension which led the United States to isolationism. But in Britain, too, the new attitudes came to the fore during the Locarno era, increasingly underlying public, political, and even official perceptions and reactions for most of the interwar period.[1] While hard-core pacifism, though stronger and

---

[1] For 'idealists' versus 'pragmatists' in British officialdom, see in P. Towle, 'British Security and Disarmament Policy in Europe in the 1920s', in R. Ahmann, A. M. Birke, and M. Howard (eds.), *The Quest for Stability: Problems of West European Security, 1918–1957* (Oxford, 1993), 127–53.

more vocal than before, remained a marginal phenomenon, there was a much wider loss of faith in the use of force in international relations, which, it was believed, was to be discarded and replaced by growing cooperation and by collective security. This change of outlook was bound up with a strong reaction against those features of the prewar political and value system which were held responsible for the war. Correspondingly came also a change of attitude towards the war itself.

By the beginning of the twentieth century the heightened international rivalries—brought about by the imperialist contest and made all the more inflammable by rapid social change—had given rise to nationalist forces and social-Darwinist notions throughout the West. Edwardian Britain (as well as Theodore Roosevelt's America) was no exception to this rule. Underlined by nationalist and racialist rhetoric and supported by political, journalistic, and academic propaganda, the Naval League, National Service League, Movement for Imperial Federation, and Movement for National Efficiency, while rarely equalling their German counterparts in chauvinist ferocity or in the extent of their official and popular support, were none the less prominent features of British public life in the prewar period.[2] When war came in 1914, these notions and forces moved closer to centre stage in all the belligerent countries.

As everywhere else in Europe, the declaration of war was greeted in Britain with widespread manifestations of popular enthusiasm. War was regarded in all countries as a defensive necessity, and after a decade of rising international tensions and repeated crises there was a common feeling, even a sense of relief, that things had to be settled once and for all, even by war. More deeply, historians have pointed out that in all countries workers seemed to have found in the war an exhilarating experience and an escape from a dull routine, and that the educated classes responded in essentially the same way. The intellectuals welcomed the war as the supreme test of nations' vitality and as a purifying and elevating experience for a mechanistic, materialistic, and decadent

[2] See G. R. Searle, *The Quest for National Efficiency* (Oxford, 1971); P. Kennedy and A. Nicholls (eds.), *Nationalist and Racialist Movements in Britain and Germany before 1914* (London, 1981); J. Gooch, 'Attitude to War in Late Victorian and Edwardian England', in *The Prospect of War: Studies in British Defence Policy, 1847–1942* (London, 1981), 35–51; A. J. A. Morris, *The Scaremongers: The Advocacy of War and Rearmament, 1896–1914* (London, 1984); M. Howard, 'Empire, Race and War in pre-1914 Britain', in *The Lessons of History* (Oxford, 1991), 63–80; P. Crook, *Darwinism, War and History* (Cambridge, 1994). Obsolete but still useful for its wealth of source material is C. E. Playne, *The Prewar Mind in Britain* (London, 1928).

mass/bourgeois society, the product of modernity.[3] In all countries the educated young, of whom society expected the most, were particularly moved by these sentiments. In Britain, the public-school ethos and response to the war can be regarded as merely a local variant of a cross-European phenomenon. While not in itself militaristic, the public-school ethos, rooted and codified in the nineteenth century, cultivated the qualities of leadership, honour, sportsmanship, chivalry, Christian masculinity, and patriotism which proved so important in 1914 and after. During late 1914 student societies all over Britain, moved by the surge in patriotic sentiments, were passing resolutions exalting the noble qualities of war.[4]

The subsequent trauma of the war and of the so-called 'lost generation', especially in its British manifestation, is a widely familiar subject. Still, a brief summary of this complex experience is in order.[5] From the point of view of its impact on national consciousness and morale, the experience was seen mainly through the eyes of the educated classes, who arguably reacted the most traumatically or, in any case, were able to make their voice heard more prominently, and who constituted the British political, social, and cultural élite. Within these classes most attention has focused on the young who enlisted and bore the brunt of the war, the 'generation of 1914', particularly the graduates of the élite public schools.

From August 1914, public-school graduates streamed in their thousands to enlist, supplying the cadre of officers for Britain's New Armies throughout the war. Their romantic enthusiasm lasted long and, artistically, came to be symbolized for generations of schoolboys by the sublime and heroic war sonnets of Rupert Brooke, who died on his way to Gallipoli in April 1915. Only gradually, with the routine of trench warfare and the climactic bloodletting of Ypres, Neuve Chapelle, Loos, and the Somme, did a new note creep in. The more sensitive

[3] See esp. R. Stromberg, *Redemption by War: The Intellectuals and 1914* (Lawrence, KS, 1982), 1–24 and *passim*; also R. Wohl, *The Generation of 1914* (Cambridge, Mass., 1979); E. J. Leed, *No Man's Land: Combat and Identity in World War I* (Cambridge, 1979); M. Adams, *The Great Adventure: Male Desire and the Coming of World War I* (Bloomington, Ind., 1990); F. Fields, *British and French Writers of the First World War* (Cambridge, 1991).

[4] See P. Parker, *The Old Lie: The Great War and the Public-School Ethos* (London, 1987); for the resolutions, pp. 61–2; for the 'code' and its role in British culture, see L. Susser, 'Fascist and Anti-Fascist Attitudes in Britain between the Wars', doctoral dissertation, Oxford University, 1988).

[5] See esp. P. Fussell, *The Great War and Modern Memory* (Oxford, 1975) and, even more, S. Hynes, *A War Imagined: The First World War and English Culture* (London, 1990).

psyches, like the front-line poets Siegfried Sassoon, Wilfred Owen, and Robert Graves, assumed a distinctively realistic tone, depicting the horror and destruction of the war, blood and mud, fear, agony, exhaustion, death and mutilation. Front-line soldiers, of British as well as of other nationalities, consistently reported a failure of communication with the civilian rear. To the soldiers' surprise, people in the rear not only continued to live their life much the same as before (in Britain much more than in the blockaded Central Powers) but also, fed on the newspapers' rosy reports from the front line, failed to comprehend the nature of life there and identify with the combatants' experience.[6] These feelings were of existential rather than ideological or political nature. Only in about late 1916, after the Battle of the Somme, were a very few dissenting voices heard among front-line officers, blaming the 'Old Men' in government for prolonging the war by rejecting a negotiated peace on the basis of the *status quo ante*.[7] Even fewer, like the war hero Siegfried Sassoon, were those who made their opinions public and became conscientious objectors, to the disdain of their front-line fellows.

On the whole, however—and this cannot be emphasized too strongly—dissent in the British armed forces was a very marginal phenomenon. While the French army, which admittedly had undergone even harsher trials than the British, suffered from widespread mutinies in the summer of 1917, and the Italian, Russian, Austro-Hungarian, and German armies, each in turn, experienced collapses of morale by the end of the war, the British army never lost its fighting spirit. (Arguably, the 5th Army came close to it in the spring of 1918.)[8] High idealism and youthful enthusiasm may have gone, but they were superseded by dogged resilience. At home, where the government used unprecedented measures to mobilize the country's resources for war, suppress opposition to it, and censor information, there was relatively little dissent and only some 16,000 conscientious objectors.[9] While people hoped that the war would end wars, they also voted in their masses in the first peacetime elections for a peace that would make Germany pay the cost of the

[6] R. Graves, *Goodbye to All That* (London, 1929), 187–8; S. Sassoon, *Memoirs of an Infantry Officer* (London, 1930), 126–44, 243–71; Erich Maria Remarque, *All Quiet on the Western Front* (London, 1929), 183–6; Hynes, *A War Imagined*, 119.

[7] Sassoon, *Memoirs*, 273–334; Graves, *Goodbye to All That*, 307–8, 318–25.

[8] A recent study on this aspect is J. G. Fuller, *Troop Morale and Popular Culture in the British and Dominion Armies, 1914–1918* (Oxford, 1990).

[9] M. Ceadel, *Pacifism in Britain, 1914–1945* (Oxford, 1980), 38–41; A. J. P. Taylor, *British History, 1914–1945* (London, 1975), 87–8.

war. The army was proud of its victory, and soldiers would deny that they were in any way disillusioned or angry at the end of the war.[10] 'Disillusionment' came much later, was particularly noticeable and potent in the victorious Western powers, and can only be understood in reference to the overall political and cultural features of those powers.

Two stages have been discerned in the interwar reaction to the war in Britain. From the coming of peace to the mid-1920s there was growing disappointment with the outcome of the war. In Britain almost as strongly as on the Continent, the upper and middle classes in particular felt disoriented in a world that appeared to have changed radically. There was a nostalgic sense of loss focusing on the old European civilization and its supposed qualities of social order, well-being, and security, which the war was believed to have destroyed. Naturally, much of this was a reaction by the old élites to a society which had been changing irrespective of the war, which was becoming more pluralistic, and in which aristocratic rule was giving way to a more bureaucratic form of government.[11] All the same, the economic depression of the early 1920s was real enough, and so was the endemic problem of the German reparations and of Germany's status in the international political and economic system. Keynes's highly influential book *The Economic Consequences of the Peace* (1920) was increasingly shaping the way educated people viewed the aftermath of the war in the United States and Britain. The book denounced the 'Carthaginian peace' imposed on Germany, demonstrating not only that the reparation sums were utterly beyond her means but that in an age of economic interdependence her ruin also hindered the economic recovery of her former enemies, who were also her past, present, and future trade partners.

The Locarno era, based on the gradual settlement of the reparation problem and the reconstruction of the European economy, and heralding a new era of political reconciliation and cooperation, completed the change of attitude to the war. It was now increasingly regarded as a senseless massacre, a disaster which European civilization had barely survived and could certainly not repeat. Reflecting and in turn shaping this change of mood were the literary memories of front-line veterans, now erupting in a remarkably dense sequence. Best-sellers such as

---

[10] See e.g. H. Essame, *The Battle for Europe, 1918* (London, 1972), 2; also Hynes, *A War Imagined*, 450.   [11] Wohl, *Generation of 1914*, 121.

Edmund Blunden's *Undertones of War* (1928), Richard Aldington's *Death of a Hero* (1929), Robert Graves's *Goodbye to All That* (1929), Erich Maria Remarque's *All Quiet in the Western Front* (1929), Ernest Hemingway's *A Farewell to Arms* (1929), and Siegfried Sassoon's *Memoirs of an Infantry Officer* (1930), all appearing almost simultaneously a decade after the war's end, were some of the most famous works that came to represent the reaction against the experience of the war. In seemingly detached, absurd, and sometime macabre tone they depicted a picture of barbarity, degradation, and day-to-day misery in trench warfare life. Overshadowing all was the sense of a terrible and senseless sacrifice, of life, youth and innocence, associated with the notion of the 'lost generation'.

To be sure, many objected to the new attitude towards the war. T. E. Lawrence, 'Lawrence of Arabia', for one, argued that the experience of the war had been much less horrible for the participants than it had been made to appear in hindsight. Indeed, it has been shown that the war authors of the late 1920s treated the war retrospectively far more negatively than they had done during the war itself. Furthermore, even at the time the 'war literature' was coming out it is doubtful if its avant-garde spirit was in any proportional sense 'representative' of the veterans' attitudes. Thus, many scholars have been critical of the shape taken by historical memory and the popular image of the war.[12] They have found it necessary to remind people that the war was not a senseless affair, that the stakes were real and high, and that a German victory and German domination of Europe would have mattered a great deal both to Britain and to the course of world history. In respect to the so-called 'lost generation', it has been pointed out that the number of Britons killed in the war amounted to no more than 12 per cent of those who had enlisted. It was smaller in absolute—and even more in proportional—terms than the number of those killed in the other belligerent powers: some 750,000, to France's 1,300,000 and to Germany's two million. None the less, it has been admitted that the more than 37,000 officers killed came unproportionally from the élite public schools and university colleges, leaving appalling gaps in their ranks. Of the 5,588 Old Etonians who served in the war, 1,159 were killed and 1,469 were wounded. In other public schools proportions were similar and even

---

[12] See e.g. Essame, *The Battle for Europe, 1918*, 2; Hynes, *A War Imagined*, 450–5; Wohl, *Generation of 1914*, 120; Howard, 'Liddell Hart', in *The Causes of War*, 239, and repeatedly elsewhere; B. Bond (ed.), *The First World War and British Military History* (Oxford, 1991), 1–2.

worse. Among Oxford and Cambridge students the death toll of about one-quarter was double the national rate. Of Liddell Hart's matriculation year in Corpus Christi, Cambridge, (1913) 27 per cent were killed in the war.[13]

Establishing facts and dispelling myths are crucial for historical understanding, but it is just as essential to recognize that facts only get their meaning within comprehensive outlooks—integrating values, sensibilities, beliefs, attitudes, interests, and expectations. These are fundamentally subjective, vary between people, societies, and cultures, and change over time. Three-quarters of a million dead are *in themselves* neither a great many nor a few; nor were the overall losses and cost of the war unprecedented in the annals of European history.[14] Whether casualties on such scale are 'acceptable' or 'unacceptable' to any given society depends on cultural attitudes and historical circumstances.[15] In Germany, which, in relation to population, had suffered twice as many casualties as Britain, there was certainly much war-weariness and a widespread loss of enthusiasm for war. The most internationally famous anti-war author, Remarque, was a German liberal and pacifist, and many other German war authors wrote in a similar vein.[16] Furthermore, it was widely realized even by right-wingers that in case of a war a superior coalition would most likely again be created against Germany, a realization that served as a strong deterrent from war. For all that, Germany was defeated, humiliated, and eager to revise the peace settlement. Nationalism, militarism, and anti-liberalism were powerful elements within its political, social, and cultural fabric. Nostalgic memories of trench camaraderie thus played an important social and political role in the aftermath of the war, as they did in Italy. Ernst Jünger's books, glorifying his experience in the trenches and exalting the qualities of war, competed with Remarque's for popularity (at least in Germany) and were personally and artistically neither less nor more

[13] For a thorough study of the statistics, see J. M. Winter, *The Great War and the British People* (London, 1986), 65–75, 85–99, concluding that there was justification to the notion of the 'lost generation'; also Wohl, *Generation of 1914*, 113–15, 120–1; Parker, *Public-School Ethos*, 16–17, 279; Hynes, *A War Imagined*, 385–6; D. French, *British Strategy and War Aims* (London, 1916), 244–7; H. Strachan, 'Liddell Hart, Cruttwell, and Falls', in Bond, *The First World War*, 42.

[14] For the latter point see also J. Mueller, *Retreat from Doomsday: The Obsolescence of Major War* (New York, 1989), 7–8, 55.

[15] This point is well made in E. Cobley, *Representing War: Form and Ideology in First World War Narratives* (Toronto, 1993), 3, 14–15, 29–70, and *passim*.

[16] See Franz Karl Stanzel and Martin Löschnig (ed.), *Intimate Enemies: English and German Literary Reactions to the Great War* (Heidelberg, 1993).

'authentic' or 'objective'.[17] If, from the late 1920s on, people in Britain increasingly came to regard the price of the war as too terrible to bear, it is because by that time they increasingly came to regard the war itself and war in general as fundamentally senseless and unnecessary. Most of them would probably not have denied that, as things turned out, Britain had defended her vital interests in the First World War. Yet, more deeply, they came to feel that under modern conditions all-out wars between great powers were in *nobody's* interest in the first place, and that the whole process that had brought the war into being, and kept it going, was the result of outdated values and misguided goals, ruinously followed by both governments and peoples.

These, of course, were old liberal notions, and indeed it was predominantly with liberal opinion that the trauma of the war was thus expressed. Those societies where liberal values were the strongest reacted the most. It was in this factor, rather then in the actual losses sustained, that the clearest correlation of the reaction against the war is to be traced. The two most extreme cases for demonstrating this argument are the United States and Serbia. The mightiest power in the world was not traumatized by heavy losses and crippling economic costs, as were the European belligerents. She suffered relatively very light casualties in her brief involvement in the war and gained tremendously from it materially, replacing Britain as the world's leading banker, creditor, and insurer. Nevertheless, it was in the United States that the disgust with and regret about participating in the war were the most rapid and sweeping. By comparison, the small and backward Serbia suffered, relative to population, the heaviest casualties of all the warring nations and was totally ravaged by the war and occupation. Nevertheless, it hardly experienced the famous 'trauma' of and 'disillusion' with the war. A modern, industrialized and liberal society was a prerequisite for these sentiments.

While Liberalism, as a movement and an ideology, may have been a minority view in Britain, liberalism, in its broadest sense, was not. It would thus be a mistake to regard the change of outlook in respect to the war as confined to a particular avant-garde group or a minority. While it was mainly among parts of the educated élite that this change first became noticeable by the late 1920s, by the 1930s, as international

[17] As mentioned before, the significant differences that existed here between liberal and non-liberal countries is not sufficiently recognized in Mueller's *Retreat from Doomsday*, esp. 53–68.

tensions were again rising, a wide consensus prevailed among the British public against involvement in another large-scale war. As mentioned before, within this consensus only a small minority were hard-core pacifists.[18] The famous Oxford Union vote of 1933 against fighting for 'King and Country' was above all a gesture, reflecting how the attitudes of youth had changed by comparison with 1914. As the 'Peace Ballot' of early 1935 revealed, the majority of the British public at least nominally seems to have believed in international cooperation to deter would-be aggressors. In any case, the public mood was unmistakable; and in the more fully democratized Britain, where universal voting rights had been introduced after the war, popular opinion made or broke governments. By 1935 collective security had become the official policy of all the major parties in Britain. Indeed, rather than merely responding to their electorate, the majority of the political class itself genuinely felt as the 1930s unfolded that a repetition of anything like the First World War was simply too horrible to contemplate.

A change in public perceptions of the military conduct of the war developed hand in hand with the change of attitude to the war itself. Winston Churchill's criticism of the war of attrition in the West and the way it was directed, already harsh in the second volume (1923) of his widely read, brilliant, and controversial *World Crisis*, became even more sweeping in the third volume (1927). Lloyd George's *War Memoirs*, published during the mid-1930s, was another major indictment of the generals. Beyond the haggling, reproaches, and recriminations among politicians and generals over the heavy toll of the war, there lay the same fundamental problem that preoccupied interwar Britain: the mass killing and economic devastation of the Great War increasingly came to be regarded as wholly out of step with the needs and sensibilities of the modern world; in case of a conflict, were there any strategic alternatives?

Crucially influenced by Fuller, Liddell Hart developed during the 1920s into a critic of the First World War. In contrast to Fuller, however, he became a staunch liberal, and was thus better positioned to articulate the political and strategic dilemma which the First World War starkly imposed on the consciousness of modern liberal-democratic societies. Aged 19 when the war started, Liddell Hart was a typical representative of the 'generation of 1914'. His intellectual development mirrored the development of that generation almost theme by theme.

[18] M. Ceadel, *Pacifism in Britain, 1914–1945* (Oxford, 1980).

Biographical

Basil Hart (he would add his mother's maiden name, Liddell, to his surname only in the early 1920s) was born in 1895. His father was a Wesleyan minister, and Basil had a typical upper-middle-class upbringing. He went to St Paul's and from there to Corpus Christi College, Cambridge, to read history. As a boy he was sensitive, a little awkward, and dreamy. His lifelong bent could already be seen in his youthful enthusiasm for games, aviation, and military history, on which he wrote both fiction and journalistic pieces with the passionate absorption and vivid imagination which would characterize his entire career. The war which broke out before the beginning of his second year in Cambridge interrupted his formal education, which he would never complete. Against his parents' wishes and with an enthusiasm his later autobiography does not fully betray, he joined the volunteers to Kitchener's New Armies. He received a temporary commission, trained with the University's OTC, and became a second lieutenant in the King's Own Yorkshire Light Infantry. As his early letters and notes reveal, he found training and army life most exciting, a feeling he never lost throughout the war.

His enthusiasm has been fully documented by his biographers. In a note of an almost archetypal nature, dated 28 November 1914, he wrote:

Before the war I, Basil Hart, was a Socialist, a Pacifist, an anti-conscriptionist and an anti-disciplinist, disapproving of all state checks on the liberty of the individual and one who hoped for internationalization. I held thinkers in greater admiration than warriors.

Now having studied the principles of warfare and undergone military training and seen the effects of it on my companions the following are my opinions:

1. I *believe* (i) in the supremacy of the aristocracy of race (and birth) (ii) in the supremacy of the individual.

2. In compulsory military service because it is the only possible life for a *man* and brings out all the finest qualities of manhood.

3. I have acquired rather a contempt for mere thinkers and men of books who have not come to full realisation of what true manhood means. . . .

4. I exalt the great general into the highest position in the roll of great men and consider it requires higher mental qualities than any other line of life.

5. I consider the Slavs, by which I indicate a greater Russia, will rule both Europe and Asia and will have world domination, being the finest and most virile civilisation and having the finest qualities of all races, and that the day of conquest and expansion is not yet over.

6. Socialism and its forms are an impossibility unless human nature radically alters.

. . .

8. Many of the German militarist ideas are sound, but I oppose the Germans because I do not consider that the German type of mind is the one to carry out their ideas.

I prefer brilliance to mechanical and methodical mediocracy. . . . I certainly believe that absolute peace is detrimental to true manhood, but 20th Century war is too frightful. If you could have war without its *explosive* horrors it would be a good thing. . . . My belief in the necessary inferiority of women is more profound than ever.[19]

Rather than a biographical curiosity, this highly revealing document deserves to be included in any anthology of the 'generation of 1914'. Here was a typical statement of a turn-of-the-century outlook which with obvious modifications could have been attributed to either of the Moltkes. However, in the background was a no less typical credo of nineteenth-century liberalism, swept aside in the enthusiasm of war but destined to return when this enthusiasm would fade away.

This was not to occur during the war. Liddell Hart arrived in France in late summer 1915 but was shortly after disabled by illness. Having pressed to return to the front, he was soon concussed by a German shell and sent home to convalesce. He returned to France in time to participate in the Somme offensive, was gassed in its third week, and was disabled again, this time for good. His writings at the time reveal not only exhilaration at his front-line experience but also naïve admiration for everything related to the British military performance, an uncritical adulation of the qualities of the British staff work, and a virtual worship of the British commanding generals.[20]

Later to become one of the most famous detractors of the experience of the First World War and the scourge of the British high command, Liddell Hart wrote before the Somme offensive: 'In the first half of the war our leadership was flawless, and it may be noted that our generalship, alone of all the nations engaged, was perfect.'[21] The ensuing battle caused no change in his opinion. Convalescing in England in September 1916, he wrote a little book entitled *Impressions of the*

[19] Liddell Hart Centre for Military Archives, King's College, London [King's], 7/1917/10; B. Bond, *Liddell Hart: A Study of His Military Thought* (London, 1977) [*LH*], 15–16.

[20] Hero-worship was prevalent among the 'generation of 1914'; for Wilfred Owen, see Parker, *Public-School Ethos*, 194.

[21] King's, 7/1916/21; the following has been fully documented in Bond, *LH*, 17–18; J. Mearsheimer, *Liddell Hart and the Weight of History* (London, 1988) [*LH*] 22–5; also, briefly, B. H. Liddell Hart, *The Memoirs of Captain Liddell Hart* (2 vols., London, 1965), i. 26.

Great British Offensive on the Somme. 'Wonderful' was probably the most recurring adjective in this enthusiastic book. In praising the preparations for the would-be notorious first day of the offensive, he wrote about 'the amazing perfection of our organization, which in generalship and work were super-German'. He maintained that 'the British G.H.Q. . . . under Haig's regime comprises the most brilliant collection of brains in the world . . . 90 percent of our general staff officers are really brilliant men, with quite a large number of men amongst them who have a genius for war'.[22] In summary he wrote:

War, at least modern war, as waged in the Western Front, is horrible and ghastly beyond all imagination of the civilian. Nevertheless it has an awe-inspiring grandeur of its own, and it ennobles and brings out the highest in a man's character such as no other thing could. Could one but remove the horrible suffering and mutilation it would be the finest purifier of nations ever known.[23]

In an early 1917 article for the *Saturday Review* Liddell Hart called civilian writers who had criticized the High Command 'armchair strategists', and argued that they failed to comprehend the nature of modern warfare.[24]

Medically unfit to return to front-line service, Liddell Hart was posted to a couple of clerical jobs before being assigned to train Volunteers, who at the decision of the War Office were being upgraded to take up the function of home defence from the Territorials, who had left for France. He performed this humble duty for the last year and a half of the war, and unwittingly it proved to be the springboard of his career. After 1916 the platoon replaced the company as the smallest independent combat unit, and there was much demand for clear directions and instructions for its drill.[25] Revealing a knack for devising, systematizing, and simplifying drill, Liddell Hart produced a number of

---

[22] King's, 7/1916/22, pp. 1, 76–85, 96. Liddell Hart's unreserved admiration for the high command can also be seen in his talk with John Buchan, who belonged to Haig's personal staff: King's, 7/1916/36.

[23] Ibid. 93. For reasons of field security the book was not authorized for publication, but Liddell Hart condensed its main arguments in an article entitled 'Great Generals of the War', published in the *Daily Express* on 21 Dec. 1916: King's, 7/1916/35.

[24] Note, King's, 7/1916/37; Liddell Hart, 'The Somme and Its Sequel': King's, 7/1917/5.

[25] See the testimony of the battle-experienced Graves, training regulars for France: *Goodbye to All That*, 304–5.

little manuals and booklets for the use of his men, which soon met with wider demand in other Volunteer units.[26]

This led to further developments after the war. In 1920, as he was struggling to stay in the army despite bad health, Liddell Hart won the patronage of General Sir Ivor Maxse, who had been inspector-general of training to the British armies in France during the later stage of the war and who was now the commander-in-chief, Northern Command. Maxse and his subordinate, Brigadier-General Winston Dugan, who had been appointed to compile the postwar infantry training manual, were favourably impressed by his work. They soon assigned him to work on the new manual which was to replace the obsolete prewar book. While getting rid of much outdated material and updating the manual in the light of the latest tactical developments of the war, Liddell Hart conceived his first contributions to infantry tactics (rather than to battle drill and methods of training). In the summer of 1920 he came up with some improvements to 'soft spots' tactics which the Allies had developed in 1918 in imitation of the famous German 'infiltration' tactics.[27] He called his improved methods of attack and defence in depth the 'expanding torrent' and 'contracting funnel' respectively.[28] Maxse and Dugan, both men of great experience in the subject who had been responsible for the training of the British armies in 'soft spots' tactics in the summer and autumn of 1918, examined his ideas and endorsed them as genuine improvements.[29] The ideas were incorporated in the new infantry training manual issued in 1921, which established Liddell Hart as an expert on infantry tactics.[30]

---

[26] Liddell Hart's numerous manuals and battle drills (King's, 7/1917; 7/1918) were compiled in his *Outline of the New Infantry Training*, later expanded and published as *New Method in Infantry Training* (Cambridge, 1918): King's, 7/1918/7; see also Liddell Hart, *Memoirs*, i. 28–33.

[27] See M. Samuels, *Doctrine and Dogma: German and British Infantry Tactics in the First World War* (New York, 1992), 7–110; P. Griffith, *Battle Tactics of the Western Front: The British Army's Art of Attack, 1916–18* (New Haven, Conn., 1994), 93–100.

[28] War Office, *Infantry Training* (1921), in King's, 7/1920; Liddell Hart, 'Memoranda of New Method and Developments of Method in Post-War Doctrine of the Army (as Embodied in 'Infantry Training') which originated with the present writer—B. H. Liddell Hart': King's, 7/1920/163; 'Autobiography' (1920–1), 17: King's, 7/1920/38; *Memoirs*, i. 43–5.

[29] Bond, *LH*, 26 and n. 29, is much closer here to the truth than Mearsheimer, *LH*, 31–2; Liddell Hart did not merely plagiarize 'infiltration' or 'soft spot' tactics, which had already been commonly known and used in the British army since 1918.

[30] Liddell Hart's lectures to the Royal United Service Institution were published as *The Framework of a Science of Infantry Tactics* (London, 1922; expanded and reissued 1923, 1926). His articles on infantry tactics appeared in British, American, Canadian, and Belgian military journals. His review of the French postwar *Réglement d'infanterie* was

But infantry tactics was only one direction in which Liddell Hart's ideas were developing. His preoccupation with training and battle drill led him to reflect upon the principles which supposedly underlay all combat activity. Stimulated by reading Foch and Colin, 'this course of thought led me to the conclusion that, on all levels, success depended on achieving a compound of "fixing, manœuvre and exploitation".'[31] This conception, which Liddell Hart termed the 'Man-in-the-Dark theory of war', is not to be confused with his infantry doctrines *per se*. Rather, it was his first, crude attempt to formulate a general theory of war.[32] At exactly that stage he made the acquaintance of Fuller, 'the greatest intellectual power I have ever come across, a titan among minnows',[33] whose influence upon Liddell Hart was overwhelming.

Liddell Hart initiated the relationship in late May or early June 1920, and it was not in connection with Fuller's expertise in the employment of tanks. This aspect of the relationship only came later. Having become aware of Fuller's lectures and articles on the principles of war, Liddell Hart sent him his *National Review* article on the 'Man-in-the-Dark' theory of war. Little impressed by what he read, Fuller reciprocated by sending a copy of his own work on the principles of war. Liddell Hart was deeply impressed. He described Fuller's work as the 'dawn of a new era in military thought'. His own rudimentary interests were stimulated and lifted to new heights by the comparatively awesome sophistication of Fuller's ideas on the science of war. On Liddell Hart's initiative, they soon met.[34]

All this helps to explain later and otherwise obscure traits of Liddell Hart's work. In the early 1920s, apart from his preoccupation first with infantry and later with armoured tactics, he was absorbed in the attempt to formulate a comprehensive theory or science of war, mostly based on

published in the *Revue Militaire Générale*. In Maxse's name he composed the greater part of the article on infantry for the *Encyclopaedia Britannica*. All in King's, 7/1919/12.

[31] *Memoirs*, i. 37–8; cf. Liddell Hart to Scammell, 1 June 1921: King's, 1/622; Liddell Hart to Fuller, 16 June 1922: King's, 1/302; 'Autobiography' (1920–1), 18: King's, 7/1928/38.

[32] See esp. 'The "Man-In-The-Dark" Theory of War: The Essential Principles of Fighting Simplified and Crystallized into a Definite Formula', *National Review* (June 1920), 473–84. The concept was integrated into other articles he wrote that year. See also 'Autobiography' (King's, 7/1928/38), 18.

[33] Liddell Hart to Scammell, 22 Feb. 1922: King's, 1/622.

[34] Fuller to LH, 7, 10 June 1920; LH to Fuller, 14 June 1920: King's, 1/302; also 7/1920/35.

Fuller's principles.[35] Partly for this reason he hailed Fuller's *The Reformation of War* as 'the book of the century',[36] and had a high regard for Fuller's much-criticized and often-ridiculed *The Foundations of the Science of War*. At that stage Liddell Hart still held Foch, whose principles had provided the initial inspiration for both Fuller and himself, in great esteem as a scientific soldier.[37] Liddell Hart outgrew his preoccupation with the principles of war in the mid-1920, and when he returned to them later it would be in a different, lighter and more sophisticated spirit.[38] But his rhetoric about the science of war, familiar to readers of his later works, remained, and so did his strong belief in a 'scientific' study of war which, as commentators have observed, characterized his 'social scientist' approach to history.[39]

There was another legacy of this phase of Liddell Hart's life. While he had entertained youthful dreams of grandeur, his innovations in infantry tactics and especially his preoccupation with the theory of war convinced him, in a way not uncommon for self-taught men discovering and walking the heights of abstract thought, that he was destined to become a great man. He was now filled with enormous pride and sense of superiority. From now on he would always have 'one eye on the future historian'.[40] In 1920-1 he wrote 13,000 words of

[35] This was the main subject of his extensive exchange of letters with his two major correspondents at the time, Fuller and Capt. J. M. Scammell of the American army, a student of Spenser Wilkinson, the Chichele Professor of Military History at Oxford: King's, 7/1921/69; Liddell Hart to Scammell, 1 June 1921: 1/622. In 1921 LH began working on a book-length MS, 'A Framework of War Founded on Man', which proved, however, beyond his capabilities at the time. See also L. V. Bond, 'The Tactical Theories of Captain Liddell Hart (A Criticism)', *Royal Engineers Journal* (Sept. 1922), 153–63; Liddell Hart, 'Colonel Bond's Criticism: A Reply', ibid. (Nov. 1922), 297–309.

[36] Liddell Hart to Scammell, 22 Feb. 1923: King's, 1/622.

[37] LH to Fuller, 16 Jan. 1922: King's, 1/302; 'Bardell' [Liddell Hart], 'Study and Reflection vs. Practical Experience', *Army Quarterly* (1923), 327; Scammell to Liddell Hart, 13 Jan. 1923: 1/622. Here also lay the root of his lifelong admiration for de Saxe. It did not stem only from the latter's renunciation of the need for battle but, echoing Fuller, was due to de Saxe's famous plea for a theory of war; J. F. C. Fuller, *The Reformation of War* (London, 1923), 24, 76; *The Foundations of the Science of War* (London, 1926), 24–5. Liddell Hart's article on de Saxe in *Blackwood's Magazine* (Aug. 1924), 143–60, was later incorporated in *Great Captains Unveiled* (London, 1927), 35–74, and, only slightly altered, in *The Ghost of Napoleon* (New Haven, Conn., 1934), 32–49.

[38] Liddell Hart, 'The Essence of War', *RUSI Journal* (Aug. 1930), incorporated in the subsequent editions of *Strategy of the Indirect Approach*.

[39] Mearsheimer, *LH*, 10. None the less, when hard-core scientism in the shape of American social sciences and game theory entered the field of strategic studies in the nuclear age, Liddell Hart found the new techniques and jargon baffling: Bond, *LH*, 211–12; L. Freedman, *The Evolution of Nuclear Strategy* (London, 1981), 307–8.

[40] King's, 7/1920/32.

'Notes for an Autobiography', outlining his background and development and detailing his achievements: his new tactical theory, new systems of infantry attack and defence, new battle drill, and 76 [*sic*] lesser new ideas incorporated in the infantry training manual.[41] Henceforth and for the rest of his life the record was stringently maintained in diary notes, memoranda, and periodical summaries of achievements on round dates, testifying to his amazing sense of superiority and craving for greatness.[42]

In the early 1920s Fuller influenced Liddell Hart decisively in respect to two subjects even more important than the principles and science of war. These were mechanization and the rejection of total war and the strategy of destruction, which will be discussed below. Correspondingly, under Fuller's direct influence and reflecting the growing doubts among the British public as a whole, came a change in Liddell Hart's attitude to the Great War and the generals who had conducted it. In 1920 or 1921 he had already noted 'How my hero-worship of 'generals' waned and disillusionment began, through close contact with the *best* of them—and finding their lack of fresh ideas—how they depended on a novice like me to show them the lessons of the war'.[43] In 1922, in a private memorandum composed in the wake of a public debate concerning Haig, Liddell Hart wrote that the fact that Haig had been an exponent of attrition in itself disqualified him from the list of great captains, whose distinctive mark was the use of surprise. He cited Fuller's 'Plan 1919' as an example of an alternative, imaginative way to have won the war.[44] By 1924 his change of attitude to the war had taken its familiar shape: 'A victory which has left us so crippled as a nation can hardly be regarded with complete satisfaction and is at least an incentive to inquire whether victory could have been hastened.'[45]

---

[41] King's, 7/1920/38, esp. p. 17; see also 'The Ideas Which I Invented during 1920, and Which I Wrote in Infantry Training 1920': 7/1920/164; 12/1920/165; 7/1921/68; 7/1922/21. Cf. Bond, *LH*, 31–2.

[42] See Liddell Hart's papers, sect. 11, including two autobiographies: King's, 11/1930/41, 11/1931/27.   [43] Cited without reference in Bond, *LH*, 20.

[44] Liddell Hart, 'Surprise v. Attrition', King's, 7/1922/26.

[45] Liddell Hart, *Army Quarterly* (Apr. 1924), 8.

3

Theory: Limited War, Moderate Peace, and the Strategy of Indirect Approach

Turning Military Theory Upside Down; Redrawing the Map of the Past

In 1923 Fuller published his first great book, *The Reformation of War*, in which he propounded the ideas which would become central to his entire thought. Echoing Keynes, he argued that the Great War

> was based on a gigantic misconception of the true purpose of war, which is to enforce the policy of a nation *at the least cost to itself and to the enemy* and, consequently, to the world, for so intricately are the resources of civilized states interwoven that to destroy any one country is simultaneously to wound all other nations.[1]

Militarily, he wrote,

> Ever since 1866 and 1870, the eyes of the General Staffs of Europe had been blinded by the brilliance of von Moltke's strategy. Soldiers had gazed on the bayonet points of Sadowa and Sedan until they were hypnotized by these great battles, and . . . dreamt of the next war as an immense 1870 operation involving unlimited slaughter. Their doctrine was founded on two tremendous fallacies. First, that policy is best enforced by destruction; secondly, that military perfection is based on numbers of soldiers.[2]

Both notions had been fallacious, claimed Fuller, because they had been rooted in a misapprehension of the nature of modern war. In the age of the internal-combustion engine, human masses had become insignificant in comparison with technological advance and technical perfection. The physical epoch had come to an end; the moral epoch was dawning. There was no longer a need literally to destroy the enemy's armies in the field, as the Allies had tried to do during the war. Aircraft using gas would disable, demoralize, and paralyse unarmoured troops,

---

[1] *The Reformation of War* (London, 1923), 75; italics in the original. Keynes's notion of a 'Carthaginian Peace' would from now on be constantly cited by Fuller.　　[2] Ibid.

surface ships, and civilian populations and infrastructures alike. Armoured forces would paralyse, demoralize, and cause the disintegration of armies by striking at their rear communications and command system in the manner Fuller had suggested by the end of the Great War in his so-called 'Plan 1919'.[3] Politically, with slaughter and destruction reduced, war would become both more humane and more rational: 'To destroy a nation is to destroy the very objective of peace; consequently, the less destruction the more complete to the winner is the victory.' 'In the future, wars will be looked upon as a means of creating a better peace and not as a means of bruising a worn-out one.'[4]

The brilliant and prophetic as well as the fanciful aspects of these ideas are obvious, and are not our concern here. The point is that they are generally associated more with Liddell Hart than with Fuller. *The Reformation of War*, 'the book of the century' in Liddell Hart's words, was the most important influence on Liddell Hart's intellectual development, determining and shaping his view of war for life. So profoundly impressed was he with the book that he simply plagiarized it almost lock, stock, and barrel in his own first important book, *Paris, or the Future of War* (1925).

This little book represents a quantum leap in Liddell Hart's writing, incomparable both in content and style with his earlier work. In a nutshell it contains all the leading ideas and historical themes that he would develop in the following years in a succession of books: *Scipio* (1926), *The Remaking of Modern Armies* (1927), *Sherman* (1929), *The Decisive Wars of History* (1929) (later *Strategy: The Indirect Approach*), *Foch* (1931), and *The Ghost of Napoleon* (1933). The writing reveals all the stylistic traits which would become his trade mark; having previously been tepid and rather undistinguished in tone, it now all of a sudden becomes brisk, compelling, supremely confident, highly provocative, and iconoclastic—all to an even larger degree than in his more mature works. There were two main reasons for this change. Liddell Hart had been invalided out of the army in 1924 and was beginning his career as a journalist, first on an occasional basis in the *Morning Post* and then, from 1925 on, as the military correspondent of the *Daily Telegraph*. Thus he was now free from military authority and from the judgement of the editors of the military periodicals, and was addressing and catering to the taste of the wider general public. Simultaneously, he

---

[3] Ibid. 102–88.   [4] Ibid. 107–8, 144, 188, and *passim*.

had been making great strides in his self-education in military history and theory. In the first half of the 1920s he developed from a humble infantry tactician entertaining dreams of glory to a dazzling, soon to be world-famous strategic thinker. There were four main influences on the development of his outlook, all of which he failed to acknowledge, with the result that they have remained undetected by historians. As mentioned, Fuller's was the primary one, and Liddell Hart's development and characteristic ideas are simply unimaginable without it. One is almost tempted to say that he sprang fully armed from Fuller's brow.

Fuller's irreverent, sweeping, and dazzling style undoubtedly set the model which the young Liddell Hart strove to emulate, though in a simplified, more popular, and more accessible form. He was also influenced decisively by Fuller's scathing criticism of the British high command and of the conduct of the First World War. By 1925 this criticism corresponded to the growing change of perspective in viewing the war and its outcome among educated public opinion in general. 'The Great War', wrote Liddell Hart,

caused the direct sacrifice of eight million lives, to which the British Isles alone contributed three-quarters of a million. So ineffectual was the treatment prescribed by the military practitioners who were called in that the illness took over four years to run its course, during which the financial temperature mounted daily, until for this country alone it reached a cost of £8,000,000 a day. Our total war expenditure was nearly ten thousand million pounds; our National Debt has been increased tenfold. Moreover, these long years of strain and want so impaired the physical health of the peoples that they fell an easy prey to epidemic diseases, and the influenza scourge of 1918 and 1919 cost, among the civilian population of the world, more than twice as many lives as were lost in battle. It is surely clear that any further wars conducted on similar methods must mean the breakdown of Western civilization . . . in these post-war years of disillusionment . . . we are justified, standing amid the *débris*, in questioning the strategic aim and direction of the war . . . it was the destruction of the enemy's armed forces in the main theatre of war.[5]

Both Fuller and Liddell Hart rejected pacifism and did not believe in the power of formal agreements to eliminate war. In a brilliant anthropological–metaphysical tract in *The Reformation of War*, Fuller, the social Darwinist, explained how war was rooted in human nature and was an inherent and indispensable part of human evolution.[6] The young

---

[5] *Paris, or the Future of War* (London, 1925), 9–10, 12.
[6] *The Reformation of War*, pp. xi, 6–23, 56–74, 256–83.

Liddell Hart, whose interests and passionate preoccupation were still almost strictly military, dismissed the whole question with little speculation.[7] His conclusion was Fullerite:

Should a millennium of Universal Peace fail to arrive, and nations still continue to settle by an appeal to force questions which vitally affect their policy, it may be that they will learn to wage war in a manner less injurious to the interwoven fabric of modern civilization, and incidentally to their own prosperity and ultimate security, than proved the case in the Great War of 1914–1918.[8]

The national objective in war must 'ensure a resumption and progressive continuance of what may be termed the peace time policy, with the shortest and least costly interruption of the normal life of the country'.[9] 'A statue of General Sherman in Washington bears this inscription: "the legitimate object of war is a more perfect peace."' Truer still, 'a more perfect peace is the only *rational* object of war.'[10]

The conduct of war itself should aim at the 'moral objective' [Fuller's] and undermine rather than literally destroy the enemy. Liddell Hart's portrayal of future warfare, in the air, on land, and at sea, was Fullerite through and through. Air power using the humane and non-destructive gas would dominate war, overwhelming in a very short period the enemy's civilian rear as well as immobilizing the obsolete mass armies. Concentrated armoured forces would travel the countryside, operating against the enemy's command and communications, his 'nerve system', in the manner Fuller had suggested in 1918. In the naval arena it would seem that, at least in closed seas, the aircraft and the submarine would displace the battleship.[11]

This was Fuller almost to the letter, yet only a couple of historians have noted this briefly. As one of them has written: 'the similarity in the approach, content and style of Fuller's *The Reformation of War* and Liddell Hart's *Paris* is striking though rarely remarked upon.'[12] To remove any doubt, this was not a case of ideas developed conjointly; nor do we have here two lines of thought running parallel, as Liddell Hart would sometimes claim in later years.[13] A comparative examination

---

[7] *Paris*, 7–9.   [8] Ibid. 22.   [9] Ibid. 25.   [10] Ibid. 91–2.
[11] Ibid. 41–89; the reference to 'Plan 1919' (pp. 82–3) is the only direct citation from Fuller. More fully on Fuller's influence and Liddell Hart's subsequent development in respect to armour doctrine see my 'Liddell Hart's Theory of Armoured Warfare: Revising the Revionists', *Journal of Strategic Studies*, 19 (1996), 1–30.
[12] B. H. Reid, *J. F. C. Fuller: Military Thinker* (London, 1987), 225; also M. Carver, *The Apostles of Mobility* (London, 1979), 43–4.
[13] See e.g. his briefing of John Wheldon, *Machine Age Armies* (London, 1968), 33–8.

of the development of Fuller and Liddell Hart respectively clearly reveals that the ideas which Fuller had developed by the early 1920s—not only regarding armoured warfare but in many other respects, including his fundamental approach to the questions of the conduct and aim of war in view of the subsequent peace—came as a revelation to the young and impressionable Liddell Hart, who made them his own. As we shall have the occasion to see, this was a pattern that would recur for years to come. Innumerable ideas used by Liddell Hart had originated in Fuller's works. Yet, although Liddell Hart's writings from the early and mid-1920 abound in references to Fuller's genius, he never acknowledged his heavy debts. Furthermore, from the late 1920s, with his own abilities and fame growing, he no longer assumed in public or in private a subordinate role to Fuller, as he had done earlier, and his attitude towards Fuller even assumed an aspect of Freudian patricide. Bearing this in mind, notwithstanding the well-documented frictions between them, Fuller behaved in an almost saintly manner. It has been pointed out that, in contrast to Liddell Hart, he showed little active preoccupation with his own reputation.[14] To know what he really thought, however, one should adopt the effective method of paying attention to his wife, the infamous Sonia, who in an angry exchange with Mrs Liddell Hart accused Liddell Hart of building his fame on her husband's ideas.[15]

Yet there were other major influences and major themes which, on the basis of Fuller's fundamental approach, went to shape Liddell Hart's evolving outlook in *Paris* and ever after. Following up on Fuller's criticism of the prewar faith in total war of destruction, Liddell Hart went beyond the Prussian model of 1866 and 1871. In this he was able to build upon three important contributions to modern military thought, which he adopted, synthesized, radicalized even beyond their originally radical thrust, expanded, and applied to reverse completely both the military theory and the picture of the past of the nineteenth century. Of these contributions, two had been well recognized but were somewhat out of the main-stream, while the third was new and sensational but fairly obscure. The first was the prominent French neo-Napoleonic school of the late nineteenth and early twentieth centuries, with its learned unravelling of the origins and nature of Napoleonic

---

[14] J. Mearsheimer, *Liddell Hart and the Weight of History* (London, 1988) [*LH*], 212.
[15] Liddell Hart to Fuller, 11 Mar. 1928, Liddell Hart Centre for Military Archives, King's College, London [King's], 1/302.

strategy and its comprehensive criticism of Clausewitz's interpretation of that strategy. The other two were Julian Corbett's rejection in the early twentieth century of the strategy of annihilation and its emphasis on the decisive battle, which Liddell Hart adapted from sea to land; and T. E. Lawrence's remarkably similar theorizing, which Liddell Hart expanded beyond its original desert guerrilla setting.

The French neo-Napoleonic school, though only hazily familiar to historians, has usually received a very mixed press.[16] Attitudes are always context-related, and, not wholly deservedly, the school's image has been associated with the growth of the disastrous doctrine of the *offensive à outrance* which almost ruined the French army, and France, in the opening phase of the First World War. Of French military studies of the period, only Jean Colin's scholarly researches on the origins of French revolutionary and Napoleonic warfare are widely recognized and held in esteem by modern historians. But Colin was merely taking part in, and building upon, the achievements of a much wider enterprise which had been central to French military thought since the mid-1880s. Stimulated by German military theory and relying on Napoleon's huge correspondence and on much other archival material, both unavailable to earlier commentators, L. Maillard, Édouard Pierron, Auguste Grouard and, especially, Henri Bonnal and Hubert Camon laid the foundations for a much deeper and fuller understanding of Napoleon's generalship and system of operations than had been offered by Jomini's seminal and penetrating analysis during the emperor's own time.[17] The few modern studies of the Napoleonic art of operations rely heavily on the work of the French school, most notably on Camon's illuminating analytical schemes.[18]

Liddell Hart's own familiarity with the authors and works of the pre-war French military school was fairly superficial even by the time he wrote *Foch* (1931). It is doubtful if he ever really read even the works of Henri Bonnal, the leading French military theorist of the period.[19] He

---

[16] For the following, see A. Gat, *The Development of Military Thought: The Nineteenth Century* (Oxford, 1992), ch. 3, esp. pp. 122–8.

[17] Cf. J. Colin's assessment, *Les Transformations de la guerre* (Paris, 1916), 253.

[18] See esp. H. Camon, *La Guerre napoléonienne* (5 vols., Paris, 1907–11), and *Le Systéme de guerre de Napolèon* (Paris, 1923); cf. D. Chandler, *The Campaigns of Napoleon* (London, 1966).

[19] The relevant sections from *Foch* were reproduced as 'French Military Ideas before the First World War', in M. Gilbert (ed.), *A Century of Conflict, 1850–1950* (London, 1966), 135–48. They were based mainly on the devastating revelations during the 1920s of Émile Mayer, with whom Liddell Hart corresponded. It should be noted, however, that

was well acquainted, however, with Camon's works, at least by the late 1920s.[20] More importantly, during the early 1920s he repeatedly referred to Colin's books, which were his chief guides to modern military history and theory. In them he could find a scholarly summary of the findings and conclusions of the French neo-Napoleonic school. Dissecting Napoleon's campaigns, Maillard and after him Bonnal laid bare the features and qualities of the emperor's strategy.[21] They emphasized his clear determination of the decisive point and line of advance, resolute and carefully coordinated marches, and rapid concentration of all forces to overwhelm the enemy. Equally, however, they highlighted the flexibility of his operational formation, the so-called *bataillon carré*, loosely dispersed until the last moment, and maintaining its freedom of action to operate and strike in all directions. Colin, developing Pierron's earlier study, showed how this mode of operation, suggested in the middle of the eighteenth century by Pierre de Bourcet, one of the authorities who had shaped the young Bonaparte's military education, had helped to leave the enemy in the dark, and guessing, regarding Napoleon's intentions and ultimate line of attack; the pattern, he stressed, had been dispersion and only then concentration, with each of Napoleon's operational plans having 'many branches', or alternative options.[22] Bonnal, more than anyone else before him, brought to light the imaginative qualities of Napoleon's genius: his mastery of decep-

much earlier he had already been aware, for example, of the distinction which has been lost in many later history books: 'the division in France in pre-war days lay between the school of Foch, Bonnal and Langlois and the modern school of Grandmaison which was adopted by the French General Staff to their cost': Liddell Hart to Scammell, 22 Feb. 1923, King's, 1/622.

[20] Both Wilkinson and Scammell detected the influence of Colin and the French school on Liddell Hart's Strategy: Wilkinson to Liddell Hart 28 Dec. 1928, King's, 1/748; Scammell to Liddell Hart, 11 Feb. 1930, 1/622. Liddell Hart admitted the similarity of his ideas to Camon's: *Army Quarterly* (Jan. 1928), 401; also Liddell Hart to Scammell, 4 Apr. 1933, King's, 1/622.

[21] The following is based on my *The Development of Military Thought: The Nineteenth Century*, 126–7. See L. Maillard, *Éléments de la guerre* (Paris, 1891), pp. x–xv, 3; H. Bonnal, *De Rosbach à Ulm* (Paris, 1903), *La Manœuvre d'Iéna 1806* (Paris, 1904), *La Manœuvre de Landshut, 1808–1809* (Paris, 1905), *La Manœuvre de Vilna, 1811–1812* (Paris, 1905).

[22] É. Pierron, *Comment s'est formé le génie militaire de Napoléon Ier?* (Paris, 1889); Liddell Hart was familiar with the work: *The Ghost of Napoleon* (New Haven, Conn., 1934), 191; J. Colin, *L'Éducation militaire de Napoléon* (Paris, 1900), 93–6; *Transformations de la guerre*, 206 ff., 221–2, English trans. *The Transformation of War* (London, 1912), 241–50, 259–60. Colin was digested by S. Wilkinson, *The French Army before Napoleon* (Oxford, 1915), 37–8, 144–51; also see *The Defence of Piedmont, 1742–1748* (Oxford, 1927), 158, 176; *The Rise of General Bonaparte* (Oxford, 1930).

tion, feints, and diversions to create surprise, disorientation, and mis-calculation on the enemy's part.

Thus, it is hardly surprising that Bonnal and his friends found Clausewitz's perception of Napoleonic strategy curiously crude and, in some respects, totally inadequate. Present-day historians, expressing uncritical reverence for Clausewitz, have tended to dismiss this affront to the great philosopher of war as nothing more than an expression of French chauvinism and wounded national pride. But although there is certainly a great deal of patriotic zeal in much of the French writings, this is totally beside the point. The French perceived very accurately that in viewing Napoleon's strategy from distant and defeated Prussia, Clausewitz had been primarily impressed by its immense energy, bold-ness, and decisiveness. Fiercely reacting against the old 'strategy of manœuvre', he had portrayed Napoleonic strategy as extremely direct and vigorously simple, and had missed a great deal of its subtlety of conception and manœuvre. They pointed out that, while it was true that Napoleon had always sought the great battle, he had never been as direct in going about it as Clausewitz had imagined. They were astonished by Clausewitz's assertion that 'Napoleon never engaged in strategic envelopment',[23] citing the many instances of Napoleon's *manœuvre sur les derrières*, the manœuvre against the enemy's rear, one of the most fundamental patterns of Napoleonic strategy. This had been the pattern which had underpinned the Marengo, Ulm, and Jena campaigns, to name only some of the most famous examples.[24]

It was these important ideas that Liddell Hart popularized, in both senses of the word, and forged into a weapon against nineteenth-century, Prussian-dominated military theory.[25] All-out war of destruc-tion and the obsession with numbers, he argued, may have originated with Napoleon. But the main culprit had been his great and influential codifier, Clausewitz, whose interpretation of Napoleon had highlighted

---

[23] *Principles of War* (Harrisburg, Penn., 1942), 49.

[24] L. Rousset (ed.), *Les Maîtres de la guerre Frédérick II, Napoléon, Moltke, d'après des travaux inédits de M le général Bonnal* (Paris, 1899), 226–7; H. Bonnal, *De la méthode dans les hautes études militaires en Allemagne et en France* (Paris, 1902), 10–11; H. Camon, *Clausewitz* (Paris, 1911); and, echoing them, Colin, *The Transformation of War*, 298–300. Cf. my *The Origins of Military Thought from the Enlightenment to Clausewitz* (Oxford, 1989), 206–9.

[25] The first three, virtually identical formulations are 'The Napoleonic Fallacy', *Empire Review* (May 1925), 510–22, King's, 7/1924/2–5; *Paris, or the Future of War* (London, 1925), 13–22; *The Remaking of Modern Armies* (London, 1927), 88–112; and repeatedly thereafter.

only crude concentration of mass and the direct, brute, and bloody clash of forces, to the neglect of all other elements of Napoleonic warfare. Clausewitz had been 'the Mahdi of mass and mutual massacre'; 'the generals of this last half century [had become] intoxicated with the blood-red wine of Clausewitzian growth'.[26] Indeed, in the same way as Clausewitz, the disciple, had been more to blame then Napoleon, his master, Clausewitz's own disciples, such as Foch, whom Liddell Hart took as typifying pre-First World War military theory, had become 'an amplifier for Clausewitz's more extreme notes'.[27] Unable to follow his complex logic and manner of speculation, they had caught only his bellicose catch-phrases and had missed his more subtle qualifying statements.[28]

The lever which enabled Liddell Hart to turn the French criticism of Clausewitz's interpretation of Napoleon into a much more sweeping and radical attack on the tenets of nineteenth-century military theory came, however, from a different source. This was T. E. Lawrence's chapters in his post-war *Seven Pillars of Wisdom* on the evolution of his military thought before and during his Arabian campaign. In this remarkable work one reads:

In military theory I was tolerably read, my Oxford curiosity having taken me past Napoleon to Clausewitz and his school, to Caemmerer and Moltke, and the recent Frenchmen. They had all seemed to be one-sided; and after looking at Jomini and Willisen, I had found broader principles in Saxe and Guibert and the eighteenth century. . . . I began to drum out the aim in war. The books gave it pat—the destruction of the armed forces of the enemy by the one process—battle. Victory could be purchased only by blood.

This, realized Lawrence, would not do for the Arab irregulars fighting the stronger Turks:

[I] was left . . . to find an alternative end and means of war. Ours seemed unlike the ritual of which Foch was priest. . . . In his modern war—absolute war he called it—two nations professing incompatible philosophies put them to the test of force. Philosophically it was idiotic . . . It sounded like a twentieth-century restatement of the wars of religion, whose logical end was utter destruction of one creed . . . This might do for France and Germany, but would not represent the British attitude. . . . [Moreover] such war depended on levy in mass, and

---

[26] *The Ghost of Napoleon* 120, 21. [27] Ibid. 133.
[28] Paris, 17–18; *The Ghost of Napoleon*, 123–6; *Strategy: The Indirect Approach* (London, 1954), 352–7. But perhaps the best statement of the argument is in *The British Way in Warfare* (London, 1931), 17–25.

was impossible with professional armies; while the old army was still the British ideal. . . . [In addition] Battles in Arabia were a mistake . . . Napoleon had said it was rare to find generals willing to fight battles; but the curse of this war was that so few would do anything else. Saxe had told us that irrational battles were the refuges of fools. . . .

In character our operations of development for the final stroke should be like naval war, in mobility, ubiquity, independence of bases and communications, ignoring of ground features, of strategic areas, of fixed directions, of fixed points. . . . Our tactics should be tip and run: not pushes but strokes. We should never try to improve an advantage. We should use the smallest force in the quickest time at the farthest place.[29]

Anyone who has ever read Liddell Hart would not fail to recognize these ideas, but they have never been traced to Lawrence and his writings. The story of the connection here requires some detective work, and (as is usually the case) Liddell Hart's own archive provides the most significant clues.

Lawrence's *Seven Pillars of Wisdom* was printed in early 1922 at the Oxford University Press, but only a handful of copies for private distribution were produced. A limited subscribers' edition appeared in 1926 but, because of Lawrence's whims, the book was not offered to the general public until 1935, after his death. Only a concise adaptation, entitled *Revolt in the Desert*, was published in 1927. However, invited to contribute an article, 'The Evolution of a Revolt', to the first issue of the *Army Quarterly* (Oct. 1920), Lawrence stitched together the two chapters from the manuscript of *Seven Pillars* dealing with his military ideas.[30] It was this article that the young Liddell Hart read when it appeared and, indeed, wrote to Lawrence about.[31] Coming as it did in conjunction with Fuller's influence and with Liddell Hart's studies of Colin's works, Lawrence's article inspired Liddell Hart's reversal of attitude to eighteenth- and nineteenth-century military thought. For, as Lawrence would later write to him: 'To provoke the

---

[29] *The Seven Pillars of Wisdom* (New York, 1936), 188–90, 196, 337.

[30] For the previously cited passages, see with some variations, T. E. Lawrence, 'The Evolution of A Revolt', *Army Quarterly*, 1 (Oct. 1920), 57–9, 64, 68. The same issue printed Fuller's 'The Foundations of the Science of War'.

[31] This first brief exchange of letters is mentioned but not included both in the printed edition of Lawrence's letters to Liddell Hart, which the latter edited, *T. E. Lawrence to his Biographer Liddell Hart* (London, 1939), 1, and in B. H. Liddell Hart, *Memoirs* (2 vols., London, 1965), i. 84. Nor is Liddell Hart's first letter to be found in his archive. However, Lawrence's reply does exist in the archive (7 July 1921, King's, 9/13/20), indicating that Liddell Hart had sent him for comment the work on principles of war with which he had then been preoccupied.

soldiers to battle on my own ground I kept on limiting what I said to irregular warfare.' But, 'for 'irregular war' you could write 'War of movement' in nearly every place, and find the argument fitted as well or ill as it did.'[32]

When in 1927 Liddell Hart, then military editor of the *Encyclopaedia Britannica*, again made contact with Lawrence to request an article on guerrilla warfare, he himself, assuming correctly that Lawrence would be reluctant to write one, raised the possibility that an adaptation of Lawrence's 1920 *Army Quarterly* article might be used. Lawrence accepted the suggestion, informing Liddell Hart that the article was in fact based on two chapters from *Seven Pillars* and advising him from whom that rare book could be obtained.[33] This was the beginning of a close friendship which lasted until Lawrence's death.

Liddell Hart cherished this friendship deeply, and not only for its snob appeal—Lawrence was a living legend, Britain's only post-war superhero. He admired Lawrence unreservedly and became his biographer, showering acclaim on his genius as a man of action and thought. However, not unlike his behaviour in Fuller's case, he pretended it was a mere coincidence that his ideas resembled so closely what Lawrence had written before.[34] Apart from the texts themselves, only Liddell Hart's voluntary references in 1921 and 1927 to Lawrence's 1920 article betray the true story. Other people, unfamiliar with Lawrence's *Seven Pillars*, were unlikely to notice; interestingly enough, not even Lawrence realized the actual sequence of events. Unlike Liddell Hart he did not keep a record of their correspondence over the years; indeed, he did not even possess a copy of *Seven Pillars* or of his 1920 article![35] As he repeatedly confessed, he had left his military interests, and his past, behind him as he moved on to new preoccupations. Thus, by 1932, after reading Liddell Hart's essay on the theory of strategy, he innocently wrote to the author: 'I may overestimate the goodness and value of your book because it hits my tender spot. In the Seven Pillars I wrote a chapter on theory, which was an expression in terms of Arabia, of very much of what you argue about the aim of war.'[36] Similarly, having read

---

[32] Lawrence to Liddell Hart, 17 Oct. 1928, in *Lawrence to Liddell Hart*, 3–4.
[33] Apart from the texts themselves, see Lawrence to Liddell Hart, 25 Oct. 1927, ibid. 1–3.   [34] '*T. E. Lawrence*': *In Arabia and After* (London, 1934), 164–75, 438–40.
[35] Lawrence to Liddell Hart, 25 Oct. 1927, in *Lawrence to Liddell Hart*, 2.
[36] Lawrence to Liddell Hart, 30 Aug. 1932, ibid. 49; the essay, 'Strategy Reframed', in *The British Way in Warfare*, was previously published in *The Decisive Wars of History* (London, 1929) later *Strategy: The Indirect Approach* (London, 1941).

The Ghost of Napoleon, he wrote to Liddell Hart: 'It has been a queer experience—like going back, in memory, to school—for by myself (though with far less knowledge, and hesitatingly) I had trodden all this road before the war.'[37] Liddell Hart officially dedicated the book 'To "T. E." who trod this road before 1914', but never hinted he had been following Lawrence's headlights.[38]

In some crucial respects Lawrence's ideas paralleled another, much greater, strategic theoretical edifice which also challenged the sacred tenet prescribing as the sole legitimate aim of war the destruction of the enemy's main armed forces in a major battle. This was Julian Corbett's thoroughgoing revision of strategic theory, culminating in his *Some Principles of Maritime Strategy* (1911). As with Lawrence's guerrilla doctrines, this book, notwithstanding its special subject, took much of its inspiration from military theory, claimed at least partial validity for all branches of war, and could thus be applied back from sea to land.

Historians have noted similarities, affinities, *and* differences between some of Corbett's ideas and Liddell Hart's conception of 'The British Way in Warfare'.[39] But since, to the best of my knowledge, Liddell Hart never cited Corbett's name or work, it has not been detected how directly and decisively he was influenced by Corbett, and in much more than the doctrine mentioned above, about which Liddell Hart diverged from as much as concurred with Corbett's argument. Corbett died in 1922 as Britain's most distinguished naval theorist and amid a controversy surrounding the publication of the official British naval history of the First World War which he had written. One may assume that Liddell Hart became acquainted with his work at that time, so crucial in his development, and it fitted in brilliantly with the influences of Fuller, Colin, and Lawrence. No 'smoking gun' for the Corbett–Liddell Hart connection can be produced. But from 1924–5 on Liddell Hart's work betrays the unmistakable and distinctive mark of Corbett's ideas.

Again, although generally treated with respect, Corbett's work has

---

[37] Lawrence to Liddell Hart, in 1933, *Lawrence to Liddell Hart*, 132. Understandably, therefore, while noting the similarity of ideas between Lawrence and Liddell Hart, Brian Holden Reid missed its source: 'T. E. Lawrence and Liddell Hart', *History*, 70 (1985), 218–31; also 'T. E. Lawrence and his Biographers', in B. Bond (ed.), *The First World War and British Military History* (Oxford, 1991), 227–59.

[38] Lawrence to Liddell Hart, 30 July 1933, ibid. 138–9; *The Ghost of Napoleon*, 5.

[39] M. Howard, 'The British Way in Warfare' (1974), repr. in *The Causes of War* (London, 1984), 193–8; followed by B. Bond, *Liddell Hart: A Study of His Military Thought* (London, 1977) [*LH*], 69, 71, 75–6.

attracted less scholarly attention than it deserves. Only recently has its stock begun to rise.[40] Its main thrust amounted to a comprehensive attack on the dominance of the parallel Nelsonian–Napoleonic models over the strategic theory of his time, as exhibited in the all-powerful and, in this respect, also parallel Mahanite–Prussian theories. 'Our teachers', wrote Corbett, 'incline to insist that there is now only one way of making war, and that is Napoleon's way. Ignoring the fact that he failed in the end, they brand as heresy the bare suggestion that there may be other ways.'[41] He questioned the doctrines of unlimited war and concentration of all forces for the decisive battle even on land,[42] and claimed they were even less universally applicable at sea. The view he propounded was, as he put it,

a direct negation of the current doctrine that in war there can be but one legitimate object, the overthrow of the enemy's means of resistance, and that the primary objective must always be his armed forces. It raises in fact the whole question as to whether it is not sometimes legitimate and even correct to aim at the ulterior object of the war.[43]

Corbett warned of the fallacy 'that war consists entirely of battles between armies and fleets'. This fallacy, he maintained, 'ignores the fundamental fact that battles are only the means of enabling you to do that which really brings wars to an end—that is to exert pressure on the citizens and their collective life'.[44] If battle were only a means to an end, he argued, then other means such as blockades, the destruction of commerce, and combined operations in selected theatres might sometimes prove no less effective.

We shall return to some of Corbett's other leading ideas later on, but first back to Liddell Hart. In *Paris*, when dealing with naval warfare, he reproduced Corbett's characteristic argument, directed against pre-First World War navalist thought, regarding the limitations of sea power. He then proceeded as follows:

---

[40] For example, the two standard textbooks, Earle's and Paret's editions of *Makers of Modern Strategy*, do not deal with Corbett (the latter does not even mention him); but see D. M. Schurman's excellent contributions in *The Education of A Navy: The Development of British Naval Strategic Thought, 1867–1914* (London, 1965), 147–84, and *Julian S. Corbett, 1854–1922* (London, 1981); E. J. Grove's Introduction to J. Corbett's *Some Principles of Maritime Strategy* (Annapolis, Md., 1988); and my *Military Thought: The Nineteenth Century*, ch. 4, pp. 212–25, on which the following is based.
[41] *Some Principles of Maritime Strategy*, 20.   [42] Ibid. 19–27, 74–5.
[43] Ibid. 74.   [44] Ibid. 97.

As with land warfare, the destruction of the enemy's main fleet is often spoken of as the objective, whereas in reality this act is but a means towards it—by the destruction of the enemy's shield the way is opened for a more effective blockade or for the landing of an army.[45]

Liddell Hart's main use for Corbett was, however, far wider than the naval sphere. In Corbett's ideas he found an additional weapon against the nineteenth century's all-pervasive 'Napoleonic fallacy', which had prescribed 'that there was only one true objective in war—"the *destruction* of the enemy's main forces on the battlefield"'.[46] In truth, he argued, echoing Corbett,

the *destruction* of the enemy's armed forces is but a means—and not necessarily an inevitable or infallible one—to the attainment of our goal. It is clearly not, despite the assertion of military pundits, the sole true objective in war. . . . All *acts*, such as defeat in the field, propaganda, blockade, diplomacy, or attack on the centres of government and population, are seen to be but means to that end.[47]

To find a wider conception of strategy than the nineteenth-century one emphasizing the total overthrow of the enemy and the decisive battle, one had to go beyond its limited experience to the wider horizons of 'universal history' and especially to the pre-revolutionary, pre-Napoleonic era which had inaugurated total war. In particular, the relatively limited warfare of the eighteenth century, which had been anathema to Clausewitz and the men of the nineteenth century, was now to be rehabilitated.[48] The inspiration for this historical revision came clearly from Lawrence, who 'had found broader principles in Saxe and Guibert and the eighteenth century',[49] but Liddell Hart's other sources were also helpful in this regard. Before the First World War there had been two major, deeply historical, independent but remarkably parallel efforts to rehabilitate eighteenth-century warfare, each carrying clear implications for strategic theory in general. The first had been made by the great historian and publicist Hans Delbrück, leading to a famous and protracted controversy with German military opinion.[50] Liddell Hart, however, read no German and was unfamiliar with the whole affair when developing his ideas. All the same, what Delbrück had performed for land warfare Corbett in his more diplomatic but no

---

[45] Liddell Hart, *Paris*, 62–3.   [46] Ibid. 14.   [47] Ibid. 26; also 33–43.
[48] Ibid. 14, 18–19.   [49] *Seven Pillars of Wisdom*, 188.
[50] See Gat, *Military Thought: The Nineteenth Century*, 103–9, and the authorities cited there.

less sweeping manner had attempted to do for war at sea. Challenging nineteenth-century navalist opinion, he had defended the historical and strategic logic of eighteenth-century *guerre de course*, relatively cautious tactics, and more limited use of battle in deciding the issue of war.[51] The suggestive nature of his argument for land warfare was all too clear. Furthermore, although Colin, Liddell Hart's other major source of inspiration, had never gone as far as rehabilitating eighteenth-century warfare, his historical studies had not only shed favourable light on the dynamics of military ideas in that period but had also explained its military practices in the context of the conditions prevailing at the time. The materials for a revision of accepted opinion were all there, and Liddell Hart's treatment of the eighteenth century in his monograph *The Ghost of Napoleon* (1933) cast Colin's historical survey into Lawrence's new perspective. For Liddell Hart, eighteenth-century warfare was not only made legitimate by reference to the historical conditions of the time but provided a shining alternative model for contemporary strategic thought. It had been a period in which states had wisely adapted their military efforts to their means and political aims, and in which war had not engulfed, and spelled ruin for, the societies which had waged it.[52]

Liddell Hart's brilliant *The Decisive Wars of History* (1929; the title was given by the publishers and would be replaced in later editions by Liddell Hart's original choice, *The Strategy of Indirect Approach or Strategy: The Indirect Approach*) developed and consolidated the ideas first raised in *Paris*. In a *tour de force* sweep through history, Liddell Hart strove to show that the achievements of the great captains of all ages had rarely been brought about by the direct clash of forces but had usually involved the prior psychological and physical dislocation of the enemy. This historical survey was followed by a no less sweeping attempt 'to construct on the fresh foundation a new dwelling-house for strategic thought'.[53]

Liddell Hart aptly took as his starting-point Clausewitz's view of strategy, defined in *On War* as 'the art of the employment of battles as a means to gain the object of war'. He rightly pointed out (for this in general had indeed been Clausewitz's intention) that this definition 'narrows the meaning of "strategy" to the pure utilization of battle,

[51] Ibid. 213–22.
[52] See esp. *The Revolution in Warfare* (London, 1946), 40–5.
[53] Liddell Hart, *Strategy*, 333. The historical survey had been foreshadowed in *Paris*, 29–33.

thus conveying the idea that battle is the only means to the strategical end'.[54] A more valid definition, he suggested, would be 'the art of distributing military means to fulfil the ends of policy', which takes into account the many alternative and complementary means other than battle which strategy possesses.[55] Clausewitz's own logic would lead to its contradiction: 'even if the decisive battle be the goal, the aim of strategy must be to bring about this battle under the most advantageous circumstances. . . . The perfection of strategy would be, therefore, to produce a decision without any serious fighting.'[56] As Lawrence had put it, the object was 'to follow the direction of de Saxe and reach victory without battle, by pressing our advantages mathematical and psychological'.[57]

Strategy is based on movement and surprise. Physically, it should take the line of least resistance, while psychologically following that of least expectation. As Bourcet–Napoleon–Colin prescribed, it must have alternative objectives or, as Sherman described it, put the enemy on the horns of a dilemma.[58] The primary principle of concentration is in need of a major revision, as suggested by Colin, Lawrence, and Corbett alike:

[it] needs to be amplified as the 'concentration of strength against weakness'. And for any real value it needs to be explained that the concentration of strength against weakness depends on the dispersion of your opponent's strength, which in turn is produced by a distribution of your own that gives the appearance, and partial effect of dispersion. . . . True concentration is the fruit of calculated dispersion.[59]

---

[54] The citation is from Clausewitz, *On War*, bk. iii. ch. 1, but the definition and the idea behind it can be found throughout Bks. ii–iv. Liddell Hart, *Strategy*, 333.

[55] Ibid. 335.

[56] Ibid. 338; also 339. Cf. Fuller: 'even in the past not a few battles have been won by surprise rather than by force of arms, and if battle can be won without suffering loss, surely this is the most economical, if not the most traditional, way of gaining the strategical object': 'Weekly Tank Notes', 31 May and 7 June, 1919, reprinted in *On Future Warfare* (London, 1928), published the year before Liddell Hart's book.

[57] *Revolt in the Desert* (New York, 1927), 66.

[58] Liddell Hart, *Strategy*, 337, 341, 343–4, 348.

[59] Ibid. 347, also 343; and *The British Way in Warfare*, 19–20. For Lawrence see *Revolt in the Desert*, 66: 'Our aim was to seek the enemy's weakest material link'; with the Arabs 'dispersal was strength. Consequently we must extend our front to the maximum.' For Corbett see *Principles of Maritime Strategy*, 'Concentration and Dispersion', 128–52; concentration, he wrote (p. 134), had become 'a kind of shibboleth'; 'victories have not only to be won, but worked for. They must be worked for by bold strategic combinations, which as a rule entail at least apparent dispersal.'

Above the operational level, or military strategy, there is, however, a higher sphere, touching upon policy, to be termed 'grand strategy'. Here the non-military means of waging war come into effect, as well as a longer view encompassing not only the object of the war but also the peace which follows it. In both respects Clausewitz's ideas are found deficient:

fighting power is but one of the instruments of grand strategy—which should take account of and apply the power of financial pressure, and, not least of ethical pressure, to weaken the opponent's will. . . . Furthermore, while the horizon of strategy is bounded by the war, grand strategy looks beyond the war to the subsequent peace. It should not only combine the various instruments, but so regulate their use as to avoid damage to the future state of peace—for its security and prosperity.[60]

Before these ideas are assessed, their underlying significance ought to be highlighted. Against a background of a sweeping reversal of attitudes in Britain towards the First World War and the phenomenon of war in general, Liddell Hart undertook a wholesale revision of the accepted precepts of military theory. Any transformation of outlook and attitude in turn involves a reinterpretation and re-creation of history. Synthesizing Fuller, Colin, Lawrence, and Corbett, Liddell Hart thus projected a mirror image of nineteenth-century military theory and view of the past, which had been formulated on the Continent in the age of nationalism. Eighteenth-century warfare, discredited and despised by the men of the nineteenth century, became an example to be emulated and revived. The Napoleonic model became the Napoleonic fallacy. Clausewitz, previously revered as the intellectual inspiration behind the Prussian triumphs, became the false prophet whose teachings had been responsible for the disastrous world war. Total war was to be replaced by limited war; and the effort to gain victory by crushing the enemy's power substituted by a calculated action, mindful of the subsequent peace. The nation-in-arms was to be replaced by a small army of professionals; the decisive clash of forces in a major battle by indirect means; concentration by calculated dispersion.

While Liddell Hart may have borrowed all of these themes, none of his sources had weaved them into such a sweeping counter-theory and

---

[60] Liddell Hart, *Strategy*, 336. Cf. the similar formulation in Fuller, *Grant*, 7, written simultaneously and also published in 1929; it is difficult to establish, though perhaps less difficult to guess, who borrowed here from whom without acknowledgement; Fuller had already used the concept in his *The Foundations of the Science of War* (London, 1926), 105.

counter-history of war *and* possessed his tenacity in hammering them out and his gifts for simplification and marketing. Coming as it did in the wake of a crisis in the old patterns of war, it is no wonder people all over the world accepted this reversal of strategic values with interest and awe, and found it thought-provoking and stimulating.[61]

Assessment and Criticisms

Criticisms of Liddell Hart's ideas can be treated in reference to two main and related themes—how serious, historically sound, and strategically valid these ideas were—which in turn hinges largely on the evaluation of Liddell Hart's treatment of Clausewitz, the focus of his criticism in his counter-theory and counter-history of war. Scepticism is all the more necessary in view of Liddell Hart's status as a popular writer, reaching out for, and aiming to influence and educate, a large uninformed and semi-informed readership. First enchanted and overwhelmed by the force and brilliance of his arguments, people often started to doubt their validity and suspect they had been tricked by the rhetoric of an extremely clever man and master of exposition. He used strong medicines to get his message across, was anything but impartial, and had little use for balance and restraint. By the standards of scholarly discussion these, of course, are dubious and unacceptable credentials. But then, Liddell Hart was playing a somewhat different game, and in a different league. He was out to reverse strategic outlook and influence public attitudes, and while in some crucial respects this may have made him a poor objective historian, it also turned him into a figure of historical significance in his own right. As an eminent historian of ideas has written, revolutionary thinkers tend

to overstate their central theses. Such exaggeration is neither unusual nor necessarily to be deplored. Those who have discovered (or think they have discovered) new and important truths are liable to see the world in their light ... Many original thinkers exaggerate greatly. ... Nor is it likely that their ideas would have broken through the resistance of received opinion or been accorded the attention that they deserved, if they had not.[62]

As critics have argued, Liddell Hart's definition of the 'indirect approach' was loose, and he stretched it even further, to explain by it

---

[61] See e.g. André Beaufre's recollections in M. Howard (ed.), *The Theory and Practice of War* (London, 1965), 138–9.

[62] I. Berlin, *Vico and Herder* (London, 1980), p. xxiv.

almost any military success. However, the core of his argument was not ambiguous at all. It amounted to the idea, advanced against nineteenth-century notions, that the enemy's psychological and physical dislocation was more crucial to its defeat than the brute clash of forces. If anything, this idea was partial and one-sided, rather than circular or tautological. The expression 'indirect approach' itself seemed lopsided to a man like Fuller, on whose ideas it had been largely based. He wrote to Liddell Hart: 'The object is to defeat the enemy and if this can be done by a direct approach so much the better.'[63] Yet the expression was largely used for provocation and effect. As T. E. Lawrence, another one of Liddell Hart's major sources who had himself found nineteenth-century military theory 'one-sided',[64] wrote to Liddell Hart:

A surfeit of the 'hit' school brings on an attack of the 'run' method: and then the pendulum swings back. You, at present, are trying . . . to put the balance straight after the orgy of the late war. When you succeed (about 1945) your sheep will pass your bounds of discretion, and have to by chivvied back by some later strategist. Back and forward we go.[65]

If Liddell Hart had been too enthusiastic and naïve to have consciously realized this himself, he certainly acknowledged the point when Lawrence made it, for he seized and repeatedly cited it in his writings.[66]

In his treatment of history, Liddell Hart's one-sidedness and partiality were compounded by other, no less significant flaws. His search for trans-historical features and instruction, problematic though perhaps not illegitimate in itself, was marred by his unhistorical and naïve disregard for the particular conditions—social, economic and political—which had shaped each period's way of doing things.[67] Admittedly, over time he improved considerably in this respect. In his still immature article on de Saxe (1924), which he would unwisely incorporate unchanged in later works, his didactic approach to his subject was ludicrously unhistorical throughout. To cite only a couple of examples, one of his praises for de Saxe was that he had 'foreshadowed the four-company system—which was only adopted in the British Army on the

---

[63] Fuller to Liddell Hart, 19 June 1929, King's, 1/302.

[64] *Seven Pillars of Wisdom*, 188.

[65] 17 Oct. 1928, in *Lawrence to Liddell Hart*, 4; see also 31 Mar. 1929 and Whit Monday 1933, ibid. 6, 132.

[66] 'A Re-definition of Strategy', *United Services Institution of India Journal* (Apr. 1929), 117, 128 (incorporated in *The Decisive Wars of History*, London, 1929); *Thoughts on War* (London, 1944), 230; *Strategy*, 363; *Memoirs*, i. 85.

[67] Bond, *LH*, 57; Mearsheimer, *LH*, 48–9.

eve of 1914!' Similarly, he regarded Saxe's recommendation of body armour as having been vindicated by the appearance of the tank.[68] The other historical articles which he had originally published in 1924 and later compiled as *Great Captains Unveiled* (1927) were equally crude. However, as he wrote *Scipio* (1926), his barely disguised allusions to the present were offered with wit and lightness of touch. And whereas *Scipio* was still a lively sketch rather than a scholarly history, Liddell Hart's *Sherman* (1929), *Foch* (1931), and history of the First World War (1930; originally entitled *The Real War*) marked his growth into an accomplished historian, relying on a fairly extensive study of the available printed sources.

To be sure, these works, too, were written for a purpose and were not without their didactic biases, intrinsic in Liddell Hart's sweeping counter-history of war. Projecting a mirror image of the nineteenth-century picture of history, he also repeated in reverse the unhistorical attitude towards other epochs and styles of warfare of which he accused it.[69] After all, the era of total war had not been just a historical aberration but had grown out of the most fundamental developments shaping Western civilization in the modern period. In contrast to Liddell Hart, Fuller, deeply conscious of historical development, related the emergence of total war to the rise of mass society and the process of industrialization. Correspondingly, from the start he argued that the demise of total war would be brought about by the emergence of a new, technological era. More than 'wrong mental attitude' was involved.

Typically, Napoleon's rise and decline were attributed by Liddell Hart in his most famous work on the subject to purely operational reasons: while 'General Bonaparte' had achieved his great victories by his masterly use of manoeuvre, surprise, and deception, the 'Emperor Napoleon' had increasingly earned diminishing strategic returns because he had impatiently misused the vast resources at his disposal in progressively more massive, head-on assaults, supported by heavy artillery concentrations.[70] It barely seems to have occurred to Liddell Hart that the reason for Napoleon's growing difficulties, and changing methods, from 1807 onward had been rooted in deeper changes in objective conditions. Not only had Napoleon's adversaries become accustomed to his methods, but the extension of French hegemony

---

[68] Cited from *The Ghost of Napoleon*, 41 and 39; *Great Captains Unveiled* (London, 1927), 54, 47–9.　　　　　　　　　　　[69] *The Ghost of Napoleon*, 20.
[70] Ibid. 101–4; also *Strategy*, 127–8, 138–41.

over the Continent had been virtually forcing them to throw greater resources into the struggle, adopt French revolutionary military innovations, and ultimately also become more united and better coordinated. Brilliant operations, relying on improvised, self-contained logistics, could no longer do the trick for Napoleon.

Liddell Hart's *Sherman* is another case in point. For Liddell Hart, Sherman's mobile operations and march through the Confederacy to the sea presented a stark contrast to the direct and bloody clash of forces in the main, eastern theatre of the Civil War, indeed a stark contrast to the reality of the Western Front in the First World War. In his opinion Sherman's model indirect approach, which cut the Confederacy in two and separated it from its bread basket, proved to be the decisive act of the war. With Fuller, who was writing *Grant* (1929) at the same time as Liddell Hart wrote *Sherman* (1929), he became involved in a bitter exchange over the relative merits and importance of their heros, in which both protagonists made some very good points.[71] Yet, as Fuller emphasized brilliantly in *Grant* and in his later *Grant and Lee* (1933), and as other critics have pointed out, the American Civil War has often been regarded as the first modern war because it had involved, and had been ultimately decided by, industrial and mass human mobilization, resulting in a protracted process of attrition. As two one-time Oxford professors of military history, Spenser Wilkinson and Michael Howard, argued independently half a century apart, the operations of Grant and Sherman must be seen as complementary efforts in this process of attrition. In Howard's vivid image, they had related to each other like two blades of a scissors.[72] Sherman's campaign could not have been carried out before the North had developed its overall material superiority over the South, and had Grant at the head of the main Union's armies not been hammering at, and pinning down, the Confederacy's main forces before Richmond.

Liddell Hart's moralizing disregard for the complexity of conditions and considerations shaping historical causation and situations was intimately linked to his strong belief in the influence of individuals, or 'great men', abstract ideas, and accidents in history. This way of looking at things, which has been related to the British historiographical tradi-

---

[71] See their correspondence between Dec. 1928 and July 1929: King's, 1/302. Apart from Liddell Hart, *Sherman* (London, 1929), see his *Strategy*, 148–53. For Fuller, see B. H. Reid, *J. F. C. Fuller: Military Thinker* (London, 1987), 112–23.

[72] Wilkinson to Liddell Hart, 28 Dec. 1928: King's, 1/748; Howard in *The Listener*, 28 Dec. 1972, 894.

tion known as the 'Whig interpretation of history',[73] often led Liddell Hart to naïve and caricaturist propositions. For example, in his polemic tracing of the manner Britain moved towards military involvement in the Continent in the decade before the First World War, Liddell Hart practically ignored the intricate political constraints and strategic considerations which had influenced British decision making.[74] Instead, one may learn from him that the whole matter resulted from the friendship forged between Foch and Henry Wilson, director of military operations at the British War Office in the years preceding the war. 'There is no exaggeration in saying that this friendship diverted the course of English history,' he wrote; it was the case of 'the influence of a French governess and a cup of tea'. The personal link was reinforced by the change of intellectual fashion as Clausewitz's influence and continental military ideas reached Britain.[75] To be sure, the scale of this latter influence, both before and during the First World War—over British military education, in the new general staff, and specifically over Haig—has been well documented by recent scholarship.[76] None the less, George Orwell's appraisal of Liddell Hart's historical analysis could probably represent the balance of scholarly opinion: 'There is something unsatisfactory in tracing an historical change to an individual theorist, because a theory does not gain ground unless material conditions favour it.'[77]

The issue at the root of all this was the traumatic First World War and its lessons for the future. Fuller and Liddell Hart contributed significantly to the interwar debate, sparked by Churchill and Lloyd George, over the conduct of the war and the performance of the British

---

[73] See Mearsheimer, *LH*, 48–9; Liddell Hart, *The Ghost of Napoleon*, 11–13; *Thoughts on War* (London, 1944), 9.

[74] See W. S. Churchill, *The World Crisis, 1911–1918* (London, 1960), 42–53; M. Hankey, *The Supreme Command* (2 vols., London, 1961), i. 69–70, 78–82; S. Williamson, *The Politics of Grand Strategy: Britain and France Prepare for War* (Cambridge, Mass., 1969); M. Howard, *The Continental Commitment* (London, 1972), 31–52; J. Gooch, *The Plans of War: The General Staff and British Military Strategy, c.1900–1916* (London, 1974), 278–98; D. French, *British Economic and Strategic Planning, 1905–1915* (London, 1982), esp. 22–38.

[75] Liddell Hart, *The Ghost of Napoleon*, 138; 'Foch and the Fate of Britain: The Influence of a French Governess and a Cup of Tea', *Reveille*, 1 Aug. 1933; also *Foch* (London, 1931), 55–62; *The British Way in Warfare*, 16–17.

[76] T. Travers, *The Killing Ground: The British Army, the Western Front and the Emergence of Modern Warfare, 1900–1918* (London, 1987), esp. 37–61, 86, 92, 96, and *passim*.

[77] George Orwell's review of *The British Way in Warfare*, *New Statesman*, 21 Nov. 1942: King's, 1/557.

high command. Both sides of this debate have since been taken up by historians, and the argument shows no signs of coming to a conclusion—nor, perhaps, can it. Here again, facts are inseparable from attitudes. At the centre of the debate stands the murderous war of attrition on the Western Front, culminating for the British in the 'carnage' of the Somme and Passchendaele. On the personal level the debate has largely focused on the generalship of the British commander-in-chief in France, Field Marshal Sir Douglas Haig.

Something like a backlash against the interwar radicals and their followers in the anti-establishment 1960s has been slowly gathering momentum among scholars. They have pointed out the predicament of the World War generals who faced very difficult objective conditions, involving a tactical and operational impasse and leaving them with very narrow strategic options other than the grinding attrition campaign on the Western Front. Historians have stressed the achievement of the British high command which, lacking the experience of its continental counterparts and virtually from scratch, succeeded in the space of a few years in creating, equipping, training, and leading into battle new mass armies which played a decisive role in containing and defeating Germany. Critics have argued that despite his indignant rhetoric Liddell Hart never really came up with a satisfactory alternative solution as to the way the war should have been conducted.[78] He took up the accusations of the tank pioneers such as Ernest Swinton, Fuller, and Churchill that the British high command had used the new machines in an unimaginative manner, thus forfeiting surprise and diminishing their effectiveness. Yet the fact remains that it had been largely owing to the generally positive response of the high command that the British had pioneered the tank, had surmounted considerable teething problems of all sorts, had produced the machine in large numbers, and had led the way throughout the war in its use. As to 'Plan 1919' with which Fuller and Liddell Hart ushered in their 1920s polemics, it had been an

---

[78] See esp. C. Falls, *The First World War* (London, 1960), continuing the line of Edmonds's official history of the war without its worst biases; J. Terrain, *Douglas Haig: The Educated General* (London, 1963); *To Win a War: 1918* (London, 1978); H. Essame, *The Battle for Europe, 1918* (London, 1972); Howard, *The Continental Commitment*, 53–61; P. Kennedy, *The Rise and Fall of British Naval Mastery* (London, 1976), 239–65; B. Bond, *British Military Policy between the Two World Wars* (Oxford, 1980), 2–6; D. French, *British Strategy and War Aims, 1914–1916* (London, 1986), p. xi and *passim*; *The Strategy of the Lloyd George Coalition, 1916–1918* (Oxford, 1995); Mearsheimer, *Liddell Hart*, 61–71; J. M. Bourne, *Britain and the Great War* (London, 1989); Bond, *The First World War*, *passim*, esp. H. Strachan, '"The Real War": Liddell Hart, Cruttwell, and Falls', 43–53.

imaginative, futuristic vision, based on machines which did not yet exist in 1918. First World War tanks had been too slow and unreliable and possessed too short a range for such enterprises.[79]

After the war Winston Churchill advanced the argument, which Liddell Hart came to support, that during the years 1916–18 the Allies should have refrained from large-scale offensives on the Western Front. Churchill claimed that these offensives had cost the Allies three casualties to every two they inflicted on the Germans, and sometimes only two to one. He suggested that a strategy of dynamic defence and limited local offensives would have sufficed to pin down the Germans while the effects of the blockade slowly took effect.[80] In a drawn-out controversy, critics and the British official history of the war rejected Churchill's figures, claiming that Allied and German casualties were roughly equal and that, given Germany's narrower manpower base, her attrition rate was considerably greater and, indeed, won the war for the Allies. Furthermore, it has been pointed out that Germany would have taken advantage of a defensive posture on the part of Western allies to concentrate even greater forces against Russia, in which case the Western powers would have been obliged to do their utmost to relieve the pressure on their ally.

All the same, still newer literature, more meticulously researched than ever before, appears to be swinging the pendulum in the other direction once again and confirming at least some of the radicals' claims. For example, two comprehensive assessments of the evidence conclude that Churchill was after all right and his many adversaries were wrong regarding the relative casualty figures of the Allies and the Germans on the Western Front.[81] Liddell Hart's relentless struggle against the distortions of the British official history of the war, flaring up with every resurfacing of 'the old lies', as he called them, is thereby vindicated.[82]

---

[79] Fuller, still restrained in *Tanks in the Great War* (London, 1920), is categorical in his *Memoirs of an Unconventional Soldier* (London, 1936), 88–350; W. Churchill, *The World Crisis, 1911–1918*, 343–59, 747, 826–9 (citing Fuller); E. Swinton, *Eyewitness* (London, 1932), esp. 294–9. For the counter-arguments, see V. Germains, *The 'Mechanization' of War* (London, 1927), 43–54; Falls, *The First World War*, 175; Terrain, *Haig*, 218–28; Reid, *Fuller*, 48–55; and even the radicals themselves: G. Martel, *An Unspoken Soldier* (London, 1949), 17–18; Liddell Hart, *The Tanks* (2 vols., London, 1959), i. 216–17.

[80] *The World Crisis, 1911–1918*, 618–39. For Liddell Hart, see e.g. 12 June 1936, King's, 11/1936/68.

[81] R. Prior, *Churchill's 'World Crisis' as History* (London, 1983), 221–30; D. Winter, *Haig's Command: A Reassessment* (London, 1991), 48, 111–13.

[82] See Liddell Hart's letters to the press in King's, 6/1946 (following the publication of the 'Passchendaele' volume of Edmonds's official history); 6/1957 and 6/1959 (debate with John Terrain); 6/1967/1.

Admittedly, the new studies reaffirm that despite Germany's considerably lower casualty rates, the attrition she suffered probably did facilitate her collapse. But was the terrible cost to the British, who shouldered much of the burden in the last phase of the war, really 'unavoidable'? On this point, too, recent studies are damning, above all in respect to Haig. It has been convincingly shown that Haig did prolong the murderous Third Battle of Ypres (Passchendaele) long after it became bogged down in the mud. Against the advice of his subordinates, who wanted a more limited offensive, he planed it as a war-winning effort and would not give up his ambition. In addition, it has been demonstrated in great detail that the British high command was indeed slow to adapt to new technologies and new tactics even in the later phase of the war, and that Haig in particular was practically incapable of grasping them. He failed to prepare the British army for modern defence in depth before Ludendorff's 1918 spring offensive. In the Allies' successful final offensives of that year, in which the British played a leading part, the strategic inspiration and planning came mainly from Foch, while tactical execution was left to the subordinate army and corps commanders, such as Rawlinson and Monash. Even Haig's supposedly stronger 'managerial' qualities, as an organizer, staff officer, and trainer, have come in for scathing criticism.[83] The dialectic progress of the debate is unlikely to end here, but Liddell Hart's critique of the British conduct on the Western Front looks much better today that it did a few years ago.

Moving to possible strategic alternatives to the deadlock on the Western Front, Liddell Hart (but not Fuller) sympathized and on occasions identified himself with the so-called Eastern school.[84] This is another controversy which never appears to die out, with most recent

---

[83] Winter, *Haig's Command*; T. Travers, *How the War Was Won: Command and Technology in the British Army on the Western Front, 1917–1918* (London, 1992) are in these respects practically unanimous in their conclusions. See also R. Prior and T. Wilson, *Command on the Western Front: The Military Career of Sir Henry Rawlinson, 1914–18* (Oxford, 1992); D. Graham and S. Bidwell, *Coalitions, Politicians and Generals: Some Aspects of Command in Two World Wars* (London, 1993), 92–125; M. Samuels, *Doctrine and Dogma: German and British Infantry Tactics in the First World War* (New York, 1992), 113–68; and, earlier, C. Barnett, *The Swordbearers: Studies in Supreme Command in the First World War* (London, 1963), 295–301. P. Griffith, *Battle Tactics of the Western Front: The British Army's Art of Attack, 1916–18* (New Haven, Conn., 1994) is more tepid. The books by Terrain and Winter (despite the latter's obvious paranoia) are the two indispensable representatives of both sides of the Haig debate; for a historiographical survey, see K. Simpson, 'The Reputation of Sir Douglas Haig', in Bond, *The First World War*, 141–62.   [84] See esp. *The British Way in Warfare*, 38–41.

historians again taking a sceptical view.[85] Little more about it will be said in the next chapter. At any rate, the Dardanelles operation, promising on paper, foundered on execution and lapsed into a debate over Churchill's responsibility for the failure.[86] As to the Salonika landing, its proponents, headed by Lloyd George, argued that if it had been carried out in early 1915 it could have created a Balkan league encompassing Serbia, Greece, Romania, and Bulgaria.[87] Critics, however, have stressed the unlikelihood of bringing together these bitterly antagonistic nations.[88] They have also pointed out that for reasons of logistics and geography it is very doubtful if the Allies would have achieved more success in the Balkans than on the Western Front, let alone bring about the collapse of Austro-Hungary. None the less, there may have been something in the argument of Lloyd George and Liddell Hart (rarely noted by their critics) that if Germany had been prevented from overrunning Romania and taking possession of her rich and vital supply of corn and oil, she could not have continued the war as long as she did.

In conclusion, it ought to be remembered that Liddell Hart wrote his most popular and best-known works when he was still relatively young, between the ages of 30 and 40, and that over time, though he would always remain above all the committed publicist, his historical senses would mature considerably and gain in depth. Thus a decade after he wrote *Scipio*, Liddell Hart no longer regarded it as a legitimate scholarly exercise.[89] Similarly, from the 1930s onwards, the more he involved himself in questions of policy and grand strategy, the more he presented Napoleon's fall as the outcome of his unrestrained and self-destructive pursuit of European hegemony rather than of operational military reasons.[90] Finally, in his *Revolution in Warfare* (1946), influenced by

---

[85] See n. 78 above.

[86] For a historiographical survey, see E. Spiers, 'Gallipoli', in Bond *The First World War*, 165–88; more recently, T. Ben-Moshe, *Churchill: Strategy and History* (Boulder, Colo., 1992), 29–69; J. Charmley, *Churchill: The End of Glory* (London, 1993), 105–25; M. Howard, 'Churchill and the First World War', in R. Black and W. R. Louis (eds.), *Churchill* (Oxford, 1993), 129–45.

[87] D. Lloyd George, *War Memoirs* (London, 1936), 1998–2002; Liddell Hart, *The British Way in Warfare*, 38–41. Liddell Hart assisted Lloyd George in the writing of his book, and it has been rightly pointed out that each reinforced the other's bias against the generals.

[88] See Lloyd George's arch-rival, W. Robertson, *Soldiers and Statesmen, 1914–1918* (London, 1926), ii. 87–8, also 175–7. D. R. Woodward, *Lloyd George and the Generals* (London, 1983), 27–47, offers a good assessment of the evidence and prospects, leaving the question open.

[89] Liddell Hart to Scammell, 31 May 1937, King's, 1/622; also *Memoirs*, i. 168.

[90] Barely hinted at in *Strategy*, 127; but see *The British Way in Warfare*, 18; *The Revolution in Warfare* (London, 1946), 43 ff.

Fuller's histories of the evolution of war, Liddell Hart produced a much more sophisticated historical survey than he had done before of the changing intensity and brutality of war from the Middle Ages to the Second World War, putting his discussion of Clausewitz's influence in a better historical perspective.[91]

Liddell Hart's treatment of Clausewitz's theories is central to his entire work and crucial to its assessment. Scholars have found much to criticize here, but to a large degree their criticisms are a reflection on the confused state of the interpretation of Clausewitz's own work. Perplexed by the contradictory ideas they have found in *On War* and failing to follow Clausewitz's tortuous intellectual development which left all these ideas mixed in his work, commentators could never really make up their minds what exactly Clausewitz meant to say. Naturally, this has made them extremely cautious. They seemed to have been able to find at least a qualifying, if not an opposite, phrase for any idea, and the ensemble of these conflicting ideas has generally been presumed to reflect Clausewitz's profundity. This has also made Clausewitz a man for all seasons, as each period has highlighted the ideas which suited its tastes and strategic requirements while explaining away those which have not.[92]

Spenser Wilkinson, the first professor of military history at Oxford and an unrivalled scholar among the occupants of the rare university posts specified for military history in Britain before the Second World War, was one of the earliest critics of Liddell Hart's attitude to Clausewitz. In the first place he claimed that Clausewitz's work was a philosophical study of the nature of war *rather than* a source of operational doctrines. This, however, was a misleading distinction which unfortunately was later to gain much currency. Although rejecting formal systems and principles, Clausewitz believed that the nature of war prescribed clear guidance for action, which he identified with fighting and the search for a major battle respectively; indeed, he felt deeply that military theory was utterly useless if it was not able to offer such guidance and merely confined itself to 'empty abstractions'. Wilkinson also tried to qualify Liddell Hart's correct assertion that Clausewitz had regarded the overthrow of the enemy's main armies as the sole legitimate means in war. At the same time, however, Wilkinson maintained, as he always had, that during the First World

---

[91] *The Revolution in Warfare*, 34–75.
[92] See my *From the Enlightenment to Clausewitz*, 190–263.

War there had been no alternative to the concentration of all forces against Germany on the Western Front.[93] No matter how justified he may have been on this point, it should serve as a reminder that Wilkinson was far from being the detached scholar passing sagacious judgement on Liddell Hart's propagandist endeavour. Rather, he himself was a distinguished and deeply committed exponent of the nineteenth-century military school, with a long and eminent career of journalistic and public campaigning over questions of national strategy and defence organization behind him.[94]

In a stream of books and articles written in the decades preceding the Great War, Wilkinson had championed a number of related causes: he had been the leading advocate of the creation of modern staff systems on the Prussian model for the British army and navy; he had striven to turn Britain into a real nation-in-arms which could match the continental powers; he had been a staunch Mahanite and the inspiration behind the creation of the British Navy League in 1894. As he put it: 'There is only one theory of war—that which is set forth, with some differences of expression and of detail, by Clausewitz, by Jomini, by Mahan.'[95] Liddell Hart's ideas were nothing new to him. Before the Great War he had already been one the most venomous critics of Julian Corbett's theories, which had challenged the navalist faith in the destruction of the enemy's navy in a major battle as the sole legitimate aim and means in war and which had suggested the desirability of limited wars and limited strategic efforts.[96] During the war Wilkinson wrote in a highly characteristic manner: 'The war that aims at striking down the enemy by the destruction of his forces is that of a successful State; the war that tries to limit its aims, and therefore its exertions, is that of the defeated.'[97] In 1911, years before he met Liddell Hart, he had argued against Norman Engell and those who had shared similar opinions that 'Peace cannot rationally be the object of policy'.[98] Finally,

[93] S. Wilkinson, 'Killing No Murder: An Examination of Some New Theories of War', *Army Quarterly* (Oct. 1927), 14–21.

[94] For Wilkinson, see J. Luvaas, *The Education of an Army* (London, 1965), 253–90.

[95] Scammell, 'Spenser Wilkinson and the Defence of Britain', *Journal of the American Military Institute*, 4 (1940), 141–2; cited by Luvaas, *The Education of an Army*, 280; for a learned account of nineteenth-century military thought, and Clausewitz, see S. Wilkinson, *War and Policy* (London, 1900), 150–4.

[96] Gat, *Military Thought: The Nineteenth Century*, 222–3.

[97] Cited by Luvaas, *The Education of an Army*, 283–4.

[98] *Government and the War* (London, 1918), 64; cited by J. Gooch, *The Prospect of War: Sudies in British Defence Policy, 1847–1942* (London, 1981), 49.

in reaction to Liddell Hart's work he wrote that the financial and economic aspects of war ought to be treated separately from the military and naval sides, to which Liddell Hart replied that, on the contrary, they had been kept in separate, watertight compartments for far too long.[99] Interpretations of Clausewitz changed with the advent of the nuclear age. It was now becoming the fashion sharply to contrast a 'good' Clausewitz with his 'bad' successors in the nineteenth-century Prussian-German tradition. In 1956 Michael Howard started to lecture on Clausewitz at King's College, London, reflecting the new 'Clausewitz renaissance' which was gathering momentum throughout the West. Diplomatically he wrote to Liddell Hart, his close friend, that he had always taken his criticism of Clausewitz's theories as having been directed against Clausewitz's disciples rather than against Clausewitz himself. But Liddell Hart held his ground, replying that he had gone over Clausewitz's work again and could not see how everything in *On War* could be explained away on the grounds of faulty interpretation. The intention in too many passages was unequivocally clear. Howard sensibly withdrew, proclaiming that a better familiarity with German philosophy of the time would be required to decide the issue.[100] However, two decades later he was to produce an excellent balanced assessment of the question in his introduction to a new translation of Clausewitz's *On War* (1976), acknowledging most of the features which Liddell Hart had criticized in Clausewitz's work. 'But the final picture Liddell Hart painted of Clausewitz's teaching', he concluded, 'was distorted, inaccurate, and unfair.[101]

So indeed it was. It was certainly inaccurate, if only because of the fact that, despite some inklings to the contrary, like most readers of Clausewitz, Liddell Hart tended to regard *On War* as an integrated whole rather than an unfinished draft whose author had completely changed his mind half-way through the work; then, in the latest parts of the work, which he had written before he died, rather than discard his old ideas, Clausewitz had striven to resolve his difficulties by trans-

---

[99] Wilkinson to Liddell Hart, 28 Dec. 1928; Liddell Hart to Wilkinson, 31 Dec. 1928: King's, 1/748.

[100] Howard commented on the passages on Clausewitz in Liddell Hart's, 'Armed Forces and the Art of War: Armies', written for *The New Cambridge Modern History*, 10 (1960), 302–30; Howard to Liddell Hart, 13 Dec. 1958; Liddell Hart to Howard, 3 Feb. 1959; Howard to Liddell Hart, 5 Feb. 1959: King's, 1/384.

[101] 'The Influence of Clausewitz', in Clausewitz, *On War* (Princeton, NJ, 1976), 39–41.

planting them into his new ones. This complex genealogy has resulted in an understandable confusion among Clausewitz's readers. Liddell Hart's picture of Clausewitz was also distorted and one-sided, though fundamentally no different from that of those commentators who in the nuclear age have subordinated one phase in Clausewitz's development to the other; although Liddell Hart cannot be recommended as a balanced authority for a study of Clausewitz, he is no worse in this regard than most of the more recent literature. Certainly, Liddell Hart was unfair to Clausewitz. Yet fairness was hardly to be expected. Liddell Hart was waging war against a highly influential conception of war and military theory which had dominated an age, and Clausewitz was an authority and a symbol which had to be dethroned.

Historians who participated in the 'Clausewitz renaissance' have lost sight of the fact that throughout his life, both in his theories and practical policy recommendations, Clausewitz was the most fervent exponent of all-out war and the strategy of destruction. Nobody in his generation formulated the Napoleonic experience in such extreme terms, not even his fellow reformers in Prussia who, like him, had been deeply shaken by their nation's disastrous defeat in 1806 and subsequent subjugation, and whose mood and opinions he generally expressed. Indeed, for all their obvious differences of character and style, a striking similarity in reverse exists between the respective historical positions and ideas of Clausewitz and Liddell Hart, something which in a sense supports the latter's allusive suggestions that he was the Prussian's equal. Both thinkers reacted to cataclysmic and epoch-making wars which had resulted in a national trauma and profound intellectual transformation. In both, their experiences produced a violent reaction against past military theory and practice, held to be responsible for the disaster; it is scarcely noted that the picture Clausewitz had painted of his predecessors was as inaccurate, distorted, and unfair as Liddell Hart's. Both advanced a new model of military theory, which they held to be universally valid and which involved an unhistorical approach to the special conditions which had determined the patterns of the past. Both were not just 'idly theorizing' but developed and preached their ideas out of consuming commitment to their countries' future. The difference between them, of course, was only that the one had stood at the dawn of total war and called on his country for an all-out national effort and on her army for a vigorous direct action, whereas a century later the other witnessed the peaking of total war and preached restraint and a return to manœuvre.

It is true that in 1827 Clausewitz's thought came to a crisis, after which, until his death, in what was above all a reaction against his own lifelong and strongly held opinions, he began to revise his theories, painfully recognizing the legitimacy of limited war and explaining it largely by the influence of policy which restrained war to suit its aims. It was these ideas that in the late nineteenth and early twentieth centuries, independent of each other, both Delbrück and Corbett developed and directed against the dominating theory of all-out war and the strategy of destruction. Thus Corbett based on Clausewitz's later theories the same ideas which Liddell Hart, Corbett's disciple, would direct against Clausewitz. This apparent paradox is rooted in the Janus face of Clausewitz's development and influence. More specifically, it ought to be noted that Clausewitz's revision of his early ideas had never gone so far as expressly to rehabilitate eighteenth-century warfare or fully to endorse alternative methods of warfare other than fighting. Both Delbrück and Corbett developed his ideas further, knowing his limitations and recognizing that he himself had never reached that far.

All the same, as critics have suggested, were not Liddell Hart's ideas regarding the subordination of war to policy and his concept of limited war in fact merely echoing Clausewitz (via Corbett)?[102] Undoubtedly, to a large degree they were. Yet they also went further, and added meaningful new dimensions to Clausewitz's line of reasoning. In Fuller's footsteps Liddell Hart developed an entire philosophy of politics, war, and peace: not only was the conduct of war to be bridled in accordance with the political aim of the war, but this aim itself had to be kept coolly in check with the view of adjusting it, beyond the inflamed emotions of an ongoing conflict, to the eventual desired state of peace. In time Liddell Hart would begin to doubt if a victorious war had ever really proved beneficial even to the victor in recent modern history. 'Victory' itself would thus appear to be a dubious aim not only in the military but also in the political sense. It is mainly in the light of these ideas that one should view Liddell Hart's assertion, in Fuller's spirit, that 'Clausewitz looked only to the end of war, not beyond war to the subsequent peace'.[103]

This was more than an abstract change of emphasis. Both Clausewitz and Liddell Hart were expressing a political ethos. Both were making

---

[102] Wilkinson, 'Killing No Murder', 20–1; Howard, 'The Influence of Clausewitz', 39–40; C. Bassford, *Clausewitz in English: The Reception of Clausewitz in Britain and America, 1815–1945* (Oxford, 1994), 133, 142.   [103] *The Ghost of Napoleon*, 121.

political statements. Both were exponents of powerful ideologies dominating their respective times, countries, and cultural circles. Although Clausewitz's work has often been naïvely proclaimed 'value-free', he in fact expressed the new attitudes in Germany of the Romantic period which in a sweeping reaction against Enlightenment ideas presented war as necessary and even beneficial.[104] These were the notions that during the nineteenth century grew to dominate German political ethos, shaped as it was by Germany's difficult course to unity and by her later struggle to win what she regarded as her proper place in the European and global order. By contrast, from the 1930s on, as the Nazi and Soviet threats presented in turn unparalleled challenges to the existing world order, Liddell Hart was to develop a fully conscious view of war which aimed to suit the needs of the liberal and politically satisfied Britain and, later, of the liberal and politically satisfied West. In the process, while building on his earlier, popular theories, Liddell Hart greatly developed and amended them. It is there, in his more mature but less-known ideas, that his main contribution to strategic theory lay, as well as the true measure of his originality and sophistication.

---

[104] Gat, *From the Enlightenment to Clausewitz*, 236–50.

4

Policy: Defence of the West (I): Containment in the 1930s

By the beginning of the 1930s, having written his history of the First World War, Liddell Hart set out to define more closely what fundamentally had 'gone wrong' with the war. He approached the question from a general point of view, reviewing Britain's historical war policy, from which he claimed she had diverged without real justification and with disastrous results in her massive continental involvement during the Great War.

He presented his interpretation of 'The British Way in Warfare' in a lecture delivered before the Royal United Services Institution in January 1931.[1] He argued that from the sixteenth century on Britain had owed much of her global pre-eminence and commanding influence in Europe to her unique strategic policy. Shielded as she had been from invasion by her insular position and naval preponderance, Britain had avoided large-scale military involvements in the great wars that had racked the Continent. Against major continental rivals, such as the Spain of Philip II and France from Louis XIV to Napoleon, she had employed a variety of other means. She had subsidized and supplied the armies of Continental allies to keep her great adversaries busy on land. While she had sent only relatively small armies to the main theatres of operations to support these allies and sustain them in the war, her amphibious expeditions and seaborne raids had distracted and tied down a great number of enemy troops. Most importantly, while Britain's naval blockade had destroyed her enemy's commerce, her overseas forces had captured his colonies, thus making Britain ever richer and all the more able to wage successfully her maritime and economic style of warfare. Finally, Britain had always known how to limit her wars to what had been politically feasible and economically

---

[1] 'Economic Pressure or Continental Victories', *Journal of the RUSI*, 76 (1931), 486–510; incorporated as 'The Historic Strategy of Britain', in *The British Way in Warfare*, (London 1932), 13–41, and *When Britain Goes to War* (London, 1935), 17–46.

profitable, and never engaged in a futile and costly effort to completely crush her enemies.

Unfortunately, argued Liddell Hart, under the influence of Clausewitz and Continental military ideas Britain had gone for an all-out war from 1914 on, building a huge army and throwing it against Germany's main forces on the Western Front. In the end she won 'victory', but the effort bankrupted her. In his speculative replay of the war, Liddell Hart suggested that once the initial German onslaught in the West had been checked, the British involvement in France should have been restricted to the stiffening of the French defence. The British forces should have been employed more profitably in more exposed theatres, exploiting the mobility and surprise offered by the Royal Navy. A more carefully planned and better coordinated Dardanelles operation could have opened communications with Russia and facilitated the formation of a Balkan league on the Entente's side. Britain certainly had had to expand her armies considerably, but should never have introduced conscription and created mass armies on the Continental model. Instead, being still by far the mightiest manufacturing and financial power in the Entente, she should have concentrated on the production of armaments and ammunition for her allies, particularly Russia. To win the war on the strength of Russia's seemingly inexhaustible reservoir of manpower had actually been the strategy of the governments and general staffs of the Western allies during the early stage of the war. Their failure to supply Russia with the resources she needed to continue the war had been regarded by Lloyd George both during and after the war as their main strategic blunder.[2] According to Liddell Hart, if Russia had not defected and if the Central Powers, subjected as they had been to the British naval blockade, had been denied the foodstuffs and raw materials of South-eastern Europe which fell into their hands in 1915–17, Germany and her allies would not have been able to continue the war for long. A satisfactory negotiated peace could then have been reached, at a much lower human and economic cost to Britain, as well as to the other belligerents.

Nothing in this historical interpretation of British strategic policy was new. As historians have pointed out, in propounding 'the British way in warfare' Liddell Hart merely restated the arguments of the so-called 'maritime school' in British history. This school, which had

---

[2] D. Lloyd George, *War Memoirs* (London, 1936), 240–88, 1998; K. Neilson, *Strategy and Supply: The Anglo-Russian Alliance, 1914–1917* (London, 1984).

figured prominently in the strategic debate in Britain since Elizabethan times, resurfaced in the late nineteenth century and, increasingly, towards and during the First World War.[3] Its principal ideas, formulated and popularized by the famous naval authors Alfred Mahan and Philip Colomb, held sway in naval circles and largely dominated official outlook as well. Although in the decade before 1914 the British government accepted the commitment of the small British regular army to France at the outset of a war against Germany, this represented no real divergence from a fundamentally maritime approach. Well into the summer of 1915 the majority of the cabinet ministers expected to leave most of the burden of land warfare to Britain's allies, and supported the search for seaborne initiatives in which it was hoped that British naval power would assist in bringing about more effective and profitable results than the campaign in France. Only later in the war did the Allies' failures in the Dardanelles and Salonika, the mounting German pressure on Russia and the drain on France's resources drive Britain to accept an increasingly significant role in the Allies' land offensives in the west. Even then, when Britain's resources and manpower were being fully committed to the land war, Lloyd George and his colleagues, in conflict with the generals, were looking for alternatives to the costly offensives on the Western Front.[4]

Churchill's *World Crisis* reactivated the debate after the war, and Liddell Hart's conception of 'the British way in warfare' was probably also influenced by the writings of Admiral Sir Herbert Richmond, the naval intellectual maverick and first commandant of the new Imperial Defence College in 1926–9. Richmond was in close touch with Liddell Hart from 1930, the two acting in alliance on a whole range of defence issues.[5] Richmond, however, held moderate, revised navalist views, influenced both by the lessons of the First World War and by the ideas

---

[3] M. Howard, 'The British Way in Warfare', in *The Causes of War* (London, 1984), 192–3.

[4] M. Howard, *The Continental Commitment* (London, 1972), 53–9; P. Kennedy, *Strategy and Diplomacy, 1870–1945* (London, 1983), 63–6; *The Rise and Fall of British Naval Mastery*, 255–9; D. French, *British Economic and Strategic Planning, 1905–1915* (London, 1982); *British Strategy and War Aims, 1914–1916* (London, 1986); *The Strategy of the Lloyd George Coalition, 1916–1918* (Oxford, 1995).

[5] Richmond is the only authority cited in Liddell Hart's RUSI lecture, which he attended and with whose thesis he generally expressed agreement in the debate that followed the lecture: Liddell Hart, *The British Way in Warfare*, 28; *Memoirs* (2 vols., London, 1965), i. 58, 284; their correspondence is in i. 598. See also B. Bond, *Liddell Hart: A Study of His Military Thought* (London, 1977) [*LH*], 75–7.

advanced even before the war by Julian Corbett.[6] None of the qualifying and more subtle notions in the work of Corbett and Richmond were embodied in Liddell Hart's tract. As we have seen before, Corbett's ideas regarding limited war and the special propensity of Britain's maritime strategy for that type of war—as opposed to the Continental total war—decisively influenced Liddell Hart's development and became central to his entire thought. However, Corbett had also been an acute critic of maritime strategy, and had emphasized its inherent limitations at least as much as its purported advantages.

To be sure, Corbett endorsed and articulated the navy's 'blue water' view, according to which the navy alone was to be entrusted with the defence of the British Isles against enemy invasion. This view was accepted in general by the Invasion Sub-Committee of the Committee of Imperial Defence which was set up to study the problem in 1907–8.[7] Corbett also advised the Admiralty committees which in 1906 and 1908 drew up the navy's proposals for a maritime strategy in a war against Germany. In the Committee of Imperial Defence which examined this problem in 1908 and again in 1911, the Admiralty objected in vain to the army's plans for the dispatch of a British expeditionary force to France on the outbreak of hostilities.[8] It is very doubtful, however, that Corbett shared the Admiralty's view on that particular point.[9] In open divergence from accepted navalist faith, one of the main themes of his voluminous scholarly study of British naval history from Drake to Nelson and of his *Some Principles of Maritime Strategy* was that British naval pressure alone had not been able to hurt a great Continental

---

[6] For Richmond's views in the relevant period, see his *National Policy and Naval Strength* (London, 1928), 27–73; *Sea Power in the Modern World* (London, 1934), esp. 75–6, 108. See also A. Marder, *Portrait of an Admiral: The Life and Papers of Sir Herbert Richmond* (Cambridge, Mass., 1952); D. Schurman, *The Education of a Navy* (London, 1965), 110–46; R. Higham, *The Military Intellectuals in Britain, 1918–1939* (New Brunswick, NJ, 1966), 31–5, 51–61.

[7] M. Hankey, *The Supreme Command* (2 vols., London, 1961), i. 66–8.

[8] Ibid. 39–40, 69–70, 78–82.

[9] Howard, 'The British Way in Warfare', 196–7, may be too definite on this point. The most that can be said is that Admiral Slade drew heavily on Corbett's material in outlining the Admiralty's proposals for economic pressure against Germany, about the immediate efficacy of which the Admiralty itself had its doubts. The objection to the dispatch of an expeditionary force to France came mainly from Fisher: Hankey, *The Supreme Command*, i. 66–8. Howard also implies that Corbett argued that a maritime power was able to apply limited power even to the attainment of the unlimited objective of total victory, whereas Corbett in fact held that this could be done only 'in concert with continental allies': Howard, 'The British Way in Warfare' 194–5; J. Corbett, *Some Principles of Maritime Strategy* (Annapolis, Md., 1988), 78.

power decisively. In opposition to navalist critics, he justified the dispatch of British armies to the Continent from Elizabethan times on. In 1907, commenting on the proposals of the Admiralty Committee, he pointed out that the capture of German colonies would have no effect on the object of the war. Two years before the outbreak of the First World War, he denied that he had ever maintained that his concept of limited maritime warfare applied to a war against Germany. During the war itself, he was sceptical of most of the schemes for amphibious and combined operations against the Central Powers.[10]

Developing the notions first advanced by Corbett, by the army's General Staff, and by Richmond, historians have left few remains of Liddell Hart's 'British way in warfare'.[11] They have argued convincingly that the dispatch of British armies to the main theatres of operations in Europe in support of Britain's allies had always been a central and essential component of her strategy. It was no smaller in fact, in terms of the manpower and money invested, than Britain's maritime and overseas efforts, or, indeed, relative to her population, than her allies' military contributions. If she was to prevent a hegemonic Continental power from establishing its supremacy over Europe, and thus control Britain's main markets and ultimately threaten her naval predominance as well, Britain simply could not risk her allies collapsing or defecting for lack of support, and of the most direct kind. Amphibious operations and raids provided no real substitute for such direct involvement, not least because their inherent complexity made them prone to fail, as their historical record clearly demonstrates. Britain employed a 'purely' maritime strategy only out of necessity, when her Continental allies were geographically remote and isolated, as Frederick the Great was in the Seven Years War; or after they had been crushed, as against Napoleon in 1807–12; or when she did not have any in the first place, as during the American War of Independence. In all these cases Britain's position was very precarious indeed.

Furthermore, in the industrial age strategic conditions changed considerably from what they had been during the early modern period. In

---

[10] 'War Plans: Secret: General Remarks on a War with Germany', Corbett Papers, Box 6; marginal note on 'Great Britain, Germany and Limited War', *Edinburgh Review*, Apr. 1912, Corbett Papers, Box 5; both cited by E. Groves, Introduction, to Corbett, *Maritime Strategy*, p. xlii.

[11] See the authorities cited in n. 1 of the Introduction to Part II (above). For Richmond's excellent analysis of most of the following points, see the references to his works in n. 6 above.

the first place, for all the clamour of the imperialist contest, the value of overseas gains for national wealth, and consequently their significance in war, decreased sharply. Secondly, while in the new global market of raw materials and goods the blockade had in fact become a far more effective instrument of war than it had been before, this was only true if the hegemonic Continental power was prevented from overrunning and occupying great stretches of the European land mass, thus making itself much less vulnerable to economic pressure. In addition, Britain herself had become even more vulnerable than her Continental rivals to a naval blockade. Thus it had become her vital interest to prevent the harbours of Western Europe from being occupied and turned into bases for enemy submarines. Finally, for the first time in history the advent of the railroad had made land transportation in the European theatre of war at least as quick and economical as sea transportation, and far more flexible. Seaborne operations on the peripheries of the Continent had thus become that much less promising and more dangerous. The advent of the aeroplane reinforced this trend, and also exposed the British Isles themselves to attack from the Continent, making Britain all the more interested in what was happening beyond her shores.

All these are perfectly valid points. The only thing is that Liddell Hart actually raised most, if not all, of them *himself*, though, admittedly, not in his well-known but superficial 1931 RUSI lecture. As it has been shrewdly put, 'it would be doing Liddell Hart an injustice' to regard that lecture as 'anything more than a brilliant piece of political pamphleteering'.[12] Indeed, even more, it would be to underestimate him considerably. There is no question that Liddell Hart was totally sincere and committed in his biases. But his 1931 lecture, although certainly programmatic in nature and directed to the future as much as to the past, was merely an abstract sketch. There was still no sign of any disturbance to peace, not even a definite enemy in view, in Europe or even in East Asia, at the beginning of the 1930s. Shortly afterwards, however, the Japanese invasion of Manchuria, Hitler's rise to power in Germany, and the subsequent actions by Germany, Italy, and Japan against the international status quo initiated a period of profound crises and once more made a great war a likely possibility. And after the tension exploded in a new world war there came yet another period of endemic crisis, with the Cold War between the communist world and the West.

---

[12] Howard, 'The British Way in Warfare', 192.

Thus, while before the mid-1930s circumstances had not really offered Liddell Hart the occasion to address any specific political situation or concrete strategic problem, from that time on questions of foreign and strategic policy were becoming his main field of concern. He was now required to adapt his hitherto abstract ideas and sweeping generalizations—including 'the British way in warfare'—to formulate much more carefully reasoned and precise policy recommendations, taking into account the particular conditions of the time and the place.[13] This he did, though not without some mistakes and the occasional blunder, with remarkable acuteness and foresight, much greater than he has been generally credited with by historians.

This, perhaps, becomes more apparent with the passage of time and the changing of historical perspectives; the opening of the British archives, for example, has altered our understanding of the 1930s, while the end of the Cold War makes possible a longer view of the fifty-year crisis. The policies which Liddell Hart advocated in relation to Nazi Germany and the Axis powers before and during the Second World War, and which he barely changed when the Soviet Union took Germany's place as the main threat to the West's interests and way of life, have become the stock-in-trade of modern strategic outlook. None the less, Liddell Hart has not been given sufficient credit as their pioneer. For all his talents for self-publicity, he himself never fully presented his case for the judgement of posterity, first, because it involved painful personal memories and second, because at the time he published his *Memoirs* in the mid-1960s events were too close to allow a wider assessment of his significance in the history of strategic thought, by himself as well as by others.

It is not the aim of this study to replay the momentous events and major decisions of the 1930s, 1940s, and 1950 and make the case for or against Liddell Hart's positions. Although discussion of available alternatives, in order to illuminate the decisions and courses of action actually taken at the time, is an essential part of historical understanding, hypothetical cases are impossible to prove or disprove and ought not be pursued too seriously. Neither is it my aim here to present Liddell Hart's role in British decision-making in any detail. By the late 1920s and early 1930s he had already become internationally famous as a military critic, theorist, and historian, and as a leading

---

[13] Cf. M. Howard, 'Liddell Hart' (1970), repr. in *The Causes of War*, 241; also J. Mearsheimer, *Liddell Hart and the Weight of History* (London, 1988) [*LH*], 99, 107.

proponent of armoured warfare. His position as the only regular military correspondent in a British newspaper and his many connections in the defence establishment and army earned him considerable influence. In the second half of the 1930s, as he moved to *The Times*, became the unofficial adviser to the War Secretary, Hore-Belisha, and regularly briefed senior politicians of all parties, his influence reached its peak. All the same, his main significance remains in the history of strategic ideas, and it is from this angle—in connection with the wider trends characterizing Western strategic thought in this century—that his policy recommendations will concern us here. For in response to the challenges facing Britain and the West from the mid-1930s on, Liddell Hart's thought expanded and assumed new dimensions. He now integrated the ideas and doctrines he had propounded in the 1920s within a fully conscious political and philosophical creed. Developing a blueprint for a strategic policy that would suit the needs of liberal and 'satisfied' nations who could no longer perceive themselves voluntarily embroiled in major great-power wars, he advanced the notions of containment and cold war, and outlined the means by which they could be implemented.

I. Collective Security

In early 1935 Liddell Hart transferred from the *Daily Telegraph* to take up the newly created post of defence correspondent of *The Times*. This new peak in his career coincided with the ending of Britain's postwar defence policy. Following the work of the Defence Requirements Committee in 1933–4 the British cabinet decided on a limited programme of rearmament to face the growing potential threats from Germany and Japan. Before assuming his new post with *The Times*, Liddell Hart conducted a comprehensive preparatory assessment of the strategic position of Britain and the Empire, whose conclusions he laid out in his first article in *The Times*. The only solution he saw for Britain's defence problems was collective security:

there could be little promise of security, so far as one can see, in adopting a policy of isolation. The most 'forceful' argument for pursuing the method of collective security is the strategic . . . the development of a collective security is not only a moral ideal but a British interest.

In emphasizing the strategic dimension of collective security, Liddell Hart reflected a wider change in British political attitudes. Collective security had previously been regarded either as an empty, if not dangerous, slogan or as a substitute for and moral alternative to rearmament. By 1935, however, in the wake of the 'peace ballot' which overwhelmingly supported collective security and military means to enforce it, the strategic aspect of this policy was taken up by the Baldwin adminstration. It was particularly identified with Eden, foreign secretary from the end of that year. Soon it would be adopted both by the Labour and Liberal parties.[14] Even Churchill, who had long treated the concept with contempt, would embrace it in the late 1930s as a disguise for the old principle of the balance of power for the purpose of blocking Germany. Liddell Hart came to advocate collective security for the same reasons as the government. While supportive of the new rearmament measures, he suggested, echoing the assessments of the responsible defence authorities, that in view of the prospective threats facing Britain, even the most extensive and expensive rearmament programme, had it been possible, would fail to achieve for Britain the kind of security she had enjoyed in the nineteenth century. Admitting that previously he had been predisposed toward isolationism, he now maintained that it was out of the question. Britain's only hope for security lay in conjunction with her allies, with whom she must work in a concerted effort to maintain the status quo. His programmatic article, overlooked by historians, was at least as important as 'The British Way in Warfare' in determining his strategic attitude during the second half of the 1930s.[15]

His position during the coming years of crises may best be clarified in reference to Britain's official policy, as it would be shaped and steered in widely divergent courses under the successive powerful personal stamp of two dominating prime ministers, Neville Chamberlain and Winston Churchill. In each case Liddell Hart supported some aspects of their respective policy lines while bitterly opposing other aspects. In his

---

[14] See esp. K. Middlemas, *Diplomacy of Illusion: The British Government and Germany, 1937–39* (London, 1972), 26–35, 144–7, 157, and *passim*; R. A. C. Parker, *Chamberlain and Appeasement: British Policy and the Coming of the Second World War* (London, 1993), 45–7.

[15] *The Times*, 14 Mar. 1935; also 'Defence of the Realm', *Listener*, 11 Mar. 1936; 'Military and Strategic Advantages of Collective Security in Europe', *New Commonwealth Quarterly*, 9 (1938) 144–55; to Barrington-Ward, 29 Mar. 1938, Liddell Hart Centre for Military Archives, King's college, London [King's], 3/108; *The Defence of Britain* (London, 1939), 45; letter to the *New Statesman*, published on 19 Dec. 1942, in reply to George Orwell's review of the new edition of *When Britain Goes to War*; here LH specifically points out that in 1935 he revised his original concept of 'the British Way in Warfare'; *Memoirs*, i. 285–6; ii, 146. The article in *The Times* and its significance are only referred to (albeit partially) by Mearsheimer, *LH*, 106, 130.

opinion, in their opposite ways both ultimately failed to square Britain's resources and aims. Indeed, as the opening of the British archives broke the monopoly of the Churchillian version of the 1930s, this view is now widely shared by historians, who have come to a better appreciation of the intricacies of the security dilemma facing Britain at that time. As one historian has put it, neither Chamberlain's policies nor Churchill's '"solved' Britain's strategic and economic dilemmas . . . both appeasement and anti-appeasement brought disadvantages; they were only a choice of evils'.[16]

Like most politically minded Britons in the second half of the 1930s, with the exception of a small minority of isolationists and extreme appeasers, Liddell Hart regarded Germany as Britain's main security problem and thought that the prevention of a German hegemony over the Continent was a vital British interest which had to be defended even by force. Equally, however, he believed, like the overwhelming majority of official and public opinion, that another total war against Germany would be a disaster, and perceived, like Chamberlain and many others in the British establishment, that it would result in the subservience of Britain to the United States and in the end of the Empire. In line with his entire philosophy of war the problem, as he saw it, was how to apply force, if necessary, to stop the revisionist powers, Germany in particular, without falling into a mutually ruinous, counterproductive, and futile total war. In his view, it was in this difficult balancing act between the two equally disastrous political opposites of appeasement and total war that the test of British policy lay.

The international situation in Europe (and the Far East) deteriorated in stages, and it was only in hindsight that events would be viewed as a single, one-way process. The Japanese invasion of Manchuria in 1931 outraged Western and British public opinion. Yet the British political and defence establishment assessed that League sanctions against Japan might be answered by her with war, which nobody wanted and for which the British armed forces, which were supposed to carry most of the burden in case of a League action, were ill-prepared. Hitler's rise to power in Germany and the first steps of German rearmament alarmed the other powers but raised no serious thoughts of armed intervention. The Versailles Treaty and the 'denial of equality' to Germany had long been regarded in Britain as a historic mistake which was better

---

[16] P. Kennedy, *The Rise and Fall of the Great Powers* (London, 1989), 413; *Strategy and Diplomacy*, 100–6.

corrected as smoothly as possible. Between 1935 and 1938 the Italian invasion of Abyssinia, the German unilateral entry into the Rhineland demilitarized zone, and the Axis Powers' intervention in Spain each made some sort of action by the other European great powers a distinct possibility. By contrast, nobody considered that anything practical could be done about the German Anschluss with Austria in March 1938. The rapid German action created a *fait accompli* which could not be reversed short of total war, and the enforced treaty separation of the two German-speaking countries was anyhow something about which the Western powers had a bad conscience. It was only from the spring of 1938, with the coming of the Czechoslovakian crisis, that European (and British) politics became dominated by the prospect of a major war.

Liddell Hart's reaction to the crises of the 1930s underwent similar development. Although he would later denounce the inaction of Britain and the League of Nations over the Japanese invasion of Manchuria as the first step of appeasement and of the collapse of collective security, he does not seem to have been troubled by the matter at the time in any noticeable way.[17] In the following years, like other Britons, he was concerned about German rearmament, though when Germany reintroduced conscription, something which went against one of his most cherished doctrines, he raised the question whether the German army was not going to lose in quality what it was gaining in quantity.[18] He, too, did not suggest that anything practical could or should be done to stop German rearmament, and like many felt that Germany was justified in repudiating the discriminatory stipulations of Versailles. After the German army had marched into the Rhineland demilitarized zone in March 1936, Liddell Hart wrote privately that Germany was doing the right thing in the wrong way. She was justified in her claim for equality and in rejecting the dictated Treaty of Versailles, but she had signed the Locarno Treaty of her own free will and therefore her unilateral action could not be justified. Could she be trusted in the future? These sentiments were common in Britain, where again practically nobody recommended armed action to eject the Germans.[19]

If the last-mentioned crises could be regarded as internal German affairs, the crises over Abyssinia, Spain, and Czechoslovakia were not. As we have seen, in early 1935 Liddell Hart came to the conclusion that

---

[17] Cf. Mearsheimer, *LH*, 132.   [18] *The Times*, 18 Mar. 1935.
[19] 7 Mar. 1936, King's, 11/1936/45; N. Gibbs, *Grand Strategy: History of the Second World War*, i (London, 1976), 227–54; B. Bond, *British Military Policy between the Two World Wars* (Oxford, 1980) 225–7.

collective security was the only conceivable method for safeguarding British security and was, therefore, a British interest. Henceforth he held firm to that doctrine, growing more persistent and vocal as each successive crisis presented an ever greater threat to British security. The strategic policy he advocated in each case was similar.

Liddell Hart's record on the Abyssinian crisis is scant but far from non-existent. As the crisis escalated over the summer and autumn of 1935, he denounced the British inaction in his private papers as short-sighted. He argued that the case was clear-cut, and reflected that it shed light on the true character of one's friends: who among them held that keeping promises was unimportant?[20] However, while commenting widely on the military operations of the war in *The Times*, he is not on record on the strategic policy he thought Britain ought to follow. This may be due to the fact that *The Times*, while strongly condemning Italy, did not support full sanctions against her. In later letters to the editor and to the assistant editor of *The Times*, the would-be ardent appeasers Geoffrey Dawson and Robin Barrington-Ward, who were arguably in a position to know whether or not what he said was true, Liddell Hart claimed that the cleavage between his opinions and their own had begun over the Abyssinian crisis when he had demanded a firm British line. He wrote that he had advocated the supply of arms to Abyssinia and supported the imposition of an oil embargo on Italy, which had been widely regarded as the only effective method of bringing her to her knees short of a war.[21] Since Britain controlled both entrances to the Mediterranean and the Italian sea route to Abyssinia, there was plenty of scope for indirect action to coerce Italy into withdrawing. Despite the scarcity of British forces in Egypt and the vulnerability of the Mediterranean route to the Italian air force and submarines, the British chiefs of staff were not very impressed by the Italian ability for effective counter-action. The reasons for the lack of determined action against Italy were mainly political: the British government saw no direct threat to British interests from the Italian occupation of Abyssinia; the British, and especially the French, were

---

[20] 30 June, 2 and 25 Sept. 1935: 11/1935/13, 28, 35.
[21] To Barrington-Ward, 30 Apr. 1937, King's, 3/107; to Dawson, 9 May 1938, 3/109; *Memoirs*, i. 287, 289. Mearsheimer, *LH*, 133–4, does not cite the references in this and the previous note. For the positions of *The Times*, Dawson, and Barrington-Ward, see M. Cowling, *The Impact of Hitler: British Politics and British Policy, 1933–1940* (Cambridge, 1975), 128–33.

reluctant to push Mussolini into Hitler's arms; and Britain was determined not to act without full French cooperation.[22]

Containment: Spain

It is obvious, however, that Liddell Hart did not feel about the Abyssinian crisis as strongly as he felt about the subsequent crises over Spain and Czechoslovakia, which strained his relations with *The Times* to the limit. From the outset, British attitudes towards the Spanish Civil War were marked by conflicting sympathies between left and right towards the warring parties, and by an even deeper official indifference. The British government believed that the outcome of the war mattered little to Britain, who would be able to maintain friendly relations with whoever won. It was in Britain's interest, however, agreed upon by all political parties, that all foreign intervention in the Spanish Civil War should be excluded. Yet by October 1936 it had become apparent that the non-intervention agreement, signed by the great powers at the end of August 1936, was almost openly disregarded by Italy and Germany, followed by the Soviet Union. In consequence, the Labour party swung against non-intervention, which remained the British and French policy up to the end of the war. Throughout 1937 Foreign Minister Eden was advocating stronger measures, including active naval surveillance, to prevent the violation of the non-intervention treaty. He was opposed, however, by his predecessor, now First Lord of the Admiralty, Sir Samuel Hoare, and by his other cabinet colleagues.[23]

Liddell Hart was similarly concerned by the course the war was taking. From November 1936 he disputed *The Times*'s editorial policy in respect to Spain and Eastern Europe, becoming ever more insistent and categorical. He protested that *The Times* was censoring information about Nationalist atrocities in order to create a false balance with Republican atrocities in this sad human and moral tale which had important public opinion implications.[24] At the beginning of April 1937 he still suggested that, as the stalemate in the Spanish Civil War went on, the Republicans' chances of holding on were improving,

---

[22] Gibbs, *Grand Strategy*, 189–222; also Bond, *British Military Policy*, 218–19; G. Post Jr., *Dilemmas of Appeasement: British Deterrence and Defence, 1934–1937* (London, 1993), 81–104.

[23] See J. Edwards, *The British Government and the Spanish Civil War, 1936–1939* (London, 1979); Parker, *Chamberlain and Appeasement*, 84–6.

[24] To Barrington-Ward, 4 Nov. 1936, and subsequent letter exchange: King's, 3/106; 19, 21 and 28 May 1937; memorandum, 'Conclusions from the Balance of Evidence', 21 May 1937; 25 Feb. 1938: all in 3/106–8; *Memoirs*, ii. 128–9.

provided that increased foreign intervention did not tip the scales against them. But from the end of that month, judging that Italian and German intervention was heavily influencing the course of the war, he is on record as opposing the British policy of non-intervention.[25] From early 1938 it was becoming clear that the Nationalists were finally winning the Civil War, a prospect which Liddell Hart viewed with the greatest anxiety. Precisely for that reason, however, he was no longer asked by *The Times* to contribute editorial leaders on Spain, and his commentaries on the war were not published. In March his article 'The Western Mediterranean', which he had originally written as a memorandum for the Secretary of State for War, Hore-Belisha, was refused publication on the grounds that it was wholly political and that its conclusions were unacceptable to the editor. From then on until the end of the Spanish Civil War in March 1939, Liddell Hart's writings on the war were regularly turned down by *The Times*.[26] Only in his articles in periodical journals was he able to express his opinions publicly.

What was he so concerned about? He was worried that if the Nationalists won the Civil War with the assistance of Italy and Germany, Spain might become a base for Axis air forces and naval light crafts and submarines. In a general European war these would close the western Mediterranean to Britain and France, and would constitute a serious threat to their naval routes around Africa and across the Atlantic. Liddell Hart argued emphatically that the gravity of this security risk was such that Britain simply could not responsibly ignore it in the hope that it would not materialize. From 1937 onward he discussed his views of the crisis with leaders of all three political parties. On two occasions he spoke with Eden, and in March and May 1938 Hore-Belisha, briefed by Liddell Hart, raised the subject of intervention in Spain in the cabinet.[27] To Liddell Hart's surprise, when discussing the question of Spain in June 1937 with the CIGS, Field Marshal Deverell, he got the impression that the latter had been entirely unaware of the strategic problem. French and British naval authorities had been aware

[25] 'Spain: Attack or Defence', *The Times*, 3 Apr. 1937; cf. *Europe in Arms* (London, 1937), 321; *Memoirs*, i. 372; to Barrington-Ward, 30 Apr. 1937, quoted ibid. ii. 132–3 (and out of context by Mearsheimer, *LH*, 136 n. 17); to Dawson, 1 Oct. 1937, quoted in *Memoirs*, ii. 135: letters in King's, 1/107.

[26] To Barrington-Ward, 25 Feb., 26 Mar., 10 Aug., 8 Nov. 1938; Barrington-Ward to Liddell Hart, 28, 29, 30 Mar., 1 Apr., and 2 Nov. 1938: all in King's, 3/108; much of this correspondence is printed in *Memoirs*, ii. 142–8.

[27] Talks with Eden, 23 Nov. 1937 and 1 June 1938: *Memoirs*, i. 136–7; King's, 11/1938/62; Cowling, *The Impact of Hitler*, 330.

of the potential danger since the beginning of the war in 1936; by late 1937 intelligence sources were reporting on Italian requests for bases in Spain. Nevertheless, it was only in March 1939 that the British chiefs of staff stressed the danger from a hostile Spain, in exactly the same terms as Liddell Hart and with equal gravity.[28]

What then did Liddell Hart suggest Britain and France should do? In his opinion, there was no need to get directly entangled in the fighting against the Italians and Germans on Spanish soil. Britain and France simply had to lift their embargo and provide the Republican forces with the arms and supplies they required. He believed that this was very likely sufficient to redress the balance and create a stalemate; in the past Spain had proved her immense capacity for absorbing foreign armies for years on end. It would then be left to the Italians and Germans to decide whether they wanted to settle the conflict at the negotiating table, or escalate it to their disadvantage:

If Germany and Italy were to reply by a large increase in the quantities of material they have already sent, France and Britain are in better strategic position than they are for such competition—since the former powers would be locking up military resources in a potentially isolated theatre. If they dared to press their objections to the point of war, we should fight with all the advantages of the defensive and under more favourable circumstances of strategic geography than we could hope for once Spain has been conquered.[29]

With France controlling the land routes to Spain and the British and French navies the sea lanes, the odds were most favourable to the Western allies. Writing his *Memoirs* in the early 1960s, Liddell Hart likened this situation to the one prevailing during the Cuban crisis in 1962. Had he lived longer, he might also have cited Vietnam and

---

[28] A talk with Deverell, 29 June 1937, King's, 11/1937/56; *Memoirs*, ii. 140; J. Edwards, *The British Government and the Spanish Civil War, 1936–1939* (London, 1979), 23, 164, 212–14; G. Stone, 'The European Great Powers and the Spanish Civil War, 1936–1939', in R. Boyce and E. Robertson (eds.), *Paths to War: New Essays on the Origins of the Second World War* (London, 1989), 220–1; Gibbs, *Grand Strategy*, i. 727.

[29] Note, 13 Mar. 1938, King's, 11/1938/30, cited in *The Defence of Britain* (London, 1937), 64, and in *Memoirs*, ii. 142. More in 'The Strategic Future of the Mediterranean', *Yale Review* (Dec. 1936), 232–45, reprinted in *Europe in Arms* (London, 1937), 100–15; 'Strategy and Commitments', *Fortnightly* (June 1938), 642–5; 'Military and Strategic Advantages of Collective Security in Europe', *New Commonwealth Quarterly* (Sept. 1938), 147 ff.; 'Britain's Military Situation', *Yale Review* (Jan. 1939), 240; 'The Defence of Western Civilization', *New Commonwealth Review* (Jan. 1939), 25; 'What Spain Means to Britain', *Picture Post*, 4 Feb. 1939; extracts from Liddell Hart's memos and writings are printed in *The Defence of Britain*, 22, 24, 39, 64, 67–70, 81–2, 90, 138, 141–2, 285; *Memoirs*, ii. 128–30, 143–4.

Afghanistan. Interestingly, a study of Germany's intentions supports his view that Hitler was careful not to get deeply involved in the Spanish Civil War and certainly did not want to see it escalate into a general war.[30] In the Abyssinian crisis, the limited and indirect course of action which was considered against Italy and which Liddell Hart supported may have succeeded had it been applied; but the strategic issue at stake, as opposed to the wider political and moral implications of the crisis, was insignificant. In the Spanish crisis the potential strategic threat to the Western allies, emphasized by Liddell Hart, was serious, and the limited and indirect course of action he advocated again appears plausible; yet, despite the Nationalists' victory, the threat did not materialize. The British government (and the editors of *The Times*) believed all along that Britain had enough economic leverage on Franco to prevent a Nationalist Spain from becoming hostile.[31] Indeed, in the event Spain would remain neutral during the Second World War, though, contrary to earlier beliefs, recent research has revealed Franco's eagerness to enter the war on the Axis side after Hitler's initial triumphs. If he did not, it was principally because Hitler was unwilling to accept his excessive colonial demands, mainly at the expense of Vichy France.[32] With the coming of the Czechoslovakian crisis, Liddell Hart viewed the potential threat as critical, and the methods he advocated were similar to those he had been advancing before. Czechoslovakia and Spain were engraved on his standard during 1938. Again he was in conflict with *The Times*, and after Munich he was in open public opposition to the British government's policy.

Containment: Czechoslovakia

Czechoslovakia was, after all, in Chamberlain's memorable phrase, 'a faraway country', inhabited by 'people of whom we know nothing'. In herself she was of practically no interest to Britain. Furthermore, whereas in the Abyssinian and Spanish crises the Western allies held the geo-strategic cards in their hands, being able to isolate the respective theatres of operations, it was Germany who held the cards in the Czechoslovakian crisis. Czechoslovakia was geographically isolated from the Western allies and, as the British chiefs of staff made clear and

---

[30] Ibid. 130; G. Stone, 'The European Great Powers and the Spanish Civil War', in Boyce and Robertson (eds.), *Paths to War*, 220–1.

[31] Dawson to Liddell Hart, 30 Oct. 1937; Barrington-Ward to Liddell Hart, 29 Mar. 1938: King's, 3/107–8.   [32] P. Preston, *Franco* (London, 1993), 343–425.

Liddell Hart himself repeatedly stressed, there was virtually nothing Britain and France could do to directly assist in her defence. Why then did Liddell Hart regard Czechoslovakia as so critical to Britain's security as to justify war to defend it, and what course of action did he propose Britain should follow?

In Liddell Hart's opinion, rather than being an embarrassing liability, Czechoslovakia was one of the most vital elements of Britain's security system. His logic, explicitly traced to his study in 1935 of Britain's defence problems, was far more comprehensive than the critics of his 'British Way of Warfare' have given him credit for. He repeatedly stressed that the development of air power and the submarine had made British security interlinked with France's security against Germany: 'If France fell under hostile domination, and her ports and air bases were available for an enemy's use, the flow of our life blood could easily be stopped. Hence her risks are our risks.'[33] In turn, French security depended on the existence of a second front against Germany in Eastern Europe. The function of France's East European alliances, with Czechoslovakia in particular, consisted of more than their potential value for offsetting Germany's military superiority, dividing her strength, and relieving some of her pressure on France. The point, in Liddell Hart's view, was that the Western allies were simply too weak to hope they would be able to defeat Germany on the battlefield in any given time-scale. Their sole potent weapon of deterrence and coercion against Germany was the blockade which, despite her efforts to achieve autarky and develop ersatz goods, her highly industrialized economy could not withstand for very long. Over 66 per cent of Germany's ores for steel production came from abroad, as did 25 per cent of her zinc, 50 per cent of her lead, 70 per cent of her copper, 90 per cent of her tin, 95 per cent of her nickel, 99 per cent of her bauxite, 66 per cent of her oil, 80 per cent of her rubber, and 10–20 per cent of her foodstuffs.[34] As Liddell Hart noted, in the age of mechanized warfare Germany's shortages in certain key raw materials such as oil and metals for the aircraft industry actually made her even more vulnerable to the blockade than she had been during the First World War.[35] However, as he clearly saw, the blockade would be effective only if its implementation

---

[33] Quotation from *The Defence of Britain*, 136.

[34] Kennedy, *Strategy and Diplomacy*, 75; *British Naval Mastery*, 307; also W. N. Medlicott, *The Economic Blockade* (2 vols., London, 1978), i. 32. Cf. Liddell Hart, *The Defence of Britain*, 40–2; also *The Second World War* (London, 1970), 23–4.

[35] *The Defence of Britain*, 41.

by Britain on the sea was not circumvented by land, as Germany had partially succeeded in doing during the First World War. As Herbert Richmond had written in 1928:

It was only owing to the fact that the land frontiers of the enemies were sealed by the armies, and that every nation of importance was either actively assisting with her navies at sea, or passively by withholding trade, that the eventual degree of isolation was procured which contributed to victory.[36]

Liddell Hart viewed the situation in the same light: 'against a Continental state, sea power can only be a serious handicap, unless its land frontiers can also be closed. In that case, unless completely self-supporting, it may be gradually starved into submission.'[37] It followed that, with France and perhaps also the Low Countries on Britain's side, Germany had to be prevented from overrunning south-eastern Europe, and the Soviet Union's political, strategic, and economic cooperation had to be secured and denied to Germany. Hence Liddell Hart's staunch opposition to the Munich settlement, opposition based entirely on strategic grounds. The great question confounding British decision making in the late 1930s, what Hitler's and Germany's future intentions might be, did not matter to him at all in weighing the issue. As he saw it, Germany could not be effectively stopped, not even by a disastrous total war, once it broke loose of its restricted territorial base.[38] The sacrifice of the Czechoslovakian bastion would bring all the countries of the Danube basin with their agricultural and mineral wealth within German reach, and give Germany the ability to sustain a prolonged war. Like the breach of a dam, concessions to Germany in south-eastern Europe implied on Britain's part the forfeiting of its only potent weapon and the total collapse of any chance of stopping Germany by limited means and limited action, or indeed *by any means at all*. Great firmness and limited effort were thus the two interdependent sides of Liddell Hart's strategic equation.[39]

---

[36] *National Policy and Naval Strength* (London, 1928), 142; see also p. 71; cited with approval by Kennedy, *Strategy and Diplomacy*, 62, also 75; British *Naval Mastery*, 254–5.

[37] *The Defence of Britain*, 144.

[38] LH's conclusions bear a striking resemblance to those of the only two rigorous studies of the question from the strategic and economic point of view: W. Murray, *The Change in the European Balance of Power, 1938–1939* (Princeton, NJ, 1984), 27, 64–7, 160, 256–63, 362–3, and *passim*; D. E. Kaiser, *The Economic Diplomacy and the Origins of the Second World War: Germany, Britain, France, and Eastern Europe, 1930–1939* (Princeton, NJ, 1980), pp. xii, 218, 262, 283, 313, 315, and *passim*.

[39] Notes, 13 Mar. 1938, King's, 11/1938/30; *The Times*, 17 June 1938; 'Strategy and Commitments', 648–9; 'Military and Strategic Advantages of Collective Security in Europe', *New Commonwealth Quarterly* (Sept. 1938), 147–52; Notes, 9, 28 Sept. 1938, 11/1938/92

However Liddell Hart's analysis might be disputed, it serves to highlight how curiously incomplete was the strategic advice given during the crisis to the British government by the chiefs of staff. The chiefs of staff were duly pessimistic about the situation, fearing that Japan and Italy might take advantage of Britain's entanglement with Germany, stressing that the Western allies were unprepared for war and could do nothing to directly assist Czechoslovakia in her defence, and judging that Czechoslovakia would not be able to resist a German attack.[40] However, even though they made it very clear that Britain's strategy against Germany rested principally on the blockade, nowhere did the chiefs of staff discuss or even mention the implications for the feasibility of that weapon of the possible loss of south-eastern Europe that might follow the abandonment of Czechoslovakia. Such an assessment had in fact been called for by Oliver Stanley, representing those in the cabinet who doubted the wisdom of Chamberlain's policy. It was blocked, however, by General Ismay, the secretary of the Committee of Imperial Defence. Thus, strange as this may appear, the problem did not figure in the political, strategic, and public debate in Britain before Munich, even though the prospect of a German-dominated *Mitteleuropa* was recognized.[41] Nor has the problem been sufficiently recognized by historians until recently.

After Munich both Romania and Yugoslavia had no choice but to concede to a series of economic treaties which gave Germany priority in exploiting their highly important oil, mineral, and food resources. By occupying the rest of Czechoslovakia in March 1939, Germany considerably expanded her economic base and enriched her meagre reserves of foreign currency and raw materials, whose condition in

---

and 103; 'Britain's Military Situation', *Yale Review* (Dec. 1938), 230–45; 'The Defence of Western Civilization', *New Commonwealth Review* (Jan. 1939), 21–30; extracts are printed in *The Defence of Britain*, 22–4, 38–42, 63, 86–7, and *Memoirs*, ii. 130–1, 140–2, 145–6, 158–64.

[40] Howard, *Continental Commitment*, 119, 122; Gibbs, *Grand Strategy*, 642–3, 646–7; Murray, *European Balance of Power*, 157–62, 209–10.

[41] W. K. Wark, *The Ultimate Enemy: Britain Intelligence and Nazi Germany, 1933–1939* (London, 1985), 207–8. The question occurred to Ismay himself, who may have been influenced in this respect by Liddell Hart without accepting his conclusions (he also mentioned the advantage of the defensive in war): see the citation (22 Sept. 1938) in Howard, *Continental Commitment*, 123. See also R. Macleod and D. Kelly (eds.), *The Ironside Diaries, 1937–1940* (London, 1962), 62, 64.

1938 was extremely serious.[42] Germany incorporated the thriving Czechoslovakian arms industry, of which the Skoda and Zbrojovka factories in particular were among the world's best, making Czechoslovakia the fourth largest exporter of arms. The military equipment captured in Czechoslovakia in vast quantities was judged first-rate by the Germans, and found sufficient to equip twenty new German divisions, including three Panzer (divisions 6–8), armed with the Czechoslovakian T35 and T38. During the 1940 campaign in the West some 40 per cent of the German medium (gun-mounted) tanks were Czech models.[43]

Indeed, the *direct* loss that the abandonment of Czechoslovakia entailed has always been recognized by historians. Czechoslovakia was a significant military power, and, as all studies of her strength emphasize, her ability to resist Germany remains an open question.[44] Her army was strong, modern, and highly motivated. It numbered 1,250,000 soldiers, organized in fifteen corps (34–5 divisions) and in additional fortress troops. It possessed around 1,200 aircrafts, more than half of which of the first line, 700 tanks, 2,200 field-guns, and 2,500 anti-tank guns. The country's mountainous frontiers with Germany were heavily fortified. On the other side, the German army of 1938 was still in the midst of its expansion. Not only the Western allies but also the chiefs of the German armed forces felt totally unprepared for a general war. The Germans planned to deploy no more than thirty-seven divisions against

[42] For the significance of Germany's economic incorporation of Czechoslovakia and south-eastern Europe, see H.-E. Volkmann's contribution to Militärgeschichtliches Forschungsamt [MF] (ed.), *Germany and the Second World War*, i (Oxford, 1990), 332–49, 451; Murray, *European Balance of Power*, esp. 256–63, 291–2; Kaiser, *Economic Diplomacy*, 264–7 and *passim*. The point is fully conceded even by the otherwise revisionist R. Overy, 'Hitler's War Plans and the German Economy', in Boyce and Robertson, *Paths to War*, 111–12, 115–16. In Kaiser's summary: 'In 1938 the Munich agreement, which removed the last effective barrier to German military expansion eastward, also laid the region's economic resources at Hitler's feet. This peaceful triumph enabled Hitler to begin war one year later and to defeat the western powers in 1940' (p. xii). For Liddell Hart, see *The Defence of Britain*, 23–4, 38–9, 87.

[43] For the impressive products of the Czechoslovakian armour industry, see W. Spielberger, *Die Panzer-Kampfwagen 35(t) and 38(t)* (Stuttgart, 1980); also W. Oswald, *Kraftfahrzeuge und Panzer der Reichswehr, Wehrmacht und Bundeswehr* (Stuttgart, 1982), 356–7. Some 4500 T38 and derivative models were built for the Wehrmacht during the war.

[44] There are several excellent studies of the strategic balance: D. Vital, *The Survival of Small States* (Oxford, 1971), 26–34; M. Hauner, 'Czechoslovakia as a Military Factor in British Considerations of 1938', *Journal of Strategic Studies*, 1 (1978), 194–222; Murray, *European Balance of Power*, 119–21, 217–63; T. Taylor, *Munich: The Price of Peace* (New York, 1979), esp. 398–9, 681–731; also see W. Murray, 'German Air Power and the Munich Crisis', in B. Bond and I. Roy (eds.), *War and Society Yearbook*, 2 (1977), 114–15; MF, *Germany and the Second World War*, i. 334.

Czechoslovakia, leaving only five, together with four reserve and fourteen Landwehr divisions, against France. Three divisions were left to defend East Prussia. Contrary to the Allies' assessments at the time, the capacity of the German army for further expansion after the outbreak of hostilities was seriously limited by lack of equipment. The German Panzer force was still inexperienced and ill-equipped. Although numbering 2,100 tanks, it possessed only light, gunless models and still practically none of the new Marks III and IV medium tanks. Germany's greatest superiority was in the air, but the Luftwaffe, too, was still experiencing severe problems in the summer of 1938, arising from the transfer to a new generation of aircraft. Only little more then 50 per cent of the machines and air crews were operationally ready.[45] Here as well, the Germans planned to throw most of their weight against Czechoslovakia.

The Germans rated Czechoslovakia's strength very highly both before the crisis and when they examined what they saw after occupying the country. All the same, they planned to conquer it in a three-week campaign. The conservative and anti-war Chief of the General Staff Beck thought it would take longer.[46] Liddell Hart believed that the Czechs might well be capable of resisting indefinitely. He echoed, perhaps knowingly, the Czechoslovakian army's plan to withdraw into the depth of the country once its frontier lines were breached and to establish new defensive lines in the Moravian hills.[47] Admittedly, as we shall see, he vastly overrated the strength of defence. However, it ought to be noted that a year later he correctly judged that the Polish army stood no chance against the Germans.

Among the conditions Liddell Hart specified for the success of Czechoslovakia's resistance were that Poland and Hungary would not intervene against her, and the support of strong air reinforcements from the Soviet Union. He was fully aware of the difficulties the Soviet Union would encounter if she wished to support Czechoslovakia. The two countries had no common frontier. The Poles were unlikely to grant the Red Army free passage through their territory. Even if the Romanians were to allow such passage, communications through the Ruthenian corridor were narrow and poor.[48] So the Soviet Union's

---

[45] W. Murray, *Luftwaffe* (Baltimore, 1985), 18.

[46] See K.-J. Müller, *Gerneral Ludwig Beck: Studien und Dokumente* (Boppard a, R., 1980), 268–311, 502 ff.

[47] See Liddell Hart's memos reprinted in *The Defence of Britain*, 56–7, 61, 74–6; cf. Hauner, 'Czechoslovakia as a Military Factor', 199–200.

[48] It was thought at the time and is believed by historians that the Romanians would not have resisted a Russian land movement through their territory and would almost

ability to support Czechoslovakia in strength on the ground was at best limited. Liddell Hart suggested that some help could come through diversion by way of a Russian attack on East Prussia, assuming again that objections from the Baltic states to the Russians crossing their territory would not constitute an obstacle. But then again, the Soviet Union's military might had just been severely weakened by the liquidation of the better half of its officer corps in the great purges of 1937–8. On balance, we may assume today that Russian air reinforcements to Czechoslovakia would have been wiped out by the Luftwaffe.[49] It is equally clear, however, that in the long run Soviet cooperation was the most important condition for a successful war against Germany.

Like the Conservative, Labour, and Liberal opposition to Munich, Liddell Hart valued Soviet cooperation highly and feared the consequences on the Soviet Union's position if Czechoslovakia was abandoned.[50] He had been regularly meeting and exchanging sympathetic views with the Soviet ambassador in London, Ivan Maisky, who during the 1938 crisis was keeping in close touch with a group of senior public figures which included Winston Churchill, Harold Nicolson, Robert Boothby, Archibald Sinclair, Hugh Dalton, Arthur Greenwood, and David Lloyd George. Maisky was urging upon everybody, and was striving to convince the Foreign Office, that the Soviet Union desired to cooperate.[51] As early as March 1935 Liddell Hart, in a conversation with the Director of Military Operations and Intelligence, General John Dill, had objected to the popular idea of diverting Germany eastward (i.e. against the Soviet Union), thus 'feeding the tiger that might turn on you; we were the ultimate obstacle to Germany's ambition, as in the past'.[52] For Liddell Hart, as for Churchill and the rest of the opposition to Munich, this was not a matter of ideology but simply a question of the balance of power. Chamberlain, however, ruled out cooperation with

certainly have turned a blind eye to aerial traffic; they expected encouragement which did not come from Britain and France. The most detailed scholarly study is J. Haslam, *The Soviet Union and the Struggle for Collective Security in Europe* (London, 1984), 169–70, 179–80; also J. Hochman, *The Soviet Union and the Failure of Collective Security, 1934–1938* (London, 1984), 157–8.

[49] Cf. Murray, *European Balance of Power*, 124–7, 238.

[50] See most of the references in n. 39 above, and specifically regarding the latter point Liddell Hart, 'Strategy and Commitments', 649.

[51] The Maisky file: King's, 1/486, faithfully referred to in *Memoirs*, ii. 167, 195; also see S. Aster, 'Ivan Maisky and Parliamentary Anti-Appeasement, 1938–39', in A. J. P. Taylor (ed.), *Lloyd George: Twelve Essays* (London, 1971), 317–57.

[52] 27 Mar. 1935, King's, 11/1935/69; quoted in *Memoirs*, i. 291.

the Soviet Union, which he distrusted and detested even more than he did Germany.

The opening of the Soviet archives may soon provide a better insight into the development of Soviet foreign policy in the 1930s than has been possible until now. In the meantime, most historians of the subject assess that the Soviet Union's paramount fear of isolation *vis-à-vis* Germany made it anxious to cooperate with the West in the mid-1930s, a goal expressed in the double policy of 'collective security' and 'popular fronts'. It is agreed that by 1938 disappointments over Abyssinia and Spain had substantially cooled Soviet attitude. During the Czechoslovakian crisis the Soviet Union's posture was reserved and its actions ambivalent. Most historians believe, however, that this was due to the correct Soviet assessment that the British government had no serious intention of cooperating.[53] Indeed, working within the 'terms of reference' laid down by the prime minister, the British chiefs of staff, in their successive assessments of the situation after the German Anschluss of Austria in March 1938 and during the September crisis, did not even discuss the possibility of cooperation with the Soviet Union, let alone insist that it was vital for a war against Germany.[54]

Chamberlain was equally reluctant to rely on support from the United States in his dealing with the Axis powers. Not without reason, following repeated disappointments during the 1930s, he did not believe that this isolationist power could be counted upon for anything but words. Aware of the United States' wish to dismantle and inherit the British Empire, he regarded a European settlement and *détente* as Britain's best option by far.[55] This made good sense, if only this option had not have proved impossible. Thus Chamberlain rejected the only major alternative to appeasement—'collective security' or a 'Grand Alliance' of Britain, France, and the Soviet Union, with the economic backing of the United States, a slogan first mooted by Churchill in Parliament in March 1938.

[53] A. B. Ulam, *Expansion and Coexistence: The History of Soviet Foreign Policy, 1917–67* (London, 1968), 234–80; Haslam, *The Soviet Union and the Struggle for Collective Security*; G. Roberts, *The Unholy Alliance: Stalin's Pact with Hitler* (London, 1989); a minority position, distrusting Soviet seriousness, is expressed by G. L. Weinberg, *Germany and the Soviet Union, 1939–1941* (London, 1954); Hochman, *The Soviet Union and the Failure of Collective Security*.

[54] Murray, *European Balance of Power*, 157–62, 287; Kaiser, *Economic Diplomacy*, 227–8; Gibbs, *Grand Strategy*, 642–3, 646–7; Hauner, 'Czechoslovakia as a Military Factor', 196–8; Bond, *British Military Policy*, 282.

[55] A good summary of attitudes can be found in C. A. MacDonald, *The United States, Britain and Appeasement, 1936–1939* (London, 1981), 19–25.

Indeed the fear of a general coalition war against Germany following a German attack on Czechoslovakia was the nightmare of the German General Staff. Beck resigned on 21 August, after having failed in his hectic efforts during the spring and summer to reverse the course of German policy. He judged that the Allies would not launch major land offensives against Germany, but insisted that in the long run they were bound to strangle her economically. Similar views were widely held by senior German officers. Beck's successor, Franz Halder, and his allies in the German army and officialdom conspired to depose the regime if the order to attack were given. They made contact with the British government through various channels, but Munich put an end to the conspiracy. The apologetic nature of the German generals' postwar testimonies, their own nationalist political views, and doubts regarding the prospects of any successful attempt against the Nazi regime made historians sceptical in their attitude towards the German opposition to Hitler. All, however, agree that the pre-Munich activity—before Hitler's bloodless victory proved him smarter than anyone—was the most serious internal threat to his leadership.[56]

Finally, German air superiority and the fear of air attacks on the British and French cities were perhaps the single most important strategic factor influencing the Western allies' decision-making before Munich. Although since the early 1930s Liddell Hart had thought the threat of air attacks on cities overrated, he was very concerned about the state of the British air defences in 1938.[57] Nevertheless, he did not think that this should affect the decision to support Czechoslovakia. In retrospect it is clear that both the effect of city bombing and the German capabilities and intent for carrying it out were vastly exaggerated.[58]

Anti-appeasement

Liddell Hart tried to convince the editors of *The Times* of the vital importance of Czechoslovakia throughout the crisis. After the summer

[56] J. Wheeler-Bennett, *The Nemesis of Power* (London, 1961), 396–424; R. O'Neill, *The German Army and the Nazi Party, 1933–1938* (London, 1966), 151–69; K.-J. Müller, 'The German Military Opposition before the Second World War', in W. Mommsen and L. Kettenacker (eds.), *The Fascist Challenge and the Policy of Appeasement* (London, 1983), 61–75; and the documents in Müller, *Beck*, 268–311, 502 ff.; G. Weinberg, 'The German Generals and the Outbreak of the War, 1938–1939', in A. Preston (ed.), *General Staffs and Diplomacy before the Second World War* (London, 1978), 24–40; K. von Klemperer, *German Resistance against Hitler: The Search for Allies Abroad, 1938–1945* (Oxford, 1992), 105–12.
[57] See e.g. *The Defence of Britain*, 153–7; also U. Bialer, *The Shadow of the Bomber: The Fear of Air Attacks and British Politics, 1932–1939* (London, 1980).
[58] See esp. Murray, 'German Air Power and the Munich Crisis', 107–18.

of 1938, publication of his articles on the subject often withheld, and he twice indicated that he might wish to terminate his employment with the newspaper. At the height of the September crisis he protested strongly against the famous *Times* leader which had suggested that the Sudleten were better handed over to Germany.[59] In the summer of 1938 he wrote: 'It would be a folly to buy momentary relief from the danger of war at the price of ultimate downfall . . . Nothing has proved more upsetting to peace-seeking calculations than the temptation of buying peace.'[60] As with other anti-appeasers, the Munich settlement was for him a turning-point which drove him into open public opposition to government policy. During and after the crisis he was often consulted by Eden, and assisted in drafting the strategic points in the latters speeches. He was in regular contact with Churchill and spoke before 'Focus', the discussion support group Churchill created at the time of Munich. Liddell Hart was also consulted by Hugh Dalton and the leadership of the Labour party, as well as by Sir Archibald Sinclair and Lloyd George of the Liberals. He spoke about the dangers of the government's policy in various public meetings, and was even invited to stand for Parliament against the government's candidates, once as a Progressive with joint Liberal and Labour backing in the Rye Division, and again as an Independent with three-party support in the by-election for the Abbey Division of Westminster.[61]

For all that, John Mearsheimer has challenged Liddell Hart's image as a staunch anti-appeaser on two main grounds. In the first place, he has argued that Liddell Hart was not seriously aroused by any of the international crises of the 1930s until and except those of Spain and Czechoslovakia as late as 1938.[62] In this Mearsheimer is generally correct, but for the small fact that *nobody* was. As mentioned before, things looked differently, and were made to look differently, in hindsight, and not only by Liddell Hart. For example, Churchill's memoirs must be read between the lines and compared with his record at the time. In the 1931–2 crisis over Manchuria Churchill was almost overtly

---

[59] To Barrington-Ward, 4 Nov. 1936, King's, 3/16; correspondence with Barrington-Ward and Dawson in Mar. 1938 and 29 July 1938; to Dawson, 10 Aug.; to Barrington-Ward, 20 Sept.; to Dawson, 5 Oct.; to Barrington-Ward, 1, 8 Nov.; from Barrington-Ward, 2 Nov. 1938: all in 3/108. Much of this is reprinted in *Memoirs*, ii. 130–1, 145–6, 159–60, 165–6, 172, 178–81.

[60] 'Strategy and Commitments', 649; cf. *Through the Fog of War* (London, 1938), 353.

[61] Eden file, King's, 1/258; Churchill file, 1/171; personal notes in 11/1938; political offers, 13/43; cf. *Memoirs*, ii. 160–5, 167–70, 174–5, 186, 195–6, 206–12.

[62] Mearsheimer, *LH*, 131–43.

sympathetic to Japan, Britain's former ally. In 1937 he was concerned by her invasion of China but only because of her connection with Germany. In any case, he did not think Britain should get involved. During the Abyssinian crisis he was at first equivocal and then opposed the sanctions which might push Italy into Germany's arms. In the Spanish crisis he stood all along for strict non-interference by Britain and France, and had little sympathy for the Republicans. He expressed concern about the approaching Nationalist victory only in early 1939. His real preoccupation was Germany: he sounded the alarm about German rearmament and called for massive rearmament on Britain's part. However, contrary to what he would later imply, he did not suggest military action against the German occupation of the Rhineland. Nor did he think there was anything practical to be done after the German Anschluss with Austria, and, like Liddell Hart, only warned of the danger to Czechoslovakia. Things really came to a head only with the Czechoslovakian crisis.

As to the other notable 'anti-appeasers', Eden resigned from the cabinet in February 1938 over the Anglo-Italian Agreement. But, as historians have shown, he differed from Chamberlain not so much on the policy of appeasement itself: the need for a 'general European settlement' involving the dismantling of Versailles and major concessions to Germany and Italy; his main objection was to Chamberlain's wish to steer unilaterally ahead in implementing such a settlement rather than cement coalitions in order to negotiate with Germany and Italy from strength and bind them to their words. Duff Cooper resigned from the cabinet after Munich. The Labour party abandoned its hostility to rearmament only with the Spanish Civil War. In 1936–7 Lloyd George was still impressed by Hitler as 'a seeker of peace and social reformer'.[63] So by what standard is Liddell Hart's anti-appeasement to be measured? The reality of the international crises of the 1930s, as opposed to the retrospective rhetoric of anti-appeasement, was that the challenges to the Western powers grew more threatening in stages, and things looked disturbing and worrying before they appeared really critical.

[63] See the relevant places in W. S. Churchill, *The Second World War*, i (London, 1955); and in M. Gilbert, *Winston S. Churchill*, v (London, 1976); N. Tompson, *The Anti-Appeasers: Conservative Opposition to Appeasement in the 1930s* (Oxford 1971) A. J. P. Taylor's letter to K. Martin, printed in *London Review of Books*, 10 May 1990, 13; Cowling, *The Impact of Hitler*, 143–176; G. Schmidt, *The Politics and Economics of Appeasement* (New York, 1986), 9–10; D. C. Watt, *Personalities and Appeasement* (Austin, Tex., 1991), 17–18; N. Rose, *Churchill* (London, 1994), 236–40; Parker, *Chamberlain and Appeasement*, 93–123; Gibbs, *Grand Strategy*, 806–7.

Mearsheimer's second main argument against Liddell Hart's image as an anti-appeaser is that even over Spain and Czechoslovakia Liddell Hart never recommended the use of force by Britain and France or proposed policies that carried a serious risk of war; that he pointed out the dangers but never proposed any solutions.[64] Now, whatever the gaps in Liddell Hart's reasoning, this is a very misleading presentation of his positions. With a remarkable lack of intellectual sensitivity to its subject, it ignores the most salient features of Liddell Hart's approach to war in general and to the political and strategic threats of the late 1930s in particular. True, Liddell Hart looked for courses of action which would prevent as far as possible the prospect of total war and which by their deterrent effect would lessen the risk of war. This was one of the pillars of his thought and surely not unreasonable as such. The other pillar, however, was that warlike action might become necessary to safeguard national interests.

As we have seen, Liddell Hart strove to apply both principles to the crises of the late 1930s. After all, there was nothing improper in coercing Italy to withdraw from Abyssinia by sanctions, oil embargo, the provision of arms to the Ethiopians, and the blocking of the Suez Canal to Italian transportation to the army in Abyssinia, while strengthening British defences in case *Italy* chose to escalate in a 'mad dog' act. Similarly, it was all the better if the Nationalists and the Axis powers could be prevented from winning in Spain simply by a massive supply of arms and provisions to the Republicans, as perhaps it could. If necessary, the Western allies' command of the sea could be used to isolate the country, and would have proved decisive if the Axis powers decided, unprudently, to escalate. True, Liddell Hart became genuinely alarmed about the situation in Spain only at the beginning of 1938, as it became clearer that the Nationalists were winning the Civil War. But then again, as long as the Republicans were able to fight back and generally hold their own, as they had been doing for a year and a half, there may have been cause for concern but what cause for alarm? Finally, ringing Germany with a two-front coalition and strangling her with an economic blockade if she chose war over Czechoslovakia was a concrete enough plan for confronting her. One may doubt its efficacy but not dismiss it or, worse, fail to give an honest idea of its content.

Mearsheimer rightly points out that, starting from his 1935 study of Britain's defence problems, Liddell Hart came to a better appreciation

---

[64] Mearsheimer, *LH*, 131–43.

of the limits of sea power and of the difficulties facing the blockade, especially under modern conditions. Liddell Hart stressed the new vulnerability of British naval power to the aeroplane, the high-speed light craft, and the submarine, and argued that in itself, without the help of Continental allies, the blockade might not prove sufficient or effective enough to contend with Germany. However, within this system of alliances Liddell Hart (and the British defence establishment as a whole) still regarded the blockade as Britain's trump card. Mearsheimer cites the following passage as evidence of Liddell Hart's scepticism concerning the blockade during the Czechoslovakian crisis: 'We must realize that we cannot win a war against Germany except by economic pressure—and it is becoming doubtful whether this weapon will remain effective enough to produce victory.' He fails, however, to mention that this assessment was written not during, but immediately *after*, the crisis, on 12 October 1938, when Liddell Hart worked out the disastrous implications of the Munich settlement and of the expected German domination over south-eastern Europe for the blockade and hence for the Western allies' ability to defeat Germany—the very danger he had been warning against throughout the crisis.[65]

So Liddell Hart opposed appeasement as strongly as anybody and supported concrete actions to check the Axis powers. But was not his insistence on limited action and limited means an unrealistic obsession which ultimately could not provide the answer to Germany's unlimited drive? Indeed, was it not the kind of policy which made possible Hitler's initial triumphs? For, whereas Liddell Hart opposed Chamberlain and *The Times* over appeasement, he was their closest ally in respect to the strategic policy known as 'limited liability', toward which the British government was moving in the years 1934–8. This strategic policy laid down that Britain's contribution in case of war in Europe would be limited to naval and air power and almost entirely exclude ground forces. The resources allocated to the army in Britain's rearmament were therefore kept below what was required to prepare it either for backing Britain's diplomatic positions in the crises of 1938–9 or for fighting a war when it came in 1939–40. Most military historians have tended to judge this policy mistaken and harmful and have pointed out Liddell Hart's share in the blame. However, most of them have also been aware of major considerations which qualified this judgement, and

---

[65] The citation is from King's, 11/1938/114; cf. Mearsheimer, *LH*, 141; also 93, 106–7, 138.

of the difficulties of pointing out a viable alternative strategic policy to the one actually pursued.[66] Moreover, no sooner had military historians issued their verdict than economic historians began to undermine it. The complexity of the strategic problems and economic constraints facing Britain's decision-makers in the 1930s was baffling, and circumstances changed considerably from year to year before 1939, altering the strategic picture more than it has been acknowledged from a teleological postwar perspective.

II. Limited Liability

The advocates of limited liability were motivated by a mixture of psychological, strategic, and economic considerations. Psychologically, the revulsion against the carnage of trench warfare on the Western Front and the reluctance to repeat that experience were something which many politicians and soldiers shared with the public at large. Strategically, Britain was overburdened by conflicting pressures and liabilities, emanating from her multi-faceted position as an island state, off the shore of Europe, and a worldwide empire whose various possessions were scattered around the globe. With relatively decreasing economic power Britain faced a growing number of simultaneous challenges. She was not prepared to let Europe fall under German domination, but she was equally committed to the defence of her empire, especially against the Japanese threat in the Far East. In addition, the security of Britain's sea communications was vital to her existence. To add to her difficulties, from 1935 on Britain had to divert some of her scant forces to the defence of her Mediterranean communications and possessions against a previously friendly Italy. Of course, as historians have stressed, Britain's various commitments were complementary as much as they were conflicting, and the maintenance of the balance of power in Europe was essential for all the rest; in the long run, if Germany would have been allowed to rule Europe Britain's naval predominance and empire would have become untenable. Still, what was the balanced solution to the intricate strategic equation with which Britain's decision-makers were grappling, if indeed there was any? As the British political and strategic establishment recognized and Liddell

---

[66] For limited liability, see esp. C. Barnett, *The Collapse of British Power* (London, 1972), 237–577; Howard, *Continental Commitment*, 96–120; P. Dennis, *Decision by Default: Peacetime Conscription and British Defence, 1915–1923* (London, 1972); Gibbs, *Grand Strategy*, 93–131, 275–322, 441–529; Bond, *British Military Policy*, 191–286.

Hart indicated in his seminal article of 1935, and as historians have clearly shown, Britain's resources were simply too small to contend by herself with the various threats to her global position, caused since the late nineteenth century by the changes in the distribution of power in the world and aggravated by the emergence of new technologies. In Liddell Hart's own expressions, 'the British Empire is on the rack, suffering a two-way stretch'; it was becoming the greatest example of strategic overextension in history.[67]

It is therefore not surprising that when from 1934 Britain began to rearm, it was mainly the chancellor of the exchequer, Neville Chamberlain, who insisted, against the recommendations of the defence requirements committee, that definite priorities had to be set for the process, and who advanced the policy of limited liability. Being the leading figure in Baldwin's cabinet and prime minister himself from 1937, he was increasingly able to carry his position through. Home and imperial defence were placed at the top of Britain's defence priorities. A Continental role for the army in support of Britain's allies was never entirely discarded, but it was progressively downgraded. Between 1934 and 1938 the army's share among the services in Britain's defence expenditure fell from second to third place, though in fact never very far behind that of the air force and the navy. Even the regular army of five to six divisions, let alone the territorial army of twelve divisions, were not allocated the resources they needed to prepare them for participation in a European war. Special priority was given to the air force, whose share in Britain's defence expenditure leaped from a distant third to first place between 1934 and 1938. The air force was intended to defend the British Isles against the rapidly expanding Luftwaffe, first by deterring attack with the threat of counter-attack by the British bombers on the German rear and later, from 1937 on, increasingly by fighter squadrons, working within the world's first integrated air defence system. In addition, the air force was viewed as a 'cleaner' and more versatile substitute for the army for intervening in the Continent, both directly from Britain and from bases in the Low Countries and France, in support of Britain's allies.

Liddell Hart became an ardent advocate of limited liability in late 1935, though he had already argued in that direction in June 1934, after

---

[67] The first expression is from 'The Defence of the Empire', *Fortnightly Review* (Dec. 1937), repr. in *The Defence of Britain*, 59; the second is cited without reference by Kennedy, *Strategy and Diplomacy*, 18.

Chamberlain had first made his case in cabinet. Among the reasons for his objection to a major Continental role for the army he stressed the army's total unpreparedness for war and its reluctance to reform. This, however, was at best only a contributory reason for his position.[68] After all, he championed limited liability largely as an adaptation of his own concept of 'the British way in warfare' which he had voiced on principled lines as early as 1931. Interestingly, there was no direct, one-way influence here between Liddell Hart and Chamberlain. There is no sign that Chamberlain was familiar with Liddell Hart's original essay. The aversion to the idea of another entanglement in the Continent was a sentiment shared by many Britons in the 1930s. In the army General Sir Burnett-Stuart in particular championed an imperial rather than a Continental role for the army, and Chamberlain's strategic ideas were initially influenced mainly by Trenchard.[69] Liddell Hart, well-informed about the deliberations in the cabinet and the army and closely in touch with both Burnett-Stuart and Trenchard, echoed all these sources in his writings.

In 1935–8, in newspaper and magazine articles, books, conversations with officials and soldiers, and as an adviser to the secretary of state for war, actively influencing the shaping and implementation of policy, Liddell Hart persistently argued, with little variation, that Britain could not be strong everywhere; that home and imperial defence had to come first; that air defence and the navy had to take priority over the army; that an expeditionary force to the Continent was not necessary, might anyway fail to arrive in time to participate in the defence of Western Europe, and might be subjected to paralysing air attacks on its land and sea communications; that air contingents would be Britain's most effective contribution to her allies.[70] As mentioned before, many of these ideas had been previously voiced by Chamberlain. In turn, Liddell Hart's active support strengthened the opinions of Chamberlain and those who held similar views, like the government's chief industrial

---

[68] *Europe in Arms*, 78, 129–30; *Memoirs*, i. 294–5, 379–81, 385–6; ii. 21–3.

[69] See G. C. Peden, *British Rearmament and the Treasury, 1932–1939* (Edinburgh, 1979), 123–5; and for Burnett-Stuart, Liddell Hart, *Memoirs*, i. 292–4; since 1930 Liddell Hart had been cooperating with Trenchard on a whole range of defence issues; the Trenchard file: King's, 1/699.

[70] *Daily Telegraph*, 25 June 1934; *The Times*, 25 Nov. 1935, 10 Feb., 6 and 23 Mar., 30 Oct., 3 and 11 Nov. 1936, 5 Mar., 29 July 1937, 17 June 1938; conversations with Duff Cooper and Halifax, 18 and 21 Jan. 1936 respectively; cited in Dennis, *Decision by Default*, 62; also Peden, *British Rearmament*, 124–5; Liddell Hart, 'The Defence of the Empire', *Fortnightly Review* (Jan. 1938), 19–30; *Europe in Arms*, 59–60, 78–19, 116–19, 124, 130–3, 138–40; *The Defence of Britain*, 59, 209–11, 265–9, 278–9, 286–93; *Memoirs*, i. 292–9, 379–83, 385–7; ii. 2–3, 51–4, 97–9, 118.

adviser, Lord Weir. When Chamberlain became prime minister and moved to make limited liability official policy, he was happy to use such a popular and authoritative strategic writer as Liddell Hart as an ally. He recommended the chapter on 'The Role of the Army' in Liddell Hart's *Europe in Arms* (1937)—which Liddell Hart had sent him—to Hore-Belisha, whom he had newly appointed to the war office to carry out his policy. And in the cabinet discussions in 1937 Liddell Hart's writings in *The Times* and memoranda to Hore-Belisha were discussed and relied upon.[71] Two opinionated amateurs, Chamberlain and Liddell Hart, found in each other an ally in their effort to effect a radical reorientation of British strategic policy.

Of course, different reasons carried different weight in the respective motives of Chamberlain and Liddell Hart for espousing limited liability. With Chamberlain the economic considerations were more prominent, whereas, 'inescapably, Liddell Hart's thought was shaped by the First World War.'[72] While recognizing new developments which were affecting war, Liddell Hart basically considered the possibility of a new war in the light of the lessons he had been attempting to draw from the First World War, with the problem of which he had been grappling both in his own histories of the war and in his work on Lloyd George's memoirs. Strongly opposing the creation of British mass armies and their commitment to the Western Front during that war, he suggested that Britain 'might have raised Kitchener's "First Hundred Thousand", but certainly not his "Last" '.[73] As the debate over the direction of Britain's rearmament dragged on, Liddell Hart became deeply suspicious that the army did not acquiesce to the government's decision to limit the commitment of British land forces to the Continent. He believed that the army was still hoping to make that commitment the basis not only for the dispatch of the whole regular and territorial armies (eighteen divisions in all) to the Continent but ultimately also for the creation of a large British 'national army' which would fundamentally replay the First World War: 'commitment, entanglement, illimitable expansion, mass conscription, futile sacrifice, and material exhaustion, leading not only to prolonged impoverishment but immediately to the weakening of our influence over

---

[71] Liddell Hart's articles in *The Times* in Nov. 1935 were filed by Weir: Peden, *British Rearmament*, 124–5, 137; see also Liddell Hart's Chamberlain file, King's, 1/159; 11/HB 1937/68; R. J. Minney, *The Private Papers of Hore-Belisha* (London, 1960), 54; Liddell Hart, *Memoirs*, ii. 38–9; Bond, *British Military Policy*, 246–7; *LH*, 105–9.

[72] Howard, 'LH', 239.

[73] *The British Way in Warfare*, 39; *When Britain Goes to War*, 43.

the restoration of peace.'[74] It would be a mistake, however, to dismiss Liddell Hart's position merely as a backward-looking, unrealistic reaction to a trauma. The policy of limited liability and Liddell Hart's understanding of it deserve serious reconsideration.

Air Force, Navy, Army, the Economy

It can hardly be disputed that the investment in the air force was the most vital element in Britain's rearmament in the 1930s. Yet it has rarely been appreciated that in this respect the order of priorities set by the British government was far sounder than the inter-service compromises proposed by the defence requirements committee, whose respective reports of 1934 and 1935 were to ensure that the air force's share in the defence budget was to remain a distant third behind that of the other two services.[75] Even with the top priority given to it, Britain's air armament, still totally inadequate at the time of the Munich crisis and lagging behind even at the outbreak of the war, was only just ready to match the Germans in 1940. It might of course be argued that if the army had been given higher priority, the Battle of France might not have been lost, and consequently there would have been no need for the Battle of Britain. Yet even if the army had been strengthened more than it was, it still could only have played a secondary role at the start of a European war, and Britain might have faced the danger of a larger Dunkirk with a weaker air defence system than the one which ultimately saved her.[76] Air force first was the logical choice of an island empire like Britain, indeed perhaps of any first-class power in the second half of the 1930s, a point about which Churchill, for example, was practically in agreement with the Baldwin and Chamberlain administrations. The RAF might also have contributed much more than it did to the Battle of France had it taken more seriously the role of close tactical support to the land forces—as both the army chiefs and Liddell Hart wanted—rather than concentrating almost solely on strategic bombing. On the other side, as claimed by John Slessor, the head of the plans branch of the Air Staff in the years preceding the war, who

---

[74] *The Times*, 26 Oct. 1937; also *Europe in Arms*, 219–21; and esp. his talk with Deverell and the Director of Military Operations, Maj.-Gen. Haining, in 12 Nov. 1936: King's, 11/1936/99; *Memoirs*, i. 382–3.

[75] The exception is the authoritative official economic history of the war: M. M. Postan, *British War Production: History of the Second World War—Civil Series* (London, 1952), 14, 29; the figures can be found in Peden, *British Rearmament*, 205.

[76] Cf. e.g. the CIGS's assessment after the fall of France: Macleod and Kelly, *The Ironside Diaries*, 370.

had always wanted a versatile air force; the RAF's concentration on strategic bombing was itself at least partly caused by the policy of limited liability which envisaged no substantial British land involvement in the Continent.[77]

As with the Air Force, it is clear that the preparedness of the Royal Navy was vital to Britain, and it, too, was still severely deficient when war came, especially the navy's air arm, and escort and anti-submarine vessels. Incidently, here also, following Fuller and Richmond, Liddell Hart held that the navy ought to invest less in battleships and more in air defence, aircraft carriers, and flotilla craft.[78]

So the question is more about the absolute size of Britain's defence budget than about the army's relative share in it. In historians' criticism of the policy of limited liability, the dominating impression has been that the army was starved of resources before 1939. In reality, while the annual expenditure on the air force, which had lagged far behind the other two services in 1934, increased eightfold by 1938, that on the army also increased more than threefold in the same period, more than the increase in the expenditure on the navy; and even in 1937–8 the annual expenditure on the three services was of roughly the same order. Similarly, the army's investment in new equipment rose sixfold between 1934 and 1938, and its share among the services rose from 19 to 25.5 per cent. (Admittedly, some of this increase was intended for the purchase of anti-aircraft guns—in 1938 about half as much as the expenditure on new equipment for the field army.[79] Thus the only reasonable query is whether Britain should not have increased her *overall* expenditure on rearmament *even more*, so as to bring the army to a state of readiness for a Continental role. However, as economic historians have shown, even if Britain could have done more, it would probably not have been that much more.

---

[77] See e.g. ibid., 394 and *passim*; Bond, *British Military Policy*, 207, 274–5, 339; Murray, *European Balance of Power*, 82–3; C. Webster and N. Frankland, *The Strategic Air Offensive against Germany, 1939–1945* (4 vols., London, 1961), i. 65–81, 94–101, 104–5; M. Smith, *British Air Strategy between the Wars* (Oxford, 1984); J. Slessor, *Air Power and Armies* (Oxford, 1936), *The Central Blue* (London, 1956), 183; A. D. Harvey, *Collision of Empires: Britain in Three World Wars, 1793–1945* (London, 1992), 644–8.

[78] See esp. *The Times*, 10 Feb. 1936; *Europe in Arms*, 92–9; Richmond, who had been the chief proponent of these ideas throughout the interwar period, is cited on pp. 94–5. Cf. S. Roskill, *Naval Policy between the Wars* (2 vols., London, 1968, 1976), i. 115–16, 224, 315, 444; ii. 56, 260. Fuller, too, repeated his earlier views along these lines: *Towards Armageddon* (London, 1937), 133–5, 196–208. See also Kennedy, *British Naval Mastery*, 282, 293, 303; Murray, *European Balance of Power*, 74–7.

[79] Again, the only historian to make these cardinal points is Postan, *British War Production*, 28, 30–1. For the expenditure on AA guns, see Harvey, *Collision of Empires*, 557.

TABLE 1. *British Defence Expenditure (£)*

	Army	Navy	Air force	% of Govt. expenditure
1934	39,691,603	56,610,010	17,607,893	14
1935	44,654,483	64,887,613	27,515,185	15
1936	55,015,395	80,976,124	49,995,697	21
1937	72,675,520	101,892,397	81,799,260	26
1938	121,542,932	132,437,403	143,499,642	38
1939	242,438,217	181,770,565	294,833,921	48

Source: R. P. Shay, *British Rearmament in the Thirties* (Princeton, NJ, 1977), 297; see also G. C. Peden, *British Rearmament and the Treasury, 1932–1939*, (Edinburgh, 1979), 205; N. Gibbs, *Grand Strategy: History of the Second World War*, i (London, 1976) 532.

TABLE 2. *The army's investment in equipment*

	Expenditure (£ m.)	% of total armed forces expenditure
1934	6.9	19
1935	8.5	20
1936	12.5	20
1937	21.4	21
1938	44.3	25.5
1939	67.6	26

Source: M. M. Postan, *British War Production: History of the Second World War—Civil Services* (London, 1952) 12, 28.

The problem here was both industrial and fiscal.[80] Run down as it had been in the lean years of the Ten Years Rule, the British arms industry lacked both the equipment and skilled labour for rapid expansion and was unable to respond to the demands of rearmament in the desired scope and speed. The bottlenecks and delays in the production of aircrafts and anti-aircraft guns in particular were the cause of repeated public outcries and parliamentary debates in 1937–38. Even when a Continental role for the regular army and the territorials was still

---

[80] For the following, see Postan, *British War Production*, 10–13; Shay, *British Rearmament*; Peden, *British Rearmament*; 'A Matter of Timing: The Economic Background to British Foreign Policy, 1937–1939', *History*, 69 (1984), 15–28; Gibbs, *Grand Strategy*, 275–322; also Howard, *Continental Commitment*, 134–6; Kennedy, *Strategy and Diplomacy*, 27, 100–2; *Great Powers*, 412–13.

envisaged, it was made clear that because of limited production capacity equipment for the latter could not be made available until well into the 1940s.[81] So the argument between those who favoured and those who objected to limited liability was in reality largely academic. Financially, the treasury's officials stressed that Britain, which was slowly but steadily recovering from the Great Depression, would simply not be able to sustain the arms race for long if rearmament were not kept within strict budgetary constraints. Otherwise, they calculated, by 1941 the economy would overheat, Britain would face a balance-of-payments crisis, and inflation would rise out of control. Since Britain's planned a protracted war against Germany, this was a major strategic consideration.

In the 1950s, 1960s, and 1970s historians were able to brandish Keynes's theories against orthodox treasury economics. But apart from the fact that those who lived through the 1980s are bound to be more sceptical about the ability to sustain large-scale 'uneconomic' expenditure on defence, economic historians have reminded us that the British government did in fact resort to large scale borrowing in 1937–8. Special defence loans financed about a quarter of the defence expenditure in 1937 and a third in 1938. There were no differences of opinion between Keynes and the treasury in this respect.[82] In 1939–40, when all financial constraints were finally dropped, Britain's defence expenditure was raised even further, so that it more or less equalled Germany's, and even surpassed it in percentage of GNP.[83] But, as the economists had predicted, Britain was bankrupt by the beginning of 1941 and could not have continued the war if it had not been for the United States' massive aid. 'The amount of cash that was needed to rebuild a two-ocean navy, to provide the RAF with both its fighter defences and its long-range bombers, and to equip the army for a European field role . . . was well beyond the industrial and financial capacity of the country.'[84] 'Experience showed', wrote Liddell Hart,

---

[81] Bond, *British Military Policy*, 199, 214, 222, 237–41.

[82] See R. A. C. Parker, 'British Rearmament 1936–9: Treasury, Trade Unions and Skilled Labour', *English Historical Review*, 96 (1981), 306–18; G. C. Peden, 'Keynes, the Economics of Rearmament and Appeasement', in Mommsen and Kettenacker, *The Fascist Challenge*, 142–56.

[83] B. A. Carroll, *Design for Total War* (The Hague, 1968), 184, 264–5; R. J. Overy, 'Hitler's War and the German Economy: A Reinterpretation', *Economic History Review*, 35 (1982), 286.

[84] Kennedy, *Strategy and Diplomacy*, 100; this verdict is an almost verbatim repetition of Chamberlain's own assessment on 25 Oct. 1936, cited and practically endorsed by Howard, *Continental Commitment*, 135.

'that to seek predominance both on land and sea overstrained the Power which attempted it. How much more probable is such a consequence when the effort has to be spread over land, sea, and air.'[85]

But if so, how could Germany, whose economy was only marginally larger than that of Britain and whose armaments industry had also been completely run down and took time to rebuild, conduct the race at such a swift pace and keep it up? In the years 1934–8 Germany spent nearly three times as much as Britain on her armed services, and even in 1938 Britain's annual defence expenditure was less than half that of Germany.[86] However, as historians have shown, apart from the fact that Germany's rearmament began earlier, which gave her a crucial head start, the answer is that she could not.[87] Assessments of the developments in Britain long suffered from the lack of a comparative perspective and from mythical popular images of German rearmament. Unlike the Conservative government in Britain, the German state intervened massively in the economy to enhance arms production. But, as in Britain, German economists were in despair about the ability of the German economy to sustain the quick pace of rearmament. It is now believed that the expenditure on armaments was only marginally significant in helping the German economy recover from the depression; and as this expenditure rose sharply after 1936, it overheated the economy and could not be kept up for long after 1939. Germany exceeded her limits in respect to raw materials, the balance of payments, and the work force. The crucial difference between Britain and Germany (and indeed Japan) was that Germany was bent on a policy of territorial expansion in Europe that would also progressively expand her economic base. As some historians have suggested, Germany's actions in 1938–9 were at least partly prompted by the economic problem, as her rearmament effort ran out of steam.[88] Finally, it might be mentioned that Germany, too, had to decide on strict priorities between the three armed services. In her case, the army and air force

---

[85] *Europe in Arms*, 221; see also *The Defence of Britain*, 46.

[86] Figures in Carroll, *Design for Total War*, 184, 264–5; Overy, 'War and the German Economy', 286; Murray, *European Balance of Power*, 20–1; MF, *Germany and the Second World War*, i. 237; Kennedy, *Great Powers*, 382.

[87] See esp. the respective contributions by Volkmann and Deist to MF, *Germany and the Second World War*, i. 157–540; Murray, *European Balance of Power*, 4–27, 48–9, and *passim*; Overy, 'War and the German Economy'; *The Nazi Economic Recovery, 1932–1938* (London, 1982); Kennedy, *Great Powers*, 394–400.

[88] See 'Debate: Germany, "Domestic Crisis" and War in 1939', *Past and Present*, 122 (1989), 200–40, for the argument between T. Mason, R. Overy, and D. Kaiser.

were allocated most of the money in 1933–9, with the navy left behind as a far third and totally unprepared for war.[89]

Britain's Allies

If Britain could not produce arms and expand her armed forces much more quickly than she actually did without undermining her economy and unbalancing her entire strategic position, what were the alternatives? Obviously they were not brilliant. The answer to the many threats and constraints with which Britain's policymakers were grappling had to be at least partly political. Chamberlain and Liddell Hart agreed that limited liability was possible only if and as long as it was backed by a complementary foreign policy, but they differed on the nature of that policy. Whereas the British government under Chamberlain combined limited liability with a diplomatic effort to meet Germany's grievances in the hope of integrating her within a stable European power system and avert conflict, Liddell Hart from 1935 on combined limited liability with strong support for collective security. Only in alliance with the powers of Western and Eastern Europe, he maintained, could Britain hope to check Germany's drive without over-exerting herself. Only if Britain was strategically able to respond to limited challenges to the status quo with less than total national mobilization and total war would she be willing to respond at all, thereby also making her deterrence posture more credible.[90]

Chamberlain's policy failed because Hitler's aims were much more far-reaching than he had assumed or was willing to accept. But were the policies advocated by Liddell Hart any more realistic? If allies in the west and east of the Continent were vital for Britain's defence, could they be expected to stand firm against Germany without the guaranteed support of a substantial British land army? In Western Europe Britain was after all the most powerful member of the alliance against Germany, and was obliged to act as a leader and show resolve if she wanted the others to follow suit. A system of collective security had its price and called for great responsibility, especially on the part of its most powerful members. Britain's non-committed attitude during and after the Rhineland crisis was one of the main reasons for Belgium's return to a policy of neutrality in 1936. That act not only made the defence of Germany much easier and that of France much harder; it also affected what was

[89] Figures in R. J. Overy, *War and Economy in the Third Reich* (Oxford, 1994), 203.
[90] See e.g. *The Defence of Britain*, 45–6, 49, 267.

considered a direct and vital British interest, namely, that Belgium's air fields and ports, just across the Channel, would not fall into Germany's hands.

It is, however, not at all clear that Britain's allies would not have been satisfied with anything less than a large British land army. They surely wanted an unequivocal British political and strategic commitment to their security and to the common cause of stopping Germany, a commitment which the British government was consistently reluctant to give. But the record shows that the Belgians, in the person of Prime Minister Paul van Zeeland, having learnt of Britain's political and strategic position and being most anxious for her cooperation, were willing to settle for no more than informal staff talks on air, naval, and industrial cooperation. Even that, however, the British government declined.[91] Similarly, both in late 1937, when the implications of the policy of limited liability were made clear to the French by Hore-Belisha, and in the Anglo-French talks in April 1938, at the beginning of the Czechoslovakian crisis, Premier Édouard Daladier and Chief of Staff Gamelin, though naturally not enthusiasticaly, were willing to recognize Britain's special strategic position and global obligations. They were willing to accept the two divisions offered by Britain rather than a large land army as a token of her European commitment. Obviously, they hoped for stronger forces later on. As the official British historian has written: 'The interesting feature of the French views was that they showed no shock at the limits on the size of Britain's contribution on land.'[92] Indeed, the veteran secretary of the committee of imperial defence, Maurice Hankey, who had earlier been working for the creation of a British expeditionary force to the Continent, changed his mind in 1937 on the grounds that the French themselves had ceased to demand such a force.[93] It should be borne in mind that until the Munich settlement and the dismemberment of Czechoslovakia, it was reasonable to suppose that France did not need a large British land force in her support or, at least, that that was not the Allies' first strategic priority.

This point underpinned Liddell Hart's strategic logic and was upper-

---

[91] See D. O. Kieft, *Belgium's Return to Neutrality* (Oxford, 1972), esp. 76–7, and 20–4, 70–2, 75–7, 80–2, 156–7, 161–6, 170–2, 187–8; also Gibbs, *Grand Strategy*, 111–14; Bond, *British Military Policy*, 228–33.

[92] Gibbs, *Grand Strategy*, 471–2, 637; also Dennis, *Decision by Default*, 132; Bond, *British Military Policy*, 275–6, 289.

[93] S. Roskill, *Hankey, Man of Secrets* (3 vols., London, 1970–4), iii. 285.

most in his mind throughout 1938. From 1936 he had insisted that Britain should not build a large army and send it across the Channel. As he perceived during the Czechoslovakian crisis, the integrity of Czechoslovakia and Soviet cooperation were essential for that policy and for the hope of stopping Germany while limiting the scale of Britain's commitments. After the abandonment of Czechoslovakia he very painfully but clearly recognized that there was no longer any question that France now needed the support of a British expeditionary force in a war against Germany.

Finally, it should be asked whether the commitment of a large British army to the Continent would have been militarily effective. Here, too, an affirmative answer is doubtful. As observers in Britain, France, and Germany pointed out at the time, the British regular and Territorial forces were composed of traditional, barely mechanized, infantry divisions, of the sort Britain's allies possessed in abundance and which could be of very limited value in a war against Germany. After all, in 1939–40 the British army *was* sent to the Continent and reinforced up to ten divisions by the time of the Battle of France, but was able to do very little to alter the outcome of the campaign.[94] One alternative was for Britain to create a fully mechanized force which could have contributed significantly in a war against Germany. That in fact was the line which the French themselves repeatedly urged the British to adopt. Both in late 1937 and in the staff talks in April 1938 the French premier Daladier, while saying that he understood that Britain's resources were not unlimited, asked that the two divisions Britain planned to send to France should at least be motorized. Similarly, in March 1938 Churchill was told by Daladier's would-be successor, Paul Reynaud, who had been championing de Gaulle's ideas in the French Chamber of Deputies and with the French public: 'We quite understand that England will never have conscription. Why do you not therefore go in for a mechanized army? If you had six armoured divisions you would indeed be an effective Continental force.' In July both Reynaud and the French military attaché in London, General Lelong, urged the dispatch of a small British mechanized force to France.[95] These pieces of evidence square with the findings of the archival research of French prewar strategic planning. It has been revealed that in the late 1930s Gamelin

<hr />

[94] Again cf. CIGS Ironside's assessment after the fall of France that more British forces would have made no difference: Macleod and Kelly, *The Ironside Diaries*, 370.

[95] See n. 92 above; Churchill, *The Second World War*, i. 252–3; Liddell Hart, *Memoirs*, ii. 193.

was positively *not* interested in British unmechanized troops (he had enough of his own). He specifically and consistently wanted an armoured British contribution to strengthen the French mobile forces against the expected penetrations of the German Panzer divisions.[96] Needless to say, the creation of a small mechanized army as the most effective possible British contribution for war in Europe had been the line pursued by the armour enthusiasts in Britain—including Liddell Hart—throughout the interwar period.[97]

Mechanization or Imperial Policing

However, as the army chiefs and the defence requirements committee concluded in 1933–4 and as historians have later emphasized, one of the main roles of the British army was to police the Empire. This role could be most satisfactorily fulfilled by traditional troops on foot and horseback, or, at best, by lightly mechanized units, rather than by a fully mechanized and heavily armoured field force, or 'robot army'. Indeed, here too, in the late 1930s, as Liddell Hart began to adapt his older ideas into specific policy programmes, he addressed the problem much more seriously, comprehensively, and in greater detail than he had done before. Being one of the main champions of the policy of home and imperial defence, coupled with limited liability in the Continent, he was obliged to come to terms with the argument against the mechanization of the British army. As an adviser to Hore-Belisha, he devised interesting schemes for the redistribution of the British forces and the creation of an imperial reserve against any contingency. In addition to the infantry for imperial police and other duties, he recommended the creation of four regular armoured divisions: two to be stationed in Britain, one in Egypt, and one in India. He also advocated the conversion to armour of four out of the twelve territorial divisions.[98] Repeatedly writing in favour of limited liability, he argued that if British forces were to be sent to the Continent at all, Britain's best aid to her allies on land could be made in the form of two or more armoured divisions. As he pointed out, these would represent a major addition to

---

[96] M. Alexander, *The Republic in Danger: General Maurice Gamelin and the Politics of French Defence, 1933–1940* (Cambridge, 1992), 202, 254–78. For more on this, see n. 198 below and related text.

[97] Cf. H. Guderian, *Achtung Panzer!* (London, 1992), 140, echoing the British armour pioneers.

[98] See esp. *The Defence of Britain*, 275–8, 326–8; a selection of Liddell Hart's memoranda to Hore-Belisha on these matters in King's, 11/HB 1937–8 is reprinted ibid. 273–93.

France's armoured divisions (66 per cent in 1939) and would be most useful for counter-offensives against German penetrations.[99] Indeed, if Britain could have done more than she actually did in her rearmament effort, this might have been the most effective field for doing it.

In the event, however, the army chiefs complained to Liddell Hart that his objection to a major continental role for the army was relied upon by the government in its decision to keep down the expenditure on the army. Among other things, this was hindering and seriously delaying the process of mechanization and the creation of the single mobile division the army was planning (later reorganized into two smaller ones, in addition to the one created in Egypt, both as Liddell Hart had been urging). The first mobile division was not yet fully operational even by the time of the Battle of France in May 1940. Furthermore, precious time and resources were wasted on the design and manufacture of light tanks for imperial defence, the role upon which the army was called upon to concentrate. Indeed, there can be no doubt that the strategic confusion regarding the role of the British army was one of the main reasons for its unpreparedness for armoured warfare, which it never fully overcame during the Second World War.[100] For his part, Liddell Hart argued that the army should have altered its priorities and invested the limited funds allocated to it in armour rather than expanding, re-equipping and motorizing its infantry divisions.[101]

Collective Security, Limited Liability, Containment

In any case, the purpose of our discussion is not to prove Liddell Hart right or wrong on one point or another, but rather to bring out the

[99] He had been arguing along these lines since early 1936 and not, as Bond, *LH*, 102–3, and Mearsheimer, *LH*, 143–4, mistakenly believe (respectively), only from June or Jan. 1938. See e.g. *The Times*, 10 Feb., 30 Oct., 2 Nov. 1936; 5 Mar. 1937; 17 June 1938; 'The Defence of the Empire', *Fortnightly Review* (Jan. 1938), 19–30; *The Defence of Britain*, 209–11, 265–9, 287, 293 (the last 3 from 1937, of which the last 2 are memoranda to Hore-Belisha for use in the Cabinet in Nov.); cf. Peden, *British Rearmament*, 175. Alexander, *Gamelin*, 263–4, 273, mistakenly assumes that Liddell Hart objected to Gamelin's desire for a mechanized force from Britain; the two were in fact of the same mind; see also n. 198 below.

[100] Conversation with Deverell, 29 June 1937, King's, 11/1937/56; *Memoirs*, i. 382; see also Gibbs, *Grand Strategy*, 524; Bond, *LH*, 108–9, 114–15; *British Military Policy*, 256, 337–8; H. Winton, *To Change an Army* (Lawrence, Kan., 1988); Mearsheimer, *LH*, 173.

[101] See *Europe in Arms*, 227–8; talk before the Compatriots Club in the House of Commons, 3 Mar. 1939, King's, 11/1939/18; *Memoirs*, i. 382, 385. Peden, *British Rearmament*, 175, relying on the documents of the Treasury and the War Office, lends support to his view; see also Murray, *European Balance of Power*, 90.

edifice of his logic in approaching the overall political and strategic problem facing Britain in the late 1930s. It will not be argued that this logic was flawless or that it was entirely consistent, for, as A. J. P. Taylor wisely concluded, 'No one was consistent in the Thirties.'[102] The problems and constraints of all sorts were too complex. But repeatedly complaining about the failure in Britain to think through the defence problem in a clear and comprehensive manner, Liddell Hart made a consistent effort to devise a comprehensive and coherent grand strategy, tailored to Britain's special political requirements and strategic dilemmas. An analysis of the problem from the perspective of time may suggest that he was not very wide of the mark.

In his verdict on Liddell Hart's advocacy of limited war and limited liability, Michael Howard has written that he 'sought to escape the dilemma of his generation by what was, in the context of his time, little more than a nostalgic wishful thinking'.[103] Perhaps he did. He certainly sought a way out of the dilemma of his age, and, indeed, perhaps there was no way out. But it would be a mistake to think that his thought was rooted in the past, as his essay on 'The British Way in Warfare' of 1931 may suggest. His ideas were remarkably modern, and directed to the present and future. Although he had no particular inclination towards economic issues, he grasped very clearly in 1935, when he undertook his comprehensive study of Britain's defence problem, the basic fact recently pointed out by a distinguished historian of the period: 'Already in 1937, Britain, like France, was spending more of its GNP upon defence than either of those countries had done in the crisis years prior to 1914, but without any significant improvement in security—simply because of far higher arms spending of the manically driven, overheated German state.'[104] Britain's problem was that, while being a liberal-capitalist status quo state, she was called upon to stop predator powers—no weaker than herself and undergoing staggering rearmament, geared for expansion—without undermining her economic and, therefore, strategic position in the process.

In the remedy prescribed by Liddell Hart there were no doubt inherent tensions between collective security and limited liability. But it was predicated on the notion that all the powers of the status quo would cooperate in standing firm against Germany, so as to create a

[102] Taylor to K. Martin, printed in *London Review of Books*, 10 May 1990, 13.
[103] Howard, 'LH', 245.
[104] Kennedy, *Great Powers*, 412; also 400–1 for the following sentence.

force large enough to prevent her from breaking out of her limited power base, and strangle her if she tried, without overstretching the resources not only of Britain (as the critics of limited liability have often claimed) but in effect of *any* of the allies.[105]

From that point of view, everything depended on the strength of the coalition assembled against Germany and on its readiness to act before she secured the resources of Eastern Europe. Here Churchill, Eden, and Liddell Hart were basically at one. In 1938 the prospects were still good. As historians now recognize, Germany's later exploits, which would bring the wealth of the entire Continent under her domination, have blurred the fact that her fundamental weakness was economic. If Germany could be contained in the west, blockaded on the sea from the rest of the world, and denied the resources of south-eastern Europe and still more of the Soviet Union, her war economy, desperately short of raw materials, could not have survived for long. Munich, however, marked a watershed. Unlike many of his contemporaries, and many historians later on, who argued that Munich at least earned Britain and her allies time to prepare for war, Liddell Hart did not doubt that the balance of power had changed drastically for the worse.[106] Germany's power base expanded, and her ability to wage a long war increased; the Soviet Union was given the cold shoulder by Britain and the West; France could no longer be expected to hold her own against Germany without the support of British land forces.

III. From Containment to Cold War

The problem of the dispatch of British ground forces to France in case of a war against Germany was the first to arise after Munich. Initially

[105] Liddell Hart, *The Times*, 27 Oct. 1937; *The Defence of Britain*, 45, 50. Studies of the Soviet Union's role make an interesting point here; as one of them claims: 'In Soviet eyes Munich was the last opportunity to halt Hitler's advance short of all-out war. The accretion of German power resulting from the annexation of Austria and the subjugation of Czechoslovakia signified to Moscow that the threat of war would no longer be enough to deter Hitler. To that extent Munich marked the final failure of collective security's original objective . . . ' : Roberts, *Stalin's Pact with Hitler*, 92. The Soviet preference for a coordinated *limited* action during the Czechoslovakian crisis is also suggested by Taylor, *Munich*, 447–56.

[106] See esp. 'Britain's Military Situation', *Yale Review* (Dec. 1939), 230–45; also published in *Contemporary Review* (Jan. 1939), 26–36; 'British Freedom', *World Review*, (Dec. 1938), 21–7; 'The Defence of Western Civilization', *New Commonwealth Review* (Jan. 1939), 21–30; *The Defence of Britain*, 22–4, 39, 46; *The Second World War*, 23–4. Cf. again Murray, *European Balance of Power*; and Kaiser, *Economic Diplomacy*.

the British government saw no reason to change its policy of sending only the smallest army contingent to the Continent, while concentrating Britain's effort in the air and at sea. But the French government and army now insisted that Britain had to make up for the loss of the Czechoslovakian army. While still expressing preference for mechanized forces, they made it clear that nothing except the dispatch of a large British army to France right from the start of a war would reassure them and satisfy French public opinion. The British government thus came to realize that a change of policy could not be avoided if France were not to be pushed into seeking her own deal with Germany. Intelligence scares in January 1939 regarding German invasions of Holland and Switzerland forced a decision. In February 1939 it was decided to allocate the money necessary for the equipment of the whole Regular army and of four Territorial divisions for a European war, and for allowing the rest of the Territorials to train. On 8 March 1939, in presenting the army estimates in Parliament, Hore-Belisha suggested that in the longer run the entire British Regular and Territorial armies would be able to participate in a war in Europe. Because of the limits of industrial capacity, however, it was to take years before this plan was to be realized.[107]

By now the money allocated to the army as well as the total defence budget was nearly doubled in comparison to 1938, and the treasury warned and the government was aware that the new levels of expenditure could not be sustained for long. But after Munich there was really no other choice for, as one historian has put it, 'it was of little use to husband resources to sustain a long war if the enemy was able to defeat you in a short one'.[108]

As we have seen before, in contrast to the British government Liddell Hart had clearly and apprehensively foreseen during 1938 that France would not be able to do without the support of a British field force if Czechoslovakia were abandoned; and in the wake of Munich he was obliged to accept that there was now no other way but to send an army to the Continent. He continued to insist, however, that the British contribution on land should take the form of an armoured-mechanized

---

[107] Dennis, *Decision by Default*, 151–62, 169, 177; Howard, *Continental Commitment*, 125–8; Gibbs, *Grand Strategy*, i. 491–514; Shay, *British Rearmament*, 235–8; Bond, *British Strategic Policy*, 287–304; Murray, *European Balance of Power*, 274–8, 296.

[108] Howard, *Continental Commitment*, 136. For the economics, see G. C. Peden, 'A Matter of Timing: The Economic Background to British Foreign Policy, 1937–1939', *History*, 69 (1984), 15–28.

force. In comparison to a larger, old-style infantry army, he claimed, such a force would be far more effective, especially in the counterattack role against German penetrations of the Western Front, and much less likely to become entangled in a First World War style of warfare. Following Hore-Belisha's speech on 8 March, while expressing regret that the intended expansion of the field force would lessen the level of motorization previously planned for the army and divert resources from the tank force, Liddell Hart none the less did not object to the new plans. He admitted that, while the army had been too big for its previous imperial role, it was now too small for its new Continental one.[109] However, a week after Hore-Belisha's speech, on 15 March, Germany invaded and dismembered the rest of Czechoslovakia, and British policy took a new and far more radical turn.

The blatant German violation of the Munich agreement was a cruel blow to Western hopes regarding Hitler's intentions and the prospects of reaching accommodation with him. The British government never gave up its hope of achieving *détente* with Germany, but public opinion was transformed after 'Prague', and there was mounting pressure in Parliament and within the Conservative Party for strong measures to prevent further German aggression. Consequently, in the weeks following Prague the government drifted into accepting two major decisions, both hastily and haphazardly arrived at, without prior consultation with the responsible professional bodies: one decision was the massive expansion of the army, first by announcing the doubling the Territorial army and three weeks later by introducing conscription; the other was the unilateral guarantee to Poland, later extended also to Romania and Greece. While both decisions had their critics at the time, most people and the majority of the immediate postwar historians accepted them with relief as signalling the end of appeasement and retreat. Liddell Hart, however, regarded both as major errors, and since the opening of the British archives historians have almost unanimously come around to his view.

[109] Talk before Churchill's 'Focus', 30 Nov. 1939; talk with Eden, 30 Jan. 1939, King's, 11/1939/6; to Barrington-Ward, 2 Feb. 1939, 3/109; talk before the Compatriots Club in the House of Commons, 3 Mar. 1939, 11/1939/18; *The Defence of Britain*, 116, 209–10, 317–19; the series 'An Army Across the Channel?' in *The Times*, 7, 8 Feb. 1939, still emphasizing the arguments against the dispatch of ground forces to the Continent, had been written in early Dec. 1938 and was held back by *The Times* for 2 months; according to Liddell Hart, it was intended to lead in a roundabout manner, and against the editorial line at the time to the conclusion that the dispatch of ground forces was now necessary; *Memoirs*, ii. 193, 196–8, 211, 223.

Conscription

After Munich the British government had been able to resist the pressure developing both from within the Conservative Party and from the French to introduce conscription in Britain. But after Prague the pressure from both directions and especially from France rose sharply. In an effort to release the pressure and avoid conscription Chamberlain on 28 March accepted Hore-Belisha's idea, raised virtually on the spur of the moment, to take advantage of the flow of volunteers to the Territorial army and double the Territorials from thirteen to twenty-six divisions. Together with the Regulars, this would give the army the paper strength of thirty-two divisions. The decision was announced in Parliament the day after without the chiefs of staff being consulted. John Slessor summarized the reaction of the bewildered military:

it was a political decision—just like that; well meaning no doubt but actually quite meaningless; there was not the remotest chance of actually getting an effective Field Force of thirty two divisions for years to come and its only immediate effect was . . . a weakening of the existing force by the inevitable dilution involved.[110]

There were simply none of the facilities, instructors, and above all the equipment necessary to make the new scheme a reality. In any case, the scheme did not succeed in alleviating the pressures on the government to introduce conscription, and French officials urged that it was absolutely vital even as a gesture for reassuring French public opinion. The integrity of the French alliance was, of course, vital, as was the government's parliamentary support. So in late April conscription was accepted, again on political grounds and without seeking the advice of the chiefs of staff. 'Very few men were actually called before the war broke out, in large part because Britain lacked the industrial capacity to equip them. In all, the decision to conscript brought a great deal more trouble than good.'[111]

Ever since the 1920s, when he had assimilated Fuller's conception of war, Liddell Hart had objected to conscription which lay at the root of mass armies. He wanted a small army of professionals which could be wholly mechanized and take full advantage of modern technology, and

[110] *The Central Blue*, 183–4.
[111] For the problems of conscription, see: Dennis, *Decision by Default*, 146, 148, 154–7, 163–5, 174, 178–81, 191–200, 206–25; Howard, *Continental Commitment*, 129–30; Gibbs, *Grand Strategy*, i. 516–21; Shay, *British Rearmament*, 272–3 (citation from 273); Bond, *British Military Policy*, 304–6, 308–10, 326–7; Murray, *European Balance of Power*, 297.

which was unlikely to repeat the First World War style of warfare. This army could be backed by a militia-type volunteers army (the Territorials). The rest of the country's population would be left in peace, and would be more profitably employed in producing the hardware essential for modern war. Liddell Hart was not impressed by the calculations of the Committee of Imperial Defence and the army, put to him by CIGS Deverell and DMO Haining in November 1936, that even after the demands of the air force, the navy, and industry for manpower were fully met, some five million men would still be left available for use by the army. He replied that the question was whether they could be *effectively* employed by the army, apart from the fact that the aftermath of the war and the avoidance of exhaustion ought also be considered. He suggested that in the technological age quality was more important than numbers.[112]

After Munich and Prague, when conscription was increasingly on the cards, Liddell Hart fought tenaciously against it in articles, lectures, and public meetings. He was supported by the authority of Sir Auckland Geddes, the director of recruiting in 1916–19. Once more in conflict with *The Times*'s editorial policy which had faithfully followed the government's turnabout on conscription, Liddell Hart again suggested to the editor that his association with the newspaper might better be discontinued. For him, conscription stood for all the bad things he had striven to avoid. By now he anchored his objection to conscription within his newly formed philosophical conception of what 'England' and the West were all about, which will be discussed later on. But his strategic arguments in themselves were formidable. By 1939 and for a long time to come the army had all the volunteers it wanted, and there was simply no equipment for the mass army projected after Prague. Furthermore, Liddell Hart anticipated that conscription would be positively harmful for the development of the army, in the first place because it would divert industrial resources from mechanization.[113]

Indeed, although after the outbreak of the war the British government, with the First World War in mind, planned the expansion of the army to fifty-five divisions, of which thirty-two would be British and the rest from the Dominions and India, it was soon realized that these

---

[112] Talk with Deverell and Haining, 13 Nov. 1936, King's, 11/1936/94; *Memoirs*, i. 382.
[113] 'British Freedom', *World Review* (Dec. 1938), 23; *The Times*, 8 Feb. and 24 Mar. 1939; to G. Dawson, 9 May 1938; talk before the Compatriots Club in the House of Commons, and throughout Liddell Hart's private notes during 1939, in King's, 11/1939; talks before the Cambridge and Oxford Unions respectively: 12/1939/39 and 44; *The Defence of Britain*, 84–5; *Memoirs*, ii. 228–37.

numbers were simply unachievable. Despite the total mobilization of manpower and industry and despite the massive American aid in war materials and equipment, the number of men and women under arms during the war in *all* of the three services never reached five million, and that of the army remained below three million. In 1944–5, despite all the efforts, the British army had no more than twenty-four divisions.[114] As Liddell Hart suggested, if the army had concentrated in 1939–40 on gradually bringing up to strength, equipping, and training the existing nineteen divisions of the Regulars and Territorials it could have possessed all the strength it needed for a very long time. In addition, it might have avoided some of the muddle created by the raising of new formations from scratch, which so unfortunately characterized its entry into both world wars.[115]

The Polish Guarantee

The decision to give Poland a guarantee that if she were attacked by Germany Britain would enter the war on her side was announced by Chamberlain on 31 March 1939, a week after Germany occupied Memel from Lithuania. Again the decision was taken by the British government in great haste and with total disregard for military advice.[116] In Parliament Lloyd George, briefed by Liddell Hart, severely criticized the decision, and although the majority of the House from all parties supported it, it is interesting to note that Churchill, for example, who welcomed the decision, was well aware of its problematic nature.[117] The main problem was the guarantee's unilateral and unconditioned nature, about which the chiefs of staff and Liddell Hart

---

[114] LH, *Memoirs*, ii 198–9; J. R. M. Butler, *Grand Strategy*, ii (London, 1957), 32–3, 255–6; W. K. Hancock and M. M. Gowing, *British War Economy: History of the Second World War—Civil Series* (London, 1949), 78; Postan, *British War Production*, 73–5, 129, 243; Macleod and Kelly, *The Ironside Diaries*, 103–6, 134, 136–7; also cf. J. Mearsheimer, *Conventional Deterrence* (Ithaca, NY, 1983), 92; Mearsheimer's strategic assessments in this book are almost antithetical to those in his later diatribe against Liddell Hart.

[115] For a defence of Kitchener's policy in the First World War, see P. Simpkin, *Kitchener's Army* (Manchester, 1988), esp. 40–6.

[116] For the following, see esp. S. Newman, *March 1939: The British Guarantee to Poland* (Oxford, 1976); A. Prazmowska, *Britain, Poland and the Eastern Front, 1939* (Cambridge, 1987); Gibbs, *Grand Strategy*, i. 689–707, 719–60, 804–6; Murray, *European Balance of Power*, 293–4, 297–305, 366–7; also Howard, *Continental Commitment*, 131–2; Dennis, *Decision by Default*, 200–5; Bond, *British Military Policy*, 306–8, 310–15, 317–19.

[117] *The Second World War*, i. 347, 375, and ch. 20; T. Ben-Moshe, *Churchill: Strategy and History* (Boulder, Colo., 1992), 110.

expressed similar concern.[118] Britain surrendered her freedom of decision on whether to go to war or not to 'the most romantic and least
realistic people in Europe', in Liddell Hart's words, giving up any
leverage she had on the Polish government before trying to make
sure that the essential preconditions for the successful fulfilment of
the guarantee were accepted by the Poles.

It was of secondary importance that the British government failed
even to secure that the guarantee would be mutual—the Poles refused
to give Romania a similar guarantee. The main point, stressed both by
the chiefs of staff and by Liddell Hart, was that the Western Allies
could not assist Poland directly, and the very little they could do to
assist her indirectly could not prevent her being overrun by Germany
within a short period of time. The chiefs of staff and Liddell Hart had
very little faith in Poland's ability to resist, given its geography and the
relative backwardness of her armed forces. Reversing their previous
attitude, though still wavering in their successive assessments of the
Soviet Union's strength and significance, the chiefs of staff now maintained, as Liddell Hart had done all along, that if Poland and the whole
of Eastern Europe were to be defended from Germany, Soviet cooperation was vital. The French, too, regarded the guarantee to Poland as
unwise, and preferred cooperation with the Soviet Union. For the
problem was that the Poles would not hear of the Red Army entering
their territory. They overestimated their own strength and underesti-
mated that of Germany. Deceived by France and Britain into expecting
Allied land and air offensive efforts in the West which would lessen the
German concentration against them, they were confident of their ability
to withstand attack. And having given the Polish government an unconditional guarantee, the Western Allies lost whatever leverage they had
had for putting pressure on it to cooperate with the Russians.

Furthermore, their unconditional commitment to go to war over
Poland lost the Western Allies most of their diplomatic leverage on
the Soviet Union as well. The driving motive behind Soviet diplomacy
in 1935–9 had been the fear that the Western powers would reach an
accommodation with Hitler, leaving the USSR isolated and dangerously
exposed. The British unilateral guarantee to Poland was therefore much
to the Soviets' advantage. Being now increasingly satisfied that

---

[118] For Liddell Hart, see his summary notes of 27 Aug. and 10 Sept. 1939, in King's,
3/109; and 11/1939, esp. 29, 31; *The Defence of Britain*, 39, 80, 95–9; *The Current of War*
(London, 1941), 142–7; *Memoirs*, ii. 214–22, 241, 249–50, 253, 255.

Germany and the Western Allies were bound for war if Poland was attacked, Stalin was in effect given a free hand to opt for neutrality at the highest price and with maximum security. The Soviet Union rather than Britain now held the European balance of power. The opinion of one historian of Soviet foreign policy is illuminating: 'There was one and only one argument that could have swayed Stalin to accept an alliance with Britain and France. This would have been a declaration that the West would *not* defend Poland *unless* the USSR joined in her defense.'[119]

Chamberlain, however, did not want a Soviet alliance anyhow. He gave the guarantee to Poland not so much with the possibility of war in mind but, first, in order to leave Hitler in no doubt that Britain meant business and thus deter him from war and bring him back to the negotiating table; and, second, because the Foreign Office suddenly became anxious that Poland might make a deal with Hitler if she could not be reassured of the Western Allies' backing. Indeed, unlike his aim in respect to Czechoslovakia in the previous year, Hitler's initial intention was to bring Poland into his camp, provided the Polish government did not object to the incorporation of the Free City of Danzig in the Reich and granted Germany extraterritorial routes to East Prussia through the Polish corridor. The winter negotiations quickly taught Hitler that there was scant chance that the Poles were going to concede to his demands. But only after the British guarantee had been given did Hitler on 3 April 1939 order his armed forces to plan a campaign for the conquest of Poland. Whether this mattered or not, there can be little doubt that, as Liddell Hart was warning, Hitler was provoked into, rather than deterred from, war by the British guarantee to Poland and possibly also by the British introduction of conscription. The Poles themselves were unenthusiastic about the British guarantee for the same reason. All the same, the important point was that if Europe was heading for war, the Soviet Union's cooperation was essential for the Western Allies; so even Chamberlain and Halifax could not for long withstand the three-party pressure in Parliament to open negotiations with her.

The Soviet–German Pact and Its Consequences

That Chamberlain and Halifax opened those negotiations reluctantly and half-heartedly is well known. Unlike their position before Munich,

---

[119] See Ulam, *Expansion and Coexistence*, esp. 266–75.

the Soviets now insisted on a full political and military Triple Alliance with Britain and France and on a guarantee to all the parties involved. The British government, which wanted no more than a Soviet participation in the guarantee to Poland, was finally forced to accept the idea of a treaty under pressure at home. Yet the slow pace of the negotiations during the spring and summer of 1939 and the story of the Anglo-French military delegation's trip to the Soviet Union in August, taking the slow sea route, composed of relatively junior representatives, and given little authority to decide on anything, did not impress the Russians that the Western Allies meant business. A week before the German occupation of Prague, Ambassador Maisky had told Liddell Hart, as he had been telling everybody who was prepared to listen and the Foreign Office, that after the Munich rebuff Stalin might turn away from the policy of cooperation with the West and into isolation.[120] On 3 May the Soviet foreign secretary, Litvinov, a Jew and the main proponent of collective security, was replaced by Molotov, an act which probably signalled Stalin's wish to widen his field of manœuvre. Secret negotiations between the USSR and Germany began seriously in late July. But only after the middle of August 1939, when the Soviets had become convinced that there was going to be no military alliance with the Western Allies, certain that Hitler intended to attack Poland very shortly, and had concluded that against his expectations this was most likely to involve Germany in war with the Western powers, did they concede to a treaty. On 22 August it was announced in Moscow, to the complete surprise of the Western powers, that the German foreign secretary, Joachim von Ribbentrop was flying to Moscow for the signing of a non-aggression pact between Germany and the USSR. The signing itself took place two days later.[121]

The Soviet–German pact changed everything, in Liddell Hart's view. As long as the West had been negotiating with the Soviet Union for military cooperation against Germany, he had not been too alarmed. Now, however, he fell into despair. At once, and more clearly than

---

[120] Liddell Hart, *Memoirs*, ii. 222; S. Aster, 'Maisky and Parliamentary Anti-Appeasement', in Taylor *Lloyd George*, 336–7.

[121] See Roberts, *The Unholy Alliance*; Haslam, *The Soviet Union and the Struggle for Collective Security*, 195–229; also J. Erickson, *The Soviet High Command* (London, 1962), 514–30. That these were indeed the Soviet calculations seems to be confirmed by the recent revelation from the Soviet archives of Stalin's speech before the Politburo on 19 Aug. 1939.

anybody, he saw the strategic implications of the new situation.[122] In the first place, nothing could now prevent Poland from being overrun by Germany; on this he was in agreement with professional opinion in the West. However, Anglo-French planning was now predicated on the assumption that in the longer run the Western powers, by fully mobilizing the resources of their empires backed by the economic resources of the United States, and by the use of economic blockade, would be able to defeat Germany; and for this assumption Liddell Hart saw no reason. He agreed that the allies' formula of 'economic and moral pressure' for the first stage of the war was their only practical strategy, but maintained that they were unlikely to assemble superior strength to defeat Germany in any time-range and argued that, as Germany now dominated Eastern Europe, the effect of the blockade might prove limited, especially if the Soviet Union were to supply Germany with the raw materials she needed.[123] Relying on the experience of both world wars, most historians now express similar assessments.[124]

But Liddell Hart's logic did not stop there. As he saw it, the political consequences of the new strategic situation were far-reaching and inescapable. During the tense week between the announcement of the Soviet–German pact and the outbreak of the war, he sent his views to Dawson as well as to a small circle of politicians with whom he had been in close touch: Eden, Cecil, Dalton, Sinclair, and Lloyd George. He claimed that there was no point in defending a hopeless cause in a war which one could not win. One had to know when and where to retreat. The Western powers had to recognize that, as the Soviet Union had changed sides, Poland could no longer be defended, or rescued from Germany. The Western powers, too, were therefore obliged to change their course, which was inevitably leading to war, while trying to get the best possible deal over Poland and for Poland. Liddell Hart argued that Hitler's demands regarding Danzig and the Corridor were not unreasonable nor unjustified. Both for the good of Poland itself—which

---

[122] For the following, see Liddell Hart's diary notes for 27 Aug. and 1 Sept. 1939; 'Summary of the Situation', 27 Aug.; 'A Personal Conclusion', 10 Sept. 1939: all in King's, 3/109 and 11/1939; *The Current of War*, 142–7, 160–1; *Memoirs*, ii. 252–5, 259.

[123] The latter point had been made by the chiefs of staff in urging cooperation with the Soviet Union in the spring, and had been also raised in the cabinet; now, however, it was optimistically underrated: Gibbs, *Grand Strategy*, i. 723–4; Butler, *Grand Strategy*, ii. 71–4; Murray, *The European Balance of Power*, 303.

[124] See e.g. Mearsheimer, *Conventional Deterrence*, 91–4, 98, which again stands in stark contrast to his *LH*. The latter completely fails to mention the Soviet–German pact as the reason for Liddell Hart's change of attitude over Poland.

might otherwise suffer heavily to for no avail—and from the point of view of the West's interests, there was no alternative to meeting those demands.

However, as Liddell Hart discovered, even if most of his correspondents found his strategic assessment of the situation hard to resist, the majority of them recoiled from his political conclusions. Lloyd George was in agreement with him, but Hugh Dalton, a previous ally in the anti-appeasement campaign, was more typical of the reactions Liddell Hart received, in raising the question what would be next: what would stop Hitler after Poland? It was much better, Dalton insisted, to go to war with Poland on Britain's side than to face Germany without her help later on. 'It is ironical', he wrote, 'that now, when *The Times*, in my view, is shaping very much better, you should have become an appeaser!'[125] Indeed what was the difference between Poland at the end of August 1939 and Munich in 1938? As Liddell Hart saw it, the difference was not in the principle and at the level of political slogans but in the harsh strategic reality: before Munich Czechoslovakia could offer stiff resistance and the Soviet Union sought cooperation with the West, so Hitler's Germany could be deterred or contained and choked; by contrast, after the Soviet–German pact Poland could not be defended and Germany could not be coerced into submission or defeated. The West was obliged to face realities and wait for better days or for a change of circumstances.

The gravity of the strategic realities was not, however, something of which British public opinion was fully cognizant. Ever since Prague, in the week leading to the outbreak of the Second World War, and even after the rapid fall of Poland, Liddell Hart had noted a complete change of mood in British public opinion and politics. He recorded with dismay what he regarded as evidence of jingoism and delusionary optimism, clearly an expression of relief from the frustrations and disappointments of the previous years. The announcement of the Soviet–German pact was not followed by an Anglo-French backdown, as Hitler expected and Liddell Hart desired, as the only rational course of action open to the Western Allies, but, to the contrary, by revival of the British bulldog spirit. On 25 August Britain signed an official treaty of mutual defence with Poland. There were now public expectations (not shared by the defence establishment) of an early Allied victory over Germany and political expressions of commitment to the

---

[125] To LH, 31 Aug. 1939, King's, 11/1939/85.

destruction of Hitlerism, both of which Liddell Hart judged to be beyond the capability of Britain and France. As he saw it, this was a swing between poles from appeasement to a bellicose pursuit of victory—both of which equally unrealistic and equally disastrous.[126] Since the signing of the Soviet–German pact his world had broken down. The worst he had striven to avert was now happening: Britain and Europe were sliding into total war, entailing total destruction and exhaustion, with no feasible aim in sight.

In June Liddell Hart had experienced a heart attack and now, in the fourth week of August, he collapsed and was incapacitated for several months. In consequence he was discharged by *The Times*, which wanted a fully active military correspondent to cover the war. Although his discharge was against his wishes—he tried hard to convince the editors that the war was not going to end soon anyhow—it did not necessarily entail an economic loss for him. He had long been tempted to write as a freelance for the popular press, which offered him much greater sums of money than *The Times*.[127] However, for several months after the outbreak of the war, though bombarded with requests for articles, he turned them down because he expected that people would not be willing to listen to what he had to say. Judging by the experience of the First World War, he had long anticipated that in times of war the newspapers would refrain from printing unpleasant material. Indeed, when he did try to offer his views on the situation to the press, the newspapers' editors declined to publish them for being too depressing for the public.[128]

But what in fact did Liddell Hart propose that the Western Allies should do at that point of time? In order fully to understand this, it is

---

[126] See in King's, 11/1939; *Memoirs*, ii. 219–20, 252–3, 257–8, 261, 276–7.

[127] In his *Memoirs*, ii. 251–2, 258–9, Liddell Hart has tried to put on a brave face over his dismissal, implying that it was largely done on his own initiative and on matters of principle. The truth is somewhat different. He had three times threatened to resign when publication of his writings were withheld: over Spain, over the state of Britain's air defence during the Czechoslovakian crisis, and over the introduction of conscription. In none of these cases had he carried out his threat, but at the end of 1938 he had succeeded in securing the right to contribute to other newspapers. In this he had long been interested for material reasons as well, using the generous offers he had been receiving from the popular press as a lever for improving his conditions with *The Times*. However, having achieved the best of all worlds, he definitely did not want to resign when the war broke out, and was practically forced to do so, mainly on account of his health. See King's, 3/108–9, and esp. his letter exchange with Dawson between 28 Aug. and 7 Sept. 1939. [128] See in King's, 11/1939; *Memoirs*, ii. 251–2, 257–8, 275.

time to examine the wider philosophical outlook he had developed in the late 1930s regarding the essence and aims of the West.

Defence of the West: Ideology and Strategy

Notwithstanding his youthful declaration of faith written in 1914,[129] Liddell Hart was not ideologically and politically aligned until the 1930s. During the 1920s he hardly ever transgressed from the strategic realm into politics. It is a mere curiosity, reflecting widespread attitudes in the West during the late 1920s, that he returned in 1928 from a tour of Italy and the Italian armed forces full of enthusiasm for the achievements of the Fascist regime.[130] By the 1930s, however, with the crisis of the democracies and the seemingly irresistible march of Nazism, fascism, and communism, politics polarized, ideology came to the forefront of public consciousness, and thinking individuals everywhere were struggling for define to themselves where they stood. Liddell Hart was no exception to this rule. While Fuller formally embraced fascism, Liddell Hart became a staunch partisan of liberal democracy.

From the mid-1930s Liddell Hart's private papers are full of statements of creed. While lamenting the mediocrity in the British army and government, he held that in the dictatorships things were far worse. His main objection to both fascism and communism was their oppressive nature. Quoting Lord Acton's famous dictum, he went on to express the following classical liberal positions, which rang far better half a century before or after than in the 1930s:

Government at the best is a necessary evil. In the light of experience, autocratic government may produce an immediate increase of efficiency, but progressively undermine the foundations of ultimate efficiency. The virtue of Parliamentary government does not lie in its government, but in its available checks on governmental abuses. . . . Full freedom may be unattainable, but the minimum condition necessary for the development of the mind is that you should be free to be true in speech to what you think.[131]

---

[129] See p. 139–40 above.

[130] The titles of his articles speak for themselves: 'Fascist Italy:—New-Born Efficiency, Traditional Courtesy', 'Pursuit of an Ideal', 'The Future: Training the Youth', 'A Patriotic Autocrat', 'The New Romulus and the New Rome': *Daily Telegraph*, 10, 11, 12, 16 Jan. 1928; *Atlantic Monthly* (July 1928); also *Yale Review*, June 1930, 665.

[131] See in King's, 11/1934; 4 Aug. 1936, 11/1936; quotation from 'Power and Freedom', 9 May 1937, 11/1937/40.

A week later, in a letter to Fuller responding to the latter's fascist writings, Liddell Hart denounced all forms of authoritarianism and the suppression of truth.[132] With their relationship already deteriorating (Liddell Hart is not even mentioned in Fuller's *Memoirs*, 1936), the breach between the two men was final. Their correspondence ceased, and they did not see each other again until 1942. The significance of this break was more than biographical, for it was now left to Liddell Hart to develop the notions he had absorbed from Fuller in the early 1920s into a strategic blueprint for a liberal-democratic West. Liddell Hart's strategic theory and political and philosophical creed became closely interconnected.

Liddell Hart defined the challenge facing Britain in the late 1930s in the opening essay of *Europe in Arms* (1937), 'The Defence of Freedom':

This island, if now less than an island strategically . . . is more than ever an island politically. . . . Will England stand rocklike amid the totalitarian tide until that tide ebbs? Our constitution for several centuries has had its roots in the growing idea of individual liberty. . . . For a time, in the last century, our example had an ever-widening influence. . . . The war of 1914–18 interrupted this liberal expansion. . . . Alike to Communism and Fascism, uniformity is an ideal, and nonconformity a crime. . . . [In Britain itself] toleration has never been so widespread, nor violence so widely disfavoured. The decline of the Liberal party . . . has helped the spread of liberal ideas through all parties. . . . The only serious danger to-day lies outside our borders. . . . It threatens not only our national existence but all that makes existence worth while.

How was the danger to be faced? If need be, inescapably, by force of arms, but with a view to the desired aim. 'Patriots' and 'pacifists' must recognize each other's point: defence was essential, but only in the cause of freedom. Freedom must become an animating ideal at home and a shining example abroad.[133]

After Munich, when for the first time in his life the alarmed Liddell Hart actively enlisted in the public political campaign in meetings, lectures, debates, and pamphlets, he amplified these ideas. Against the peace movements he argued that peace was worth having only for the purpose of maintaining justice, freedom, free speech, and the conditions conducive to the life and growth of the individual. In the same way, fiercely campaigning against conscription, he declared repeatedly that totalitarianism must not be fought by totalitarian means. Individual rights were superior to state rights, and the end could never

[132] To Fuller, 16 May 1937, King's, 1/302.   [133] *Europe in Arms*, 1–7.

justify the means. Britain must safeguard and cultivate freedom, which is humanity's greatest achievement and the underlying direction of its development.[134]

Ideals, of course, are not an independent sphere but form part of a wider reality. As Liddell Hart grasped, a fundamental fact about Britain's political position in the 1930s was that, while already being a satisfied imperial power, she had progressively become a consumerist, liberal-democratic society with no interest in major wars unless the status quo was seriously threatened. In this, as in so many other aspects of the development of 'modernity', Britain and the strategic problems she faced might be seen as paradigmatically foreshadowing the condition of the 'West' as a whole later on. As already mentioned, Liddell Hart was the first to try to work out the theoretical framework of a grand strategy suited for this new or emerging model.

In his important 'Attack or Defence' series in *The Times* in late 1937 Liddell Hart put forward the outline of this grand strategy. He argued that Clausewitz's claim that, while being stronger than attack, defence was unable to produce a decision was true only 'so far as the positive overthrow of the enemy was necessary for the fulfilment of the purpose in war'. That object, however, was no longer necessary for the purpose of a non-aggressive Britain and her friends:[135]

Military action should be ruled by its head: the national object. We may be drawn into war to defend our interests and ensure, in face of an aggressor, the continuance of liberal civilization, those larger ideas which we epitomize when we speak of 'England'. To attain that object, need not imply on our part a war *à outrance*. For the aggressor, aiming at conquest, the complete overthrow of the opposing forces and the occupation of the opponent's territory may be necessary to his success. But not for ours. Our object is fulfilled if we can convince the enemy that he cannot conquer.[136]

Searching for apt historical models for the new political and strategic requirements, Liddell Hart came up with one which had been held in

---

[134] See e.g. ibid. 219–21; 'Democratic Service', *Student Forum*, 30 Nov. 1938; 'British Freedom', *World Review*, Dec. 1938, 21–7; *The Defence of Britain*, 86; and the extensive documentation throughout King's, 11/1939; *Memoirs*, ii. 206–7, 210.

[135] Clausewitz himself had become increasingly aware of this; see my *The Origins of Military Thought from the Enlightenment to Clausewitz* (Oxford, 1989), 213, 260; and 'Clausewitz on Defence and Attack', *Journal of Strategic Studies*, 10 (1988), 20–6. Liddell Hart, *The Times*, 26 Oct. 1937, repr. in *The Defence of Britain*, 106–7.

[136] *The Times*, 27 Oct. 1937; repr. in *The Defence of Britain*, 42–3. Originally in a memorandum for the record: 23 Sept. 1937, King's, 11/1937/75.

contempt by the men of the nineteenth century who had exalted national vigour and decisive victories. This was the Byzantine tradition of imperial defence which, as Liddell Hart claimed, safeguarded Byzantium for more than 1,000 years—a feat unequalled in history—and must be judged a tremendous success in terms of adjusting means and ends:

This new–old and strength conserving strategy of imperial defence does not imply a purely passive resistance. Its aim is to convince the enemy that it has nothing to gain and much to lose by pursuing a war. Its guiding principle is to eschew the vain pursuit of a decision by the offensive on our part. Its method is not merely to parry, but to make the enemy pay as heavily as possible for his offensive efforts. This implies in the military sphere an active and mobile defence, in which the effect of direct resistance is extended by *ripostes* both strategic and tactical as well as by continual harassing action. In this offensive–defensive strategy there is a part for mobile land forces as well as for the sea and air forces. And economic pressure in turn will be used to extend the wearing down process in the military sphere.[137]

These ideas formed the basis for a new chapter, 'Grand Strategy', which together with another new chapter—on Byzantine wars—was to be incorporated in the second edition of Liddell Hart's major theoretical work *The Strategy of Indirect Approach* (1941).

If Britain is viewed as 'the first modern nation', paradigmatically reflecting, as it were, 'the way of the future', the United States, the other English-speaking, oceanic, liberal-democratic, and capitalist-consumerist great power, is equally famously cast in a similar position. To demonstrate the idea of this study regarding the historical background and significance of Liddell Hart's work, one might turn to the United States for obvious parallels. Here was another nation whose experience of the First World War—though much briefer and less agonizing than Britain's, and economically far more rewarding—had resulted in a traumatic backlash. This had led to the ascendence of isolationism, which owing to more fortunate geopolitical conditions would be sustained longer than in Britain. Then, in the late 1930s, when the international crises across both the Pacific and Atlantic oceans posed challenges of a high order, what were the political and strategic notions which Roosevelt and the American adminstration began to toy with, no matter for the moment how seriously? Starting from Japan's invasion of China in the summer of 1937 and the signing of the tripartite Anti-Comintern Pact in November of that year (which was perceived in

---

[137] *The Times*, 27 Oct. 1937; repr. in *The Defence of Britain*, 120–2.

Washington as a global military alliance against the status quo powers), the notions of a coordinated policy of sanctions and containment against the aggressors were increasingly aired by the president. The idea was first embodied in his famous 'quarantine speech' on 5 December 1937. As Roosevelt told both his cabinet and the British ambassador in mid-December: 'We want to develop a technique which will not lead to war. We want to be smart as Japan and Italy. We want to do it in a modern way.' He argued that the Axis powers were pursuing a policy of 'undeclared war' which ought to be answered in kind. During the Czechoslovakian crisis Roosevelt called for a 'siege' of Germany. He suggested that the Allies ought to close their borders with Germany, even without declaring war, and stand on the defence, relying on the economic blockade to do the job. The United States would back them economically (everything except 'troops and loans'). Offensive actions would only result in 'terrific casualties' and, in view of German military power, would prove futile. Finally, after Munich and during 1939 Roosevelt stressed the importance of Soviet cooperation.[138]

Obviously, these notions were very hazily defined, took the form of presidential speculations rather than of official policy, lacked the support of Congress and of the majority of Americans, and therefore inspired little faith abroad. For example, without an American guarantee (which was not forthcoming) that the United States would join the war if Britain were attacked by Japan following a policy of sanctions, Chamberlain had no intention of risking such a policy in 1937-9 (as indeed in 1931 and 1934). It was finally implemented against Japan by the United States only in the summer of 1941.[139] All the same, it is Roosevelt's general trend of thought which is of interest to us. Liddell Hart was barely concerned about the Far East, and there was probably little if any consequential link between his own ideas and those being entertained across the Atlantic. Only the historical circumstances of and the strategic challenges facing Britain and the United States revealed an underlying similarity, and the same was true of the respective proposed solutions.

[138] See D. Reynolds, *The Creation of the Anglo-American Alliance, 1937–1941* (London, 1981), 17, 30–31 (quotation), 35, and *passim*; R. Dallek, *Franklin D. Roosevelt and American Foreign Policy, 1932–1945* (New York, 1979), 163–4, and *passim*; C. Macdonald, 'Deterrence Diplomacy: Roosevelt and the Containment of Germany, 1938–1940', in Boyce and Robertson *Paths to War*, 297–329; D. C. Watt, *Succeeding John Bull: America in Britain's Place, 1900–1975* (Cambridge, 1984), 82–3.

[139] That this amounted to a strategy of containment is again noted by J. Mueller, *Retreat from Doomsday: The Obsolescence of Major War* (New York, 1989), 75–7.

The grand strategy which Liddell Hart developed in the late 1930s for 'England' and the West was devised as an antidote to what he labelled 'camouflage war' or 'war by points', which he maintained had already been taking place for several years around the world against the interests of the Western powers.[140] This grand strategy was defensive in aim and, as we have seen in reviewing Liddell Hart's positions in respect to the successive international crises, it was based on containment and deterrence, economic coercion, peripheral war by proxy, blockade, and limited war, in that order. It was defensive because Liddell Hart assessed that Britain and her allies (the fully committed, not including the United States) were simply not strong enough to crush a major rival like Nazi Germany; and that any attempt to do so, even assuming this goal could be achieved, would bankrupt them in every respect, while being strictly unnecessary for the attainment of their fundamental aims. Defensive also because Liddell Hart grew to believe that the very concept of 'victory' was a mirage and a boomerang which more often than not created resentment in the defeated side, gave rise to new rivals, and sowed the seeds of the next round of conflict. By 1935 Liddell Hart wrote privately that he had lost faith in solutions by force.[141] This was typical of the way large sections of the British élite during the interwar period came to interpret modern and recent historical experience. Soundly or not, they were contrasting the heritage and durability of the victories and settlements of 1807, 1871, and 1919 on the one hand with those of 1815 and 1866 on the other. According to Liddell Hart, the West had to check the hostile forces but not embark on a crusade to crush them, which would 'only lead to mutual suicide, and the collapse of civilization'.[142]

Cold War

In Liddell Hart's view, all these considerations only grew in force after the outbreak of the war and Germany's overrunning of Poland in September 1939. As mentioned earlier, with the fall of Czechoslovakia and Germany's increasing domination of south-eastern Europe, Germany had become much less susceptible to economic coercion. The Soviet–German pact had made her even less susceptible, as well as practically nullifying the prospects of defeating her by force. Liddell

---

[140] For these concepts, see e.g. *The Defence of Britain*, 26; Note, 15 Mar. 1938, King's, 11/1938/32.　　　　[141] 26 Dec. 1935, King's, 11/1935/55.
[142] *The Defence of Britain*, 19, also 20–1, 26, 35–8, 43; diary notes of 4 Aug. 1939, printed in *The Current of War*, 140–1.

Hart had been against going to war under these circumstances in the first place, and now he thought, like Lloyd George and Beaverbrook, that Britain and France ought not to reject Hitler's peace offers but to strive for a negotiated settlement.[143] Victory may be desirable in abstract in view of the nature of the Nazi regime, but it was simply unattainable. The alternative presented to the British people between either total victory or total defeat was unhistorical and irrational.[144] In the meantime Liddell Hart proposed that Britain and France should publicly declare that they were renouncing the offensive in the defence of Western civilization and the struggle against aggression. This would give the Allies the moral advantage, and provide less provocation for Germany to attack in the West.[145]

What does all this amount to? Having lost their ability to contain Germany within her old frontiers, choke her economically if she attempted to break out of them, and indeed win a war against her, the Allies' only desirable option, as Liddell Hart saw it, was in effect armed coexistence alongside her. Central and south-eastern Europe could not be rescued from Germany's domination (though Liddell Hart did not spell this out), at least until Germany fell out with the Soviet Union.[146] What the Western Allies ought to concentrate upon in terms of grand strategy was the security of the Western bloc or Western civilization. Until a satisfactory peace with Germany could be negotiated, there was to be no more than a continuation of the 'Twilight' or 'Phoney War' which was already prevailing on the Western Front—in effect, 'cold war'.

To that end, no provocative offensive action was to be attempted by the West, for no promising course of action could be envisaged anyhow and any Western offensive initiative would only drive Germany into action and lead to escalation. Here also the interesting point is that Liddell Hart's grand design was matched by very acute specific strategic

---

[143] After the fall of Poland, Lloyd George and Liddell Hart were practically unanimous about the war. Regarding the possibility of peace, Lloyd George thought in terms of an 'ethnic Poland', stripped of her German, Belorussian, and Ukrainian provinces and populations: P. Addington, 'Lloyd George and Compromise Peace in the Second World War', in Taylor *Lloyd George*, 361–84, esp. 367–71.

[144] Memorandum, 7 Nov. 1939, King's, 11/1939/128; other notes, memoranda, and articles are printed in *The Current of War*, 161–2, 185–92.

[145] 8 Sept. 1939, King's, 11/1939/100; published after a long delay as 'Is There a New Way to Fight This Strange War?', *Sunday Express*, 10 Dec. 1939, and reworked in many subsequent articles; the original memo was reprinted in *The Current of War*, 151–7, also 162–3; cf. *Memoirs*, ii. 275, which makes no mention of the actual content of the article.

[146] See ibid. 260, 276.

analyses. As the French and British high commands were agreed, the Allies would not be able to carry out for years to come a land offensive in the West. The bombing of the Ruhr and of German cities was clearly not in the Allies' interest, for they, and especially France, were more vulnerable than Germany to such attacks and because the Luftwaffe held the advantage in the air.[147] When in the winter of 1939–40 the idea of Anglo-French expeditions to Scandinavia captured the imagination of Allied public opinion, Liddell Hart rejected it outright. There was much enthusiasm for armed intervention in defence of the heroic Finns against the Soviet Union, and Hore-Belisha, for example, was not untypical when talking about the prospects of occupying Leningrad and smashing the Soviet Union, as an indirect move against Germany. Liddell Hart, however, saw very clearly that the Red Army's initial defeats created a false impression as to its real strength, and that in the end it was bound to conquer. He argued that the Soviet Union's demand for the removal of its border with Finland from the gates of Leningrad was strategically understandable and that its offer of a territorial exchange with Finland was reasonable. Finally, and most importantly, he stressed that to add the Soviet Union to the West's enemies and push it further into Germany's arms was total madness. On these grounds he also rejected the plans for bombing the Black Sea oil shipping to Germany and the Soviet Union's Caucasian oilfields from the Allies' Mediterranean air bases. These ideas were seriously considered, especially by the French, and widely publicized by the press. Only the collapse of Finland's resistance put an end to these schemes.[148]

The Allies' planned expedition to Finland was largely conceived as an excuse for cutting off the transport of the Swedish iron ores destined for Germany via neutral Norwegian waters. Liddell Hart totally opposed this idea, which had been championed in Cabinet by Churchill since the beginning of the war. Critics have remarked that in this he appears to have gone against his own major doctrines of the indirect approach and the British way in warfare. In a sudden about-turn he equated the proposed Norwegian scheme with the Salonika operation in

---

[147] See e.g. Liddell Hart, 'Will the Cities Be Bombed?', *Sunday Express*, 11 Feb. 1940; repr. in *The Current of War*, 195–201. The British official history of the war in the air still blamed the French for their lack of courage: C. Webster and N. Frankland, *The Strategic Air Offensive against Germany, 1939–1945* (4 vols., London, 1961), i. 137–43; but see Butler, *Grand Strategy*, ii. 166–71.

[148] To HB, 25 Feb. 1940, King's, 11/HB 1940/28; *Evening Standard*, 10 Feb. 1940, repr. in *The Current of War*, 220–6, also 216, 227–35; on the Soviet oilfields: *Evening Standard*, 2 March 1940, repr. *The Current of War*, 236–43; *Memoirs*, ii. 275–6.

the First World War, which he now presented as a failure. However, apart from the fact that Liddell Hart obviously never claimed that *any* indirect operation was necessarily good, the point is, of course, that he viewed the proposed Norwegian operation as undesirable in terms of the overall grand strategy he advocated, *as well as* being, specifically, strategically unsound. The Swedish ores were sufficiently important for Germany to provoke her into action, whereas the Allies were not strong enough to prevent her from overrunning Norway. When the alarmed Germans responded to the Royal Navy's action in Norwegian territorial waters by a pre-emptive invasion of Denmark and Norway, Liddell Hart, while urging that speed was now the most essential requirement of the Allies' response, regarded the ensuing events as a deserved punishment for a reckless folly.[149]

So we are back again to square one. The war against Germany could not be 'won', for she could not be either strangled or crushed by Britain and France. The Allies' only viable option was to continue the low-intensity 'phoney war' which would lessen the provocation for Germany, to escalate the war against them and which, by demonstrating to her that she also could not win and had much to lose from the continuation of the war, would pave the way for a negotiated settlement. This recurring theme in Liddell Hart's writings from 1937, emphasized in *The Defence of Britain* published on the eve of the war, appears to have been echoed virtually verbatim by Chamberlain, who after the outbreak of the war wrote to Roosevelt (and to his sisters) that Britain would not win the war 'by a spectacular and complete victory, but by convincing the Germans that they cannot win'. 'Hold out tight, keep up the economic pressure, push on with munition production and military preparations with the utmost energy', but 'take no offensive unless Hitler's begins it.'[150]

Interestingly enough, on the other side of the hill as well attitudes after the Polish campaign remarkably corresponded to Liddell Hart's trend of thought. The German high command, led by the army's commander-in-chief and by the chief of the army's General Staff, Generals Brauchitsch and Halder, who were supported by all three

---

[149] Liddell Hart's articles at the time are reprinted in *The Current of War*, 248–96; Bond, *LH*, 130.

[150] For these often-quoted extracts, see R. J. Overy, *The Origins of the Second World War* (London, 1987), 77; J. Charmley, *Chamberlain and the Lost Peace* (London, 1989), 210; Chamberlain may have also been intentionally responding to Roosevelt's ideas cited above. See also Mueller, *Retreat from Doomsday*, 70.

army group commanders, was almost unanimously against launching any offensive in the West. Most high-ranking German generals did not believe Germany was capable of decisively defeating the Allies, and feared such an offensive would develop into a high-intensity war of attrition which could only be to Germany's disadvantage. They thought that Germany ought to sit quietly and concentrate on absorbing the wealth of Eastern Europe. In the words of General Alfred Jodl of the OKW: 'There was, particularly in the army, a widespread opinion that the war would die a natural death if we only kept quiet in the West.' It was Hitler who forced the reluctant army into planning and executing an offensive in the West. His pressure gave rise to another round of conspiracy to overthrow him, involving most of the army's high command, including Reichenau, hitherto the regime's strongest supporter within the army. The conspiracy came to an end when Brauchitsch collapsed in an audience with Hitler. Hitler wanted to attack in the West because he did not trust the Allies not to move into the Low Countries and thus seriously threaten the Ruhr; because he wanted to pre-empt the build-up and arrival in France of large British forces; because he did not trust the Soviet Union and feared an American intervention; and because he had long thought that the final settling of accounts with France was necessary for the establishment of his new European order.[151] Liddell Hart argued later that if it were not for the Allies' provocative actions Hitler would not have taken the offensive in the West.[152]

To bring things into focus, what Liddell Hart was advocating was containment and something approaching cold war prior to the advent of nuclear weapons. Yet, in the absence of that Great Deterrent, what was there to prevent total war? In the first place, there was the general fear of rapid and mutual destruction from the air which was perceived by the men of the 1930s in terms quite similar to those by which the nuclear threat would be perceived later on. Secondly, there was the general trend of major wars between the great powers, as demonstrated in the First World War, to become ever more costly in all respects as well as increasingly more alien to the values and interests of modern

---

[151] H. Deutsch, *The Conspiracy against Hitler in the Twilight War* (Minneapolis, 1968); W. Warlimont, *Inside Hitler's Headquarters, 1939–1945* (New York, 1964), 36, 59; Wheeler-Bennett, *The Nemesis of Power*, 466–72; Müler, *Beck*, 190–206; B. Stegmann's and H. Umbreit's contributions to MF, *Germany and the Second World War*, ii. 9, 232–8; Mearsheimer, *Conventional Deterrence*, 101–12, quotation from 102.

[152] *The Current of War*, 210.

societies. The latter argument at least may have held force for the West, but was hardly compatible, for instance, with Hitler's world-view and vision of the future and of the 'modern'. But then, Liddell Hart was also advocating a calculated policy which would renounce all offensive action on the Allies' part in order to decrease the chances of a German pre-emption and of escalation. In addition, he was seeking any other element to strengthen deterrence and underline the futility of war. It was against this background that he made the greatest blunder of his career, preaching the growing strength and complete superiority of tactical and operational defence over attack. This time his grand strategic design seriously biased his judgement of practical strategy, though even here he demonstrated dazzling foresight in some crucial respects.

IV. Defence versus 'Blitzkrieg'

Mearsheimer has rightly pointed out that Liddell Hart's new emphasis on the superiority of defence was intimately related to his preoccupation in the 1930s with policy and grand strategy.[153] In 1931–2, consulted by the British government regarding the position to be adopted in the coming disarmament conference in Geneva, Liddell Hart adopted and developed the scheme of 'qualitative disarmament', as opposed to the 'quantitative' approach around whose implementation the contentions between France and Germany in particular revolved. He thought that the best way to bypass the differences in the national points of view and deter aggression was to abolish 'offensive weapons', such as the heavy tank (above 5, 8, or 10 tons) and heavy gun (above 4-inch calibre), which had been developed as 'tin-openers' to overcome defensive lines and military stalemate. The temptation of a quick victory would thus be reduced. The new development in his thought was not easy for Liddell Hart because, as he admitted, it went against all that he had struggled for during the 1920s: precisely to overcome defensive lines and military stalemate, chiefly by the use of the tank. However, as he pointed out, this had to be sacrificed for the 'wider view' of deterring aggression. 'There is a higher point of view than the general's—that of a statesman', he replied to Fuller's scathing criticism; 'Prevention is better than cure—and once war has begun, any cure is a highly uncertain one.' Furthermore, Liddell Hart's reflections on the 'British way in warfare' the year before had already taught him that Britain in

[153] *LH*, 109–16.

particular, with her 'preservative policy, insular position, limited resources, and inherent slowness in preparing for war', had little to gain from lightning land campaigns.[154]

The problem of defining certain weapon systems as either defensive or offensive is not our concern here. Winston Churchill anticipated the arguments against that distinction when he said in Parliament, after the idea had become official British policy, that it was a 'silly expedient', since the character of weapons was determined by the way they were used and by the politics they served rather than by their inherent qualities. Liddell Hart made the opposite case no less ably in his response in the the *Daily Telegraph*.[155] It might be noted that 'qualitative disarmament', aimed at enhancing deterrence, was to become a guiding principle in the nuclear age, but then, nuclear weapons have made the rationale much clearer, at least in principle.

Other factors contributed to Liddell Hart's new trend of thought. By 1931 he had completed *Foch*, in which he had delved into the problematic development of military ideas between 1871 and 1914. Having in addition dealt with the American Civil War in *Sherman*, he became very conscious that the face of future war had all too often been reflected in earlier wars, but had been radically misinterpreted because of wishful thinking and lack of intellectual courage to face reality.[156] Now, with even greater attentiveness than before, he would always keep one eye on the First World War.

At first, in 1933–5, Liddell Hart argued that since the armies of the great powers retained their traditional character, being composed predominantly of infantry masses, the stalemate of trench warfare was most likely to recur in case of a war. Under these conditions air power would only add to the paralysis of movement on the battlefield, unless really strong air forces were created. Armoured forces, operating deep in the enemy's rear—as Liddell Hart had been advocating—have the best chances of success, but they barely existed at the time. By contrast, motorized (lorry-mounted) formations, beginning to appear in all armies, would again only strengthen the defender by enabling him to rush machine-gun troops to threatened sectors of his front and block enemy advances. The best use of these forces in the offensive would be

---

[154] 'Would the Scrapping of Heavy Guns and Tanks Cripple the Aggressor's Power?', *Daily Telegraph*, 1 Feb. 1932; 'Aggression and the Problem of Weapons', *English Review*, July 1932, 71–8 (a reply to Fuller), quotation from 71–2; *Memoirs*, i. 183–93, 207–10, quotation from 186.   [155] *Memoirs*, i. 207–8. See also *Europe in Arms*, 143–4.
[156] See e.g. ibid. 339–56; *The Defence of Britain*, 118–20.

in combining the threatening strategic attack, or leap forward, with the tactical defence when the enemy is obliged to move out to check the advance. This was to be Sherman's 'baited offensive' revived. In sum, however, Liddell Hart claimed that the defence retained, if not increased, its superiority, leaving little prospect for successful aggression.[157]

From 1935 on, as rearmament began in earnest and armoured divisions were increasingly being formed in all the major European armies, a new stage began. Would these new divisions break the stalemate, as Fuller, Liddell Hart, and the other armour enthusiasts had believed in the 1920s? By the second half of the 1930s both Fuller and Liddell Hart had grown sceptical about it, and as always it had been Fuller who had led the way. From the late 1920s he had been developing his concept of the dialectic and spiralling evolution of the offensive and defensive means of war, which in his view had always inaugurated new eras in military history. He had been giving ever-growing weight to the anti-tank gun and mine as the tank's equals. They would be used within a new system of defence in depth, in which the tank itself, concentrated in reserve for the counter-offensive, would play a major role.[158] Liddell Hart, always highly attentive to whatever Fuller was saying, picked up and elaborated on these ideas. In late 1935, discussing the British army's decision to create the Mobile Division which he desired so deeply, he wrote:

It is setting expectations high to count on the programme of modernization to bridge the gulf that now separates armies from their desire for successful attack. My own view is that these potential developments in offensive power are far exceeded by the actual growth, largely unrecognized, of defensive power . . . Not only fire, but the means of obstruction and of demolition, may now be moved more swiftly to any threatened spot to thwart a hostile concentration of force.[159]

Liddell Hart now increasingly used the very same arguments against overly optimistic expectations of tanks and of tank forces which he had rejected in the 1920s. It was as if he were paraphrasing Victor

---

[157] Ibid.; *Spectator*, 17 Nov. 1933, 738–40; *New York Times Magazine*, 2 Dec. 1934, 3, 18; *The Times*, 17 Aug., 19 Sept., 27 Nov. 1935, 21 Aug. 1936.

[158] Fuller, 'One Hundred Problems of Mechanization', pt. ii, *Army Quarterly*, 19 (1929), 256–8. For a balanced assessment from the second half of the 1930s, see Fuller, 'The Problem of Tank and Anti-Tank Weapons', *Fighting Forces*, 14 (1937), 42–5.

[159] *The Times*, 26 Nov. 1935, repr. in *Europe in Arms*, 83; see also *The Times*, 23 Mar. 1936.

Germains; indeed he probably was. Only a couple of examples will be quoted here:

> It should not be forgotten that the extraordinary successes gained in the World War by British and French tanks at Cambrai, Soissons, and Amiens, were nothing else but surprises under conditions that would not occur again. They were gained (and they could only be gained) against a defence practically non-existent, impoverished with the most primitive of means, and completely inexperienced; and they could be expanded into decisive action only because the tank (at that time) was shrouded in the veil of the 'tank terror'.

> It is true that tanks have been improved and increased, but anti-tank weapons have made still more rapid progress—and, being cheaper, can be multiplied faster.[160]

In his generally acute analyses of the strategic lessons of the Spanish Civil War, Liddell Hart highlighted evidence which supported his view that 'the defence is paramount at present' and most likely to create stalemate. It is true that while the performance of mechanized troops in Spain was widely regarded at the time as falling short of the radical expectations pinned upon them, he at first pointed out correctly that these troops were mainly no more than motorized infantry which did not possess offensive tactical capability. He called attention to the fact that the tanks used were early light models which all armies were in the process of replacing with heavier ones, and that in many cases these tanks were employed in small numbers and over unsuitable ground.[161] However, in time he also began to stress that the Spanish Civil War demonstrated that large-scale tank breakthroughs were already a thing of the past.[162]

---

[160] LH, *The Times*, 21 May 1937; 'Military and Strategic Advantages of Collective Security in Europe', *New Commonwealth Quarterly* (Sept. 1938), 144, repr. in *Europe in Arms*, 54. For the same ideas, see also: *The Times*, 30 Oct., 2 Nov. 1936, repr. in *Europe in Arms*, 118; ibid. 125–9, 138–9; *The Defence of Britain*, 120–1. None of these passages was marked by Liddell Hart for inclusion in the list of his successful forecasts (13/3), which he carefully compiled for the writing of his *Memoirs*. Cf. V. Germains, *The 'Mechanization' of War* (London, 1927), 47–54, 74–89.

[161] 'Spain: Attack or Defence', *The Times*, 3 Apr. 1937; repr. in *Europe in Arms*, 323–32.

[162] *The Times*, 21 May 1937. The growth of anti-tank defence was recognized at the time even by the armour enthusiasts; cf. Tukhachevsky, citing the evidence from Spain and extensively quoting from Liddell Hart: 'In modern war the strength of the defence is steadily growing'; 'The Red Army Field Service Regulations', *Red Star*, 6 May 1937, in Richard Simpkin, *Deep Battle: The Brainchild of Marshal Tukhachevskii* (London, 1987), 161–2. None the less, Tukhachevsky, like Guderian, continued to hold that by virtue of its superior mobility it would be possible decisively to concentrate the tank in selected sectors of the front.

As mentioned before, this development in Liddell Hart's views was influenced by, and subordinated to, his 'wider view' concerning Britain's and the West's favoured policy and grand strategy. Pronouncing the superiority of defence was one of his chief means for alleviating the tension between the doctrines he championed of collective security and limited liability (together making containment), and for enhancing deterrence, particularly against war assuming a total form. In late 1937, as British strategic policy was being decided upon, Liddell Hart wrote in his programmatic 'Defence or Attack' articles:

So great is the power of the defensive nowadays that a small reinforcement may suffice to establish a deadlock . . . comparatively slight provisions of up-to-date material—such as aircraft, anti-aircraft, artillery, and machine-guns—would have sufficed to make permanent and general the temporary and local stalemates which the aggressor repeatedly suffered. That provision would have made but a small drain on the resources of the Powers which had supported the principle of collective security, thereby removing the fear that they might be appreciably weakened in meeting other contingencies. . . .

These reflections lead to speculation on the future of war. Will the effect of a spreading recognition of its indecisive trend, combined with the present mutual fear of air reprisals, lead to its full operation only against states which lack the means to resist on land or retaliate in the air; and to a self-imposed limitation if great powers become engaged? In other words, even though such powers may be drawn into war against each other through some clash of interests, will they perhaps in self-preservation confine themselves to strokes against out-lying forces on the remote parts of each other's territory, rather than risk a mutual holocaust of their great cities and a vain employment of their armies?[163]

Here was the outline of the strategic policy which Liddell Hart would advocate in the following years. The more he crystallized containment, limited liability, and deterrence into a comprehensive security programme against Germany, the more extreme he became in advocating the superiority of defence, with which he cemented together the whole concept.[164] The idea that Germany, or the Allies, might launch a successful attack could have ruined any of the pillars of this concept, which Liddell Hart put together as the only way of achieving security reasonably, without mutual devastation. Therefore, everything had to be done in order to eradicate that idea. Liddell Hart's motivated bias

---

[163] 'The Futility of Aggression', *The Times*, 27 Oct. 1937; repr. in *Europe in Arms*, 49–50.

[164] The connection is well made by Mearsheimer, *LH*, 110–11, 115–16.

regarding the strength of tactical defence was getting ever stronger during the crisis years before the war.

As the British army was resuming more serious training for war, Liddell Hart was publicly criticizing any trace of training for the offensive. He claimed that the offensive was deeply rooted in military tradition and in the soldier's creed, and suspected that the army was in effect preparing itself for an offensive Continental strategy in opposition to government policy.[165] The CIGS, Deverell, and the director of military operations and intelligence, Haining, tried to convince him that he was exaggerating about this. 'Haining also suggested that in my view of the superiority of the defence, I was relying too much on the experience of the last war. He remarked—"History never repeats itself"'—a view which Liddell Hart rejected.[166] When in late 1937 Deverell returned deeply impressed from the German army's manœuvres, in which Panzer forces were employed for the first time on a large scale, his fate was sealed. It did not help that the Germans had in fact been emulating the British model and closely studying Liddell Hart's writings.[167] 'He had come back from the German manœuvres with the report that the French could not stand against them, that the Maginot line would not hold, and that the offensive would succeed.'[168] The stupidity of the man became so obviously dangerous in the eyes of Liddell Hart and Hore-Belisha that they decided to get rid of him. After a careful preparation of the political ground they acted swiftly. On 30 November the Cabinet authorized the removal of Deverell and of his deputy, Knox, as well as a thorough purge of the army council. Gort, Hore-Belisha's military secretary who was on friendly relations with Liddell Hart, was pushed upwards to become the new CIGS. In December the memorandum 'On the Role of the Army' which Liddell Hart had prepared for Hore-Belisha was approved by the Cabinet.[169] Limited liability became official policy. The revolution was complete.

[165] See e.g. *The Times*, 14 Aug., 10 Sept. 1937; the latter repr. in *The Defence of Britain*, 374–5.
[166] Meetings between Liddell Hart and Deverell, 12 Nov. 1936, King's, 11/1936/99 (Haining attending); 29 June 1937, 11/1937/56; 18 Nov. 1937, 11/1937/94; cf. Liddell Hart, *Memoirs*, i. 382–3, in which Haining's remark is not cited.
[167] A. Gat, 'British Influence and the Evolution of the Panzer Arm', *War in History*, 4(2) (1997), 150–73; 4(3) (1997), 316–38.
[168] Talk with Hore-Belisha, 15 Oct. 1937, King's, 11/HB 1937/56; not cited in *Memoirs*. See also Wark, *The Ultimate Enemy*, 95–6.
[169] Liddell Hart's paramount role as the spirit behind Hore-Belisha and as kingmaker is amazingly revealed in his files: King's, 11/1937/96 ff., 11/HB 1937–8; partly printed in *Memoirs*, ii. 62–74.

To use an analogy which Liddell Hart would have appreciated, it was a repetition in reverse of the famous 1911 Michel affair within the French high command: the head of the army, who foresaw the outline of the German attack in the approaching war, was removed by the civilian minister of war, supported by the 'Young Turks' in the army who had little faith in their chief. While in France this affair had been largely caused by, and had led to the victory of, the spirit of the *offensive à outrance*, in Britain it was prompted by what one of his contemporaries aptly dabbed Liddell Hart's doctrine of the *défense à outrance*.[170]

Défense à outrance

The supremacy of the defence and its relation to the doctrines of collective security and limited liability were vital to Liddell Hart's approach to the security of France and of her East European allies. The ideas that Britain need not send an expeditionary force to the Continent (or send at most a small mechanized force); that France could hold her own against Germany, but that no major offensive against Germany in the West was possible even if France were reinforced by the British; and that, given Soviet support, Czechoslovakia could resist the Germans for a very long time—were all closely interdependent and largely based upon the power of the defence.[171]

Hence Liddell Hart's strategic position throughout the Czechoslovakian crisis of 1938. It was a strategy similar to the one Churchill had proposed in his *World Crisis* for the First World War. The Western Allies should remain in defence, refrain from large-scale, murderous, 'Passchendaele' offensives in the West, and confine themselves to limited selective attacks. This would suffice to pin down large German forces and ease the pressure on the Western powers' East European allies. Germany would be defeated in the long run by the strength of economic blockade.[172] As with Churchill's original proposal, scholars have pointed out, the trouble with this strategic scheme was that Germany was not going to be distracted from her target in the East by limited, mainly demonstrative Allied offensives in the West. Germany planned an overwhelming concentration against Czechoslovakia,

---

[170] Cited by Mearsheimer, *LH*, 118.

[171] See most strikingly in Liddell Hart's paper on 'The Military Situation in Europe', given at the Staff College in Dec. 1937; printed in *The Defence of Britain*, esp. 55, 57, 59–60.

[172] *The Times*, 17 June 1938; 'Military and Strategic Advantages of Collective Security in Europe', *New Commonwealth Quarterly* (Sept. 1938), 147–52; Notes 9 and 28, Sept. 1938: King's, 11/1938/92, 103; *The Defence of Britain*, 74–6, 86–7.

leaving only a small fraction of her forces on the French frontier. Especially if one believed, as Liddell Hart did, that Czechoslovakia was able to hold out for a very long time, thus allowing the Western Allies (France in particular) time to mobilize, it was inescapable that the Allies should have launched large-scale offensives against Germany in the West in order to divert her from her prey in the East and keep her forces divided. Given the German forces' weakness in the West in 1938, these attacks were in fact not without prospects of success. A pure double-defensive strategy against an enemy like Germany, who was expected to utilize very aggressively the interior lines in order to gain overwhelming concentrations on one front at a time and defeat each of its enemies separately, was an unpractical notion for the Allies.[173]

While being much less hopeful over the defence of Poland, Liddell Hart's basic strategic scheme during the Polish crisis changed only slightly from the one he had espoused during the Czechoslovakian crisis. He recognized very well that Poland could not hold her own in the defence against Germany, but continued to object to more than limited Allied offensives against the Siegfried Line.[174] Now, if the Soviet Union were to participate in the war against Germany, as Liddell Hart expected as a *sine qua non* until the signing of the Soviet–German pact in late August 1939, this was again an impractical strategy for the Allies, and for the same reasons. But if the Soviet Union could not be counted as an ally, as became clear after the signing of the Soviet–German pact, there was probably no other strategy for the West. In the first place, both the German army as a whole and the German forces on the French border (Army Group C) had practically doubled since 1938. Secondly, Germany was likely to overrun Poland much too quickly for the Western Allies to be allowed the time to mobilize and carry out large-scale offensives before German forces could be brought back westward.

During these years the fear that the French might take the offensive and drag the British along with them and into a massive Continental commitment was paramount in Liddell Hart's mind.[175] As the war approached, he grew increasingly alarmed about this, insisting that only the offensive could lose the war for the Allies. After the defection

---

[173] See e.g. Liddell Hart, *The Defence of Britain*, 78–9; for Mearsheimer's just criticism, see *LH*, 139–41.

[174] 'Gamelin', *Life Magazine*, 20 Feb. 1939, 63; *The Defence of Britain*, 209.

[175] See e.g. 'The Defence of the Empire', *Fortnightly Review* (Jan. 1938), 27–9; *The Times*, 17 Sept. 1938; *The Defence of Britain*, 209–10.

of the Soviet Union, the Allies were indeed incapable of attacking in the West; and their high commands recognized this very well and acted accordingly during the period known as the 'Phoney War'. But every rumour from general headquarters inflamed Liddell Hart's suspicions that offensive schemes were being entertained.[176]

In May–June 1940, within six weeks, the Low Countries and France fell before a lightning German campaign. Liddell Hart was as surprised as anybody. As his biographers have already revealed and contrary to what he himself claimed, he had not foreseen even the possibility of a German victory. Quite the reverse: for years he had been insisting that France was virtually secure from a German attack. Two of the major doctrines he had been advocating now appeared in a disastrous light. First, his insistent claim that the strength of modern defence was paramount and was continuing to grow was revealed to be fallacious. As Mearsheimer has shown, in later years Liddell Hart would do his utmost to eradicate this central and unhappy idea of his from historical memory, often by unscrupulous means.[177] His *Memoirs* barely mention it. Secondly, limited liability, of which Liddell Hart had been one of the chief exponents, now appeared to have been totally misguided and irresponsible. More than a decade before the fall of France, Germains had articulated ideas common among many army officers:

'A National Force, maintained at a high standard of efficiency, can only be produced by the works of years' . . . if we do not [take this to heart], and whether we have mechanized armies or not . . . we shall be very lucky indeed if the next war produces only Sommes and Paschendaeles, and not a swift and overwhelming defeat.[178]

Similarly, in January 1936 Colonel Henry Pownell of the secretariat of the Committee of Imperial Defence wrote in his diary against the advocates of limited liability:

---

[176] 'The Need for a New Technique', repr. in *The Current of War*, 152; cf. Roosevelt's phrase, n. 138 above and related text. Liddell Hart repeatedly wrote about Gamelin in very favourable terms: 'Gamelin', 56–63; *Sunday Express*, 29 Oct. 1939 and 18 Feb. 1940; *The Current of War*, 205, 209; Mearsheimer, *LH*, 124. His unfavourable testimony in *Memoirs*, ii. 18, tilts the original record. It might be noted, however, that before the war Gamelin was highly regarded by both the British and the Germans.

[177] *LH*, esp. 179–81, 216–17.

[178] *The 'Mechanization' of War*, 249–50. Cf. Montgomery-Massingberd's bitter charges against Liddell Hart shortly before Germany attacked in the West: 29 Apr. 1940, King's, 6/1940/5, 11/1940/29.

if war with Germany comes again (whether by Collective Security, Locarno or any other way) we shall again be fighting for our lives. Our effort must be the maximum, by land, sea and air. We cannot say our contribution would be 'so and so' and no more, because we cannot lose the war without extinction of the Empire. The idea of the 'half hearted' war is the most pernicious and dangerous in the world. It will be 100 per cent—and even then we may lose it.[179]

The nightmare of the 'Westerners' in the British strategic debate during the era of the two world wars, which had almost been realized during Ludendorff's spring offensives in 1918, came true. The security of France and of the Low Countries was simply too vital for Britain to risk on 'a too fine calculation'. Liddell Hart could reasonably claim that building a strong army for Europe had in any case been beyond Britain's economic capability, and that everything had changed and containment had broken down with Munich and with the rejection of Soviet cooperation. All the same, as with the even more promising Japanese case the year after, the policy of containment, economic coercion, and cold war floundered when the enemy did the unthinkable and in a highly successful lightning campaign broke down the walls built up against him. In his meeting with Daladier on 28–29 April 1938, Chamberlain justified limited liability by claiming that the power of the defensive in warfare had increased with modern methods and modern weapons: forms of attack previously thought of as irresistible, he argued, could now be met with a sufficiently organized defence. The official British historian who cites this wonders where Chamberlain found the inspiration for these views. But the answer to this, given the wording as well as the content of Chamberlain's argument, should not be too difficult to find.[180] Responsibility for the collapse of France could at least partly be laid at Liddell Hart's door. Consequently, his prestige suffered heavily, and justly. Apart from anything else, he was made to look silly.[181]

It must have been an awful feeling for Liddell Hart, and his first apologetic efforts in his early wartime books to explain France 1940—and the later Blitzkrieg victories—often read rather patheti-

---

[179] B. Bond (ed.), *Chief of Staff: The Diaries of Lieutenant-General Sir Henry Pownall* (London, 1972), 99.

[180] Gibbs, *Grand Strategy*, i. 637. Similarly, at the beginning of the war Chamberlain maintained that it was necessary to remain firm until the Germans saw the obvious—that in modern war the defensive side had the advantage; cited by Charmley, *Chamberlain*, 210.

[181] His painstaking efforts to save face are documented in sect. 6 of his papers; a selection can be found in Mearsheimer, *LH*, 152–4.

cally.[182] He argued, for example, that he had been obliged to conceal his real views about the Allies' weakness in order not to assist the enemy, and that he had developed his preference for the defensive before the war because he had known that the Allies possessed no real offensive weapon in the form of large mechanized forces. In truth, however, Liddell Hart favoured a defensive posture for the West predominantly because of what he regarded to be its ultimate political aims, and in order to deter and limit war; only then did he increasingly convince himself that the defensive was tactically and operationally becoming ever stronger. Also, while he did claim (justly) that Britain lacked armoured forces suited for the offensive, this was mainly a contributing factor to his argument.[183] He did not believe the offensive would work for the Germans either.

Despite his continued criticism of many aspects of the mechanization of the British army, Liddell Hart in fact was generally much encouraged by the process finally set in motion in the British and French armies as they rearmed in the late 1930s[184] He found reassurance in the growth in the number of French mobile formations and in the quality of the French newest tank models; and this was partly, but not wholly, due to his desire to create a favourable impression of the French ability to confront the Germans without the support of a substantial British army. He was fully informed of the British intelligence reports which throughout the period portrayed a fairly good picture of the strength, structure, and doctrine of the tank formations of the main antagonists. Before the war he accurately informed his readers that while the Germans possessed more armoured divisions than the French, the French had more and heavier tanks with their infantry.[185] The belief that by the 1940 campaign the Germans had managed to achieve overwhelming numerical superiority in tanks over the Allies was widely held just before and immediately after the German victory, and Liddell Hart

[182] For his 'apologia', see mainly his *Dynamic Defence* (London, 1940), 12–41, 57–64; *The Current of War*, 15–125, 193–4, 208–9, 214, 316, 320–2, 328–9, 337–8; *The Revolution in Warfare* (London, 1946), 15–16, 28–9; *The Defence of the West* (London, 1950), 3–11; *Memoirs*, ii. 28, 242–4, 280–1.

[183] *Europe in Arms*, 116–40; *The Times*, 25 Oct. 1937; also 2 Nov. 1936.

[184] In view of that development, he did not even strongly object to the mechanization of the cavalry, adopted in both Britain and France (and Germany) alongside the expansion of the armour corps. More surprisingly, during that period he also did not take a stand against the design and acquisition of special 'infantry tanks' by both the French and British armies; *Europe in Arms*, 122–3, 228.

[185] *The Times*, 23 Dec. 1935, 19 July 1938; *Fortnightly Review* (Jan. 1938), 26–7; *Life*, 20 Feb. 1939, 62; *Europe in Arms*, 43–4, 49–51; also Mearsheimer, *LH*, 122–3.

used it to excuse himself in his wartime writings. But by the end of the war it became clear that the earlier estimates had been all too accurate, and that it was in fact the Allies who held the superiority in tank numbers in May 1940, as well as enjoying rough parity in tank quality.[186]

So we turn to armoured doctrine. After 1940 Liddell Hart stressed that the Germans had applied the doctrine of armoured warfare which Fuller, himself, and the other British armour pioneers had evolved. Contrary to misconceptions which have recently gained the ascendancy in Anglo-American historiography, this was quite true.[187] However, was not this fact much depreciated by Liddell Hart's loss of faith in the late 1930s in sweeping armoured offensives? Here too the answer is much more intriguing than recent critics of Liddell Hart have allowed.

Mechanized Defence in Depth

It ought to be made clear that Liddell Hart's advocacy of the strength of defence by no means involved a withdrawal from the idea of armoured warfare. The battlefield and the sort of defence he foresaw before the war was markedly modern. It was dominated by mobile mechanized forces working closely with aircraft, but also by the anti-tank gun and other anti-tank measures which would be engaged in a constant struggle for supremacy with the tank.[188] So long as they survived, traditional foot and horse-drawn troops would be relegated to a secondary and subsidiary role, except on special ground. The defence itself would take the form of mobile defence in depth, in which armoured and mechanized divisions, stationed in the defender's rear, would counter-strike to check and destroy large-scale penetrations by the enemy's mechanized formations.

A prevailing impression regarding the German 'Blitzkrieg method' is that it came as an almost total surprise to the Allies. This was not at all the case. Throughout the late 1930s the Allies' intelligence services and high commands had possessed a good picture not only of the strength and composition of the Panzer troops but also of their doctrine and intended method of employment. The old French fear of a German *attaque brusquée*, now to be carried out with armoured and mechanized

---

[186] In Mar. 1940, while correctly assessing the number of German mobile divisions, Allied intelligence estimated the German tank force at 5,800–7,500, two to three times the actual number: F. H. Hinsley, *British Intelligence in the Second World War*, i (London, 1979), 134. But see e.g. Guderian to LH, 14 Dec. 1948: King's, 9/24/62.

[187] Gat, 'British Influence and the Evolution of the Panzer Arm'.

[188] See e.g. Liddell Hart, *The Times*, 21 May 1937.

divisions which, without prior warning, would overrun the French defensive lines, penetrate deep into the country, and disrupt the French mobilization, was paramount in the Allies' strategic considerations and was widely discussed.[189] Gort's comment to Liddell Hart was prophetic but not entirely uncommon:

May it not be possible for Panzer divisions and concentrated air forces to effect a breach and this attack can take place with little previous warning? If by rapidity, deception and surprise it is possible to make a bridgehead then the war will pass into open country once more. I feel novelty lies in some such direction as this as Belgium is hackneyed.[190]

To this, and to Deverell's similar suggestion in a conversation with Liddell Hart, the latter replied that the chances for such break-throughs were doubtful and that modern and mobile defence, integrating armoured forces for counter-offensives, was likely to prove more effective.[191]

In the years 1935–7 Liddell Hart further developed his doctrine of large-scale armoured breakthroughs, which remarkably anticipated the outline of future 'Blitzkrieg' and which, indeed, profoundly influenced the creators of the Panzer arm.[192] However, while foreseeing amazingly accurately the prospects of such offensives, he also foresaw their limitations. Time and again during those years he concluded his scheme of how deep armoured breakthroughs might be achieved with the following qualifying remarks:

it would be necessary to follow up the strokes [of the armoured forces] with reinforcements and occupying forces. Here would lie the invader's hardest problem . . . It is conceivable that an attacker by extraordinary foresight, by gauging the trend of developments exactly, and by perfectly calculated measures to diminish his own vulnerability while maintaining his strength, might succeed in producing the internal collapse of his adversary without courting his own—but such foresight has never been shown by any makers of war.[193]

---

[189] See e.g. Liddell Hart, *Europe in Arms*, 27–8, 48; *The Defence of Britain*, 101. For the British picture of German armour, see Wark, *The Ultimate Enemy*, 93–101. For the French, see R. Young, 'French Military Intelligence and Nazi Germany, 1938–1939', in E. R. May (ed.), *Knowing One's Enemies: Intelligence Assessment before the Two World Wars* (Princeton, NJ, 1984), 288–9.

[190] Gort's comments on LH's 'Defence or Attack', 6 Nov. 1937, King's, 11/1937/73.

[191] Conversation with Deverell, 29 June 1937, King's, 11/1937/56; Macleod and Kelly *The Ironside Diaries*, 38.

[192] See my 'Liddell Hart's Theory of Armoured Warfare: Revising the Revisionists', *Journal of Strategic Studies*, 19 (1996), 1–17; 'British Influence and the Evolution of the Panzer Arm'.   [193] 'The Next Big War', *Listener*, 15 Mar. 1936.

There is little doubt that the new mechanized divisions which the European armies now possess will be used in the first hours of war with the aim of penetrating the enemy's frontier and opening the way for the subsequent general advance . . . But there is reason to doubt whether this mechanized spearhead will produce the decisive advantage which is sought. The chances are against this, unless the enemy is not only taken unaware but is himself unmechanized.

The main problem would be deliberate obstruction and counterattacks by mechanized forces brought forward against the threat.[194] Finally,

The general deduction that the defensive has a great and growing superiority does not, of course, imply that the offensive can never succeed. It is likely to succeed, as already noted, in a campaign where the defender has no effective counter-weapons to nullify such offensive instruments such as aircraft and tanks. It may possibly succeed against an opponent of similar equipment if the attacker displays a great superiority of art, and thereby produces a great local superiority of fire and psychological threat.[195]

Anyone familiar with the theme of 'the rise and fall of Blitzkrieg' during the Second World War cannot fail to be impressed by these insights. For Liddell Hart France 1940 was an accident, albeit a terrible and fateful one. During the second half of the 1930s he consistently emphasized the role of armoured formations which would be kept in the rear for counterattacks against enemy armoured penetrations within a modern system of mobile defence in depth.[196] For Liddell Hart this was the story of the 'expanding torrent' versus the 'contracting funnel' of the later stage and immediate aftermath of the First World War all over again, only by means of mechanized rather than infantry forces and, consequently, on a wider scale and at a much quicker pace. While valuing the Maginot Line, he pointed out that it was intended mainly as

---

[194] *Atlantic Monthly* (Dec. 1936), 693; similar ideas in 'Future Warfare', *English Review* (May 1937), 529–43, and 'The Defence of the Empire', *Fortnightly Review* (Jan. 1938), 19–30.

[195] *The Times*, 25 Oct. 1937; this extract is repr. in *The Defence of Britain*, 105. None of the above passages is cited by Mearsheimer; after conceding that, defensively employed, the tank 'can thwart a blitzkrieg', he writes that in Liddell Hart's 'pieces on the strength of the defense, especially those written in the late 1930s, he failed to discuss the significant offensive potential of the tank when a defender does not understand how to employ tanks on the battlefield (i.e. he fails to emphasize that a blitzkrieg was possible under certain circumstances)': Mearsheimer, *LH*, 113–14.

[196] The Soviets developed the same idea far more systematically in their 1936 Field Service Regulations, and it was also well recognized by the Germans; see Simpkin, *Deep Battle*, 47–8, 172–3; Ritter von Leeb, *Defence* (Harrisburg, Penn., 1943; originally in *Militärwissenschaftliche Rundschau*, 1936–7), 109–10.

a covering and delaying line against a sudden German attack and would require strong mobile reserves behind it. This was precisely the role he persistently advocated for the British armoured formations in conjunction with the French mobile divisions.[197]

France and Belgium

Indeed, as recent research has shown, this was also the role the French themselves envisaged in the second half of the 1930s for their new heavy armoured divisions (DCR: *Division Cuirassée de Réserve*), which were to be reinforced by a British armoured contribution and further supported by the French cavalry-type armoured divisions (DLM: *Division Légère Mécanique*) and motorized infantry divisions. Serious attention was given in France during those years to operational planning for mobile defence in depth. To be sure, French tank production was lagging, and the British armoured contribution failed to be ready in time for the Battle of France. Nevertheless, by the time of that battle, the French had been hastily creating their third and beginning to create their fourth DCR, which, as their title indicates, were specifically intended for the counter-offensive role against the Panzer divisions and destined for deployment as a strong mobile reserve in the area of Laon, Rheims, and Châlons-sur-Marne, at the centre of the French line. While these heavy formations were still inexperienced and suffered from many deficiencies, the three DLMs, although also inferior to the all-round combat concept of the German Panzer divisions, were well trained and incorporated the new and excellent SOMUA medium tanks. Finally, the seven French motorized divisions in fact slightly outnumbered their German counterparts.[198] Although the doctrine of the French army during the interwar period negated the idea of a mobile battle of manœuvre, the chances of these mobile formations to check German armoured penetrations were not altogether unfavourable, had not things turned out so badly for the Allies.

For the Allies' collapse in the West in 1940 was not predestined, but

---

[197] *The Times*, 30 Oct. 1936; 'The Defence of the Empire', *Fortnightly Review*, Jan. 1938, 24–9; *Europe in Arms*, 27–8, 47–8; *The Defence of Britain*, 55, 60, 104–5, 210, 307, 376–81.

[198] See H. Dutailly, *Les Problèmes de l'armée de terre française (1935–1939)* (Paris, 1980), 141–59, 314–37; M. Alexander, *The Republic in Danger: General Maurice Gamelin and the Politics of French Defence, 1933–1940* (Cambridge, 1992), 201–2; R. A. Doughty, *The Seeds of Disaster: The Development of French Army Doctrine, 1919–1939* (Hamden, Conn. 1985), 161–77. Liddell Hart was well informed about these developments at the time: *Europe in Arms*, 43–4.

involved a strong element of chance. Until the beginning of 1940 the Germans had planned a fairly conventional and limited advance into Holland and Belgium, spearheaded by their armoured and mechanized divisions. To this the Allies intended to respond by an advance into Belgium, led by their own mobile troops, either to the line of the River Scheldt (Plan E) or, more ambitiously, to the line of the River Dyle (Plan D). Both Liddell Hart and Fuller pointed out at the time that a campaign in the West would be an entirely different ball game from that experienced by the Germans in Poland. Belgian and Dutch territory was cut by rivers and water channels, posing great difficulty for mechanized forces, and in addition the Germans would face adversaries with modern equipment.[199] Senior German officers held the same view. In Halder's opinion: 'Techniques of Polish campaign no recipe for the West. No good against a well-knit army.' According to General Leeb, also rejecting the Polish comparison, 'the high value of the French army and its leadership must not be underrated and the equipment with armoured units and anti-tank weapons of the French and English armies must not be forgotten'.[200]

It was only during February–April 1940 that both sides changed their plans. The Germans adopted Manstein's plan, which switched their main offensive trust, including most of their mobile divisions, southwards to the Ardennes region. Almost simultaneously the Allies, still expecting the main offensive to come from the north, adopted an even more ambitious version of the Dale plan, incorporating the so-called Breda extension. The plan envisaged a rapid deep advance into Holland by the Allies' extreme left, verting the cream of the French mobile divisions (and the semi-mobile British Expeditionary Force) westward. Only after that advance had been completed were these divisions planned to be withdrawn once more to the role of strategic reserve.[201] In view of the new German plans, the Allies' order of battle was thrown disastrously out of balance. Not only were the Allies' best troops deployed in the wrong direction, but their mobile strategic reserve was left dangerously weak. Despite desperate efforts, this situation

---

[199] For Fuller, see his 'Tanks Won't Do Much', *War Weekly*, 19 Nov. 1939, King's, 11/1939/146; for Liddell Hart, see e.g. *The Defence of Britain*, 55–60, and 11 May 1940, repr. in *The Current of War*, 301.

[200] Quoted by Mearsheimer, *Conventional Deterrence*, 102, 108.

[201] The best analysis of the Allies' strategic considerations is J. A. Gunsburg, *Divided and Conquered: The French High Command and the Defeat of the West, 1940* (London, 1979).

proved impossible to remedy when the full significance of the German breakthrough in the Ardennes became clear. Consequently, the German mechanized forces were only haphazardly and sporadically opposed during their breakthrough and race to the Channel. The conditions which Liddell Hart had specified for the complete success of a lightening mechanized campaign, and had regarded as exceptional, were disastrously realized.

Thus in his efforts to excuse himself after 1940 Liddell Hart argued that the fall of France had not been inevitable but had been caused by extraordinary strategic blunders on the part of the Allies' high command. In the immediate aftermath of the defeat, he himself wavered on the exact line the Allies should have taken.[202] But on the main issue, the French total neglect of the Ardennes, which had been traditionally regarded as unsuitable for the operations of large formations,[203] Liddell Hart possessed a good personal record upon which to base his criticism. For after travelling through the Ardennes in 1928 he came to the conclusion that, contrary to Allied perceptions in 1918, this region was not unsuitable for the movement of large formations, a point he repeated in the following decade in his successive books on the First World War.[204] In May 1936, after the German occupation of the Rhine demilitarized zone and more than a year before Gort would suggest to him the possibility of a German armoured breakthrough in a sector different from the traditional Belgian route, Liddell Hart had a talk (which he recorded at the time) with Ronald Adam and Col. Bernard Paget:

I remarked that there was still a danger interval before the new Belgian defence were completed, or those of the French along the German frontier. I suggested that we ought not overlook the possibility that if the French took the offensive, the Germans while meeting them defensively, would launch a

---

[202] See initially, LH, *The Defence of Britain*, 216–19; then, *Dynamic Defence* (London, 1940), 18; *The Current of War*, 209, 316, 337; finally, 'Could the 1940 Collapse in the West Have Been Averted?', *Sunday Pictorial*, 28 Sept. 1947; repr. in *The Defence of the West*, 3–19; and as an Introduction to A. Goutard, *1940: The Battle of France* (London, 1958).

[203] Although recent research has done much to show logic behind the Allies' plans, it reaffirms that they (and Gamelin in particular) totally blundered regarding the Ardennes: R. J. Young, *In Command of France: French Foreign Policy and Military Planning, 1933–1940* (Cambridge, Mass., 1978), 169; Umbreit's contribution to MF *Germany in the Second World War*, ii. 271; C. Paillat, *Le Désastre de 1940*, i (Paris, 1983), 191–6; Alexander, *Gamelin*, 199–200.

[204] *The Decisive Wars of History* (London, 1929), 225; similarly, see *The Real War* (London, 1930), 461; *Foch* (London, 1931), 383; *A History of the First World War* (London, 1934), 577.

flank counter-stroke through Belgian Luxembourg with their 3 Mechanized divisions [*then in existence*].

Paget said that the chances were that the Belgians would have sufficient time to man their fortifications, but Liddell Hart replied that the Germans might attack by surprise.[205]

These various observations, made in different contexts, do not imply that Liddell Hart in any way 'predicted' the route the Germans would choose in 1940. He did not. No one, including the Germans, did or could have. They simply demonstrate that Liddell Hart had been clearly and more than most aware of the passibility of the Ardennes for large formations, including modern mechanized ones; and it was largely on this awareness that the campaign in the West in 1940 hinged, and was lost. In 1939 Liddell Hart's comprehensive and carefully weighed survey of the various strategic options open to the antagonists on the Western Front was on the whole optimistic about the prospects of the defence in the Ardennes sector, assuming the right measures would be adopted. The region, he wrote,

might prove a strategic trap for an invader if he fails to cross the Meuse. . . . For the Belgians, the obvious plan of defence is to make sure of holding the Meuse moat, together with the Liège bridge-head beyond it, while utilizing the Ardennes as a spring-buffer to absorb the shock of any hostile advance which come through that way. The Ardennes offer such a series of fine defensive positions that it would be desirable to employ here sufficient forces to develop the full delaying power of this vast obstacle. It is difficult, however, for the Belgians to do so from their own resources without jeopardizing their main position on the Meuse. Moreover, they have to reckon with the possibility of having to meet danger from a new direction, where they are more vulnerable— on their Dutch flank. . . . The full development of the potentialities of the Ardennes as an obstacle thus depends on whether, and how soon, the limited Belgian forces here can be reinforced by those of a guarantor Power. During a recent tour . . . it was revealing to find how immensely strong by nature were the series of positions—the gorge of the Semois, the heights north of Sedan, and the Meuse—upon which the French might have stood [in 1914], yet which in the event they so swiftly abandoned.[206]

The concept in itself was impeccable, and in step with the ideas Liddell Hart had been developing in the second half of the 1930s regarding flexible defence in depth. Lacking the benefit of hindsight,

---

[205] 15 May 1936: King's, 11/1936/64; cited by Bond, *LH*, 101, 232–3, but not by Mearsheimer, *LH*, 182–3.   [206] *The Defence of Britain*, 217–19.

it kept all the options open. Given the uncertainty regarding the direction of the German main offensive effort, and especially the possibility of a German turning movement through Dutch territory, Liddell Hart saw the Ardennes as a scene of a delaying manœuvre on the Allies' part. Relying on the topographical features of that region, field fortifications, field forces, and wide-scale obstruction should be used to delay enemy columns long enough for the Allies to take up their main fortified line of defence along the heights overlooking the Meuse and deploy their mechanized reserves behind it. The attacking spearheads would then find themselves in an awkward position, experiencing logistic problems and having limited room for deployment and mutual support.

This assessment of the situation, made the year before the war, underpinned Liddell Hart's reactions when the German offensive in the West was launched on 10 May 1940. On the 11th he noted that the German advance through Holland, upon which all eyes in the Western camp were fixed, had been expected, but also pointed out that it might be a diversion. Two days later, before the German thrust through the Ardennes became publicly known and the centre of attention, his overall survey of the Front again mentioned the Ardennes as a scene for delaying action. On the 15th, as the Ardennes offensive and the German crossing of the Meuse became known, Liddell Hart wrote that the attack had been expected, but that now that the Germans had reached Sedan the situation had become serious. He maintained, however, that French armour was designed specifically to meet such a German breakthrough, and even on the 19th, when all was lost, argued that the danger must not be exaggerated, for the German armoured penetration would hopefully lose its momentum. At the beginning of June he was still hoping for Allied counter-offensives which would stop the Germans as in 1918, and only on the 6th he finally resigned himself to the idea that the armour required for counter-attacking was simply not in place.[207]

Wholly concentrating on the Dutch and Flanders routes, the Allied high command left the Ardennes covered by only thirteen, mostly second- and third-class divisions. These forces were not designed to push strong delaying forces into the Ardennes, and were incapable of it. When the German Army Group A, totalling forty-four divisions, including seven Panzer and three motorized, and massively supported by the Luftwaffe, rolled into the Ardennes, the French were only able to

---

[207] Repr. in *The Current of War*, 299–300, 304, 309–10, 315–17, 338–44.

push in one horse cavalry division and several infantry battalions. Thus, even though the Belgian delaying forces performed quite effectively, especially on 10 May, the German mechanized spearheads encountered little opposition and no wide-scale obstruction. By the end of 13 May the Germans had begun to cross the Meuse, which the weak French forces in the area again proved incapable of holding. Since the French high command was slow to realize what was happening, the battle by then was practically lost.[208]

The Fall of 'Blitzkrieg'

So what does all this prove, first, in respect to Liddell Hart's ideas on defence? There is no doubt that his overriding concern during the 1930s to prevent the eruption of a new total war and lay down the ground rules for a limited strategic response to the Nazi challenge biased his judgement, most notably regarding the superiority of the defensive. He was all too eager to seize on new developments which were only beginning to take shape, such as the Allies' acquisition of tanks and anti-tank guns and creation of mobile formations, as if they were already a reality, rather than an incomplete and greatly deficient process. In addition, although the battlefield he foresaw was dominated by modern mobile forces rather than by the traditional arms of the First World War, he portrayed it all too frequently, if not as static, then at least as frozen in the operational sense as the battlefields of the Western Front in the previous war. On this he probably exaggerated, even in the long run. Nevertheless, viewed from a more distant perspective, was he on the whole that wrong, or mainly over-hasty?

As Liddell Hart would repeatedly point out for the rest of his life, by the second half of the Second World War all armies had learnt how to contend with armoured breakthroughs and had developed the techniques and the means for blunting them. These, he would claim, were the techniques of mobile defence in depth which he had advanced in the second half of the 1930s. By 1942, both in Russia and in North Africa, such techniques put an end to the spectacular spate of 'Blitzkrieg' successes. Thereafter, in Italy, Western Europe and the Eastern Front

---

[208] On the whole operation, see R. A. Doughty, *The Breaking Point: Sedan and the Fall of France, 1940* (Hamden, Conn., 1990). For the Belgian and French reading of German intentions regarding the Ardennes, see Bond, *France and Belgium, 1939–1940* (London, 1975), 60–1, 64–5, 76–7, 78–80; F. H. Hinsley, *British Intelligence in the Second World War*, i. (London, 1979) 129–36; Paillat, *1940*, ii (Paris, 1984), 299–354; Doughty, *The Breaking Point*, 73–7.

the war again became a gigantic struggle of attrition. Offensive operational success was now only achieved under conditions of overwhelming superiority in *matériel*, the very conditions Liddell Hart in his prewar writings had insisted would be required. More remarkably, he did not make this argument of self-justification retrospectively but in fact advanced it well before the event. In late 1940, after the dramatic fall of France and *prior* to the occurrence of even one instance of a successful defence in depth against mechanized forces, Liddell Hart wrote in *Dynamic Defence*, referring of course to himself:

> the knowledge gained in developing the new offensive technique led to the discovery of an effective counter-technique. But it had taken fully ten years to gain official acceptance for the former, and even then in a half-hearted way. So it was perhaps too much to expect that the antidote could have been approved and prepared in time, unless the war had been postponed until 1945!

He repeated his forecasts from the preceding years:

> While it is axiomatic that the attacker enjoys the advantage of the initiative, it may not carry him far save where he is met by slow-moving forces. The advantage is likely to be short-lived if the defender disposes of adequate mechanized forces. The advance of the attacker's armoured units through the defence, if they are in depth, is likely to be slower than the bringing up of the defender's armoured units along unobtrusive roads, or across country that they know. On arrival they can strike the attacker's armoured force at the moment when it is likely to be somewhat disorganized by its fighting advance.

This would be 'a reversed form of "soft spot" tactics', supplementing 'gradually contracting funnels' of defensive dispositions, in which 'the lanes would now be hedged with anti-tanks guns'.[209]

So if one were to take a very favourable view of the development of Liddell Hart's ideas, one could suggest that, rather than being—like the proverbial generals—always ready for the last war, he was consistently one war ahead in his thought: in the 1920s he anticipated the sweeping mechanized offensives of 1939–42; in the second half of the 1930s he was looking ahead to the curbing of 'Blitzkrieg' in 1942–5; and from the late 1930s he was calling for a strategy and policy of containment and cold war. But then, even if we were to present Liddell Hart's views in

---

[209] *Dynamic Defence*, 26, 52–4; see also his opinions *at the time* regarding the Soviet Union's prospects of defence in June 1941 and regarding the Western Desert, where he was interestedly following Rommel's use of anti-tank guns and defensive tactics within an offensive strategy: *This Expanding War* (London, 1942), 72–3, 138–40; *The Revolution in Warfare*, 15–23, 29; *The Rommel Papers* (London, 1953), 451–60; *Memoirs*, ii. 281.

this very favourable manner, how practical were these subsequent sets of ideas *in and for their times*? Was the vision of wide-ranging armoured warfare, developed in the 1920s, readily applicable? In many crucial respects—strategic, economic, and technological—it was not; yet it was meant as a programme for future development. Could 'Blitzkrieg' have been checked in the early stage of the Second World War? In France and the Low Countries in 1940 it was not, but perhaps it might have been, had Allied preparations been somewhat better focused or had their strategic conduct been less unfortunate. Finally, and most intriguingly, could containment have worked in the late 1930s, and cold war in the early 1940s? Some of the arguments relevant to these questions have been widely discussed by historians in different contexts, and speculation here is best cut as short as possible.

Containment in the 1930s: Conclusion

In hindsight it is clear that a diplomatic and strategic Great Power coalition against Germany was, as it were, the order of the day in the late 1930s if Germany were to be stopped. Whether under the mantle of 'collective security' or more soundly in accordance with the older principle of the 'balance of power', this was simply a vital interest of Britain, France, and the Soviet Union, backed by a favourably neutral United States. Whether the Western powers and the Soviet Union could really cooperate with one another on a sustained basis is an open question. A policy of 'Grand Alliance', no less than the alternative one of appeasement was full of uncertainties, risks, and pitfalls. Assuming that the West would have been willing to cooperate, Stalin's USSR was a notoriously difficult client. On the other hand, it feared being isolated *vis-à-vis* Hitler's Germany more than anything and anyone. A Grand Alliance, had it existed, would in the first place have had a great deterrence value, either for Hitler himself or for other power brokers in Germany who might have stopped him at an early stage and even short of war. This was the outlook Liddell Hart shared with more prominent public figures, such as Eden, Lloyd George, and Churchill. The opinion of one historian of the period, dwelling on the same problem in no relation to Liddell Hart, is interesting: 'The Eden–Baldwin policy, if it had been continued after 1936, might have advanced through deterrence the sort of stalemate created since the 1950s by nuclear stockpiles.'[210] Within a grand strategy

---

[210] Middlemas, *Diplomacy of Illusion*, 454.

of containment against the Axis powers, there was then much scope for the means Liddell Hart was striving to develop: economic pressure, supply of arms to small allies, war by proxy, naval isolation of outlying theatres of war, and limited war.

If deterrence against major war had failed, a coalition of West and East would have been even more necessary for stopping Germany. This coalition could not, however, have worked strictly on the basis of a pure 'double-defensive' strategy, a defence on both fronts, as Liddell Hart advocated. Active cooperation between the Allies in the East and West would have been essential both politically and strategically if Germany were not to defeat its enemies separately. On this point Liddell Hart's First World War trauma and ideas regarding the superiority of the defence led him seriously astray. However, assuming that Germany was contained in her 1938 or even 1939 frontiers, which would have left her ecenomically choked. Could the war then have been significantly limited and destruction and self-exhaustion decreased by burden-sharing between the Allies, and by the pursuit of a fundamentally defensive policy on their part which would have restricted their war aim to the termination of hostilities on the basis of the *status quo ante*, with or preferably without Hitler? On the face of it this is not inconceivable. But there is really no point in pursuing the 'ifs' any further.

The problems become all the more involved when considering Liddell Hart's position in favour of a cold war against Germany once the Soviet–German pact had abolished, at least for a time, the idea of a Grand Alliance and had made the Allies' prospects in a war against Germany strategically dubious. After the fall of France, this again was the option Liddell Hart was to advocate for Britain. During the Second World War he would be relegated to the wilderness as far as his official and public standing was concerned, not only because he was largely discredited by the fall of France but mainly because he would pose as an out-and-out opponent of Churchill's policy of total war against Germany.

5

Policy: Defence of the West (II): Cold War–Hot War

I. The Second World War

Liddell Hart's opposition to Britain's war policy during the Second World War relegated him to the wilderness. He still had many connections in the army, and a few high-ranking officers like Tim Pile and Percy Hobart (themselves unpopular) remained loyal to their old friendship. He still travelled extensively to visit army units and manœuvres. But the war office and the general staff, now largely occupied by his contemporaries and former friends, were closed to him, as was Whitehall. His collaboration with Churchill during the Munich crisis was over. Most of his previous political connections had been serving in Churchill's government and following his direction of the war. Eden was now politely acknowledging receipt of Liddell Hart's memoranda but nothing more. Their relationship ended for good. Hugh Dalton was minister of economic warfare and Archibald Sinclair was secretary of state for the air, both supervising policies which Liddell Hart criticized sharply. The only man in the cabinet who gave him any attention at all, and it too was not excessive, was the former isolationist Beaverbrook. Outside government during 1940 Lloyd George was preparing his return to the premiership to save the nation once Churchill's war policy had failed. When this did not happen, Lloyd George's star was rapidly eclipsed.

Thus Liddell Hart, who only shortly before had been well connected in government, adviser to all political parties, 'kingmaker' in the war office, and Britain's most popular and influential strategic publicist, was cut off from any involvement in the shaping of policy and strategy during his country's greatest and most desperate war. Showing considerable moral courage and psychological strength, he expressed views which were deeply unpopular with the large majority of the British people. He now crossed the line between the status of an unconventional iconoclast and that of an 'unsafe' fringe figure. The consequences for his career would be long-term. Thereafter, during the formative years of the Cold War, although he was consulted once or twice by the Labour secretary of state for war, Emanuel Shinwell, and remained in good terms with Field Marshal Montgomery, the government and defence establishment remained closed to him. Only with the coming of a younger generation of politicians and soldiers and during the anti-establishment 1960s did his popularity rise again. This time, however, he was cast as a vintage sage. Liddell Hart's practical involvement in, and influence upon, the shaping of policy were over by 1940. This is one of the reasons why our treatment of his views in this chapter can be cut shorter than before. Another reason is that he had crystallized practically all his ideas regarding Britain's and the West's desired defence policy by 1937–41, and would not change them from then on.

After the fall of France British policy was personified by the new prime minister, Winston Churchill. Liddell Hart's feelings toward him were mixed. During the 1920s Churchill had everything which qualified him to rank very highly in Liddell Hart's esteem. Churchill's criticism of the British high command's conduct in the First World War, his Easternism, and his views regarding the need for a limited and mostly defensive strategy on the Western Front were picked up and echoed by Liddell Hart. Churchill was a radical, a promoter of reform in the navy, one of the creators of the tank, a champion of air force, and an admirer of Lawrence. The only problem was that Churchill did not return Liddell Hart's love. His rudeness to friend and foe alike is famous. Liddell Hart was stung by his scornful dismissal of the idea of 'quali-tative disarmament', and by his arrogance at several meetings in which both of them participated during the early 1930s. So his attitude cooled. Lloyd George's ambivalence towards his former ally, lieutenant, and rival reinforced this change in the mid-1930s. Churchill, in any case, was by now no longer regarded as a radical but as an anachronism, and was universally believed to be politically finished.[1] For all that, Liddell Hart's relationship to Churchill was ultimately determined by their respective positions on policy and strategy. On this ground they co-operated during the Munich crisis, and departed thereafter. With the outbreak of the war Churchill became the main force in the cabinet

---

[1] See very positively: Liddell Hart in the *Daily Telegraph*, 4 Mar. 1927; *The Remaking of Modern Armies* (London, 1927), 175, 281–91; *A History of the World War, 1914–1918* (London, 1934), 112–13; *'T. E. Lawrence': In Arabia and After* (London, 1934), 46–7; 'The New British Doctrine of Mechanized War', *English Review* (1929), 688–9; in the 1920s Liddell Hart was sending Churchill his books; for a cooler attitude, see King's, 11/ 1936/28, 40; *Memoirs*, i. 301–6; ii. 74–5; the Churchill file: 1/171.

pressing for the utmost effort and offensive ventures. He was the driving force behind the Norwegian project. After the fall of France it was he who would chart the course of British policy.

Despite sharp differences in basic attitudes and rhetoric, there is little real disagreement among most historians regarding Churchill's strengths and weaknesses as a war leader.[2] In his crusade against Churchill both during and after the Second World War, Liddell Hart pointed out most, if not all, of the weaknesses that would later be brought to the fore by revisionist historians. During the interwar period Churchill lost touch with the development of the tank which he had helped to pioneer and, against his earlier views, accepted the Admiralty's underrating of the potential of the aircraft in sea warfare and of the submarine. He was full of combative spirit and overflowed with brilliant but amateurish operational schemes which he pursued enthusiastically, with a mixture of eloquence and bullying, against professional opposition, without first ensuring that the means to realize them were in place. Hence the series of disasters and débâcles, from the Dardanelles on, with which his career had always been and would continue to be associated well into the Second World War. Above all there was the fundamental question of Churchill's overall direction of the war—the goals he set, the policies and strategies he advocated and implemented, and the postwar world his actions helped to shape. This was the main battleground for Liddell Hart, as well as for Churchill's later critics and defenders.

Can Britain 'Win' by Herself?

Churchill's crucial decision, by which he stamped his mark on history, was to keep Britain in the war after the fall of France and to continue the fight with total commitment of all resources until Nazi Germany was overthrown and 'victory' achieved. He succeeded in rallying the British people to that cause, inspiring them with hope and impressing the rest of the world (especially the USA) with Britain's determination. In government and in the defence establishment this 'act of faith' was

---

[2] See esp. J. R. M. Butler, *Grand Strategy: History of the Second World War*, ii (London, 1957), 562; J. M. A. Gwyer, *Grand Strategy*, iii (London, 1964), 432–3; M. Howard, *The Mediterranean Strategy in the Second World War* (London, 1968); 'Churchill and the First World War' and the other contributions to R. Black and W. P. Louis (eds.), *Churchill* (Oxford, 1993); T. Ben-Moshe, *Churchill: Strategy and History* (Boulder, Colo., 1992); J. Charmley, *Churchill: The End of Glory* (London, 1993); and for a summary of Liddell Hart's decades-long crusade, see his 'The Military Strategist', in A. J. P. Taylor *et al.* (eds.), *Churchill: Four Faces and the Man* (London, 1969), 155–202.

expressed in and sustained by the more rational and systematic language of professional political and strategic assessment. From the spring of 1940 an overall strategy was devised by which it was believed that Britain would not only survive but defeat Germany. This strategy guided Britain's war effort so long as she remained alone in the war against Germany and Italy, and even later. In hindsight historians agree that this strategy as a whole, as well as each of its component parts, was based on unsustainable and naïvely optimistic assumptions which had no prospect of materializing. Liddell Hart, however, assessed all that *at the time*.[3] He had no quarrel with Churchill's decision to continue the war, maintain Britain's independence, and resist Germany's domination of Continental Europe. He, too, believed deeply that Britain had to be the core around which Western civilization would be rebuilt. However, he assessed that Britain had no chance of defeating Germany militarily.

Devised by the chiefs of staff in May 1940 to take account of the expected fall of France and reaffirmed in September at the height of the Battle of Britain, British strategy held that Britain would never be able to create a land force strong enough to invade the Continent and defeat the German army head on. It was assumed, however, that German power, now spreading over the whole of Continental Europe, could be weakened by the application of combined pressures which ultimately, and relatively quickly, might lead to its collapse. The effort was to consist of three principal means—the blockade, strategic bombing, and subversion in the occupied countries—leading to armed insurrections against the Germans, supported by small, amphibious British expeditionary forces. This strategic conception was, of course, the 'Maritime', 'indirect', 'British Way in Warfare' which Liddell Hart had espoused. Churchill and the generation that now occupied Whitehall and the General Staff shared the same experiences and strategic notions which had shaped Liddell Hart's own thought. From 1935, however, Liddell Hart had considerably amended, qualified, and partly withdrawn from the simplistic sketch he had drawn in 1931. Like the responsible defence authorities, he, too, repeatedly stressed that Britain's only viable strategy after the fall of France was maritime and

---

[3] See esp. Butler, *Grand Strategy*, ii. 209–17, 343–4, and *passim*; D. Reynolds, 'Churchill and the British "Decision" to Fight On in 1940: Right Policy, Wrong Reasons', in R. Langhorne (ed.), *Diplomacy and Intelligence during the Second World War* (Cambridge, 1985), 147–67. LH's wartime books, in which he did not hesitate to include journalistic articles and private memoranda of a necessarily transitory nature, are often remarkable documents; from the beginning of 1941 he was covering the war for the *Daily Mail*.

indirect.[4] But like Corbett he maintained that this strategy would never be able to bring down a great power like Germany that ruled most of the Continent.

Despite Germany's occupation of Western Europe, domination over central and south-eastern Europe, and economic access to the Soviet Union—all of which were recognized by the British chiefs of staff—the latter none the less continually expressed their belief that Germany was critically dependent on raw materials, food, and especially oil from overseas. The chiefs of staff thus maintained that a British blockade would bring Germany's war economy to a halt within several months and create widespread famine. It was widely believed that the foundations of the Nazi regime were shaky, that morale of the German home front was very low, and that both might collapse at any moment. Although Germany's unexpected collapse in 1918 was in people's minds, it seems incredible today that professional opinion, which should have been well aware of the preconditions that had led to that collapse, could subscribe to such wishful thinking. But it universally did. Only in June 1941 (before the German invasion of the Soviet Union) was it realized that earlier expectations had been unrealistic, although it was still believed that the German war economy would collapse within two years.[5] Liddell Hart, however, had assessed after Munich, and especially after the signing of the Soviet–German pact in August 1939, that the economic blockade could no longer be regarded as a decisive weapon. It might have serious disruptive value, but it was no longer able to strangle the German war economy and win the war. Obviously, he did not change his mind after the fall of Western Europe.

With varying emphases, the authors of British strategy evaluated the efficacy of the blockade in conjunction with the effects of a strategic bombing campaign, targeted at the German war economy. In September 1940, after the first salvos of city bombing, Churchill went further than his military advisers, suggesting that Germany's control of Europe limited the potential of the blockade and claiming that the main hope for winning the war lay with Bomber Command.[6] The strategic bomb-

---

[4] *Dynamic Defence* (London, 1940), 43, 53; *The Current of War* (London, 1941), 402–3 (7 Jan. 1941); *This Expanding War* (London, 1942), 41–3 (3 May 1941).

[5] W. N. Medlicott, *The Economic Blockade* (2 vols., London, 1978); Butler, *Grand Strategy*, ii. 212–13, 215–16, 343–4; Gwyer, *Grand Strategy* iii. 21–3; F. H. Hinsley, *British Intelligence in the Second World War*, i. (London, 1979), 223–48, 305–11.

[6] Medlicott, *The Economic Blockade*, i. 420–1; Butler, *Grand Strategy*, ii. 234, 403.

ing campaign which had been evolving for some time was now unleashed with ever greater effort and ferocity.

Although highly charged, the facts about how city bombing began and escalated during the Second World War are in little real dispute among historians. In the mid-1930s there was great enthusiasm for strategic bombing in all the major air forces. However, by the second half of the decade the Great Powers' leaderships were increasingly considering the desirability of keeping the civilian populations out of the air war, a goal which Chamberlain took up more actively on the eve of the war. Hitler, too, repeatedly proposed that air bombing should be restricted to the zone of military operations. In September 1939 both Britain and Germany declared their agreement with President Roosevelt's proposal not to bomb civilians and unfortified cities. To be sure, the Germans appalled Western public opinion with their devastating air attacks on Guernica in 1937, Warsaw in 1939, and Rotterdam in 1940. However, all these cities were defended military strongholds within the combat zone and were attacked as such, even if the so-called 'collateral damage' and terror effect were hardly discouraged. By the outbreak of the war the Luftwaffe was mainly geared for cooperation with the army, though it never relinquished its aspirations towards a truly 'strategic' role. In any case, at least in the West, terror bombing of civilians was positively *not* desired by Hitler. By an order issued on 1 April 1940, he specifically instructed that the air war in the coming campaign should not be allowed to escalate into city bombing. Hitler cannot, of course, be suspected of any humanitarian scruples. But against opponents who were able to retaliate, he was very sensitive to the safety of the German civilian rear. For similar reasons, he did resort to the use of poison gas during the Second World War. The RAF, for its part, wanted to bomb the Ruhr from the beginning of the war but was restrained partly by the British government, partly by the French. On 15 May 1940, following the German bombing of Rotterdam and after Churchill became prime minister, permission to bomb industrial targets east of the Rhine was given. The air raids did negligible damage, but British bombing became a link in a series of mutual irritations that were to push both sides to escalate.

During the Battle of Britain the Luftwaffe was under strict orders not to bomb civilian targets. Only Hitler could authorize such attacks. On 24 August, however, residential areas in London were bombed by mistake, and the next night the RAF retaliated by bombing Berlin. This was a major cause for the German decision to begin raids on

London on 7 September. Nevertheless, the attacks were still aimed at strategic targets in the capital. Hitler rejected requests from the Luftwaffe to bomb residential areas, which he wanted to reserve as a last resort to deter the British from bombing German cities. On 19 September Bomber Command was ordered to start a full-scale bombing offensive against Germany. Once the Germans, like the British before them, were forced to switch to night bombing, any discrimination between civilian and strategic targets became almost impossible, even if the belligerents so desired, which they increasingly did not. Churchill, who had always objected to restrictions on the bombing of civilians, pushed for all-out bombing of Germany's cities from September 1940. It was the air staff that objected, still hoping to pinpoint Germany's economic vitals, especially the oil industry. As the British bombing campaign began in earnest in 1941, restrictions on the deliberate bombing of civilians were quickly dropped—in retaliation for the Blitz and for operational reasons, when targets could not be located. During the year it gradually became clear that Bomber Command was not even remotely hitting its targets. By the end of 1941 it was therefore decided to concentrate on the bombing of cities—the only targets big enough to be located and hit—with the view of breaking the German morale. This policy was to be ruthlessly pursued by the new chief of Bomber Command, Air Marshal Sir Arthur Harris.[7]

Liddell Hart viewed these developments with alarm and despair. By the mid-1930 he no longer believed in out-and-out air attacks on the enemy civilian rear, as he had, in Fuller's footsteps, in *Paris*. In 1939 he supported the elimination of such attacks by agreement (though on the outbreak of the war he apparently took no chance, for he moved out of London). During the 'Phoney War' he objected to attacks on the German civilian rear for reasons mentioned in the previous chapter. During the summer and autumn of 1940 he anxiously recorded what he

---

[7] See U. Bialer, ' "Humanization" of Air Warfare in British Foreign Policy on the Eve of the Second World War', *Journal of Contemporary History*, 13 (1978), 79–96; G. Best, *Humanity in Warfare* (New York, 1980), 273; R. J. Overy, *The Air War, 1939–1945* (London, 1980), 24, 104; C. Webster and N. Frankland, *The Strategic Air Offensive against Germany, 1939–1945* (4 vols., London, 1961), i. 134, 144–53; Butler, *Grand Strategy*, ii. 410–12, 567–70; the contributions by K. A. Maier and H. Rohde to Militärgeschtliches Forschungsamt [MF] (ed.), *Germany and the Second World War* (Oxford, 1990–   ), ii. 33–43, 121, 338, 386–91; the contributions by O. Groehler, M. Messerschmidt, and H. Boog to Boog and MF (eds.), *The Conduct of the Air War in the Second World War* (New York, 1992), 279–97, 298–309, 373–404; Overy, *The Air War*, 104; L. Kennett, *A History of Strategic Bombing* (New York, 1982), 105–41; and most recently J. W. Legro, *Cooperation Under Fire: Anglo-German Restraint During World War II* (London, 1995).

recognized at the time as steps in a slide into bombing of civilian population, claiming that German air doctrine did not prescribe city bombing. As early as January 1941 he already assessed, and repeated thereafter, that a bombing match between England and Germany was unlikely to be decisive, and that its only result would be vast, indiscriminate devastation and exhaustion. In April he accused Churchill of repeating Passchendaele in the air.[8]

The bombing campaign was to prove one of the biggest strategic disappointments of the Second World War. Yet, as historians have argued, strategic bombing was untried, and after Britain had been thrown out of the Continent it became her only means of striking at Germany. The point Liddell Hart was making was, however, more subtle and compelling. Not only did he regard the bombing of the enemy's civilian rear as barbaric, judging at the time that it would bring a great deal of misery but no decision; he also argued that in a bombing match between Germany and Britain, Germany, possessing air bases in France and the Low Countries, in close proximity to Britain, was bound to inflict on her much heavier punishment. It was a contest under wholly unequal terms, as the bombing campaign during the winter of 1941 demonstrated. The German invasion of the Soviet Union in June 1941 was to distract the Luftwaffe from Britain for the rest of the war; but the attack on the Soviet Union was not known when the British bomber offensive was launched, could have failed to take place, or might have ended differently. Under the circumstances prevailing at the time, Liddell Hart maintained that initiating or escalating a bombing campaign against Germany's civilian rear was a wholly irrational strategy for Britain. He believed that every effort should be made to de-escalate the air war, and held that Churchill's warlike nature and instinctive aggressiveness were pushing him again into a disastrous venture whose prospects for success and probable outcome had not been fully thought out.[9]

---

[8] 'War in the Air', *Helios* (1934), 235–41; also in *New York Times Magazine*, 28 Jan. 1934; *Europe in Arms* (London, 1937), 319–42; *The Defence of Britain* (London, 1939), 147–62, 188–94; July–Oct. 1940, King's, 11/1940/76–8, 92, 117–22; to the Bishop of Chichester, George Bell, 2 Nov. 1940, also 25 June 1943, 11/1943/37; *The Current of War*, 404 (7 Jan. 1941), and *This Expanding War*, 43 (3 May 1941), 258–63 (6 Aug. 1941); 17 Feb. 1941, 11/1941/3; 12 Apr. 1941, 11/1941/21. See also *The Revolution in Warfare* (London, 1946), 70, 72, 86.

[9] *The Current of War*, 404 (7 Jan. 1941), and *This Expanding War*, 43 (3 May 1941). The only historian to mention this crucial point is Best, *Humanity in Warfare*, 276; it has been picked up and made the centre of discussion in Legro, *Cooperation under Fire*. In the spring of 1941 a parliamentary group proposed a de-escalation of city bombing, but their initiative was rejected by the government: Kennett, *Strategic Bombing*, 132–3.

Britain's third strategy for the defeat of Germany after the fall of France was subversion, backed by amphibious sallies or even landings. Here too, however, once again anticipating the arguments against his own earlier theories, Liddell Hart saw no prospect for significant success. In November 1940 he poured cold water on Hore-Belisha's enthusiasm, writing to him that he had checked and found out that the overwhelming majority of amphibious operations carried out in the previous three centuries had been failures. While he agreed that action against Italy—especially in Africa—was the most promising strategy for Britain, he wrote that if Italy were ever to be brought to the point of collapse, German troops would overrun her with ease. British expeditionary forces would stand no chance against the strong, modern German army, and landing attempts would only lead to new Dunkirks.[10]

The Greek campaign was a case in point. Churchill sought to consolidate a Balkan front against the Axis from the beginning of the war, and British diplomatic activity in the capitals of this region was intensive throughout 1940. Yet the British military authorities claimed that Britain had no forces to spare and that whatever she sent would be swept away by the Germans. The Italian invasion of Greece at the end of October raised the question again. The chiefs of staff still thought that no aid to Greece could be spared or would be of any practical use, but Churchill succeeded in pressuring the reluctant secretary of state for war, Eden, and the commander-in-chief in the Middle East, Wavell (who was then husbanding resources for his planned counter-offensive against the invading Italian army in Egypt), to send scarce equipment to Greece. In the meanwhile, the Greeks succeeded in defeating the invaders by themselves and pursued them into Albania. The British then began to toy with the idea of gaining a foothold on the Continent, especially air bases from which the Romanian oilfields could be attacked. This, however, was precisely the sort of British involvement the Greeks did not want. They sought to avoid, not provoke, a German invasion. Indeed Hitler, who decided at the end of 1940 to attack the Soviet Union rather than pursue a Mediterranean strategy, was anxious to avoid any distractions. However, alarmed by the British activity and the potential threat to the Romanian oilfields, he felt that an invasion of Greece might become unavoidable.

---

[10] To Hore-Belisha, 21 Nov. 1940, King's, 11/HB 1940/47; also *The Current of War*, 403 (7 Jan. 1941).

In view of the German army's concentrations in Romania and entry into Bulgaria, and following the Italian defeat in Libya and the fall of Benghazi, Churchill renewed his pressure to have British forces sent to Greece. As the Greeks themselves were changing their minds, Eden, now foreign secretary, became supportive of the operation and the British high command was finally giving in. By then, however, Churchill himself was beginning to have doubts. He left the decision on the whole operation to Eden and the CIGS, Dill, both sent to confer with Wavell in the Middle East. Weary of months of harassment and bullying by the prime minister, Wavell reversed his earlier position and came to support the initiative. The renewal of the offensive in North Africa was postponed, and British forces began to disembark in Piraeus in the beginning of March. By that time Hitler decided that the occupation of Greece had indeed become unavoidable. By the end of the month, as Yugoslavia was coerced into joining the tripartite pact (but not to allow Axis troops through her territory), a pro-British coup took place in Belgrade. It led to a swift German invasion which occupied both Yugoslavia and Greece in less than a month. British prestige again suffered a severe blow, as the British expeditionary force had to be evacuated, leaving most of its equipment and 11,000 men behind. A month later the humiliation was completed with the fall of Crete. Whereas after the war it was believed that the Balkan campaign may have delayed Hitler's invasion of the Soviet Union and thus contributed to its failure, later studies have shown that its effect was almost negligible.[11]

Liddell Hart did not take any strong position in his commentaries during the Greek crisis. He was oblivious both of Hitler's overall strategic intentions and of the behind-the-scenes activity on the British side. Before the campaign he anticipated a possible new Dunkirk in case of a British involvement, but did not come out against it. He also pointed out that the completion of the British offensive in North Africa

---

[11] Butler, *Grand Strategy*, ii. 365–88, 439–59, 554; J. S. Koliopoulos, *Greece and the British Connection, 1935–1941* (Oxford, 1977); S. Lawlor, *Churchill and the Politics of War, 1940–1941* (Cambridge, 1994), 115–256; Ben-Moshe, *Churchill*, 132–63; G. Craig, 'The Political Leader as Strategist', in P. Paret (ed.), *Makers of Modern Strategy from Machiavelli to the Nuclear Age* (Princeton, NJ, 1986), 500. The German generals testified to Liddell Hart that the spring mud and river overflow had prevented an earlier invasion of the Soviet Union: *The Other Side of the Hill* (London, 1948), 249–55; M. van Creveld, *Hitler's Strategy, 1940–1941: The Balkan Clue* (Cambridge, 1973), 151–76, has shown that the German army needed the extra time to complete its preparations; he does mention, however, that the 12th Army was subtracted from the invasion of the Ukraine (p. 135).

would have to be postponed. As the defeat in Greece became clear, he returned to his more principled line, claiming that a Balkan strategy had been beyond Britain's capabilities. As Lloyd George, who was continuously in touch with Liddell Hart, said in Parliament, any idea of invading Europe was 'fatuous'. Liddell Hart maintained that British decisionmakers continued to ignore realities and, failing to think through the consequences, had encouraged the governments of Yugoslavia and Greece 'to over-estimate the chances of successful resistance'. As one historian has written: 'Churchill was convinced that it was the right or even the duty of great powers to sacrifice small neutrals for the sake of victory over Nazism.' Liddell Hart, however, charged that the sacrifices were made to no avail. In September 1941 he concluded that Churchill had dragged one small neutral after another into the war and Nazi occupation by means of foolish provocations that merely alarmed the Germans into action. After the war he argued that the Greek diversion had prolonged the war in North Africa for two years, because it allowed Rommel time to arrive and launch his counter-offensive in March and April 1941.[12]

Cold War

So Liddell Hart perceptively assessed that the strategy devised in Britain after the fall of France for the purpose of defeating Germany was based on illusions, and that the means it deployed were often counter-productive and recklessly dangerous. But what did he propose Britain should do instead? He had already crystallized his views on this matter during the Phoney War, when he assessed that even in alliance with France it was difficult to see how Britain could positively win the war against Germany. With Britain alone in the war, he initially thought, as did Lloyd George and the majority in the cabinet, that Britain should first try to strengthen her hand after the disaster in the Low Countries and France by repulsing Hitler's offensive and proving that she could not be defeated. Hitler might then agree to a more favourable peace than he had been willing to conclude in the summer of 1940.[13] However, once

[12] *This Expanding War*, 16–17 (18 Mar. 1941), 24 (6 Apr.), 38 (26 Apr.); P. Addison, 'Lloyd George and Compromise Peace', in A. J. P. Taylor (ed.), *Lloyd George: Twelve Essays* (London, 1971), 361; for the neutrals: van Creveld, *Hitler's Strategy*, 141; Liddell Hart, 6 Sept. 1941, 11/1941/62; but see also Lawlor, *Churchill*, 250; Liddell Hart, *Defence of the West*, 12–19.

[13] 3 and 14 Sept., and 12 Oct. 1940, King's, 11/1940/81, 87, 90, 91. For Lloyd George and Churchill's cabinet after the fall of France, see Addison, 'Lloyd George and Compromise Peace', 362, 375–83; D. Reynolds, 'Churchill and the British "Decision" to Fight On'.

the critical stage of the Battle of Britain was over, Liddell Hart no longer mentioned a negotiated peace with Germany. Instead he proposed a comprehensive programme for what was effectively a policy of cold war against her.

Liddell Hart maintained that historically the concept of 'victory' proved to be a ruinous but persistent delusion. In any case, Britain was unable to liberate occupied Europe by force. Thus, rather than exhaust herself in futile offensive efforts which would only bring American and Soviet domination of the world, Britain ought to adopt a long-term view of the conflict. The bombing campaign should, as much as possible, be de-escalated and then brought to an end. The blockade, which could only bring misery to the inhabitants of occupied Europe but no decision, should be adjusted and applied with discrimination. The mass army still planned should be scaled down, and resources invested in a smaller and highly mechanized force, as well as diverted from the military altogether. Britain's defences should be made impregnable, but all offensive efforts should be renounced. Britain should try to return to a state of normality and in collaboration with the United States resume economic growth and foster prosperity. Her best weapon would be the building up of a free and just society at home which would serve as a shining model and as an attractive alternative to the German 'New Order' in Europe. This model would be constantly subversive to German rule, until in time it might lead to its disintegration from within. For that purpose all the 'totalitarian' measures and restrictions on free speech adopted in wartime Britain should be withdrawn. About these measures, which in his view included conscription, Liddell Hart felt most deeply, and he tirelessly enlisted in every public campaign against them.[14]

Liddell Hart formulated this new strategic outlook into the language of theory in a new chapter on grand strategy which he added to the second edition of his *The Strategy of Indirect Approach* (1941). He repeated the distinction he had made in his 1937 *Times* article between 'acquisitive' and 'conservative' states, the latter being 'primarily concerned with the preservation of its security and the

---

[14] The argument was gradually perfected: 3 Sept. 1940, King's, 11/1940/81; *Dynamic Defence*, 53–6; *The Current of War*, 403–6 (7 Jan. 1941); 17 Mar. 1941, 11/1941/18; 12 Apr. 1941, 11/1941/21; *This Expanding War*, 43–5 (3 May 1941). For the propaganda, restrictions on speech, and repressive measures in wartime Britain, see C. Ponting, *1940: Myth and Reality* (London, 1990), 152–6. See also B. Bond, *Liddell Hart: A Study of his Military Thought [LH]* (London, 1977), 126–8.

maintenance of its way of life'. What would be the best strategy for this type of state?

It is a folly to imagine that the aggressive types . . . can be bought off—or, in modern language, 'appeased' . . . But they can be curbed. Their very belief in force makes them more susceptible to the deterrent effect of a formidable opposing force. This forms an adequate check except against pure fanaticism . . . While it is hard to make a real peace with the predatory types, it is easier to induce them to accept a state of truce—and far less exhausting than an attempt to crush them . . . The experience of history brings ample evidence that the downfall of civilized States tends to come not from direct assaults of foes but from internal decay, combined with the consequences of exhaustion in war.

The policy of armed truce and deterrence has its difficulties, not least the psychological:

A state of suspense is trying—it has often led nations as well as individuals to commit suicide because they were unable to bear it. . . . [furthermore] Peaceful nations are apt . . . to court unnecessary danger because, when once aroused, they are more inclined to proceed to extremes than predatory nations.[15]

Here were the leading ideas which, developed and discussed, would gain universal currency in the late 1940s and during the 1950s, with the Cold War. In retrospect they appear extremely interesting and intriguing. Yet two questions immediately suggest themselves. First, was not Liddell Hart unduly pessimistic after all? Was not British strategy, Churchill's in particular, based on the assumption that the United States would join the war, tip the scales against Germany, and make possible her defeat? Secondly, could the Nazi and Soviet cases be compared at all? And were not nuclear weapons anyhow essential for a cold war regime? We shall deal with the first question here and defer treatment of the second.

The American and Soviet Alliances

Although British strategy after the fall of France presupposed only American *economic* assistance, Churchill believed, and assured his cabinet colleagues and the defence establishment, that the United States would enter the war before long. This was an important psychological factor in the British decision to fight on. In turn, Britain's resolve greatly impressed the United States. American economic aid was indeed

---

[15] *The Strategy of Indirect Approach* (London, 1941), 205, 210–11; from the 1954 edn. on: pp. 368, 372.

forthcoming in great volume with Land-Lease from the beginning of 1941, though at a cost. It was given only after the US made sure that Britain had no more money to pay and had liquidated all her disposable foreign assets; and it included strict stipulations which secured American domination of world trade at Britain's expense. American entry into the war remained, however, a dubious matter. In the summer of 1940 Churchill believed that the US would enter the war after the presidential elections in November. This did not happen. By late spring 1941, as disillusionment with the efficacy of both the blockade and strategic bombing was growing in Britain, and following the defeats in Greece and North Africa, the British high command concluded, revising its earlier views, that full American participation in the war would be necessary for defeating Germany. However, with a declaration of war by the US not yet in sight and with Roosevelt apparently telling different people different things according to what they wanted to hear, waves of gloom began to spread through the British government and defence establishment. It was widely felt, and resented, that it was now the US who was employing Britain's traditional strategy and, taking advantage of American geographical isolation and economic might, was holding the world balance without risking herself in the fray. 'We are their Hessians,' was a common feeling in British official circles during the summer and autumn of 1941.[16]

We shall interrupt our treatment of the United States' position for a moment to take account of Hitler's invasion of the Soviet Union. As in Germany, American and British official assessments after the invasion held that the Soviet Union would be defeated in a matter of weeks or a few months. Soviet resistance was considered mainly as a valuable distraction for Germany from offensive action in the West in 1941. Churchill publicly expressed total support for the Soviet Union's struggle but, in contrast to Eden's more forthcoming response, did not intend to offer more than rhetoric and token material aid.[17] Liddell Hart, however, writing two days after the German invasion, immediately realized that the face of the war had changed completely. There was now a chance of positively defeating Germany, although, if Hitler's gamble paid off, he would be able to turn all his forces against Britain

---

[16] D. Reynolds, *The Creation of the Anglo-American Alliance, 1937–1941* (London, 1981); Gwyer, *Grand Strategy*, iii. 16–23.

[17] Butler, *Grand Strategy*, ii. 543–5; Gwyer, *Grand Strategy*, iii. 90; S. Lawlor, 'Britain and the Russian Entry into the War', in Langhorne (ed.), *Diplomacy and Intelligence*, 168–83.

with the resources of the Soviet Union at his disposal. Liddell Hart fully comprehended the enormity of Hitler's gamble. Explicitly going against Western professional opinion and the apparent implications of the Finnish war, he gave a remarkably accurate and balanced picture of the Red Army's enormous strengths, as well as weaknesses. He pointed out the great strides it had made in mechanized and modern techniques of war, as well as the traditional toughness of its rank and file. He judged that the Soviet Union's survival would depend on her ability to absorb the thrusts of the German mechanized forces by using her vast space for elastic defence and mechanized counter-offensives. He even suggested that Hitler's aim might be the Baltic, the Ukraine, and the Caucasus oil. Liddell Hart's commentary throughout the summer campaign remained very perceptive, and always cautiously optimistic. He noted that because of the stubbornness of the Soviet resistance and the enormity of their space, the Blitzkrieg—aiming at a speedy paralysis rather than physical annihilation of the enemy—was encountering serious difficulties.[18]

Still, even though Liddell Hart accurately judged in June 1941 that the Soviet Union stood a good chance of withstanding the German onslaught and that there now existed a possibility of victory over Germany, the realization of that possibility rested largely with the United States; and the prospects for her entry into the war remained foggy. During the summer of 1941 the US extended Land-Lease to the Soviet Union, took over the battle against the German submarines in the western half of the Atlantic, and garrisoned Iceland. In August Roosevelt and Churchill signed the Atlantic Charter, a declaration regarding the face of the post-war world. It was, however, clear to the British that American entry into the war was not to be expected in the near future. The majority of Americans and members of Congress still objected to the war, and Roosevelt's own intentions are unclear. He was surely not going to allow Britain to fall, and probably would have used the United States' growing weight to steadily increase American influence on the course of the war. But was he waiting for more progress to be made in US rearmament, and using the time to prepare American public opinion for its eventual participation in the war? Or was he quite satisfied with the existing situation, in which Britain and the Soviet Union were doing the fighting with massive American political and

---

[18] *This Expanding War*, 70–3 (24 June 1941), also 254 (6 Aug. 1941); 88–91 (31 July 1941); the campaign is followed on pp. 67–123.

economic support but without full American participation? This question remains in dispute and can probably never be decided. It is doubtful if Roosevelt himself knew. It was only Japan's surprise attack and the subsequent German declaration of war on the United States that finally decided the issue—as the German invasion of the Soviet Union had done for the USSR. Both of Britain's mighty allies in the coalition against Germany entered the war against their will.[19]

Whether Hitler's ultimate aims and the pressures of the war and of the war economy would anyhow have driven Germany into war with both the Soviet Union and the United States is difficult to tell. History is not preordained. It should be noted, however, that in the same way as Soviet participation did not necessarily mean victory over Germany until the United States joined in, American participation still left the path to victory very unclear had not the Soviet Union been brought into the war and survived to engage the lion's share of the German land forces. The participation in the war of both powers was necessary. Only the development of the atomic bomb can be cited as a sure way to victory for the West in the absence of Soviet participation.[20] All the same, what one historian has written regarding Lloyd George's peace policy may also be cited in respect to Liddell Hart's proposal for a cold war against Germany: 'Churchill won his great war and thus his great victory, but some alternative line would have to have been devised in the absence of the Russian and American alliances, or in the event of the rapid defeat of Russia in 1941 and continued benevolent neutrality of the United States.'[21] One might further add that Liddell Hart's proposed policy of cold war so long as Britain remained alone in the war left room for possible future escalation to active warfare once conditions had changed. It was to Churchill's attempt actively to win the war on

---

[19] Gwyer, *Grand Strategy*, iii. 111–24; R. Dallek, *Franklin D. Roosevelt and American Foreign Policy, 1932–1945* (New York, 1979), 285; in recent years historians have become increasingly sceptical regarding American intentions of joining the war: Reynolds, *The Anglo-American Alliance*, esp. 214–19; Charmley, *Churchill*, 332; *Churchill's Grand Alliance* (London, 1995), 16–17, 38–44, 356; J. Keegan, 'Churchill's Strategy', in Blake and Louis (eds.), *Churchill*, 338–9; N. Rose, *Churchill* (London, 1994), 276, 288; G. L. Weinberg, *A World at Arms: A Global History of World War II* (Cambridge, 1994), 238–45 (citing recently discovered documentation).

[20] Interestingly enough, here too—though, of course, he was not privy to the development of the atom bomb—Liddell Hart took care to leave a loophole in his analysis by repeatedly mentioning 'the possible discovery of some revolutionary new weapons of paralysing effect' as one way of breaking the German hold over occupied Europe: *The Current of War*, 403–4 (7 Jan. 1941); *This Expanding War*, 257–8 (6 Aug. 1941).

[21] Addison, 'Lloyd George and Compromise Peace', 383.

Britain's own strength, and to the means employed for that purpose, rather than to his decision to leave Britain in the war, that Liddell Hart objected before the Grand Alliance came into being. After Pearl Harbor his advocacy of a cold war against Germany, which spanned the years 1939–41, was over.

Unconditional Surrender

Liddell Hart's views and proposals during the remainder of the Second World War will be reviewed here only briefly. In principle they represent little that is new beyond the ideas he had been developing since the 1920s; and seen from the transitory point in time in which this book is written, they appear less important. Although the grounds shifted considerably after the Grand Alliance took shape, Liddell Hart only intensified his opposition to the British and Western Allies' war policy. While the military defeat of Germany had now become a very real possibility, he concluded that a victory achieved at the end of a protracted total war would completely bankrupt Britain and cause her to lose her empire. As he wrote: 'Spain, Sweden, Holland, France and Austria all exhausted themselves through overstraining themselves in offensive war-efforts that were beyond their capability.' Furthermore, echoing Corbett, Liddell Hart pointed out that, relative to her Continental rivals, Britain had always been a small nation which had never been able, nor had attempted, to crush her enemies completely.[22] He endlessly reiterated that history had proved the concept of 'victory' to be illusory and called for a cool view forward, free from the passions of war, into the ensuing state of peace. He judged that the pursuit of victory would lead to American and Soviet domination of the world and only saw the seeds of the next conflict. Liddell Hart thus returned to advocate a negotiated settlement to the war. He believed that once the odds had changed against Germany, a new German leadership might arise which, provided that German independence and national integrity were maintained, would seek peace on terms that could be acceptable to the West. This would help to restore the European and global balance of power and keep the Soviet Union in check. In October 1943 Liddell Hart predicted that the war would leave the Soviet Union in control of eastern and central Europe, including part of Germany, with the West in control of the other part. Thus, in contrast to some present-day revisionist critics of Churchill, Liddell Hart advocated peace with

---

[22]   29 July 1942, King's, 11/1942/59; repeated in May and 4 July 1943, 11/1943/26.

Germany, not when German power was at its apogee, but from 1942, when it could be checked again. On one occasion he even wrote to Robert Graves that Britain had always known how to get out of wars in which her former allies continued to fight (presumably implying departing from the Soviet Union rather than the United States).

All this focused from the summer of 1943 into out-and-out opposition to the demand made by Roosevelt and Churchill in Casablanca for 'unconditional surrender' by the Axis powers. Liddell Hart hastily sent the British government a memorandum arguing against that demand. In his view, unconditional surrender, which closed the door to a negotiated end to the war, would leave no way out for the German people and opposition, thus playing into Hitler's hands. These were the themes he reiterated in his books at the end of the war and ever after. In the general jubilation of VE day he grimly concluded that his predictions had come true: Europe lay ruined and divided, communism was rampant, and Britain was exhausted and rendered economically dependent. As the Cold War broke out, Liddell Hart wrote that the only possible response to the Soviet threat was to retract the Western Allies' mistake and rearm the Germans as quickly as possible—a measure which would be taken after the Korean War.[23] Indeed, with the coming of the Cold War, criticism of the policy of unconditional surrender and of the Western Allies' alleged failure to consider the Soviet threat during the Second World War became widespread. Even Churchill in his memoirs misleadingly attempted to play down his involvement in the proclamation of unconditional surrender. He and others similarly created the enduring legend that well before the defeat of Nazi Germany he had been gravely concerned about the future Soviet threat and had tried to direct Western strategy accordingly. In truth, it has been shown that Churchill refused to consider the shape of the post-war world until Nazi Germany had been defeated, and began to contemplate the Soviet threat only in the very last months of the war. 'First catch your hare' was his slogan.[24]

---

[23] 3 Sept. 1942, King's, 11/1942/70; 24 Jan. 1943, 11/1943/3; 17 Apr. 1943, 11/1943/26; 31 July 1943, 11/1943/47; 11 Aug. 1943, 11/1943/49; 1 Oct. 1943, 11/1943/62; 1 Dec. 1943, 11/1943/75; to Graves, 3 Oct. 1942, 1/327; some of this already in the 1941 ed. of *The Strategy of Indirect Approach*, 203, 208–10; *Why Don't We Learn from History?* (London, 1944) 7 May 1945, 11/1945/5; Liddell Hart to George Bell, 19 Feb. 1948.

[24] Howard, *The Mediterranean Strategy*, pp. ix–x, 56, 63–5; *Grand Strategy: History of the Second World War*, iv (London, 1972), 281–5; Charmley, *Churchill*, 464–74, 521; Ben-Moshe, *Churchill*, 225–44, 277–324; D. Reynolds, 'Great Britain and the Security "Lessons" of the Second World War', in R. Ahmann, A. M. Birke, and M. Howard (eds.), *The Quest for Stability: Problems of West European Security, 1918–1957* (Oxford, 1993), 301–4.

In June 1942, after five years of separation, Liddell Hart again met Fuller, and the two outcasts, each for different reasons, made up. They were both campaigning against total war and the bombing offensive— ideas which Liddell Hart had adopted from Fuller twenty years earlier. Liddell Hart was also in touch with other leading critics of total war and air bombing such as George Bell, the Bishop of Chichester. With Soviet participation closing the holes in the blockade and the American Eight Air Force joining British Bomber Command, Liddell Hart no longer claimed that the air offensive and the blockade were not harming the German war effort significantly. Rather, he emphasized their barbaric and wasteful nature, which only escalated the war and would lead to exhaustion through attrition. In 1941 he had already suggested that Hitler's Blitzkrieg was more humane than Britain's air offensive and blockade. He now insisted that the blockade had always been used by Britain in limited wars for limited aims, whereas its employment in a war to the finish was wholly barbaric. Again reversing his older ideas, he took up his critics' arguments of the 1920s, denouncing the Allies' Sherman- and Mongol-like warfare against civilians. By the end of the war he was able to reaffirm that the strategic air offensive had failed to achieve its goals.[25]

As the US Air Force strategic bombing surveys would show, although Germany's cities were destroyed, German civilian morale did not collapse, and German military output actually rocketed in 1943–4, during the height of the bombing offensive. Admittedly, that offensive diverted the Luftwaffe from the Eastern Front to the defence of Germany, and diverted German industry from the production of bombers to fighters. Industrial resources, raw materials, and (mainly second-grade) manpower were also diverted to air defence and recon- struction. Furthermore, if it had not been for the bombing, German military production would probably have risen even more than it actually did. Yet, as the bombing offensive probably absorbed more than a third of the Western Allies' war production, the question of cost- effectiveness and possible alternative usage of resources is bound to arise. Although the Allies' (namely, American) resources were huge, they were not boundless. For example, tactical air cooperation with the army was inadequate until 1943–4, and Western tank models never

[25] 17 Mar. 1941, King's, 11/1941/18, and *This Expanding War*, 260 (6 Aug. 1941); 12 Jan. 1943, 11/1943/26; 3 July 1943, 11/1943/40; *Why Don't We Learn from History?*, 87; *The Revolution in Warfare*, 24–5, 74–5.

caught up with those of Germany (and the Soviet Union). The supply of landing craft proved to be another crucial bottleneck for Allied strategy. Critics have also suggested the possibility of more accurate, versatile, and discriminating alternatives within the strategic air offensive option to the high-altitude 'carpet' bombing by heavy four-engine aircraft.[26]

The arguments against Liddell Hart's views on these contentious issues are as strong as, or even stronger than, his own. Indeed, they question his entire system of thought. While thinking Hitler and the Nazi regime tyrannical, brutal, and despicable, he clearly did not grasp the scope and intensity of their murderous racial vision, the lengths to which they would go in implementing their policies, and their success in winning the support of the German people. For him, they were not the first and probably not the last of their kind that Britain and the West had faced and would still have to face. He would not accept that the Second World War was fundamentally different from earlier wars. He soberly pointed out that it was a common psychological phenomenon, arising from the passions of war and the needs of propaganda, to regard the current enemy—Louis XIV, Napoleon, Kaiser Wilhelm—as different, more barbaric and more menacing than earlier ones.[27] A. J. P. Taylor has remarked that in the First World War German atrocities were universally believed in but were in fact rare, whereas in the Second World War atrocity stories were generally discounted even though they were in fact all too true.[28] However, Liddell Hart did not change his position much even after the war, when the horrendous reality became known. His bias was clearly motivated. It was crucial to his critique of the Allies' aims and conduct of the war. He would never concede that 'victory' in the Second World War mattered or that the

---

[26] D. MacIsaac (ed.), *The United States Strategic Bombing Survey* (10 vols., New York, 1976), Webster and Frankland, *The Strategic Air Offensive*, ii and iii, Butler, *Grand Strategy*, ii. 527–33; Overy, *The Air War*, 122–5; M. Smith, 'The Allied Air Offensive', in J. Gooch, *Decisive Campaigns of the Second World War* (London, 1990), 67–83; MF *Deutschland und der zweite Weltkrieg*, vi (Stuttgart, 1990), 560–5; A. D. Harvey, *Collision of Empires: Britain in Three World Wars, 1793–1945* (London, 1992), 644–8, 703–6. The bombing effort is improbably estimated by Webster and Frankland, *The Strategic Air Offensive*, i. 92, at 10% of British war production; A. J. P. Taylor estimates it at more than a third: *The Second World War* (London, 1975), 129, accepted by M. Hastings, *Bomber Command* (New York, 1979), 107, and Kennett, *Strategic Bombing*, 181; Overy places the air war investment of all the warring powers at 40–50% of which the bombers took the lion's share on the Allies' side: 'Air Power in the Second World War', in H. Boog and MF (eds.), *The Conduct of the Air War in the Second World War* (New York, 1992), 12, also 18.

[27] *Why Don't We Learn from History?*, 51. [28] Cited in Bond, *LH*, 168.

Soviet Union—tyrannical and brutal as she was—posed a less sinister threat to the West and to humanity than Nazi Germany.

Unconditional surrender may not have been the most subtle diplomacy. Many in both the American and British administrations thought so at the time, including Foreign Secretaries Hull and Eden. But it was extremely effective for the aims set by its initiators. As Louis Namier would write to Liddell Hart, negotiations with Germany would have rapidly strengthened her hand by allowing her to play the partners of the Grand Alliance—who were deeply suspicious of each other—against one another, as Talleyrand had done in 1815.[29] The bombing offensive, too, terrible and strategically blunt as it was, was largely a political tool. From late 1941 Churchill no longer believed that it would win the war. But it was one of the very few things the Western Allies were able to offer the Soviet Union in 1942–4 as a substitute for a Second Front, and it drove the war and defeat home to the German people.

Both Roosevelt and Churchill thought it necessary to completely eradicate Nazism, leave the Germans in no doubt that they had been totally defeated, and prevent the repetition of the post-1918 survival of the German nationalist tradition. It is very doubtful whether during the middle phase of the war, and until it became too late to matter, any alternative German government would have been able to come to power or accept peace on terms acceptable to the West. No alternative government was also likely to be other than conservative-nationalist. Roosevelt in particular, who in the late 1930s had been entertaining ideas similar to Liddell Hart's regarding the need for developing a 'new technique' of waging war, based on containment and cold war, now wanted complete victory in order to shape a new world order in which Germany and Japan would be democratized and collective security enforced by the victors.[30] The outcome of the war may have divided Europe, but it created a Western bloc which encompassed the world's most advanced industrial societies, except the Soviet Union. For this purpose it may have been necessary to destroy Germany and Japan first and then build them up again—futile as this may be made to sound by critics. The

---

[29] Namier to Liddell Hart, 24 Mar. 1951, King's, 1/539; A. J. P. Taylor, from whom Liddell Hart expected more sympathy, argued the same thing: see their letters of 2 and 27 Mar., 9 and 12 Apr. 1961, 1/676.

[30] Dallek, *Roosevelt and American Foreign Policy*, 359, 373–8; Reynolds, *The Anglo-American Alliance*, 251–66; J. L. Gaddis, *Strategies of Containment: A Critical Appraisal of Postwar American National Security Policy* (New York, 1982), 10.

West was not merely preserved by the war—the goal Liddell Hart had desired—but widely expanded. Contrary to the views of Liddell Hart and modern, enlightened opinion in interwar Britain, this time at least military victory in war decisively shaped history, as that nineteenth-century man, Winston Churchill, had always believed it had.

Cold War against Nazi Germany: Conclusion

Many of these arguments may also apply to Liddell Hart's advocacy of a policy of cold war against Germany during the period when Britain stood alone. Liddell Hart was remarkably perceptive in most of his strategic judgements, and correct in assessing that by herself Britain stood no chance of defeating Germany. But was a policy of cold war any more viable? Can the later successful implementation of that policy against the Soviet Union be taken as a comparable model? Some of the differences are obvious. The Western bloc that would face the communists would include the world's most advanced industrial societies, and even then the security and psychological burden would be felt by them to be almost too heavy. By contrast, in 1940–1 Britain stood alone, with only the United States behind her. As for the opponent, the Soviet leadership would always be much more conservative and cautious in its policies than Hitler. It is not only that he corresponded more to the category of 'fanatics', which Liddell Hart suggested were difficult to contain; Germany was also driven to adventurist and aggressive policies by her lack of economic self-sufficiency, whereas the Soviet Union was largely autarkic. It is doubtful that Hitler would have agreed to settle into a state of indefinite cold war with Britain and the US, especially if the blockade was to continue, albeit in a modified form. In any case, the US would have probably been able to prevent Britain from falling. But it is difficult to see how Britain could have relaxed her defence effort sufficiently to return to a state of normality and resume economic growth and prosperity, as Liddell Hart wished and as the West would be able to do during the Cold War. As to the end of the Cold War, the Soviet collapse would be caused primarily by economic failure, whereas there is no reason to suppose that a German economic circle would have become similarly inefficient. While German terror was rivalled by the Soviet, it was genocidal towards the Jews, gypsies, and other special groups, and semi-genocidal towards the Slavs. Repression, however, neither brought about by itself nor allowed the disintegration of the Soviet bloc, and can scarcely be expected to have done so in the case of Germany's New Order, even if some mellowing of the regime might have occurred after Hitler was gone. Britain emerged exhausted from the war, but a policy of cold war was unlikely to have conserved her forces any better. It was her good fortune that Hitler's Germany became embroiled in war with both the Soviet Union and the United States.

Finally, there is the question of the viability of a Cold War regime before the advent of nuclear weapons. There is no question that that 'great deterrent' concentrated the minds of the Cold War antagonists wonderfully and created that type of powerful inhibition to war that Liddell Hart had sought in vain in preaching the doctrine of the superiority of defence. Nuclear weapons thus made a Cold War regime much more stable and endurable than it could ever have been before. It would be a mistake, however, to think that it was solely the nuclear factor that brought that regime into being.[31] As a leading historian of the Cold War has pointed out, it is all too often forgotten that when the policy of containment and the Cold War regime against the Soviet Union were being evolved after the Second World War, the US had a monopoly on nuclear weapons and theoretically had every reason to pre-empt and force her way without fear of retaliation.[32] Had the Soviet Union or Nazi Germany, rather than the United States, possessed a nuclear monopoly, there can be little doubt that they would have pressed for the massive production of nuclear weapons and carried out a worldwide policy of conquest and coercion. The notions of containment and cold war, already discernible before the Second World War in both Britain and the United States, pre-dated the Bomb and the Cold War, and their roots went deeper into the modern 'Western condition'.

II. The Nuclear Age

The advent of the atom bomb made very little change in Liddell Hart's thought. He immediately recognized it to be not 'just another new weapon'—as many military experts who were struggling to digest its significance held—but a revolutionary one, for which no satisfactory defence existed or could be envisaged in the foreseeable future. At the

---

[31] I here stand between the two poles represented by Mueller, *Retreat from Doomsday: The Obsolescence of Major War* (New York, 1989), and 'The Essential Irrelevance of Nuclear Weapons: Stability in the Postwar World', *International Security*, 13 (2) (1988), 55–79, and M. van Creveld, *The Transformation of War* (New York, 1991).

[32] J. L. Gaddis, 'The Origins of Self-Deterrence: The United States and the Non-use of Nuclear Weapons, 1945–1958', in his *The Long Peace: Inquiries Into the History of the Cold War* (New York, 1987), 104–46.

same time, however, Liddell Hart viewed nuclear weapons as only the last step in a long process which had been increasing the cost and destructiveness of war so as to threaten the very existence of civilization and render total war irrational. Since he continued to believe, again in contrast to another prevailing view of the Bomb, that armed conflict and war would continue until international society underwent fundamental transformation—limiting sovereignty, curbing nationalism, and strengthening forms of European and World Federation and world order—the problem for him remained unchanged: how to limit war effectively, while making the most of its still considerable strategic potential. The means he foresaw for this dual purpose also remained as before: qualitative disarmament and control of nuclear weapons; deterrence, mutual restraint, and collective security; subatomic conventional warfare, to be carried out by small, fully mechanized armies relying on mobility and calculated dispersion, as well as by airborne forces for the role of imperial strategic reserve; indirect approach, 'camouflage war', peripheral war, infiltration, subversion, and guerrilla and non-violent techniques.

Liddell Hart advanced this remarkable blueprint for the nuclear age in the very first months after Hiroshima and Nagasaki, and had no trouble in incorporating it as a postscript to his *The Revolution in Warfare* (1946), which he wrote before the conclusion of the Second World War and the introduction of the Bomb, but which contained fundamentally the same ideas.[33] Although in time the book would be recognized as pioneering, the scope and perceptiveness of its vision are becoming all the more apparent as the Cold War era can be viewed in perspective and, one dares venture, as the outline of the post-Cold War world is emerging. During the formative years of the nuclear age Liddell Hart had no access to classified technological and strategic information, nor did he have to deal with the practical, day-to-day problems and constraints with which politicians and soldiers were

---

[33] See already in Liddell Hart to Hobart, 21 Aug. 1945, King's, 1/376; *The Revolution in Warfare*, 83–93; also 'War, Limited', *Harper's Magazine* (Mar. 1946), 193–202. The pros and cons of the balance of power, unification, or federation are first discussed in the 1941 edn. of *The Strategy of Indirect Approach*, 203–4. See also M. Howard, 'The Classical Strategists', in his *Studies in War and Peace* (London, 1970), 159, and 'Liddell Hart', in his *The Causes of War*, 246; L. Freedman, *The Evolution of Nuclear Strategy* (London, 1981), 97–100. Bond, *LH*, 164–214, provides the sole extensive summary of Liddell Hart's work in the nuclear age. The only new idea in *The Revolution in Warfare* was the automatization of warfare, which was in fact borrowed unacknowledged from Fuller's much earlier works: cf. p. 34 above.

grappling. For these same reasons, however, he was again free to take the longest view.

Liddell Hart's view regarding the policy to be adopted in respect to the Soviet Union was also similar to the one he had developed against the German threat in 1937–41: 'The military policy of a peaceful minded nation, aiming at self-preservation but not at expansion, should . . . concentrate . . . *primarily on defence.*'[34]

The more one weighs all the factors, the more probable it appears that there could be no victory in a war between the Western Powers and the Soviet Union, but only a common loss. . . . There is a school of thought—more common in triumphant America that in war-weary Britain—which regarding war with Russia as bound to come, is inclined to force the issue. It talks of the importance of being ready 'to strike first' regardless of the basic fact that America's comparative remoteness entails delay in exerting her weight, and of the risk that war might be needlessly precipitated in the attempt. It ignores the likelihood of initial Russian success, the long road to recovery in consequence, and the irreparable damage that civilization would suffer in the process. It underrates the difficulties of gaining so-called 'victory' over Russia when the balance of strength has turned.[35]

For all that, Liddell Hart's pioneering formulation of the doctrines of containment and cold war has not been recognized. Partly this was because he lost public stature and was himself deeply scarred by his wartime isolation. He no longer developed his views as effectively as he had done in 1937–41, and the popular illustrated magazines to which he occasionally contributed in the second half of the 1940s, for handsome sums of money, were no substitute for the wide and influential readership of *The Times*. In addition, the hub of world power which during the interwar period, owing to Germany's collapse and the partial retreat of the United States and the Soviet Union from the international scene, had at least appeared to reside in Britain—giving the ideas of Fuller and Liddell Hart extra resonance—moved away, to the United States. And, as is always the case, the centre of strategic thought was moving in the same direction. Global policies and strategies were now decided in Washington, and it was there that intellectuals were coming forth to stimulate, articulate, and criticize them. It was left to a younger and fresher voice than Liddell Hart to stamp his name on the doctrine of

---

[34] 'War, Limited', 201; similarly *The Revolution in Warfare*, 87.
[35] 'What War with Russia Would Mean', *John Bull*, 30 Nov. 1946, 7, 9; repr. in *The Defence of the West* (London, 1950), 149–50.

Containment. This was George Kennan (b. 1904), probably the greatest of the Cold War intellectuals. The political and strategic programme for the West which he advanced in the early post-war years bears a stunning resemblance to that which Liddell Hart had developed during the struggle against Germany.

Kennan and Containment

During the Second World War, as a career diplomat who was serving in central and eastern Europe and was in contact with the German opposition, Kennan did not believe in any sort of compromise solution to the war with Germany. He felt that Nazi Germany had to be completely crushed, and the country repartitioned into small states. In retrospect he would come to look at this with astonishment, believing that the Western Allies missed opportunities for dealing with the German conservatives and army leaders. He also expressed the opinion that over time Hitler's empire would have collapsed of its own repressive nature and corruption, but that the damage that it would have done would have been too heavy to bear. All the same, when in 1945–7 Kennan developed the notion of the containment of the Soviet Union, he stressed that, threatening to the West as it was, the Soviet Union was different from Nazi Germany in possessing more time and in being more cautious.[36] It was this and not the nuclear factor that made the difference for him. As he would specifically point out, the idea of containment was formed in a fundamentally non-nuclear set of mind and derived from pre-1945 experiences.[37] The atom bomb is not even mentioned in either his 'Long Telegram' from Moscow of February 1946 or his famous 'X' article of 1947. It should be remembered that it was universally believed until the Soviet surprise of 1949 that it would take the Soviet Union much longer to develop nuclear weapons. Moreover, Kennan insisted throughout the second half of the 1940s that the US must refrain from using nuclear weapons as an active instrument of diplomacy and war, and he would have liked to see them abolished by agreement.

[36] Kennan's 'Long Telegram' from Moscow, 22 Feb. 1946, printed in *Memoirs* (2 vols.; Boston, 1967, 1972), i. 557–8, also 116–19, 239; his 'X' article in *Foreign Affairs*, 25 (1947), repr. in *American Diplomacy* (New York, 1985 (1951)), 118–21, also 87–8. In Kennan's unpublished lectures, some of which are confidential, given at various official and unofficial forums and now deposited at the Seeley G. Mudd Manuscript Library, Princeton [Mudd], see 8 Jan. 1948, King's, 17/1; 17 Sept. 1948, 17/11.

[37] *American Diplomacy*, pp. vi–vii.

Kennan had always been a 'realist', believing in a firm and dispassionate line towards the Soviet Union. He gradually developed the notion of her containment from the end of the Second World War. However, he would remember his period as one of the deputy commanders at the newly established National War College, from September 1946 to May 1947, as 'enormously stimulating and interesting' for him. 'It was at that time—in the background reading, in the attendance at lectures by distinguished outsiders, in the agonizing over my own lectures—that some of the ideas were conceived that have been basic to my views on American policy ever since':

we had, as it turned out, virtually nothing in the way of an established or traditional American doctrine which we could take as a point of departure for our thinking and teaching. . . . We found ourselves thrown back, perforce, on the European thinkers of other ages and generations: on Machiavelli, Clausewitz, Gallieni—even Lawrence of Arabia. We had the admirable compilation *Makers of Modern Strategy*, edited by E. M. Earle to draw on . . . But it was obvious that in no instance was the thinking of these earlier figures fully relevant or remotely adequate to the needs of a great American democracy in the Atomic age. . . .

The precedents of our Civil War, of the War with Spain, and of our participation in the two world wars of this century, had created . . . an unspoken assumption that the normal objective of warfare was the total destruction of the enemy's ability and will to resist and his unconditional capitulation. . . .

The most significant of the appreciations to which I came during that year at the War College was that this approach to the cultivation and use by our country of armed forces would no longer work. I doubted that it had been a sound one even in the pre-atomic age. It seemed to me that in each of the two world wars, the application of it, while successful in the immediate military sense, had complicated—very gravely indeed—the problems of the peace. . . .

This meant, it seemed to me, a need for return to much earlier concepts. The doctrine of total war had been a doctrine of the nineteenth and twentieth centuries. We would now have to revert to the concepts of limited warfare prevalent in the eighteenth century. The aims of warfare, accordingly, would have to become limited. If weapons were to be used at all, they would have to be employed to temper the ambitions of an adversary, or to make good limited objectives against his will—not to destroy his power, or his government, or to disarm him entirely. . . .

From these two appreciations . . . I went ahead to develop a concept of the peacetime requirements of our armed force establishment which laid emphasis on the maintenance of small, compact, alert forces, capable of delivering at short notice effective blows on limited theaters of operation far from our own shores.[38]

From the mid-1950s these ideas would become commonplace among strategic theorists, but they were not so in 1946–7. Although it is the argument of this study that it was the West's overall political and strategic conditions that produced the strategy of containment, the question whether Kennan was in any way influenced by Liddell Hart's strikingly similar ideas arises, and is one for which the present author has no definite answer. Liddell Hart's name is conspicuously not among the authorities cited by Kennan, either in the passage quoted above or in his lectures at the time, now held at the Seeley G. Mudd Manuscript Library at Princeton. After the war Liddell Hart was in eclipse, and an unwise choice as an ally. The chapter devoted to him in Earle's *Makers of Modern Strategy*, the book Kennan cites, was very critical. However, Liddell Hart's 'War, Limited' appeared in the March 1946 issue of the popular American intellectual journal *Harper's Magazine*, and his *The Revolution in Warfare*, which contained exactly the same strategic ideas and historical interpretation as would be espoused by Kennan, came out in Britain in 1946 and was published in America by Yale University Press in 1947. It seems unlikely that a book by such a well-known writer, relating to the new strategic challenges of the era and issued by a prestigious American publishing house, was unknown to those at the new War College who exactly at that time were struggling to form their minds in respect to US defence policy. Indeed the book, and Liddell Hart's earlier works that express similar ideas—the 1941 edition of *The Strategy of Indirect Approach*, reissued in 1946, *The Current of War* (1941), *This Expanding War* (1942), *Thoughts on War* (1944), and *Why Don't We Learn from History?* (1944)—all exist in the original editions in the library of the National Defence University to which the War College now belongs.[39]

Either way, Kennan's notion of containment against the Soviet Union took shape in early 1947, and was offered to the public in an article signed 'X' in the July issue of *Foreign Affairs*. When it was revealed that

[38] *Memoirs*, i. 308–11; these recollections, published in 1967, mention the nuclear factor far more prominently than Kennan's writings at the time. This is also pointed out by Gaddis, *The Long Peace*, 112–13.

[39] My attempts to raise the question in letters to Mr Kennan himself have been unsuccessful, his secretary replying that owing to his many commitments and advanced age he was not responding to any queries: T. Bramley to the author, 27 Oct. 1994 and 24 Apr. 1995.

the author was the nominated head of the newly established Policy Planning Staff at the State Department, it immediately gained great publicity. Coming as it did in close proximity to the announcement of the Truman Doctrine and the Marshall Plan, it was generally taken as an almost official expression of policy. In the article Kennan argued that the Soviet Union was fundamentally hostile to the capitalist world and ideologically committed to its destruction. There was no prospect for it being drawn into peaceful coexistence and cooperation with the West. In contrast to Napoleon or Hitler, however,

it is more sensitive to contrary force . . . and thus more rational in the logic and rhetoric of power. On the other hand it cannot be easily defeated or discouraged by a single victory on the part of its opponents. . . . In these circumstances it is clear that the main element of any United States policy towards the Soviet Union must be that of a long-term, patient but firm and vigilant containment of Russian expansive tendencies. It is important to note, however, that such a policy has nothing to do with outward histrionics: with threats or blustering or superfluous gestures of outward 'toughness'. . . . Like almost any other government, [the Kremlin] can be placed by tactless and threatening gestures in a position where it cannot afford to yield even though this might be dictated by its sense of realism.[40]

Kennan suggested that the Soviet Union suffered from many problems and internal tensions: her success was achieved at the price of tremendous economic and human toll; her people were war-weary and disillusioned; the occupied nationalities of her empire were ever a source of unrest; and she was overall weaker than the West. For her part, the US must strive to solve her internal problems and project to the rest of the world an attractive model and a vital and confident vision. It must never adopt the methods of its enemy. Rejecting both options of retreat and pre-emptive war, the United States ought to work together with local allies, particularly in Western Europe, so as to create a strong enough coalition against the Soviet Union and share the burden of containment against her, a burden which the United States could not carry alone. In this way,

the United States has it in its power to increase enormously the strains under which Soviet policy must operate, to force upon the Kremlin a far greater degree of moderation and circumspection than it has had to observe in recent years, and in this way to promote tendencies which must eventually find their

[40] 'The Sources of Soviet Conduct', *Foreign Affairs*, 25 (1947), repr. in *American Diplomacy*, 118–19.

outlet in either the break-up or the gradual mellowing of Soviet power. For no mystical, Messianic movement . . . can face frustration indefinitely . . .[41]

Once again the similarity between Kennan's ideas and those which Liddell Hart had developed in respect to Nazi Germany is striking, though a circumstantial explanation for their likeness cannot be ruled out: many of the notions which both men expressed were derived from the Allies' planning during the Second World War; some were 'in the air', as the perceived Soviet threat increasingly dominated American consciousness. In addition, Kennan's knowledge of Soviet and European affairs was infinitely superior to Liddell Hart's. Kennan held strong views on foreign affairs, and his powers of observation, deduction, and articulation were tremendous.

Be that as it may, given the similarity of their respective positions, it is not surprising that Kennan's image developed in a way similar to Liddell Hart's. During the immediate post-war period (like Liddell Hart in respect to Germany during the Munich crisis) Kennan was perceived as a hard-liner for mistrusting the Soviet Union and advocating her containment. In his capacity as head of the Policy Planning Staff at the State Department, a position he held until January 1950, he played a leading role in shaping American policy during the formative stage of the Cold War. However, by the end of his tenure and thereafter, as the Cold War was becoming dominated by the threat of nuclear war and as the United States became entangled in messy local conflicts, especially in east Asia, Kennan thought that American policy was veering in the other direction and he became progressively more critical of it. Consequently, he was now viewed as 'soft' and 'unsafe', and found himself increasingly isolated from official circles.[42] He believed all along that the Soviet threat, and hence containment itself, was mainly political rather than military, and that the Russians had no practical intention of invading Western Europe.[43] For his War College students he developed

---

[41] Ibid. 120–1, 126–7. On more specific points, see also Kennan's 'long telegram' of Feb. 1946, ibid. 559; 6 Nov. 1947, in A. K. Nelson (ed.), *The State Department Policy Staff Papers, 1947–1949* (3 vols., New York, 1983), i. 130 and *passim*; 26 June 1950, King's, 17/18.   [42] See esp. *Memoirs*, ii. 249–61.

[43] Kennan's position in this respect at the time, unclear to readers of Mr X and only revealed in his *Memoirs*, i. 358–9, is fully confirmed by the archival evidence. See e.g. 22 Oct. 1946, Mudd, 16/17; 10 Apr., 9 May, 28 July, and Dec. 1947, 16/29, 32, 33, 39 and 40; 8 Jan. 1948, 17/1. See also T. H. Etzold and J. L. Gaddis (eds.), *Containment: Documents on American Policy and Strategy, 1945–1950* (New York, 1978), 64–81, 90–7, 154, 173–211; Nelson *Policy Staff Papers*, i. 129; ii. 281–92, 490–6. Finally see Kennan, *Realities of*

a catalogue of 'Measures Short of War' which were the most suitable in the struggle to contain the Soviet threat.[44] He rejected the common view that the victory of the communists in China and the conflicts in Korea and Vietnam were Moscow-inspired and represented a world-wide, coordinated communist bid for power. As he saw it, these were predominantly indigenous conflicts, involving local forces which were very likely to fall out with the Kremlin, did not constitute a significant threat to the United States, and called for as little as possible high-handed American meddling in the affairs of desperately poor and help-less peoples.[45]

Kennan supported the initial American intervention to reinstate the status quo in Korea, but was deeply concerned that the conflict would escalate into total war:

The thought of a war with Russia . . . was particularly alarming and abhorrent to me because of my acute awareness . . . that in a war of this nature the American side would have no realistic, limited aims. Falling back on the patterns of the past and seized by wartime emotionalism, we would assuredly attempt once again to achieve the familiar goals of total enemy defeat, total destruction of the enemy's armed forces, his unconditional surrender, the complete occupa-tion of his territory, the removal of the existing government and its replacement by a regime that would respond to our concept of 'democratization'. . . . I had tried to bring home to my War College students, that in a war between the United States and the Soviet Union, there could be no complete military victory. Neither country was occupiable by the forces of the other. Both were simply too large, too different—linguistically, culturally, and in every other way.[46]

Kennan always held that the horrible and suicidal nature of nuclear weapons made them sterile and impractical as instruments of Western strategic policy. Within the adminstration, he was against the develop-

---

American Foreign Policy (Princeton, NJ, 1954), 64–5; *Russia, the Atom and the West* (New York, 1958), 16–19 and *passim*.

[44] 16 Sept. 1946, Mudd, 16/12.

[45] Etzold and Gaddis *Containment*, 226–8; Nelson, *Policy Staff Papers*, ii. 121–3, 412–51; Kennan, 'America and the Russian Future', *Foreign Affairs*, 29 (1951), repr. in *American Diplomacy*, 152; beautifully stated in *Realities of American Foreign Policy*, 96–99; and *Russia, the Atom and the West*, 66–82; also *Memoirs* ii. 23–60.

[46] This is the wording of *Memoirs*, ii. 94–5; see similarly: 'America and the Russian Future', in *American Diplomacy*, 129–30; ibid., 101–2; *Realities of American Foreign Policy*, 79–81. Similarly in the classified material of the late 1940s: 26 June 1950, Mudd, 17/18; Etzold and Gaddis *Containment*, 173–211, 344–64; Nelson, *Policy Staff Papers*, ii. 372–411: 'United States Objectives with Respect to Russia' in peace and war, Aug. 1948.

ment of thermonuclear weapons by the United States and called for an agreement with the Soviet Union to prohibit their deployment.[47] Later, he rejected both the notion of 'massive retaliation' and the reliance on tactical nuclear weapons for the defence of Europe. He maintained that there should never be a 'first use' of nuclear weapons by the West, and that at most they should be reserved for deterrence against similar weapons. He argued that if war was to come it had to be kept limited and conventional. He believed that a Soviet attack on Western Europe, the sceptre which dominated Western strategic policy, was unlikely, and suggested once that even if it came, Europe would be better off relying on guerrilla resistance by paramilitary militias and on civil disobedience rather than on rigid forward defence by armies.[48] While he repeatedly pointed out the ethnic diversity of the Soviet empire as a source of endemic trouble and weakness, he ruled out any attempt by the West to encourage the occupied nationalities to revolt, or to lead a crusade for their liberation. He believed that this would only push the Soviet Union to extreme actions, make war imminent, and court disaster for the entire world.[49] He believed that Western defence policy must be defensive. The West's most potent offensive weapon was the long-term alternative it presented to the Soviet system. The West must have patience, and do its utmost to demonstrate to the peoples of the communist world that it is not their enemy. Historical evolution was bound to change the Soviet Union from within. No regime based on evil and terror was durable. 'If . . . anything were ever to occur to disrupt the unity and efficacy of the Party as a political instrument, Soviet Russia might be changed overnight from one of the strongest to one of the weakest and most pitiable of national societies.'[50]

Increasingly critical of Western policy, Kennan began to argue that much of the responsibility for the escalation and militarization of the Cold War rested with the West, whose hard-line measures, resulting from misconceptions of Soviet intentions and actions, alarmed the Soviets into stronger and largely protective measures of their own.

---

[47] See e.g. 23 Jan. 1947, Mudd, 16/21; memorandum to Dean Acheson, 20 Jan. 1950, in Etzold and Gaddis *Containment*, 373–81.

[48] *Realities of American Foreign Policy*, 84–5; *Russia, the Atom and the West* (New York, 1958), 52–65; *Memoirs*, ii. 246–9.

[49] 'America and the Russian Future', in *American Diplomacy*, 140–2; *Realities of American Foreign Policy*, 76–81; *Memoirs*, ii. 97–102.

[50] 'The Sources of Soviet Conduct', in *American Diplomacy*, 125; see also 'America and the Russian Future', in *American Diplomacy*, 148–53; *Realities of American Foreign Policy*, 79, 92–3.

Kennan believed that the exhausted and cautious Soviet Union, while never forsaking its hostile designs against the West, never realistically intended to invade Western Europe. Both by ideology and in view of the political and strategic realities, the Soviets' favoured methods were subversion, infiltration, propaganda, and political influence. The Soviet Union therefore interpreted the unilateral reconstruction and militarization of West Germany and Japan by the West, the creation of Nato as a *military* alliance, and the Western reliance on nuclear weapons (all of which Kennan criticized) as offensive actions against her.[51] In this line of argument Kennan foreshadowed much of the revisionist analysis of the origins of the Cold War. Needless to say, he also again strikingly paralleled many of the arguments Liddell Hart had advanced regarding British and Allied policy towards Germany and was in fact advancing in respect to Western policy towards the Soviet Union.

Interestingly, the two men first made personal contact when Kennan held a visiting fellowship at Oxford during the academic year 1957–8 and delivered his BBC Reith Lectures on Russia, the West, and the nuclear threat. Commenting on Liddell Hart's paper 'Basic Problems of European Defence' which Liddell Hart had sent him, Kennan wrote: 'I read it with utter amazement, and much gratification, at the fact that our minds should have run so closely together . . . had I read your paper at an earliest date I should have suspected myself of subconscious plagiarism.'[52]

Liddell Hart: Deterrence and Defence

Indeed, Liddell Hart and Kennan held remarkably similar views. While Liddell Hart supported the resurrection and rearmament of Germany within some sort of a European federation and combined European defence system,[53] he too maintained that, despite the Soviets' aggressive appearance, they were war-weary, mostly concerned about their own security, and conscious of the realities of the global balance of

---

[51] Etzold and Gaddis, *Containment*, 101, 135–44, 153–8; *Memoirs*, i. 397–448; ii. 137–8, and Kennan's masterful dispatch from Moscow of 8 Sept. 1952, ibid. 327–51; *Russia, the Atom and the West*; Gaddis, *The Long Peace*, 63–71.

[52] To Liddell Hart, 29 Oct. 1957, King's, 1/415. While they met during the year on official and academic occasions and corresponded extensively—as usual, on Liddell Hart's urging—Kennan evaded any personal relationship, politely declining Liddell Hart's persistent invitations to come to his nearby Buckinghamshire house.

[53] The 'European idea' already mooted in the 1941 edition of *The Strategy of Indirect Approach*, 203–4, is regarded as essential in the *Sunday Pictorial*, 24 Aug. 1947, and repeatedly in the following years.

power. Their most promising strategy was subversion and 'camou-
flaged' or 'cold' war. He predicted that, for the West, 'the best chance
might lie in an internal split, starting near the top—since it is almost
impossible to overthrow a totalitarian regime from below, by popular
revolt'. The Soviet explosion of a nuclear device in 1949 strengthened
Liddell Hart in his view that the West could not rely on nuclear
weapons for anything other than deterring a nuclear attack. In view
of their horrific nature, nuclear weapons provided neither credible
deterrence nor defence against either a Soviet invasion of Western
Europe or any other sort of non-nuclear threat around the globe.
The West's only rational option was non-nuclear and limited. It should
be noted that Liddell Hart wrote all this in the late 1940s, before Korea
and before the idea of limited war and the opposition to 'massive
retaliation' was taken on by Western defence intellectuals. Furthermore,
Liddell Hart who had pioneered the idea of limited war during the
1920s, had become increasingly cautious and circumspect about the
circumstances of its implementation long before Vietnam would cool
the defence intellectuals' enthusiam for it.[54]

Liddell Hart maintained that for the defence of Western Europe
conventional forces must be created. He continued to reject mass conscript armies of the old type, which would be slow to mobilize and
unable to respond quickly enough to a surprise Soviet attack. Instead,
he restated his previous advocacy for two types of force. One, always
kept in a state of high alert, was to be an élite, high-tech, professional
striking force, composed of some twenty wholly armoured and fully
mechanized divisions, a number of airborne divisions, and a powerful
air force. The other was to comprise militias on the pattern of the
British Territorials, locally resisting and obstructing the enemy's
advance. Civil disobedience, for all its problems against a ruthless
adversary, should also be considered. Civil defence and the protection
of industry must be seriously taken up.[55]

In the second half of the 1950s a fast-growing community of defence
intellectuals and strategic analysts was forming in the United States and

---

[54] Similarly, Liddell Hart amended his views regarding guerrilla warfare, now under-
lining its destructive effect and long-term harmful legacy to those who practised it:
Liddell Hart, *Defence of the West*, 53–7, expanded and incorporated into the 1967 edn.
of *Strategy: The Indirect Approach*.

[55] Liddell Hart's articles from the second half of the 1940s were collected in *Defence of
the West*; see esp. 57, 88, 94–5, 97–8, 125–6, 129–30, 132, 136–40, 144–5, 148–50, 188–90,
216–42, 328–38, 366–80; quotation from p. 132. Also see *Deterrent or Defence* (London,
1960), 5, 16 and *passim*.

Britain. In 1954 Liddell Hart took part in the creation of the Military Commentators Circle, which in 1958 would develop into the Institute for Strategic Studies. The new strategic community held almost unanimously, as Liddell Hart and Kennan had done all along, that with the Soviet Union possessing nuclear and thermonuclear capability, a Western defence policy based on a massive nuclear attack lacked credibility in response to anything but a massive Soviet nuclear attack.[56] A wave of literature espousing the idea of limited war rose in the second half of the 1950s, naming, however, Clausewitz's later ideas as its classical source of inspiration. Where the defence intellectuals were mostly divided was over the desirability of relying on tactical nuclear weapons which had been developed and had begun to enter service toward the mid-1950s. Liddell Hart had rejected their use well before the argument started, pointing out that the devastation to Europe would be unlimited. Like Kennan, he continued to insist that conventional forces were the only viable option for Western defence policy.[57]

The argument over the West's reliance on nuclear weapons for the defence of Europe was to continue with new twists and turns until the collapse of the Soviet empire. Liddell Hart, however, retired in 1960 from participation in current strategic debates. He dedicated the last decade of his life to completing his *Memoirs* and *History of the Second World War*, while also maintaining extensive contacts with, and offering help and much encouragement to, young scholars from all over the world. Knighted in 1965, he died in 1970.

Assessment

Again, weighty arguments could be, and have been, advanced against Liddell Hart's (and Kennan's) philosophy of war, as applied to the Cold War. These are the sort of arguments that will probably always be contested in the debate between 'hawks' and 'doves' over the Cold

---

[56] For Liddell Hart's immediate rejection of the American 'New Look' and of the similar British defence thinking represented by the chief of the Air Staff, Sir John Slessor, see *Daily Mail*, May 1954, 26–7; *World*, 1 June 1954; Preface to the 1954 edn. of *Strategy: The Indirect Approach*, 14–15; *Deterrent or Defence*, 17–26. Reviewing the latter book for the *Saturday Review*, 3 Sept. 1960, 17–18, presidential candidate Senator John F. Kennedy made it a vehicle for outlining his critique of the outgoing adminstration's defence policy. Interestingly, Liddell Hart was a well-known figure to him: Kennedy's remarkably mature and comprehensive Harvard dissertation, which turned into a national bestseller, *Why Britain Slept* (New York, 1940), had cited him widely. The Liddell Hart–Kennedy correspondence file) King's, 1/418.

[57] *Picture Post*, 19 Feb. 1953; *Deterrent or Defence*, 24, 58–62, 74–81. For Kennan, see *Russia, the Atom and the West*, 56–65.

War; while information about the conflict will certainly become more abundant and accurate over time, historical alternatives can never be tested, and differences of perspective, temperament, and values among commentators are inherent in the intellectual construction which is 'historical judgement'.

Thus, it may be claimed that conditions of nuclear abundance, achieved only in the 1960s, had to be reached before the nonsensical, suicidal nature of a full-scale nuclear war between the superpowers was fully realized. Even then, and certainly before, however irrational the Western threat to *initiate* the use of nuclear weapons may have been, the risk that the threat would be carried out was horrifying enough to deter a Soviet attack on Western Europe, if indeed the Soviets ever seriously contemplated such an attack. The nuclear race was thus a stabilizing as well as a destabilizing force in the Cold War. Because of their economic, social, and political priorities, the conventional defence option proved beyond the reach of the countries of Western Europe. Only their reliance on the American nuclear force gave the Europeans a measure of protection, and psychological reassurance. This may have been an irresponsible defence policy, and it certainly appeared so at the time, but in the event it contributed to Western Europe's remarkable political and economic recovery. Indeed, it was the protracted and wasteful arms race—both nuclear and conventional—that proved too heavy a burden for the Soviet Union and contributed to its collapse. How crucial a contribution was it to an economy that was failing for other, more fundamental reasons is still to be assessed.

Going deeper, one may argue that war, even when 'cold', involves risks, anxieties, and passions which it would be simply unrealistic to rule out, even in the name of the most realistic and sober calculations. In a conflict involving animosity, fear, gaps in information, and suspicion, there is a mutual quest for wider margins of safety, occasional scares over imagined or real dangers, a great deal of waste, and much non-linear logic. From this point of view, Liddell Hart's approach— and Kennan's—may appear too 'sensible' and sensitive, too detached and rational for a phenomenon like war. Even assuming that their vision of cold war proved in the end more comprehensive and far-sighted than others, did they not shrink from the passions and violence of conflict and war that had to be endured on the way? Did they not have too clinical a view of the role of mass psychology and of the necessity of mobilizing and keeping attuned to public opinion, especially in democracies?

Whatever position one may take on these points, the argument of this study is that Liddell Hart, followed by Kennan, expressed and pioneeringly codified a new and emerging view of war which is in some fundamental way typical of advanced Western and 'Westernized' liberal-democratic societies. The ideas of containment, cold war, and limited war—their core ideas—reflected a growing aversion in these societies to the phenomenon of war in general. War was becoming increasingly in conflict with their domestic values and practices. It was more and more out of place and debilitating within the system of global trade in raw materials, manufactured goods, finance, services, and information, upon which their economic prosperity was increasingly based. It was progressively at odds with the social and economic expectations of the people, whose volatility Liddell Hart and, more deeply, Kennan, distrusted, but who with the decline of authority and relaxation of social control increasingly refused to shoulder its burden. Among Western élites there was now growing awareness of the limitations of military force, especially under modern conditions, and of the complexity of exchanging military victories into political gains; a growing tendency to try to understand and take account of the other's point of view; and a growing demand to curb the passions to which conflict and war gave rise.

Under these conditions, 'defence', that is, the maintenance of a political, economic, and international order that was working in accordance with Western interests, came to be regarded as the only sensible and legitimate strategic policy for the West. It was thus the political and strategic techniques that promised maximum defence at minimum cost and with minimum bloodshed, and made use of the West's strongest assets—its economic power and technological supremacy—that came to the fore in the shape of containment, cold war, economic coercion, and limited war. Nuclear weapons tremendously strengthened this trend, but only as one of a much wider set of factors underlying Western strategic policy. The new strategic attitudes were in the ascent before the advent and proliferation of nuclear weapons, and, with some differences, they also largely characterize the Western approach towards non-nuclear antagonists.

The new strategic paradigm and the trends that had brought it into being have widened and deepened momentously during the twentieth century. They have long been implicit in the philosophy and realities of economic and political liberalism that since the eighteenth century has been increasingly manifest in Western Europe and North America. And it is no coincidence that it was among 'enlightened' public opinion, in the leading liberal-democratic powers, Britain and the United States, in the wake of the First World War and the Versailles settlement, that such factors became a potent political force. As economic and political liberalism expanded rapidly all over the developed world after the Second World War, so did the attitudes towards war that grew out of it. To some extent these attitudes have always expressed themselves in pacifism, isolationism, and support for unilateral disarmament. But in a world in which conflict and the threat of war remained a possibility, they have also led to an ongoing search for defence policies that would be the least in conflict with the new political, economic, social, and cultural modes.

Kennan himself—another early twentieth-century Mid-Westerner, born and raised in Milwaukee, Wisconsin, and deeply nostalgic for the America of the small community and 'whitewashed fences'—has been a lifelong critic of the ills of modernity, as he saw them: uninformed and volatile democracy; self-indulgent and permissive society; rampant consumerism; vulgar and corrupting media; overdevelopment, urban decay, and destruction of the environment; and the decline of communal values. In the 1930s he devised a scheme for a new form of élite, meritocratic, and hierarchic political system to replace mass democracy, and he would express similar views even in 1947. At the same time, however, he cherished above all the classical liberal rights and civic freedoms of the Anglo-American and Western tradition.[58] His memorandum to Secretary of State Dean Acheson, in which he expressed in a remarkably similar language the same ideas which Liddell Hart had formulated more than a decade earlier, is in this respect most revealing:

Whether or not war on a grand scale can achieve positive aims for an aggressive totalitarian power, it is my belief that it cannot achieve such aims for a democracy. It would be useful, in my opinion, if we could recognize that the real purposes of the democratic society cannot be achieved by large-scale violence and destruction; that even in the most favorable circumstances war between great powers spells a dismal deterioration of world conditions from the standpoint of the liberal-democratic tradition; and that the only positive function it can fulfil for us—a function, the necessity and legitimacy of which I do not

[58] 18 June 1947, King's, 16/34; *Memoirs*; also the 3 biographies: B. Gellman, *Contending with Kennan* (New York, 1984), 83–105, and *passim*; A. Stephanson's hostile *Kennan and the Art of Foreign Policy* (Cambridge, Mass., 1989), 211, 216–21, 232–8, and *passim*; D. Mayers, *George Kennan and the Dilemmas of US Foreign Policy* (New York, 1988).

dispute—is to assure that we survive physically as an independent nation . . . For such positive purposes as we wish to pursue, we must look to other things than war: above all to bearing, to example, to persuasion, and to the judicious exploitation of our strength as a deterrent to world conflict.[59]

It is a telling fact that Liddell Hart, the man who first translated the new conditions and sensibilities of the modern world into the language of strategic theory, did so while increasingly identifying himself with the liberal creed. As we have seen, by the second half of the 1930s his newly developed views regarding Britain's desired defence policy of containment and cold war went hand in hand with what he perceived and strongly affirmed as her liberal political culture, institutions, and values (though also her worldwide imperial interests). At that time Liddell Hart sought to maintain his position as an 'impartial' strategic adviser to all parties. But by 1945 he had lost this position anyhow, and had become more committed than ever. From being a conscientious liberal, he now came out openly as a Liberal. He enlisted in the party's electoral campaigns in both 1945 and 1950, speaking in public meetings on its behalf and serving on the Liberal campaign fund national committee.[60] Since he was a man of his times, his liberalism was of the 'New Liberalism' mould of the late nineteenth and early twentieth centuries. Like Kennan, he advocated social reform as well as individual rights, was more liberal then democratic, and thought men and women fundamentally unequal. Like Kennan he also rejected the Messianic and crusading brand of Wilsonian liberalism.

The Liberal Party which Liddell Hart joined was reaching the nadir of its long decline. However, as he wrote in 1937, the decline of the Liberal Party came with the adoption of liberal values by all parties and the incorporation of these values throughout the fabric of British society. To be sure, even the most 'Western' regions of the 'West' have never been solely or perhaps even principally dominated by liberalism—politically, socially, economically, or philosophically. Yet liberalism, in all these aspects, has been for centuries the agent and expression of these regions' development of modernity, and it is as such that it has won its status as the West's 'defining' characteristic. In this sense, like John Locke or John Stuart Mill, although representing no

---

[59] Memorandum from Kennan to Acheson, 20 Jan. 1950, in Etzold and Gaddis, *Containment*, 378–9.

[60] His file of correspondence and activities connected with the Liberal Party is King's, 5/21; for his speeches in meetings, see also 12/1945/1, 12/1950/3, 4, 7.

more than one school of thought or even a minority opinion, Liddell Hart was a quintessentially 'English' thinker. At the same time, however, to the extent that the liberal–democratic model would come to dominate the developed world in the course of the twentieth century, he developed in the language of theory the strategic paradigm of the future.

6

Conclusion: 'The Western Way in Warfare', Past and Future

This study suggests that Liddell Hart's contribution to strategic theory goes much further, and is more serious, than the popular doctrines, such as the 'indirect approach' or the 'British way in warfare', which won him fame in his youth.[1] This contribution, and Liddell Hart's more substantial claim for originality, should be understood in their historical context. New and significant intellectual constructions usually emerge at times of fundamental change or paradigmatic shifts, when prevailing ways of interpreting and coping with reality no longer seem adequate. Rather than being alone in their views, the thinkers who generate them usually make their names by early sensing, conceptualizing, and turning into philosophical and political programmes the feelings and notions which are beginning to emerge, more or less hazily, around them. From the perspective of time, the reaction against the First World War—particularly noticeable among the West's most liberal and increasingly democratic societies, Britain and the United States—can be seen as marking such a paradigmatic 'break'. For leading sectors of public opinion and of the political élite in those societies the idea of a major war, involving massive loss of life and wealth, was simply becoming unacceptable. Liberal-democratic, status quo powers, whose wealth was based on manufacturing and vast global trade, called for a wholly different set of strategic ideas from those required by etatist-nationalist, still largely agrarian, politically expansionist, or disunited, or revisionist, and economically less secure powers, whose wars had provided the model for nineteenth-century strategic theory.

It had fallen mainly to Clausewitz personally to experience, internalize, and formulate in the language of strategic theory the marrying of etatism and surging nationalism which had made its debut on the

[1] Cf. M. Howard in 'Liddell Holmes', *Listener*, 28 Dec. 1972, 896. For his contribution to armoured doctrine, again see my 'Liddell Hart's Theory of Armoured Warfare: Revising the Revisionist's', *Journal of Strategic Studies*, 19 (1996), 1–30; and 'British Influence and the Evolution of the Panzer Arm: Myth or Reality?', *War in History*, 4(2) (1997), 150–73; 4(3) (1997), 316–38.

European scene with the French Revolution. While still representing only a minority view in Prussia and pushed to the political fringes with the post-1815 European order, Clausewitz was riding the wave of the future in nineteenth-century Europe. True, during the last years of his life he came to recognize, against his own strongly held views throughout his career, that limited war and indecisive strategy—associated with the discredited eighteenth-century type of warfare—was a 'legitimate' option for belligerents whose circumstances and policy so dictated. Nevertheless, the implications and practical strategies for that type of war were left to be worked out by later societies, for which limiting war was again becoming not just a *theoretical* option. For these societies, military 'victory' increasingly appeared, while not disconnected from, more and more difficult to identify with a successful peace and an overall gain—a notion still alien to Clausewitz. A major reformulation of strategic theory was thus required, was first attempted, even before the First World War, by Julian Corbett— another Edwardian liberal—and was then developed during the interwar period by Liddell Hart.

The sort of ideas that Keynes articulated in his *The Economic Consequences of the Peace* were to become widespread among Western élites by the 'Locarno era', and a general abhorrence of war would gain massive popular hold in the West by the 1930s. It was in this context that Liddell Hart crystallized his early doctrines in the 1920s, developing them further in his more mature, less known, and largely discredited writings of the second half of the 1930. The doctrines he now advanced for the West were those of strategic, economic, and ideological containment and cold war. Liddell Hart was not alone in thinking along these lines. No longer able to embrace isolationism, both the British and American adminstrations attempted policies which veered between political accommodation and economic reward on the one hand ('appeasement') and containment and economic coercion on the other (e.g. Roosevelt's notions of 'quarantine' and 'a modern technique').[2] Neither Britain nor the United States embarked on all-out war until forced into doing so by the surprising collapse of their defences in May–June 1940 in Western Europe and in December 1941 in the Pacific. Indeed, this political and strategic order of priorities, along a

---

[2] For the origins of this posture in that 'first "reasonable" nation', Britain of the second half of the nineteenth century, see P. Kennedy, *Strategy and Diplomacy, 1870–1945* (London, 1983), 15–39.

scale stretching from isolationism to appeasement, containment and cold war, limited war, and only reluctantly fully fledged war, became the pattern for the West.[3]

While the experience of Hitler and the Second World War was to stiffen attitudes again for a while, the same aversion to and loss of faith in war were soon to return on a much wider scale and with ever-increasing force throughout the West and among those affected by its model. These attitudes now manifested themselves not only in those fortunate countries which historically had been sheltered by sea from invasion and large-scale land warfare and had experienced relatively little serious border or nationalist problems; they have, for example, become strongly evident in that quintessential 'Continental' country, the democratized and liberalized West Germany, and increasingly potent within the formerly heavily mobilized Israeli society from the 1980s on. Aware of the still major defence problems facing their countries, many observers in the West were much concerned about their societies' 'loss of belligerency' which seemed to border on an irresponsible flight from reality. By and large, however, the West's record does not look too bad, either by luck or, more probably, because, belligerent or not, Western societies have enjoyed supremacy in resources and technology over their rivals.

Scholars' attitude to Liddell Hart is likely to remain ambivalent, and not only because of the unflattering revelations about him. Too much of what he wrote is considered dogmatic, superficial, or unhistorical. These, indeed, are the very same charges that have been levelled since the eighteenth century against the liberal doctrine and liberal thinkers by their sometimes more sophisticated critics. None the less, whatever its philosophical and practical shortcomings, an amazing part of the liberal programme came to be realized simply because it proved to be almost inseparably intertwined with the West's course into modernity. And much the same may apply to Liddell Hart's ideas as well. More balanced minds than his have criticized, qualified, or rejected them. Yet, viewed from a longer perspective, his dogmatism appears to have had a Gordian knot-cutting greatness about it, cutting through genuine complexity, to be sure, but riding the most powerful currents of the age, anticipating the course of things to come. Thus, for example, Liddell

---

[3] For a concentrated elaboration of this thesis, see my 'Isolationism, Appeasement, Containment, Limited War: Western Strategic Policy from the Modern to the "Post-Modern" Era', in A. Gat and Z. Maoz (eds.), *War in A Changing World* (in preparation).

Hart's theories have often been dismissed wryly on the grounds that he advocated wars without the spilling of blood. Yet the profound reaction in the West to the casualty list of the First World War signalled a new and ultimately much enhanced unwillingness on the part of individuals and society as a whole to accept the sacrifice of life in war. Indeed, as the twentieth century draws to a close this has become an overwhelming social imperative and a reality which no government in any advanced society can ignore.

Partly for that reason and because of a decreasing willingness by civil society to enlist at all, partly because of worldwide commitments, and partly because of the growing sophistication and cost of modern weapon systems—as mechanization was followed by another revolutionary wave of electronics, affecting armies as it had air forces and navies—professionals, as opposed to conscripts, are increasingly in vogue in the developed world. Even in a country like Israel, the most extreme case to be sure, where traditionally all available manpower has been mobilized for war and where preparations for large-scale land warfare continue to be made, a change is increasingly noticeable, and was under way even before the collapse of the Soviet Union and the great advances in the peace process. The nation in arms is still there in Israel and is likely to remain, for military as well as symbolic reasons, but both for the capital-intensive, high-tech battlefield and for the lowly 'policing' of hostile populations smaller forces of professionals are increasingly preferred to the masses of reservists.

As the West at present no longer confronts a technologically advanced Second World, either Axis or Soviet, the strategic challenges it faces are obviously considerably altered and lightened. Yet much of what became the pattern of international relations during the interwar period—when the modern global industrial and trading system which had been emerging since the end of the nineteenth century took shape—seems to be enduring, deepening, or even returning. War appears increasingly removed from any obvious or immediate interest of Western societies. However, local conflicts and 'aggressive' actions by local powers, either close by or further away around the globe, pose disturbing problems. Some of these conflicts affect Western interests and spheres of influence in ways not very different from how similar conflicts affected the formal empires of the interwar period. Some, however, appear wholly irrelevant to these interests and, as then, only arouse concern either in public opinion for humanitarian reasons or as an undesirable example for others. The economy, ecology, demography, communications, cultural transfers, and nuclear proliferation are making the world increasingly interdependent. Yet the ability of advanced societies to isolate themselves from problems beyond their borders is still considerable; and their willingness to pay the price of intervention—armed or not—or ability to achieve much by it are very limited. Furthermore, as before, the West is far from being a monolith, and it is difficult to unite its members for concerted action, or prevent them from 'defecting' or from pursuing 'selfish' national interests. Under these conditions there are inherent and frustrating tensions—first experienced during the interwar period—between isolationism, a search for some sort of world order and collective security regimes, and traditional *Realpolitik* or balance-of-power considerations.

When force is applied, it is usually along the lines first mooted during the 1930s and championed by Liddell Hart. The favoured techniques include economic sanctions; the provision of money and hardware to cement coalitions and strengthen local forces against adversaries; blockade; naval and aerial actions, in which advanced countries possess a clear superiority; and limited, 'surgical' operations by highly mobile and technologically superior striking forces. Direct large-scale warfare, especially on land where casualties might be high, would tend to be avoided. Heightened awareness of the elusiveness of victory and of the intricacy of military and political causes and effects—as well as self-imposed restrictions on ruthlessness and, increasingly, nuclear proliferation—result in half-way measures, stop/go strategies, and a general indecisiveness.

These methods have had a mixed and often disappointing record, from the 1930s onward. They are politically and strategically difficult to apply, often ineffective, and they bring their own sort of psychological strains for those who practise them. Still, given the nature of modern Western societies, of their foreign affairs, strategic requirements, and cultural sensibilities, this way of war-making appears to be their norm, as much as all-out war was for their predecessors.

BIBLIOGRAPHY

ARCHIVES

Bundesarchiv-Militärarchiv, Freiburg im Breisgau.
J. F. C. Fuller's Papers, Rutgers University, New Brunswick, NJ.
George Kennan's Papers, Seeley G. Mudd Manuscript Library, Princeton University.
Liddell Hart Centre for Military Archives, King's College, London.

BOOKS AND ARTICLES

ADAMS, M., *The Great Adventure: Male Desire and the Coming of World War I* (Bloomington, Ind., 1990).
ADAMSON, W., 'Fascism and Culture: Avant-Garde and Secular Religion in the Italian Case', *Journal of Contemporary History*, 24 (1989), 411–35.
—— 'Modernism and Fascism: The Politics of Culture in Italy, 1903–1922', *American Historical Review*, 95 (1990), 359–90.
—— 'The Language of Opposition in Early Twentieth-Century Italy: Rhetorical Continuities between Prewar Florentine Avant-Gardism and Mussolini's Fascism', *Journal of Modern History*, 64 (1992), 22–51.
—— *Avant-Garde Florence: From Modernism to Fascism* (Cambridge, Mass., 1993).
ALEXANDER, M., *The Republic in Danger: General Maurice Gamelin and the Politics of French Defence, 1933–1940* (Cambridge, 1992).
ATKINSON, J. L., 'Italian Influence on the Origins of the American Concept of Strategic Bombardment', *Airpower Historian*, 4 (1957), 141–9.
BALBO, I., 'Guerra aerea', in *Enciclopedia italiana*, xviii (Rome, 1938), 92–3.
BARNETT, C., *The Swordbearers: Studies in Supreme Command in the First World War* (London, 1963).
—— *Britain and Her Army, 1509–1970* (London 1970).
—— *The Collapse of British Power* (London, 1972).
—— (ed.), *Hitler's Generals* (London, 1989).
BASSFORD, C., *Clausewitz in English: The Reception of Clausewitz in Britain and America, 1815–1945* (Oxford, 1994).
BAYLEY, S., 'Dead as a Flat Battery', *Times Literary Supplement*, 18 Aug. 1995, 25.

BECKER, J. M., *Nationalism and Culture: Gabriele d'Annunzio and Italy after the Risorgimento* (New York, 1994).

BENEWICK, R., *The Fascist Movement in Britain* (London, 1972).

BENJAMIN, W., 'The Work of Art in the Age of Mechanical Reproduction', in *Illuminations* (New York, 1968), 243–4.

—— 'Theorien des deutschen Faschismus', in *Walter Benjamin: Gesammelte Schriften*, iii (Frankfurt, 1977), 238–50; trans. in *New German Critique*, 6 (1979), 120–8.

BEN-MOSHE, T., *Churchill: Strategy and History* (Boulder, Colo., 1992).

BENNETT, E., *German Rearmament and the West, 1932–1933* (Princeton, NJ, 1979).

BERLIN, I., *Vico and Herder* (London, 1980).

BEST, G., *Humanity in Warfare* (New York, 1980).

BEYERCHEN, A. D., *Scientists under Hitler* (New Haven, Conn., 1977).

BIALER, U., '"Humanization" of Air Warfare in British Foreign Policy on the Eve of the Second World War', *Journal of Contemporary History*, 13 (1978), 79–96.

—— *The Shadow of the Bomber: The Fear of Air Attacks and British Politics, 1932–1939* (London, 1980).

BILLIG, M., *Fascists* (New York, 1978).

BLACK, R., and Louis, W. R. (eds.), *Churchill* (Oxford, 1993).

BONADEO, Al., *D'Annunzio and the Great War* (Madison, Wis., 1995).

BOND, B. (ed.), *Chief of Staff: The Diaries of Lieutenant-General Sir Henry Pownell* (London, 1972).

—— *France and Belgium, 1939–1940* (London, 1975).

—— *Liddell Hart: A Study of His Military Thought* (London, 1977).

—— *British Military Policy between the Two World Wars* (Oxford, 1980).

—— (ed.), *The First World War and British Military History* (Oxford, 1991).

BONNAL, H., *Les Maîtres de la guerre Frédérick II, Napoléon, Moltke, d'après des travaux inédits de M le général Bonnal*, ed. L. Rousset (Paris, 1899).

—— *De la méthode dans les hautes études militaires en Allemagne et en France* (Paris, 1902).

—— *De Rosbach à Ulm* (Paris, 1903).

—— *La Manoeuvre d'Iéna 1806* (Paris, 1904).

—— *La Manoeuvre de Landshut, 1808–1809* (Paris, 1905).

—— *La Manoeuvre de Vilna, 1811–1812* (Paris, 1905).

BOOG, H., and Militärgeschichtliches Forschungsamt (eds.), *The Conduct of the Air War in the Second World War* (New York, 1992).

BOURNE, J. M., *Britain and the Great War* (London, 1989).

BOYCE, R., and ROBERTSON, E. (eds.), *Paths to War: New Essays on the Origins of the Second World War* (London, 1989).

BRACHER, K. D., 'Tradition und Revolution im Nationalsozialismus', in *Zeitgeschichtliche Kontroversen* (Munich, 1976), 62–78.

BUTLER: see *Grand Strategy*

CAMON, H., *La Guerre napoléonienne* (5 vols., Paris, 1907–11).

—— *Clausewitz* (Paris, 1911).

—— *Le Système de guerre de Napoléon* (Paris, 1923).

CAPPELLUTI, F., 'The Life and Thought of Giulio Douhet' (dissertation, Rutgers University, 1967).

CARROL, D., *French Literary Fascism* (Princeton, NJ, 1995).

CARROLL, B. A., *Design for Total War* (The Hague, 1968).

CARSTEN, F., *The Reichswehr in Politics, 1918 to 1933* (Oxford, 1966).

CARVER, M., *The Apostles of Mobility* (London, 1979).

CAVENDISH, R., *A History of Magic* (London, 1977).

—— *The Magical Arts* (London, 1984).

CEADEL, M., *Pacifism in Britain, 1914–1945* (Oxford, 1980).

CEVA, L., and CURAMI, A., *La Meccanizzazione dell'esercito italiano dalle origini al 1943* (Rome, 1989).

CHACE, W., *The Political Identities of Ezra Pound and T. S. Eliot* (Stanford, Calif., 1973).

CHANDLER, D., *The Campaigns of Napoleon* (London, 1966).

CHARMLEY, J., *Chamberlain and the Lost Peace* (London, 1989).

—— *Churchill: The End of Glory* (London, 1993).

—— *Churchill's Grand Alliance* (London, 1995).

CHESNEAUX, J., *The Political and Social Ideas of Jules Verne* (London, 1972).

CHURCHILL, W., *The World Crisis, 1911–1918* (London, 1960).

—— *The Second World War* (6 vols., London, 1948–55).

CLAUSEWITZ, C. VON, *Principles of War* (Harrisburg, Penn., 1942).

—— *On War* (Princeton, NJ, 1976).

COBLEY, E., *Representing War: Form and Ideology in First World War Narratives* (Toronto, 1993).

COLE, W., *Charles A. Lindbergh and the Battle against American Intervention in World War II* (New York, 1974).

COLIN, J., *L'Éducation militaire de Napoléon* (Paris, 1900).

—— *Les Transformations de la guerre* (Paris, 1911); trans. as *The Transformation of War* (London, 1912).

COOPER, M., *The Birth of Independent Air Power* (London, 1986).

CORBETT, J., *Some Principles of Maritime Strategy* with introd. by E. Grove (Annapolis, Md., 1988).

COWLING, M., *The Impact of Hitler: British Politics and British Policy, 1933–1940* (Cambridge, 1975).

CROOK, P., *Darwinism, War and History* (Cambridge, 1994).

CROSS, C., *The Fascists in Britain* (London, 1961).

CUENO, J., *The Air Weapon, 1914–1916* (Harrisburg, Penn., 1947).

DAHRENDORF, R., *Society and Democracy in Germany* (London, 1968).

DALLEK, R., *Franklin D. Roosevelt and American Foreign Policy, 1932–1945* (New York, 1979).

D'ANNUNZIO, G., *Gabriele d'Annunzio: combattente al servizio della regia marina*, ed. G. Po (Rome, 1931).

——— *Gabriele d'Annunzio: scritti, messaggi, discorsi e rapporti militari*, ed. G. Po (Rome, 1939).

DE FELICE, R., *Fascism* (New Brunswick, NJ, 1977).

DENNIS, P., *Decision by Default: Peacetime Conscription and British Defence, 1915–1923* (London, 1972).

DEUTSCH, H., *The Conspiracy against Hitler in the Twilight War* (Minneapolis, Minn., 1968).

DOUGHTY, R. A., *The Seeds of Disaster: The Development of French Army Doctrine, 1919–1939* (Hamden, Conn., 1985).

——— *The Breaking Point: Sedan and the Fall of France, 1940* (Hamden, Conn., 1990).

DOUHET, G., *L'Automobilismo, sotto il punto di vista militare: schema di un sistema automobilistico per uso militare* (Turin, 1902).

——— *A proposito dell'articolo: gli automobili e la loro applicazione nell'arte della guerra* (Rome, 1902).

——— *Automobilismo militare e pesante* (Genoa, 1904).

——— *Cenno sommario sullo stato attuale dell'elettrotecnica* (Turin, 1905; date of composition 1903).

——— *I Problemi dell'aereonavigazione* (Rome, 1910).

——— *L'Arte della guerra* (Turin, 1915).

——— *Come finì la Grande Guerra* (Rome, 1919).

——— *L'Onorevole che non potè più mentire: racconto dei tempi ante-guerra* (Rome, 1921).

——— *Diario critico di guerra* (2 vols., Rome, 1921–2).

——— *Il Dominio dell'aria* (Rome, 1921; second enlarged edn. 1926), trans. as *The Command of the Air* (London, 1943).

——— *La Difesa nazionale* (Rome, 1925).

——— *Probabili aspetti della guerra futura* (Palermo, 1928).

——— *Le Profezie di Cassandra* (Genoa, 1931).

——— *La Guerra integrale* (Rome, 1936).

——— *Giulio Douhet: scritti inediti*, ed. A. Monti (Gennaio, 1951).

DUTAILLY, H., *Les Problèmes de l'armée de terre française (1935–1939)* (Paris, 1980).

EARLE, E. M. (ed.), *Makers of Modern Strategy from Machiavelli to the Second World War* (Princeton, NJ, 1943).

EDGERTON, D., *England and the Aeroplane: An Essay on a Militant and Technological Nation* (London, 1991).

EDWARDS, J., *The British Government and the Spanish Civil War, 1936–1939* (London, 1979).

EKSTEINS, M., *Rites of Spring: The Great War and the Birth of the Modern Age* (New York, 1990).

ERICKSON, J., *The Soviet High Command* (London, 1962).

ESSAME, H., *The Battle for Europe, 1918* (London, 1972).

ETZOLD, T. H., and Gaddis, J. L. (eds.), *Containment: Documents on American Policy and Strategy, 1945–1950* (New York, 1978).

Evolution of Soviet Operational Art, The, i: 1927–1964, trans. H. S. Orenstein, foreword and introd. by D. Glantz (London, 1995).

FALLS, C., *The First World War* (London, 1960).

FIELDS, F., *British and French Writers of the First World War* (Cambridge, 1991).

FISHMAN, R., *Urban Utopias in the Twentieth Century: Ebenezer Howard, Frank Lloyd Wright, and Le Corbusier* (New York, 1977).

FLUGEL, R., 'United States Air Power Doctrine: A Study of the Influence of William Mitchell and Giulio Douhet at the Air Corps Tactical School, 1921–1935' (dissertation, University of Oklahoma, 1965).

FREEDMAN, L., *The Evolution of Nuclear Strategy* (London, 1981).

FREI, N., 'Wie modern war der Nationalsozialismus?', *Geschichte und Gesellschaft*, 19 (1993), 367–87.

FRENCH, D., *British Economic and Strategic Planning, 1905–1915* (London, 1982).

—— *British Strategy and War Aims, 1914–1916* (London, 1986).

—— *The British Way in Warfare, 1688–2000* (London, 1990).

—— *The Strategy of the Lloyd George Coalition, 1916–1918* (Oxford, 1995).

FRITZSCHE, P., *A Nation of Fliers: German Aviation and the Popular Imagination* (Cambridge Mass., 1992).

FULLER, J. F. C. [books only; a full bibiliography of articles in journals can be found in Reid, *J. F. C. Fuller*, 261–4]:

—— *The Star in the West: A Critical Essay upon the Works of Aleister Crowley* (London, 1907).

—— *Hints on Training Territorial Infantry* (London, 1913).

—— *Training Soldiers for War* (London, 1914).

—— *Tanks in the Great War, 1914–1918* (London, 1920).

—— *The Reformation of War* (London, 1923).

—— *Sir John Moore's System of Training* (London, 1924).

—— *British Light Infantry in the Eighteenth Century* (London, 1925).

—— *On Future Warfare* (London, 1928).

—— *The Generalship of Ulysses S. Grant*, (London, 1929).

—— *Yoga: A Study of the Mystical Philosophy of the Brahmins and Buddhists* (London, 1925; 2nd edn. 1933).

—— *The Foundations of the Science of War* (London, 1926).

—— *Grant* (London, 1929).

—— *India in Revolt* (London, 1931).

—— *Armoured Warfare* (London, 1943; originally *Lectures on FSR III*, 1932).

FULLER, J. F. C. *War and Western Civilization, 1832–1932: A Study of War as a Political Instrument and the Expression of Mass Democracy* (London, 1932).

—— *The Dragon's Teeth: A Study of War and Peace* (London, 1932).

—— *Grant and Lee* (London, 1933).

—— *The Secret Wisdom of the Qabalah: A Study of Jewish Mystical Thought* (London, 1936).

—— *The First of the League Wars* (London, 1936).

—— *Memoirs of an Unconventional Soldier* (London, 1936).

—— *Towards Armageddon* (London, 1937).

—— *Thunderbolts* (London, 1946).

—— *Armament and History* (London, 1946).

—— *The Conduct of War, 1789–1961: A Study of the Impact of the French, Industrial and Russian Revolutions on War and its Conduct* (London, 1961).

FULLER, J. G., *Troop Morale and Popular Culture in the British and Dominion Armies, 1914–1918* (Oxford, 1990).

FUSSELL, P., *The Great War and Modern Memory* (Oxford, 1975).

FUTRELL, R. F., *Ideas, Concepts, Doctrine: A History of Basic Thinking in the United States Air Force, 1907–1964* (Maxwell Air Force, Alabama, 1971).

GADDIS, J. L., *Strategies of Containment: A Critical Appraisal of Postwar American National Security Policy* (New York, 1982).

—— 'The Origins of Self-Deterrence: The United States and the Non-use of Nuclear Weapons, 1945–1958', in his *The Long Peace: Inquiries Into the History of the Cold War* (New York, 1987), 104–46.

GAT, A., 'Clausewitz on Defence and Attack', *Journal of Strategic Studies*, 10 (1988), 20–6.

—— *The Origins of Military Thought from the Enlightenment to Clausewitz* (Oxford, 1989).

—— *The Development of Military Thought: The Nineteenth Century* (Oxford, 1992).

—— 'Liddell Hart's Theory of Armoured Warfare: Revising the Revisionists', *Journal of Strategic Studies*, 19 (1996), 1–30.

—— 'British Influence and the Evolution of the Panzer Arm: Myth or Reality?', *War in History*, 4(2) (1997), 150–73; 4(3) (1997), 316–38.

—— 'Isolationism, Appeasement, Containment, Limited War: Western Strategic Policy from the Modern to the "Post-Modern" Era', in A. Gat and Z. Maoz (eds.), *War in a Changing World* (in preparation).

GELLMAN, B., *Contending with Kennan* (New York, 1984).

GERMAINS, V. W., *The 'Mechanization' of War* (London, 1927).

GEYER, M., *Aufrüstung oder Sicherheit: Die Reichswehr in der Krise der Machtpolitik, 1924–1936* (Wiesbaden, 1980).

GIBBS: see *Grand Strategy*

GILBERT, M., *Winston S. Churchill*, v (London, 1976).

GLANTZ, D., *Soviet Military Operational Art: In Pursuit of Deep Battle* (London, 1991).

GOLDSTEIN, L., *The Flying Machine and Modern Literature* (London, 1986).

GOOCH, J., *The Plans of War: The General Staff and British Military Strategy, c.1900–1916* (London, 1974).

—— 'Attitude to War in Late Victorian and Edwardian England', in *The Prospect of War: Studies in British Defence Policy, 1847–1942* (London, 1981), 35–51.

GOODRICK-CLARKE, N., *The Occult Roots of Nazism* (New York, 1985).

GOUTARD, A., *1940: The Battle of France* (London 1958).

GRAHAM, D., and BIDWELL, S., *Coalitions, Politicians and Generals: Some Aspects of Command in Two World Wars* (London, 1993).

Grand Strategy: History of the Second World War, vol. i. by N. Gibbs (London, 1976); ii, by J. R. M. Butler (London, 1957); iii, by J. M. A. Gwyer (London, 1964); iv, by M. Howard (London, 1972).

GRAVES, R., *Goodbye to All That* (London, 1929).

GREGOR, A. J., *The Ideology of Fascism* (New York, 1969).

—— 'Fascism and Modernization', *World Politics*, 26 (1974), 370–84.

—— 'Fascism and the "Countermodernization of Consciousness"', *Comparative Political Studies*, 10 (1977), 239–58.

GREIL, A., 'The Modernization of Consciousness and the Appeal of Fascism', *Comparative Political Studies*, 10 (1977), 213–38.

GRIFFIN, R., *The Nature of Fascism* (London, 1991).

GRIFFITH, P., *Battle Tactics of the Western Front: The British Army's Art of Attack, 1916–18* (New Haven, Conn., 1994).

GRIFFITHS, R., *Fellow Travellers of the Right* (London, 1980).

GUDERIAN, H., *Achtung Panzer!* (London, 1992; German original 1937).

—— 'Schnelle Truppen einst und jetzt', *Militärwissenschaftliche Rundschau*, 4 (1939), 237–8.

—— *Panzer Leader* (London, 1952).

GUNSBURG, J. A., *Divided and Conquered: The French High Command and the Defeat of the West, 1940* (London, 1979).

GWYER: see *Grand Strategy*

HADDOW, G. H., and GROSZ, P., *The German Giants: The Story of the R Planes, 1914–1919* (London, 1969).

HAMILTON, A., *The Appeal of Fascism* (London, 1971).

HANCOCK, W. K., and GOWING, M. M., *British War Economy: History of the Second World War—Civil Series* (London, 1949).

HANKEY, M., *The Supreme Command* (2 vols., London, 1961).

HARPER, G. M. (ed.), *Yeats and the Occult* (Canada, 1975).

HARRIS, J. P., *Men, Ideas and Tanks: British Military Thought and Armoured Forces, 1903–1939* (Manchester, 1995).

HARVEY, A. D., *Collision of Empires: Britain in Three World Wars, 1793–1945* (London, 1992).

HASLAM, J., *The Soviet Union and the Struggle for Collective Security in Europe* (London, 1984).

HASTINGS, M., *Bomber Command* (New York, 1979).

HAUNER, M., 'Czechoslovakia as a Military Factor in British Considerations of 1938', *Journal of Strategic Studies*, 1 (1978), 194–222.

HENDRIX, J., 'The Interwar Army and Mechanization: The American Approach', *Journal of Strategic Studies*, 16 (1993), 77–81.

HERF, J., *Reactionary Modernism* (Cambridge, 1984).

HEWITT, A., *Fascist Modernism: Aesthetics, Politics, and the Avant-Garde* (Stanford, Calif., 1993).

HIGHAM, R., *The Military Intellectuals in Britain, 1918–1939* (New Brunswick, NJ, 1966).

HINSLEY, F. H., *British Intelligence in the Second World War*, i (London, 1979).

HOCHMAN, E., *Architects of Fortune: Mies van der Rohe and the Third Reich* (New York, 1989).

HOCHMAN, J., *The Soviet Union and the Failure of Collective Security, 1934–1938* (London, 1984).

HOMZE, E., *Arming the Luftwaffe* (Lincoln, Nebr., 1976).

HOUGH, G., *The Mystery Religion of W. B. Yeats* (Brighton, Sussex, 1984).

HOWARD, M. (ed.), *The Theory and Practice of War* (London, 1965).

—— *The Mediterranean Strategy in the Second World War* (London, 1968).

—— 'The Classical Strategists', in *Studies in War and Peace* (London, 1970).

—— *The Continental Commitment* (London, 1972).

—— 'Liddell Hart' (1970) and 'The British Way in Warfare: A Reappraisal' (1974), repr. in *The Causes of War* (London, 1984), 189–207, 237–47.

—— 'Empire, Race and War in pre-1914 Britain', in his *The Lessons of History* (Oxford, 1991), 63–80.

—— See also *Grand Strategy*.

HOWE, E., *The Magicians of the Golden Dawn: A Documentary History of a Magical Order, 1887–1923* (London, 1972).

—— *Astrology and the Third Reich* (Wellingborough, Northants, 1984).

HUGHES, T., *American Genesis: A Century of Invention and Technological Enthusiasm, 1870–1970* (New York, 1989).

HUGHES, T., and HUGHES, A. (eds.), *Lewis Mumford* (Oxford, 1990).

HURLEY, A., *Billy Mitchell: Crusader for Air Power* (New York, 1964).

HYDE, H. M., *British Air Policy Between the Wars* (London, 1976).

HYNES, S., *A War Imagined: The First World War and English Culture* (London, 1990).

INGOLD, F. P., *Literatur und Aviatik: Europäische Flugdichtung, 1909–1927* (Basel, 1978), 26–49.

ITALIAANDER, R., *Italo Balbo* (Munich, 1942).

JAMESON, F., *Fables of Aggression: Wyndham Lewis, the Modernist as Fascist* (Berkeley, Calif., 1979).

JOES, A. J., 'On the Modernity of Fascism', *Comparative Political Studies*, 10 (1977), 259–68.

JOHNSON, D. L., *Frank Lloyd Wright versus America: The 1930s* (Cambridge, Mass., 1990).

JOLL, J., 'F. T. Marinetti: Futurism and Fascism', in his *Three Intellectuals in Politics* (New York, 1965), 133–78.

JONES, H. A., *The War in the Air*, v and vi (Oxford, 1935 and 1937).

JORDAN, M., *Machine-Age Ideology: Social Engineering and American Liberalism, 1911–1939* (Chapel Hill, NC, 1994).

JOSEPHSON, M., *Edison* (London, 1961).

JÜNGER, E., *Sämtliche Werke*, i (Stuttgart, 1978), vii (1980), viii (1981).

—— 'Die Technik der Zukunftsschlacht', *Militär-Wochenblatt*, 1 Oct. 1921, 287–90.

—— *Storm of Steel: From the Diary of a German Storm-Troop Officer on the Western Front* (New York, 1929).

—— *Copse 125: A Chronicle from the Trench Warfare of 1918* (London, 1930).

KAISER, D. E., *Economic Diplomacy and the Origins of the Second World War: Germany, Britain, France, and Eastern Europe, 1930–1939* (Princeton, NJ, 1980).

KAYSEN, C., 'Is War Obsolete? A Review Essay', *International Security*, 14 (1990), 42–63.

KENNAN, G. F., *American Diplomacy* (New York, 1985).

—— *Realities of American Foreign Policy* (Princeton, NJ, 1954).

—— *Russia, the Atom and the West* (New York, 1958).

—— *Memoirs* (2 vols., Boston, 1967, 1972).

KENNEDY, J. F., *Why Britain Slept?* (New York, 1940).

KENNEDY, P., *The Rise and Fall of British Naval Mastery* (London, 1976).

—— and NICHOLLS, A. (eds.), *Nationalist and Racialist Movements in Britain and Germany before 1914* (London, 1981).

—— *Strategy and Diplomacy, 1870–1945* (London, 1983).

—— *The Rise and Fall of the Great Powers* (London, 1989).

KENNETT, L., *A History of Strategic Bombing* (New York, 1982).

—— *The First Air War, 1914–1918* (New York, 1991).

KEYNES, J. M., *The Economic Consequences of the Peace* (London, 1920).

KIEFT, D. O., *Belgium's Return to Neutrality* (Oxford, 1972).

KLEMPERER, K. VON, *German Resistance against Hitler: The Search for Allies Abroad, 1938–1945* (Oxford, 1992).

KOLIOPOULOS, J. S., *Greece and the British Connection, 1935–1941* (Oxford, 1977).

KRAFT, B., *The Peace Ship: Henry Ford's Pacifist Adventure in the First World War* (New York, 1978).

LACEY, R., *Ford: The Men and the Machine* (Boston, 1986).

LARSEN, B., *Lindbergh of Minnesota* (New York, 1973).

LARSEN, S. T., HAGTVET, B., and MYKLEBUS , J. P. (eds.), *Who Were the Fascists?* (Bergen, 1980).

LAWLOR, S., *Churchill and the Politics of War, 1940–1941* (Cambridge, 1994).

LAWRENCE, T. E., 'The Evolution of A Revolt', *Army Quarterly*, 1 (Oct. 1920).

—— *Revolt in the Desert* (New York, 1927).

—— *The Seven Pillars of Wisdom* (New York, 1936).

—— *T. E. Lawrence to his Biographer Liddell Hart*, ed. B. H. Liddell Hart (London, 1939).

LE BON, G., *The Crowd: A Study of the Popular Mind* (London, 1896).

—— *The Psychology of Peoples* (London, 1899).

LE CORBUSIER, *Aircraft* (New York, 1988, original 1935).

LEDEEN, M., *The First Duce: D'Annunzio at Fiume* (Baltimore, 1977).

LEEB, RITTER VON, *Defence* (Harrisburg, Penn., 1943; originally in *Militärwissenschaftliche Rundschau*, 1936–7).

LEED, E. J., *No Man's Land: Combat and Identity in World War I* (Cambridge, 1979).

LEGRO, J. W., *Cooperation Under Fire: Anglo-German Restraint during World War II* (London, 1995).

LEVINE, I. D., *Mitchell: Pioneer of Air Power* (New York, 1943).

LIDDELL HART, B. H. [books only]:

—— *New Methods in Infantry Training* (Cambridge, 1918).

—— *The Framework of a Science of Infantry Tactics* (London, 1922; expanded and reissued 1923, 1926).

—— *Paris, or the Future of War* (London, 1925).

—— *A Greater than Napoleon: Scipio* (London, 1926).

—— *Great Captains Unveiled* (London, 1927).

—— *The Remaking of Modern Armies* (London, 1927).

—— *Sherman* (London, 1929).

—— *The Decisive Wars of History* (London, 1929); later *Strategy: The Indirect Approach*, rev. and enlarged edns.: 1941, 1946, 1954, 1967.

—— *The Real War* (London, 1930); enlarged as *A History of the World War, 1914–1918* (London, 1934).

—— *Foch* (London, 1931).

—— *The British Way in Warfare* (London, 1932).

—— *The Ghost of Napoleon* (New Haven, Conn., 1934).

—— *'T. E. Lawrence': In Arabia and After* (London, 1934).

—— *When Britain Goes to War* (London, 1935).

—— *Europe in Arms* (London, 1937).

—— *Through the Fog of War* (London, 1938).

—— *The Defence of Britain* (London, 1939).

—— *Dynamic Defence* (London, 1940).

—— *The Current of War* (London, 1941).
—— *This Expanding War* (London, 1942).
—— *Thoughts on War* (London, 1944).
—— *Why Don't We Learn from History?* (London, 1944).
—— *The Revolution in Warfare* (London, 1946).
—— *The Other Side of the Hill* (London, 1948).
—— *The Defence of the West* (London, 1950).
—— (ed.), *The Rommel Papers* (London, 1953).
—— *The Tanks* (2 vols., London, 1959).
—— *Deterrent or Defence* (London, 1960).
—— *Memoirs* (2 vols., London, 1965).
—— *The Second World War* (London, 1970).
'Liddell Hart: The Captain Who Taught Generals', *Listener*, 28 Dec. 1972.
LINDBERGH, A. M., *The Wave of the Future: A Confession of Faith* (New York, 1940).
—— *The Flower and the Nettle: Diaries and Letters, 1936–1939* (New York, 1976).
—— *War Within and Without: Diaries and Letters, 1939–1944* (New York, 1980).
LINDBERGH, C., *The War Time Journals of Charles A. Lindbergh* (New York, 1970).
—— *Autobiography of Value* (New York, 1978).
LLOYD GEORGE, D., *War Memoirs* (London, 1936).
LOOSE, G., *Ernst Jünger* (New York, 1974).
LUNN, K., and THURLOW, R. (eds.), *British Fascism* (London, 1980).
LUVAAS, J., *The Education of an Army* (London, 1965).
MACDONALD, C. A., *The United States, Britain and Appeasement, 1936–1939* (London, 1981).
MACISAAC, D. (ed.), *The United States Strategic Bombing Survey* (10 vols., New York, 1976).
MACKSEY, K., *Guderian: Panzer General* (London, 1975).
—— *The Tank Pioneers* (London, 1981).
MACLEOD, R., and KELLY, D. (eds.), *The Ironside Diaries, 1937–1940* (London, 1962).
MAIER, C., 'Between Taylorism and Technocracy: European Ideologies and the Vision of Industrial Productivity in the 1920s', *Journal of Contemporary History*, 5(2) (1970), 27–61.
MAILLARD, L., *Éléments de la guerre* (Paris, 1891).
MARDER, A., *Portrait of an Admiral: The Life and Papers of Sir Herbert Richmond* (Cambridge, Mass., 1952).
MARINETTI, F. T., *Selected Writings* (New York, 1972).
MARKOV, V., *Russian Futurism: A History* (Berkeley, Calif., 1968).
MARTEL, G. Le Q., *In the Wake of the Tank* (London, 1931).
—— *An Outspoken Soldier* (London, 1949).

MARTIN, A., *The Mask of the Prophet: The Extraordinary Fictions of Jules Verne* (Oxford, 1990).

MASON, T., OVERY, R. and KAISER, D., 'Debate: Germany, "Domestic Crisis" and War in 1939', *Past and Present*, 122 (1989), 200–40.

MATTIOLI, G., *Mussolini Aviator, and His Work for Aviation* (Rome, 1939).

MAY, E. R. (ed.), *Knowing One's Enemies: Intelligence Assessment before the Two World Wars* (Princeton, NJ, 1984).

MAYERS, D., *George Kennan and the Dilemmas of US Foreign Policy* (New York, 1988).

MEARSHEIMER, J., *Conventional Deterrence* (Ithaca, NY, 1983).

—— *Liddell Hart and the Weight of History* (London, 1988).

MEDLICOTT, W. N., *The Economic Blockade* (2 vols., London, 1978).

MESSERSCHMIDT, M., *Die Wehrmacht im NS-Staat: Zeit der Indoktrination* (Hamburg, 1969).

MIDDLEMAS, K., *Diplomacy of Illusion: The British Government and Germany, 1937–39* (London, 1972).

MILFORD, J. (ed.), *The Attraction of Fascism: Social Psychology and Aesthetics of the 'Triumph of the Right'* (New York, 1990).

Militärgeschitliches Forschungsamt (ed.), *Germany and the Second World War* (Oxford, 1990–); German original: *Das deutsche Reich und der zweite Weltkrieg* (10 vols., Stuttgart, 1979–).

MINNEY, R. J., *The Private Papers of Hore-Belisha* (London, 1960).

MITCHELL, W., *Our Air Force* (New York, 1921).

—— *Winged Defence* (New York, 1925).

—— *Skyways* (Philadelphia, 1930).

—— *Memoirs of World War I* (New York, 1960).

MOMMSEN, H., 'Nationalsozialismus als vorgetäuschte Modernisierung', in *Der Nationalsozialismus und die deutsche Gesellschaft* (Hamburg, 1991), 405–27.

MOMMSEN, W., and KETTENACKER, L. (eds.), *The Fascist Challenge and the Policy of Appeasement* (London, 1983).

MORRIS, A. J. A., *The Scaremongers: The Advocacy of War and Rearmament, 1896–1914* (London, 1984).

MORROW, J., *The Great War in the Air* (Washington, DC, 1993).

MOSLEY, O., *My Life* (London, 1968).

MOSSE, G., *The Crisis of German Ideology* (New York, 1964).

—— *The Nationalization of the Masses* (New York, 1975).

—— *Nazism* (Oxford, 1978).

—— (ed.), *International Fascism* (London, 1979).

—— *Masses and Man: Nationalist and Fascist Perception of Reality* (Detroit, 1987).

MUELLER, J., 'The Essential Irrelevance of Nuclear Weapons: Stability in the Postwar World', *International Security*, 13 (2) (1988), 55–79.

—— *Retreat from Doomsday: The Obsolescence of Major War* (New York, 1989).

MÜLLER, K.-J., *Das Heer und Hitler: Armee und nationalsozialistisches Regime, 1933–1940* (Stuttgart, 1969).

—— *General Ludwig Beck: Studien und Dokumente* (Boppard a.R., 1980).

—— *The Army, Politics and Society in Germany, 1933–45* (Manchester, 1987).

MUMFORD, L., *Technics and Civilization* (London, 1934).

—— *The Culture of Cities* (London, 1938).

MURRAY, W., 'German Air Power and the Munich Crisis', in B. Bond and I. Roy (eds.), *War and Society Yearbook*, 2 (1977), 114–15.

—— *The Change in the European Balance of Power, 1938–1939* (Princeton, NJ, 1984).

—— *Luftwaffe* (Baltimore, 1985).

NEHRING, W., *Kampfwagen an die Front!* (Leipzig, 1934).

—— *Die Geschichte der deutschen Panzerwaffe, 1916 bis 1945* (Berlin, 1969).

NEILSON, K., *Strategy and Supply: The Anglo-Russian Alliance, 1914–1917* (London, 1984).

NELSON, A. K. (ed.), *The State Department Policy Staff Papers, 1947–1949* (3 vols., New York, 1983).

NEWMAN, S., *March 1939*: The British Guarantee to Poland (Oxford, 1976).

NOIRAY, J., *Le Romancier et la machine: l'image de la machine dans le roman français (1850–1900)*, ii (Paris, 1982).

NOLTE, E., *Three Faces of Fascism* (New York, 1969).

NYE, D., *Henry Ford: 'Ignorant Idealist'* (New York, 1979).

NYE, R. A., *The Origins of Crowd Psychology: Gustave Le Bon and the Crisis of Mass Democracy in the Third Republic* (London, 1975).

OGORKIEWICZ, R., *Armoured Forces* (London, 1970).

O'NEILL, R., *The German Army and the Nazi Party, 1933–1939* (London, 1966).

OSWALD, W., *Kraftfahrzeuge und Panzer des Reichswehr, Wehrmacht und Bundeswehr* (Stuttgart, 1982).

OVERY, R. J., 'From Uralbomber to Amerikabomber: The Luftwaffe and Strategic Bombing', *Journal of Strategic Studies*, 1 (1978), 154–78.

—— *The Air War, 1939–1945* (London, 1980).

—— *The Nazi Economic Recovery, 1932–1938* (London, 1982).

—— 'Hitler's War and the German Economy: A Reinterpretation', *Economic History Review*, 35 (1982).

—— *The Origins of the Second World War* (London, 1987).

—— *War and Economy in the Third Reich* (Oxford, 1994).

PAILLAT, C., *Le Désastre de 1940* (2 vols., Paris, 1983, 1984).

PARET, P. (ed.), *Makers of Modern Strategy from Machiavelli to the Nuclear Age* (Princeton, NJ, 1986).

PARKER, P., *The Old Lie: The Great War and the Public-School Ethos* (London, 1987).

PARKER, R. A. C., 'British Rearmament, 1936–9: Treasury, Trade Unions and Skilled Labour', *English Historical Review*, 96 (1981), 306–18.

PARKER, R. A. C., *Chamberlain and Appeasement: British Policy and the Coming of the Second World War* (London, 1993).

PAYNE, S., *Fascism: Comparison and Definition* (Madison, Wis., 1980).

—— *A History of Fascism, 1914–1945* (Madison, Wis., 1995).

PEDEN, G. C., *British Rearmament and the Treasury, 1932–1939* (Edinburgh, 1979).

—— 'A Matter of Timing: The Economic Background to British Foreign Policy, 1937–1939', *History*, 69 (1984), 15–28.

PIERRON, É., *Comment s'est formé le génie militaire de Napoléon Ier?* (Paris, 1889).

PLAYNE, C. E., *The Pre-War Mind in Britain* (London, 1928).

PONTING, C., *1940: Myth and Reality* (London, 1990).

POST, G. Jr., *Dilemmas of Appeasement: British Deterrence and Defence, 1934–1937* (London, 1993).

POSTAN, M. M., *British War Production: History of the Second World War—Civil Series* (London, 1952).

PRAZMOWSKA, A., *Britain, Poland and the Eastern Front, 1939* (Cambridge, 1987).

PRESTON, A. (ed.), *General Staffs and Diplomacy before the Second World War* (London, 1978).

PRESTON, P., *Franco* (London, 1993).

PRINZ, M., and ZITELMANN, R. (eds.), *Nationalsozialismus und Modernisierung* (Darmstadt, 1995).

PRIOR, R., *Churchill's 'World Crisis' as History* (London, 1983).

—— and WILSON, T. *'Command on the Western Front: The Military Career of Sir Henry Rawlinson', 1914–18* (Oxford, 1992).

RAUCH, M., 'Anti-Modernismus im Nationalsozialistischen Staat', *Historisches Jahrbuch*, 107 (1987), 94–121.

REID, B. H., 'T. E. Lawrence and Liddell Hart', *History*, 70 (1985), 218–31.

—— *J. F. C. Fuller: Military Thinkers* (London, 1987).

REMARQUE, E. M., *All Quiet on the Western Front* (London, 1929).

RENNEBERG, M., and WALKER, M. (eds.), *Science, Technology and National Socialism* (Cambridge, 1994).

REYNOLDS, D., *The Creation of the Anglo-American Alliance, 1937–1941* (London, 1981).

—— 'Churchill and the British "Decision" to Fight On in 1940: Right Policy, Wrong Reasons', in R. Langhorne (ed.), *Diplomacy and Intelligence during the Second World War* (Cambridge, 1985).

—— 'Great Britain and the Security "Lessons" of the Second World War', in R. Ahmann, A. M. Birke, and M. Howard (eds.), *The Quest for Stability: Problems of West European Security, 1918–1957* (Oxford, 1993), 301–4.

RICHMOND, H., *National Policy and Naval Strength* (London, 1928).

—— *Sea Power in the Modern World* (London, 1934).

ROBERTS, G., *The Unholy Alliance: Stalin's Pact with Hitler* (London, 1989).

ROBERTSON, W., *Soldiers and Statesmen, 1914–1918* (London, 1926).

ROSE, N., *Churchill* (London, 1994).

ROSEMAN, M., 'National Socialism and Modernisation', in R. Bessel (ed.), *Fascist Italy and Nazi Germany: Comparisons and Contrasts* (Cambridge, 1996), 197–229.

ROSKILL, S., *Naval Policy between the Wars* (2 vols., London, 1968, 1976).

—— *Hankey, Man of Secrets* (3 vols., London, 1970, 1974).

SAMUELS, M., *Doctrine and Dogma: German and British Infantry Tactics in the First World War* (New York, 1992).

SASSOON, S., *Memoirs of an Infantry Officer* (London, 1930).

SCHENBAUM, D., *Hitler's Social Revolution* (New York, 1966).

SCHILDT, A., 'NS-Regime, Modernisierung und Moderne', *Tel Aviver Jahrbuch für deutsche Geschichte*, 23 (1994), 3–22.

SCHMIDT, G., *The Politics and Economics of Appeasement* (New York, 1986).

SCHONBACK, M., *Native American Fascism during the 1930s and 1940s* (New York, 1985).

SCHURMAN, D. M., *The Education of a Navy: The Development of British Naval Strategic Thought, 1867–1914* (London, 1965).

—— *Julian S. Corbett, 1854–1922* (London, 1981).

SCHWARZ, H.-P., *Der konservative Anarchist: Politik und Zeitkritik Ernst Jüngers* (Freiburg, 1962).

SCHWELLER, R., 'Domestic Structure and Preventive War: Are Democracies More Pacific?', *World Politics*, 44 (1992), 235–69.

SEARLE, G. R., *The Quest for National Efficiency* (Oxford, 1971).

SENFF, H., *Die Entwicklung der Panzerwaffe im deutschen Heer zwischen den beiden Weltkriegen* (Frankfurt a.M., 1969).

SERGÈ, C., *Italo Balbo: A Fascist Life* (Berkeley, Calif., 1987).

—— 'Douhet in Italy: Prophet without Honor?', *Aerospace Historian*, June 1979, 69–80.

—— 'Giulio Douhet: Strategist, Theorist, Prophet?', *Journal of Strategic Studies*, 15 (1992), 351–66.

SHAND, J., 'The Reichsautobahn: Symbol for the Third Reich', *Journal of Contemporary History*, 19 (1984), 189–200.

SHAY, R. P., *British Rearmament in the Thirties* (Princeton, NJ, 1977).

SIMPKIN, P., *Kitchener's Army* (Manchester, 1988).

SIMPKIN, R., *Race to the Swift: Thoughts on Twenty-First Century Warfare* (London, 1985).

—— *Deep Battle: The Brainchild of Marshal Tukhachevsky* (London, 1987).

SKIDELSKY, R., *Oswald Mosley* (London, 1981).

SLESSOR, J., *Air Power and Armies* (Oxford, 1936).

—— *The Central Blue* (London, 1956).

SMITH, M., *British Air Strategy Between the Wars* (Oxford, 1984).

—— 'The Allied Air Offensive', in J. Gooch (ed.), *Decisive Campaigns of the Second World War* (London, 1990), 67–83.

SOKOL, C., *The German–American Bund as a Model of American Fascism, 1924–1940* (Ann Arbor, Mich., 1979).

SPENGLER, O., *Decline of the West* (London, 1926).

SPIELBERGER, W., *Die Panzer-Kampfwagen 35(t) and 38(t)* (Stuttgart, 1980).

STANZEL, F. K., and Martin Löschnig (eds.), *Intimate Enemies: English and German Literary Reactions to the Great War* (Heidelberg, 1993).

STEPHANSON, A., *Kennan and the Art of Foreign Policy* (Cambridge, Mass., 1989).

STERN, J. P., *Ernst Jünger* (New Haven, Conn., 1953).

STERNHELL, Z., *Neither Right nor Left* (Berkeley, Calif., 1986).

STRACHAN, H., 'The British Way in Warfare', in D. Chandler (ed.), *The Oxford Illustrated History of the British Army* (Oxford, 1994), 417–34.

STROMBERG, R., *Redemption by War: The Intellectuals and 1914* (Lawrence, Kan., 1982).

SURETTE, L., *The Birth of Modernism: Ezra Pound, T. S. Eliot, W. B. Yeats, and the Occult* (London, 1993).

SUSSER, L., 'Fascist and Anti-Fascist Attitudes in Britain between the Wars' (dissertation, University of Oxford, 1988).

SWINTON, E., *Eyewitness* (London, 1932).

SYMONDS, J., *The Great Beast: The Life and Magic of Aleister Crowley* (London, 1971).

TAYLOR, A. J. P. et al. (eds.), *Churchill: Four Faces and the Man* (London, 1969)

—— (ed.), *Lloyd George: Twelve Essays* (London, 1971).

—— *British History, 1914–1945* (London, 1975).

—— *The Second World War* (London, 1975).

—— Letter to Kingsley Martin, printed in *London Review of Books*, 10 May 1990, 13.

TAYLOR, B. B., *Le Corbusier: The City of Refuge, Paris 1929/33* (Chicago, 1987).

TAYLOR, T., *Munich: The Price of Peace* (New York, 1979).

TERRAIN, J., *Douglas Haig: The Educated General* (London, 1963).

—— *To Win a War, 1918* (London, 1978).

TIMMS, E., and COLLIER, P. (eds.), *Visions and Blueprints: Avant-Garde Culture and Radical Politics in Early Twentieth-Century Europe* (Manchester, 1988).

TISDALL, C., and BOZZOLLA, A., *Futurism* (London, 1977).

TOFFLER, A. and TOFFLER, H., *The Third Wave* (New York, 1980).

—— *War and Anti-War* (New York, 1993).

TOMPSON, N., *The Anti-Appeasers: Conservative Opposition to Appeasement in the 1930s* (Oxford 1971).

TOWLE, P., 'British Security and Disarmament Policy in Europe in the 1920s', in R. Ahmann, A. M. Birke, and M. Howard (eds.), *The Quest for Stability: Problems of West European Security, 1918–1957* (Oxford, 1993), 127–53.

TRAVERS, T., 'Future Warfare: H. G. Wells and British Military Theory, 1895–1916', in Brian Bond and I. Roy (eds.), *War and Society* (London, n.d.), 67–87.

—— The Killing Ground: The British Army, the Western Front and the Emergence of Modern Warfare, 1900–1918 (London, 1987).

—— How the War Was Won: Command and Technology in the British Army on the Western Front, 1917–1918 (London, 1992).

TRIANDAFILLOV, V. K., The Nature of the Operations of Modern Armies, with foreword by J. Kipp and introd. by J. Schneider (Ilford, Essex, 1994).

TRYTHALL, A. J., 'Boney' Fuller: The Intellectual General (London, 1977).

TURNER, H. Jr. (ed.), Reappraisals of Fascism (New York, 1975).

ULAM, A. B., Expansion and Coexistence: The History of Soviet Foreign Policy, 1917–67 (London, 1968).

VAN CREVELD, M., Hitler's Strategy, 1940–1941: The Balkan Clue (Cambridge, 1973).

—— The Transformation of War (New York, 1991).

VERGANO, P., Origins of Aviation in Italy, 1783–1918 (Genoa, 1964).

VERNE, J. J., Jules Verne (New York, 1976).

VITAL, D., The Survival of Small States (Oxford, 1971).

VOGELSANG, T., 'Hitlers Brief an Reichenau vom 4. Dezember 1932', Vierteljahrshefte für Zeitgeschichte, 7 (1959), 429–37.

WAGAR, W., H. G. Wells and the World State (New York, 1961).

WARK, W. K., The Ultimate Enemy: British Intelligence and Nazi Germany, 1933–1939 (London, 1985).

WARLIMONT, W., Inside Hitler's Headquarters, 1939–1945 (New York, 1964).

WATT, D. C., Succeeding John Bull: America in Britain's Place, 1900–1975 (Cambridge, 1984).

—— Personalities and Appeasement (Austin, Tex., 1991).

WEBB, J., The Occult Establishment (La Salle, Ill., 1976).

WEBER, E., Varieties of Fascism (Princeton, NJ, 1964).

WEBSTER, C., and FRANKLAND, N., The Strategic Air Offensive against Germany, 1939–1945 (4 vols., London, 1961).

WEINBERG, G. L., Germany and the Soviet Union, 1939–1941 (London, 1954).

—— A World at Arms: A Global History of World War II (Cambridge, 1994).

WEISS, J., The Fascist Tradition (New York, 1967).

WELLS, H. G., Anticipation of the Reaction of Mechanical and Scientific Progress upon Human Life and Thought (London, 1902).

—— The War in the Air (1908).

—— The World Set Free (1914).

—— Italy, France and Britain at War (New York, 1917).

—— The Outline of History (London, 1920).

—— The World Set Free (London, 1927).

—— The Shape of Things to Come (1933).

—— Experiment in Autobiography (New York, 1934).

WHEELER-BENNETT, J., The Nemesis of Power: The German Army in Politics, 1918–1945 (New York, 1967).

WHELDON, J., *Machine Age Armies* (London, 1968).

WIK, R., *Henry Ford and Grass Roots America* (Ann Arbor, Mich., 1972).

WILKINSON, S., *War and Policy* (London, 1900), 150–4.

—— *The French Army Before Napoleon* (Oxford, 1915).

—— *Government and the War* (London, 1918).

—— *The Defence of Piedmont, 1742–1748* (Oxford, 1927).

—— 'Killing No Murder: An Examination of Some New Theories of War', *Army Quarterly* (Oct. 1927), 14–21.

—— *The Rise of General Bonaparte* (Oxford, 1930).

WILLIAMSON, S., *The Politics of Grand Strategy: Britain and France Prepare for War* (Cambridge, Mass., 1969).

WINTER, D., *Haig's Command: A Reassessment* (London, 1991).

WINTER, J., *The Great War and the British People* (London, 1986).

—— *Sites of Memory, Sites of Mourning: The Great War in European Cultural History* (Cambridge, 1995).

WINTON, H., *To Change an Army: General Sir John Burnett-Stuart and British Armoured Doctrine, 1927–1938* (Lawrence, Kan., 1988).

WOHL, R., *The Generation of 1914* (Cambridge, Mass., 1979).

—— *A Passion for Wings: Aviation and Western Imagination, 1908–1918* (New Haven, 1994).

WOLLGAST, S., '"Technikphilosophie" während der Herrschaft des deutschen Faschismus', in his and G. Kovács (eds.), *Technikphilosophie in Vergangenheit und Gegenwart* (Berlin, 1984).

WOODWARD, D. R., *Lloyd George and the Generals* (London, 1983).

WOOLF, S. J. (ed.), *European Fascism* (New York, 1969).

YOUNG, R. J., *In Command of France: French Foreign Policy and Military Planning, 1933–1940* (Cambridge, Mass., 1978).

Index

Acheson, Dean 303
Acton, Lord 233
Adam, Ronald 259
Aldington, Richard 135
Aristotle 17 n.

Bacon, Francis 17 n., 25
Badoglio, Pietro 68–9
Balbo, Italo 67–9, 75, 102, 109
Baldwin, Stanley 186, 207, 210, 264
Barès, Commandant 52
Barrington-Ward, Robin 189, 193, 202
Beaverbrook, Lord 239, 266
Beck, Ludwig 90, 91, 97, 98, 99, 120, 198, 201
Bell, George Bishop of Chichester 284
Benjamin, Walter 47, 88 n.
Benn, Gotfried 101
Bergson, Henri 22
Berkeley, George 16, 17
Bernardi, Mario de 69
Bernhardi, Friedrich von 80
Bètunda, Mario 48
Blériot, Louis 48, 55, 63
Bloch, Ivan 10, 25
Blomberg, Werner von 89–100, 102, 115
Blunden, Edmund 135
Bolling, Raynal C. 71
Bonaparte, Napoleon 24, 48, 58, 91, 150–5, 158, 159, 161, 162, 165–6, 178, 182, 285
Bonnal, Henri 22, 151–3
Boothby, Robert 199
Bottomley, Horatio 76

Bourcet, Pierre de 152, 161
Brook, Rupert 132
Brusati, General 60
Burnett-Stuart, John 208
Buzzi, Paolo 48

Cadorna, Luigi 51, 52, 60, 61
Caemmerer, Rudolf von 154
Calderare, Mario 48
Camon, Hubert 151–3
Caproni, Giovanni Battista 50–1, 52, 56, 61, 71, 72, 74
Carlyle, Thomas 9, 14
Cecil, Lord 230
Chamberlain, Neville 186, 187, 193, 196, 199, 200, 203, 205, 207–9, 210, 215, 224, 226, 228, 229, 237, 241, 252, 271
Chamier, J. A. 77
Churchill, Winston 27, 78, 128, 138, 167, 168, 169, 171, 180, 186, 187, 199, 200, 202, 203, 210, 217, 221, 226, 240, 244, 249, 264, 265, 266, 267–8, 269, 270, 271, 272, 273, 274, 275, 276, 278, 279, 280, 281, 282, 283, 286
Clausewitz, Carl von 25, 34, 115, 153–4, 159, 160–1, 162, 163, 167, 172–7, 179, 235, 292, 306–7
Coffin, Howard 71
Colin, Jean 143, 151–3, 155, 157, 160, 161, 162
Colomb, Philip 180
Comte, Auguste 7, 9, 16, 17
Condorcet, M. J. A. N. Marquis de 34

Cooper, Duff 203
Copernicus, Nicolaus 25
Corbett, Julian 151, 157–62, 173, 176, 181–2, 270, 282, 307
Crowley, Aleister 16–19, 24, 26
Curtiss, Glenn 48

Daladier, Édouard 216, 217, 252
Dalton, Hugh 199, 202, 230, 231, 266
D'Annunzio, Gabriele 5, 43–5, 48, 49–50, 51, 52, 53, 55, 56, 61, 62, 64, 67, 78, 122
Darwin, Charles; Darwinism; social Darwinism 8, 12, 14, 15, 22, 23, 25, 26, 35, 39, 43, 131, 148
Davis, D. 117
Dawson, Geoffrey 189, 193, 202, 232
Déat, Marcel 5
De Gaulle, Charles 116, 217
Delbrück, Hans 159, 176
De Man, Henry 5
Descartes, René 17, 25
Deverell, Cyril 191, 225, 248, 255
Dewey, John 109
Dill, John 199, 275
Don Juan 48
Doriot, Jacques 5
Douhet, Giulio 52–62, 65–7, 70, 71, 72, 73, 74, 75, 109, 121
Drake, Francis 181
Dreyfus, Alfred 7
Driant, Émile 48
Dugan, Winston 142

Eden, Anthony 186, 190, 191, 202, 203, 221, 230, 264, 266, 274, 275, 286
Edison, Thomas Alva 105, 107
Eliot, T. S. 18
Engell, Norman 173
Engels, Friedrich 116

Ferrarin, Arturo 69
Fichte, Johann Gottlieb 17
Fisher, John 181 n.
Fiske, Bradely 73
Foch, Ferdinand 25, 29, 96, 143, 144, 151, 154, 167, 170, 244
Ford, Henry; Fordism 27, 93, 105–7, 108, 110, 115
Fourier, Charles 7, 9, 11
Franco, Francisco 193
Frederick II, of Prussia 182
Fritch, Werner von 90, 97
Frunze, M. V. 116
Fullam, William 73
Fuller, John Frederick Charles 13–42, 43, 59, 60, 66, 73, 75, 77, 78, 85, 87, 96, 109, 110, 115, 117–19, 121, 123, 124, 127, 138, 143–50, 155, 156, 157, 161 n., 162, 164, 165, 166, 167, 168, 170, 172, 176, 225, 233, 234, 243, 245, 258, 272, 284, 290

Gallieni, Joseph Simon 292
Gamelin, Maurice 216, 218, 251 n.
Gardner, Lester 74
Garibaldi, Giuseppe 5
Geddes, Auckland 225
Germains, Victor 40–1, 118, 119, 246, 251
Ginsburg, Moses 115
Goebbels, Joseph 101
Goering, Herman 103, 110
Goethe, J. W. 37
Goltz, Colmar von der 80
Gorrell, Edgar S. 71
Gort, Lord 248, 255
Gramsci, Antonio 114
Grandmaison, F. J. L. L. de 21, 22
Graves, Robert 82, 133, 135, 283
Greenwood, Arthur 199
Grey, C. G. 77
Gröner, Wilhelm 91

Grouard, Auguste 151
Guderian, Heinz 32, 96, 97, 98,
  99–100, 120, 218n., 246 n.
Guibert, A. H. 25, 154, 159
Guidoni, A. 74
Gurdjieff, G. I. 26, 108
Gusev, S. I. 116

Haig, Douglas 141, 145, 167, 168,
  170
Haining, R. H. 225, 248
Halder, Franz 95, 201, 258
Halifax, Viscount 228, 229
Hamley, Edward 23
Hankey, Maurice 27, 216
Hannibal 58
Harris, Arthur 272
Hegel, G. W. F. 17, 37
Hemingway, Ernest 135
Heraclitus 15
Hess, Rudolf 18
Hesse, Kurt 85 n., 87
Himmler Heinrich 18
Hindenburg, Paul von 94
Hitler, Adolf 18, 21, 38, 80, 81, 89,
  90, 92, 94, 95, 96, 98, 99–103,
  109, 115, 122, 183, 187, 189, 192,
  193, 195, 201, 203, 215, 223, 228,
  229, 231, 239, 241, 242, 243, 264,
  265, 271, 272, 274, 275, 276, 279,
  280, 281, 283, 284, 285, 287, 288,
  291, 308
Hoare, Samuel 190
Hobart, Percy 266
Hoover, Herbert 109
Hore-Belisha, Lesley 185, 191, 209,
  216, 218, 222, 223, 224, 240, 248,
  274
Houston, Lady 77
Howard, Michael 166, 174
Hull, Cordell 286
Hume, David 17

Huxley, Thomas 8, 14, 15, 17, 25

Ismay, H. L. 196

Jackson, Robert 25
James, William 22, 26, 39, 109
Jaurès, Jean 116
Jefferson, Thomas 106
Jodl, Alfred 242
Jomini, Antoine Henri 23, 24, 25,
  154, 173
Jünger, Ernst 79, 81–9, 102, 115, 136

Kamensky, Vasily 114
Kant, Immanuel 14, 17
Keim, August 80
Kennan, George 291–8, 300, 301,
  302, 303, 304
Kennedy, John F. 300 n.
Kerr, Mark 77
Keynes, Hohn Maynard 34, 35 n., 37,
  134, 146, 213, 307
Kid, Benjamin 14, 15, 26
Kitchener, H. H. 139, 209, 226 n.
Knox, Harry 248
Korda, Alexander 11
Kuhn, Fritz 107
Külental, Colonel 93

Laing, Samuel 14
Langlois, Hippolyte 21
Lawrence, D. H. 18
Lawrence, T. E. 76, 78, 102, 135, 151,
  154–7, 159, 160, 161, 162, 164,
  267, 292
Le Bon, Gustave 9, 21–2
Lecky, W. E. H. 14
Le Corbusier (Charles Edouard
  Jeanneret) 5, 78, 115
Leeb, Ritter von 258
Lelong, General 217
Lenin, Vladimir Ilich Ulyanov 114,
  115

Lewis, Wyndham 18, 46
Liddell Hart, Basil Henry 40, 75, 85, 96, 117–9, 124, 127–310
Lindbergh, Anne Morrow 110–13
Lindbergh, Charles A. 104, 105, 110–12
Lippman, Walter 109
Litvinov, Maxim 229
Lloyd, Henry Evans 25
Lloyd George, David 138, 167, 171, 179, 180, 199, 202, 203, 209, 226, 230, 231, 239, 264, 266, 267, 276, 281
Locke, John 25, 304
Londonderry, Lord 77
Louis XIV, of France 178, 285
Ludendorff, Erich 38, 80, 170

MacDougal, William 22
Machiavelli, Niccolo 292
Macmillan, Norman 77
Mahan, Alfred 158, 173, 180
Maillard, L. 151, 152
Maisky, Ivan 199, 229
Malebranche, Nicholas de 17
Malevich, Kazimir 114
Marinetti, Filippo Tommaso 5, 43, 45–9, 53, 55, 56, 58–9, 64–5, 78, 86, 88 n., 114
Marshall, George 294
Martel, Giffard Le Q. 29, 30, 117
Martin, Rudolf 48
Marx, Karl; Marxism 11, 34, 88, 114–21, 123
Maude, F. M. 24
Maud'huy, Louis de 21, 22
Maxse, Ivor 142
Mayakovsky, Vladimir 114
Mead, George Herbert 109
Melnikov, Konstantin 115
Mermoz, Jean 78
Michel, Victor 249
Michels, Robert 44

Miliutin, N. A. 115
Mill, John Stuart 304
Mitchell, William (Billy) 71–5, 105, 109–10
Molotov, Vyacheslav 229
Moltke, Helmuth von 58, 98, 140, 146, 154
Monash, John 170
Montgomery, Bernard 267
Montgomery-Massingberd, Archibald 251 n.
Moore, John 21
Mosca, Gaetano 44
Mosley, Oswald 5, 6, 13, 37–8, 41, 43, 77, 114
Mumford, Lewis 109
Mussolini, Benito 21, 44, 45, 49, 62–5, 69, 100, 101, 102, 103, 109, 110, 114, 115, 122, 189

Namier, Louis 286
Nehring, Walter 120
Nelson, Horatio 158, 181
Newton, Isaac 25
Nicolson, Harold 199
Nietzsche, Friedrich 9, 36, 37, 43, 45, 63, 82, 108

Orwell, George 167
Ouspensky, P. D. 26, 108
Owen, Wilfred 133, 140 n.

Paget, Bernard 259, 260
Papini, Giovanni 45
Pareto, Vilfredo 44, 45
Pearson, Karl 15, 22, 25, 26, 39
Philip II, of Spain 178
Pierce, Charles Sanders 109
Pierron, Édouard 151, 152
Pile, 'Tim' 266
Pinedo, Francesco de 69
Plato; Platonism 9, 17
Porro, Carlo 61

Porsche, Ferdinand 54
Pound, Ezra 18
Pownell, Henry 251
Prezzolini, Giuseppe 45
Pythagoras 17

Radek, Karl 118
Ramsay, William 11
Rand, Ayn 108
Rawlinson, Henry 170
Reichenau, Walter von 90, 92, 94–9
Remarque, Erich Maria 82, 135, 136
Reynaud, Paul 217
Ribbentrop, Joachim von 229
Richmond, Herbert 73, 180, 182, 195
Roe, A. V. 77
Röhm, Ernst 101
Rommel, Erwin 263 n., 276
Roosevelt, Franklin D. 236–7, 241,
    271, 280–1, 283, 286
Roosevelt, Theodore 109, 131
Rosenberg, Alfred 18
Rotheremere, Lord 76
Rundstedt, Gerd von 90
Russell, Bertrand 78
Rutherford, Ernest 11

Saint-Exupéry, Antoine de 78
Saint-Simon, Henri de 7, 8 n., 9, 11,
    16
Salveneschi, Nino 71
Sassoon, Siegfried 82, 133, 135
Saxe, Maurice de 25, 154, 155, 159,
    161, 164–5
Scammell, J. 144 n., 152 n.
Schelling, Friedrich von 17
Schliefen, Alfred von 98
Seeckt, Hans von 91, 119
Sempil, Baron 76
Shaw, George Bernard 8, 9, 37
Sherman, William T. 149, 161, 166,
    244
Shinwell, Emanuel 267

Sikorsky, Igor 50–1
Sims, William E. 73
Sinclair, Archibald 199, 202, 230, 266
Slade, Edmond 181
Slessor, John 211, 224, 300 n.
Smuts, Jan Christian 75
Soddy, Frederick 11
Soffici, Ardengo 45
Sorel, Georges 45, 114
Spanknoeble, Heinz 107
Speer, Albert 101
Spencer, Herbert 7, 9, 16, 17, 25, 39
Spengler, Oswald 37, 39, 82, 115
Spinoza, Benedict 17
Stalin, Joseph 109, 115, 120, 228, 264
Stanley, Oliver 196
Steiner, Rudolf 90
Stoppiani, Mario 64
Strasser, Otto 101
Stülpnagel, Joachim von 91, 98
Sueter, Murray 76
Swinton, Ernest 27, 28 n., 29, 168
Sykes, Frederick 75

Talleyrand, Charles Maurice de 286
Taylor, A. J. P. 220, 285, 286 n.
Taylor, Frederich; Taylorism 27, 78,
    93, 109, 115
Thorne, Andrew 96
Thwaites, Norman 77
Tirpitz, Alfred 80
Toynbee, Arnold 39
Trenchard, Hugh 71, 75, 208
Triandafillov, Viktor K. 118–9
Trotsky, Leon 116
Truman, Harry 294
Tukhachevsky, Mikhael 116–20,
    246 n.

Van der Rohe, Mies 101
Van Zeeland, Paul 216
Verkhovskii, A. I. 119
Verne, Jules 6–8

Vesnin, brothers (Alexander, Victor, Leonid) 115
Voroshilov, Klementi 121

Wagner, Richard 18, 43
Wallace, Graham 9, 109
Ward, Lester Frank 109
Warlimont, Walter 93
Wavell, Archibald 274, 275
Webb, Sidney and Beatrice 8
Weblen, Thorstein 109
Weir, William 75, 209
Wells, H. G. 6, 7, 8–12, 20, 30, 45, 48, 60 n., 78, 102

Wilhelm II, Emperor 285
Westminster, Duke of 77
Wilkinson, Spenser 144 n., 152 n., 166, 172–4
Willisen, Wilhelm von 154
Wilson, Henry 29, 36, 167
Wilson, Woodrow 130, 304
Wright, Frank Lloyd 105, 108–9, 115
Wright, Wilbur (and brothers) 10, 47–8, 55, 105

Yeats, W. B. 17, 18